Capitalism by Gaslight

EARLY AMERICAN STUDIES

Exploring neglected aspects of our colonial, revolutionary, and early national history and culture, Early American Studies reinterprets familiar themes and events in fresh ways. Interdisciplinary in character, and with a special emphasis on the period from about 1600 to 1850, the series is published in partnership with the McNeil Center for Early American Studies.

CAPITALISM
BY
GASLIGHT

Illuminating the Economy
of Nineteenth-Century America

Edited by
Brian P. Luskey
and
Wendy A. Woloson

PENN

UNIVERSITY OF PENNSYLVANIA PRESS

PHILADELPHIA

Published by
University of Pennsylvania Press
Philadelphia, Pennsylvania 19104-4112
www.upenn.edu/pennpress

Printed in the United States of America on acid-free paper
1 3 5 7 9 10 8 6 4 2

Library of Congress Cataloging-in-Publication Data

Capitalism by gaslight : illuminating the economy of nineteenth-century America / Brian P. Luskey and Wendy A. Woloson. — 1st ed.
p. cm. — (Early American studies)
Includes bibliographical references and index.
1. Capitalism—United States—History—19th century. 2. Informal sector (Economics)—United States—History—19th century. 3. United States—Economic conditions—19th century. 4. United States—Social conditions—19th century. I. Luskey, Brian P. II. Woloson, Wendy A., 1964– III. Series: Early American studies.
HC105.C23 2015
330.973'05—dc23

2014028631

CONTENTS

Capitalism by Gaslight

Introduction

BRIAN P. LUSKEY AND WENDY A. WOLOSON

The gaslight of Philadelphia's street lamps illuminated the work of the successful entrepreneur James Francis during the Civil War era. He managed a crew of employees in two businesses. In the colder months, his team cleaned chimneys. When the weather turned warmer, he became Philadelphia's "Dog-Killer-in-Chief," leading his men in the grisly work of rounding up stray dogs and rendering them into wheel grease. He also caught stray pigs. This work purportedly helped him clear $1,000 a year, although the evidence suggests that he was able to save little from these earnings. The *Evening Telegraph* reported that a friend, the city's fire marshal Alexander Blackburn, paid for Francis's medical care, "Christian consolation" on his deathbed, and burial in 1864.

The fact that this man, an African American, had cultivated the regard of a white official was certainly noteworthy for the era. But such news did not lead to more widespread respect for his clear achievements. The *Telegraph*'s obituary largely ignored Francis's good business sense and his vital role as a provider of essential services to the city's residents and employment for a number of workers. Instead, the newspaper announced that Francis's passing marked the "Death of a Well-Known Character." He would be missed more for his comforting presence in the panorama of urban street life than for the economic ingenuity and hard work by which he had carved a niche for himself and other black men at the center of the city's economy and society. His white contemporaries marginalized Francis and his crew of laborers, obscuring his endeavor and their toil in the shadows of social experience and the historical record.[1]

James Francis and the markets he helped make have eluded the attention of historians for one hundred and fifty years because many scholars have looked elsewhere to identify the creators of capitalist transformation. Economic historians have examined the exploits of elite merchants and financiers and have traced the flow of credit, capital, and commodities across oceans, rivers, canals, and railroads in order to assess macroeconomic issues of development and growth.[2] Social historians have explored the ways in which the wrenching economic and social changes of a "market revolution" unsettled time-honored standards of household independence and produced conflict in the workplace, in the home, and on the streets.[3] Scholars have also charted the development of consumer cultures in which shopkeepers and customers crafted refined spaces of display, sought access to cultural capital through their transactions, and gave new meanings to leisure, shopping, and goods.[4] More recently, compelling new cultural histories have emphasized the ways capitalism "took command" in nineteenth-century American life—an "anonymous," pervasive, and "revolutionary" system that cultivated new practices of selfhood, ways of knowing, methods of dealing, and platforms for governance.[5]

Francis used ingenuity and moxie just to get by. It would strain the limits of the available evidence to claim that he was, or thought himself to be, a capitalist. His white contemporaries certainly would not grant him the label's social stature as they made light of, rather than illuminated, his impressive efforts. Yet ordinary people, through their varied struggles to survive and succeed, created capitalism as much as captains of commerce and industry did. The purpose of this volume is to examine the many people, goods, transactions, strategies, and economic practices that have been obscured by nineteenth-century debates about the meanings of economic activity and more recent arguments about what constituted capitalism. The gaslight lamps of nineteenth-century cities provide a useful metaphor for us. In *Capitalism by Gaslight*, we bring these economies out of the shadows and illuminate them in order to better understand what capitalism was in the nineteenth century.[6]

White Philadelphians' patronizing dismissal of Francis is as much a part of nineteenth-century capitalism as Francis's hard work: Americans at the time paid quite a bit of attention to what petty entrepreneurs were doing in order to lend moral legitimacy to the markets and activities they deemed respectable and appropriate. Within these cultural debates, we can see capitalism as a contest for meaning, especially among the privileged few who had access to economic and cultural resources that enabled them to control the discourse materially and rhetorically. Merchant princes reaped the economic rewards of other people's economic activity and also accumulated cultural capital by obscuring the exertions and creativity of those petty producers and entrepreneurs in order to validate and ennoble their own.

The markets we investigate here, often labeled "marginal" by contemporaries and historians, were actually central to the economy and to individuals' struggles for survival and their efforts to achieve ambitions. The story of nineteenth-century American capitalism that emerges in this collection reveals a multitude of people who made markets by navigating a range of new financial instruments, information, and transactions, the fluid mobility and mutable value of people and goods, and the shifting geography and structure of commercial institutions, even as powerful capitalists denigrated the activities of petty entrepreneurs in order to legitimate their own. What is more, by uncovering what ordinary individuals actually *did*, the contributors to this volume go far beyond illuminating the economic and cultural past. They recover a forgotten social history as well, for petty entrepreneurs who sold used clothing or struggled to make do by pilfering cotton were simply living their lives.

We see this collection as part of a scholarly project that has begun to show, as Rosanne Currarino has argued, that capitalism was a "contingent," "contested," and "historical" process that arose and attained shape out of "the messy minutiae of daily life."[7] It is our contention that the "messy minutiae" that shaped the practices, habits, and worldviews of people such as James Francis helped to constitute capitalism in nineteenth-century America, a process that was gradual, highly contested, and certainly not monolithic. In order to make such a claim stick, we must establish the significance of market activity that historians have by and large dismissed as "underground," "marginal," and "informal" (and even "black," "illicit," or "gray"). These terms not only marginalize significant forms of commerce at the core of daily life but also exclude these activities from the larger history of capitalism.

This volume represents an attempt to gain a deeper understanding of Americans' economic activities in the nineteenth century and, in the process, to develop a more complete picture of American capitalism.[8] The essays here contain revised and expanded versions of many of the papers presented at a conference jointly sponsored by the McNeil Center for Early American Studies and the Library Company of Philadelphia. This conference brought together scholars embarking on innovative research projects focused on nineteenth-century economic activity of the sort that has, to date, remained relatively unexplored by historians. The provocative papers and lively conversation over the conference's two days signaled to us, the co-organizers, the need for further exploration of the subject.[9]

Taken together, these essays illuminate how the capitalist system worked and how people worked the system. Commercial exchanges defined by movement, transience, and change have particularly confounded our understanding of certain market participants and their activities, because buyers, sellers, and service providers are not always who they claim to be, commodities often defy easy categorization, the medium of exchange can be in flux, and the goods that make it to market can be as counterfeit as their makers. As these essays show, economic enterprise was often by degrees legal or illegal, legitimate or illegitimate, making it that much more difficult for contemporaries to track and police them and for those studying them today to gauge their contributions to the larger economy. Transactions sometimes occurred in back alleys, basements, and places with nondescript façades and hidden entrances. And they also took place in the full light of day but, as criminal enterprises, ran afoul of the law.

Arguably, people operating within these markets had to possess greater amounts of commercial acumen because they had to know the rules and systems in both legal and illegal spheres, all the while being cognizant of and being able to elude (or collude with) the authorities. The economies these people helped to create were characterized not by their fixity and reliability—like those of established businessmen with storefronts, ready access to stock, and dependable credit networks—but rather by their instability. These petty entrepreneurs had no choice but to make their own way, enjoying neither the benefits of formal apprenticeships nor the camaraderie of professional trade groups. In fact, their occupations were sometimes so interstitial that they were the only ones employed in those lines of work. They recognized market developments and met evolving consumer needs. These economic worlds operated interdependently, and because of that, we who study them today should not disaggregate them into distinct categories of "black," "white," and "gray" markets. It is more useful and accurate (yet certainly more challenging) to consider the range of economic activity as a spectrum shaded by nuance rather than attempt to delineate sharp contrasts between the darkness of the illicit and the brightness and purported purity of the licit.

The historiographical debate about the "market revolution" relied upon similarly clear distinctions and fostered a rancorous divide among scholars seeking to understand the transition to capitalism in early America. "Market" historians contended that most Americans welcomed opportunities to envision and engage with broader markets, while "social" historians argued that "precapitalist" farmers, planters, and artisans opposed the new terms of credit and organization of labor foisted on them by capitalist merchants and manufacturers. Will B. Mackintosh transcends this debate in his essay on the Loomis Gang, a family of horse thieves that would otherwise fall through the cracks of these rigid analytical categories. Mackintosh argues that we should understand that this family, whose criminal network extended from upstate New York to Pennsylvania and Canada, contributed to the larger social and economic changes unfolding in the Erie Canal corridor in the middle decades of the nineteenth century. The Loomises sought profit and social mobility in the very region that historians have long associated with the triumph of new models of business organization and the pious, domestic values of the emerging middle class. The Loomises' market revolution mirrored and distorted the practices and institutions of law-abiding capitalists, and ultimately produced violence when neighbors lashed out in an attempt to destroy the alternative version of the market that the gang represented. But, like the activities of others described in this volume, the Loomises' activities were only by degrees distinct from so-called legitimate commerce.

Americans did not just debate the question of legitimacy when people trespassed moral boundaries. They were also concerned with the ways goods circulated and changed meanings as they did so. Robert J. Gamble demonstrates how fluid movement and amorphous legal categories complicated early officials' attempts to control public markets. Gamble explores the cultural forces behind the drive to categorize, legislate, and patrol petty entrepreneurs and commodities as they circulated promiscuously through Early Republic Philadelphia and Baltimore. Popular representations of the vast array of commodities moving through the cities' sprawling secondhand marketplace—recycled, bartered, pawned, counterfeited, or stolen—show just how complicated this process could be.

Value was also fluid and contested, since it was time-sensitive, situational, and contingent upon people's faith in an ephemeral medium of exchange. To explain how Americans assessed value, Joshua R. Greenberg examines shinplasters, a historiographically neglected category of paper money printed by commercial entities and towns. A necessary yet particularly unstable form of currency, these dubiously legal bills circulated liberally at particular moments of national economic crisis or when state monetary laws changed, alleviating the problems associated with the shortage of available money. Ultimately, shinplasters destabilized Americans' trust in all paper money issued by banks, and politicians responded by attempting to harness that anxiety into support for their partisan perspectives on the banking issue more generally. In the years following the Panic of 1837, the meaning of the term "shinplaster" came to include legal bank bills of doubtful value as well. Thus, the circulation of shinplasters helped antebellum Americans facilitate economic transactions and determine what paper money was worth.

An examination of another type of rags—secondhand clothing—and the Jewish men who collected, patched, and resold them illuminates how ethnicity factored into commercial interactions. Adam Mendelsohn explains that rag traders not only appreciated the economic potential in others' cast-offs but also applied ingenuity and hard work to create value where others saw worthlessness. Anti-Semitic observers disputed these entrepreneurs' respectability—even though they were operating within the bounds of the law and providing necessary garments for many classes of people—and cast the trade as a disreputable one. And yet, in spite of their detractors' efforts to cordon off New York's Chatham Street and London's Petticoat Lane—the main sites of old clothes commerce—from more reputable marketplaces, secondhand dealers circulated widely. As a result, at least in the American context, Jews resorted to peddling, a valuable (if informal) apprenticeship that often led them to successful careers as clothing manufacturers and shopkeepers.

The large-scale influx of Irish and German immigrants on American shores, another example of the circulation of people during the nineteenth century, offered opportunities for unscrupulous native-born businessmen to nestle into a lucrative but culturally contested market niche based upon their exploitation of the newcomers. Brendan P. O'Malley takes up Mendelsohn's transatlantic approach and analyzes the world of a group of nefarious middlemen, the "emigrant runners" who took advantage of immigrants to American shores in the middle decades of the nineteenth century. Runners, in some respects hated and distrusted as much as the foreigners they duped, offered transportation and temporary housing to immigrants. Keenly sizing up the needs of a vulnerable population, they were able to envision a business opportunity and capitalize on it. They evaded regulation in part by immersing themselves in the violent urban subculture of the era. Moreover, their black deeds intersected with those of corrupt politicians, exposing the blurry boundaries between "legitimate" and "illegitimate" business practices and highlighting the need for—and limits of—institutional reform.

In this vacuum of oversight, opportunities to dupe and defraud proliferated, making the debate about moral legitimacy more shrill but also ripe for popular entertainment as Americans came to understand these issues by reading about the frauds of the day. Corey Goettsch examines New York's notorious mock auctions, in which by-bidders worked in league with crooked auctioneers to hoodwink passersby into purchasing goods of dubious value. Pretending to sell precious items such as gold watches at incredibly low prices, mock auctions capitalized on both Americans' growing desire to participate in the bustling marketplace of consumer goods and their questionable ability to judge the quality and value of such goods. Mock auctioneers and the "Peter Funks" who abetted them emerged—like Jewish secondhand dealers and immigrant exploiters—as capitalism's bogeymen, figures whom contemporaries thought most aptly personified fraud in their society. Because these men were highly skilled entrepreneurs who knew and could work every angle to exploit their victims, they also symbolized the ways in which every capitalist could be a Peter Funk.

In this cultural milieu, assertions about character became ever more significant, even (and especially) among participants in the most morally troubling markets. Craig B. Hollander returns us to the Atlantic Ocean to describe the risks that Americans took and the rewards they reaped in the illegal slave trade in the years following the War of 1812. After 1807, a nefarious but lawful commerce became illegal under British law. And yet, even with the United States following suit in the next year to clarify the distinctions between legitimate and illegitimate, slave trade financiers and ship captains in the United States and Cuba maintained and strengthened their economic networks. They also forged ties with merchants not explicitly engaged in the slave trade but who hoped to profit from trade in the markets that slavers visited. Like many of the other essays in this collection, Hollander's work illustrates the ways in which illicit trade could end up supporting legal institutions and forms of exchange. In addition, it demonstrates how financial incentives encouraged many to engage in lucrative and immoral business practices.

Even within slave society, the boundaries of legitimacy were also up for debate. Slaveholders passed laws that prohibited commercial exchange between slaves and white people who did not own them. Hemmed in by these constraints, slaves and nonslaveholders nevertheless participated in commercial networks that were embedded within and contributed to the larger movement of goods in the Atlantic economy. Michael D. Thompson examines the ways slaves and their white abettors seized opportunities to steal cotton and other staple goods from Charleston's waterfront during the antebellum period. The problem of theft also intersected with the questions of legitimacy that surrounded slavery, as slaveholders tried to explain away slaves' pilfering as an outgrowth of their moral deficiency and the influence of the enterprising whites who were in league with them. Hardly a marginal activity, the theft of staple goods on Charleston's wharves registered on the account books of the city's slaveholders and merchants, and in no small measure shaped the markets in those commodities.

Their boundaries blurry and porous, nineteenth-century criminal and quasi-criminal economies thrived. Ever elusive, this kind of commerce was impossible to police, quantify, and control. The most successful criminal entrepreneurs attempted to bridge the worlds of legitimate and illegitimate, knowing how to finesse the various legal, economic, and cultural systems. Katie M. Hemphill's essay on the business of prostitution in Baltimore encourages historians to reconsider the line between exploitation and opportunity. A form of illicit commerce, prostitution was nevertheless a robust trade and in fact developed in tandem with the city's commercial and transportation infrastructures. The popularity of glamorous hotels and restaurants and the proximity of a local clientele of male clerks and merchants made the older model of "brothel"—an establishment that housed men and offered them many domestic services beyond sex—largely obsolete. Madams began to specialize—to adopt a term that business historians have applied to this era of transformation—in providing sexual services (often to city elders, police officials, merchants, clerks, and other respectable men in the community) even as they diversified by offering clients the types of sociability often associated with middle-class gentility. In essence, enterprising madams disguised their quests for profits by domesticating a hurly-burly environment.

Hemphill's essay and the ones that follow it suggest that we must pay closer attention to the ways in which entrepreneurs both specialized and diversified their operations to get by in the nineteenth-century economy. Paul Erickson argues that we must situate the nineteenth-century book trade within a broader commercial context. In fact, his vignettes portraying bookselling barbers, smut-peddling purveyors of "fancy goods," and profit-minded reformers confound scholars' assertions that a clearly defined "book trade" was separated from the retailing of other commodities. These salesmen and their customers, participants in an economy that was about more than books, unsettled distinctions between respectable and disreputable trade for their contemporaries even as they add complexity to our understanding of nineteenth-century business organization.

The people showcased in these essays encountered immense barriers for getting by and getting ahead, demonstrating amazing ingenuity and a willingness to rethink the concepts of value in order to survive. The story of Robert M. Budd, the dealer in old newspapers who is the subject of Ellen Gruber Garvey's concluding essay, illustrates new themes that would emerge at the end of the century while also showing how Budd's line of work was closely linked to earlier secondhand dealers, such as Mendelsohn's used clothing sellers. Focusing on a man known by his contemporaries as "Back Number Budd," Garvey describes an innovative entrepreneur and early participant in an information revolution in the late nineteenth and early twentieth centuries. As a business owner, Budd saw profit in materials that others had devalued. He saved old newspapers and created a system of filing that lawyers and newspaper correspondents paid him to access. A pioneer of the time, Budd recognized the value of commodifying information and succeeded for a time in cornering the market for that information in New York City.

These essays reveal that during the nineteenth century the rules of economic engagement were still being established, meaning that definitions of terms such as legal and illegal, moral and immoral, acceptable and disdained were up for debate. At a time when many Americans condemned the social upheaval and economic inequality resulting from capitalism, some prominent merchants, ministers, reformers, journalists, and authors of fiction sought to establish wholesale and retail trade as legitimate norms against which all other trafficking should be judged. Historians have adopted these moral categories of legitimacy a little too faithfully, taking for granted the value judgments placed on so-called aberrant economic ventures and ignoring or marginalizing them in their own scholarship. In fact, "upstanding" men of commerce engaged in illegal, semilicit, and morally suspect economic practices of their own, whether by pressing their thumbs on the scale, marking up goods to reap unreasonable profits, dealing with black-market suppliers, or patronizing brothels. By the same token, those who defied the law outright were still tied to legitimate markets, as goods and money were recirculated and obtained new values and new meanings, moving through the market's porous membranes from legal to illegal and back again.

These essays illuminate the economies of people whom contemporaries relegated to the shadows of capitalism's dramatic triumph in the nineteenth century. When exposed to light, these otherwise hidden forms of commerce become flashpoints revealing the tensions, fissures, and inequities inherent in capitalism itself. Indeed, this was capitalism.

CHAPTER 1

The Loomis Gang's Market Revolution

WILL B. MACKINTOSH

Just before dawn on the morning of Sunday, June 17, 1866, a mob of angry citizens gathered in the semidarkness about a mile from the Loomis farm in Sangerfield, New York. The Loomis dogs had been poisoned the night before, and the vigilantes quickly rousted the family from their beds and set fire to the house and barns. They hanged two family members from a nearby tree in order to extract confessions for a series of recent crimes; no one was killed, but the mob left in the early morning light with a Loomis son in irons, bound for the county jail. The Loomises were clearly not an ordinary farm family; this remarkable operation of "lynch law" capped a twenty-year career of large-scale larceny, horse thieving, and fencing of stolen goods. Their criminal activity stretched from Pennsylvania to Ontario and from Vermont to Ohio, and made their large family conspicuously prosperous. They conducted their business proudly and publicly, and they seemed to relish their wide social and political influence. The 1866 lynching ended the family's criminal enterprise, but not before they had achieved local, statewide, and even international fame as one of the most effective, efficient, and well-organized criminal operations of the 1850s and 1860s.

The story of the rise and fall of the "Loomis Gang" has provided grist for the mills of local historians and romance novelists, but for scholars of the nineteenth-century American economy, it poses a deeper set of questions.[1] After all, the Loomises' flamboyant criminal behavior and the vigilante justice that brought them down did not take place in a dim precommercial past or on some distant, isolated frontier. The Loomis farm lay less than twenty miles from the bustling manufacturing and Erie Canal port city of Utica, in a region of central New York State that was an epicenter of the infrastructural developments and market intensification that have been described as a "market revolution" by Charles Sellers.[2] How was the Loomis Gang able to pursue such a large-scale and open criminal enterprise right in the very heart of the market revolution? Why did victimized local residents turn to vigilante action—what contemporaries called the "California solution"—in the rapidly modernizing Erie Canal hinterland? How did the Loomis family thrive in the buckle of the middle-class, evangelical "burned-over district," where their neighbors were busily constructing a new moralistic, domesticated ideology of family?

The answers to these questions lie in a rejection of the dichotomies I have just posed. The Loomises were not an aberration at the heart of the market revolution. Rather, they were an idiosyncratic example of the transformation of American social and economic life in these years. Their gang was hierarchically organized and operated over a wide region, working across a number of different local markets and jurisdictions, and so they were able to pursue their criminal activities efficiently and at minimum risk. The Loomises, like many of their contemporaries, believed that the individualistic pursuit of profit trumped all other considerations. Their family, like others throughout the antebellum North, reflected refinement and the desire to enhance their position in market society. In all of these ways, the Loomis family embodied the social and economic changes unfolding in nineteenth-century America. They were as well-suited to their political and economic moment as the prosperous hop farmers and influential canal merchants among whom they lived.

Yet the Loomises were also obviously different from their neighbors; their market revolution was not the same market revolution celebrated by their contemporaries and analyzed by Sellers. Their practices trespassed across the boundaries that local businessmen and state politicians were busily tracing to justify their own success and shape the economic behavior of others. Boosters of the market revolution in New York State celebrated the personal independence that came from market activity, lionized assertive entrepreneurs who seized the "main chance," and reconceived of government as a primary enabler of economic growth.[3] The Loomises interpreted this spirit of the age as license to take what they wanted, bully their opponents, and manipulate authority in pursuit of their own success. The Loomises' market revolution intertwined opportunity and violent repression, a dynamic that Joshua Rothman has recently described on the antebellum southwestern frontier.[4] The story of the Loomis Gang suggests that the market revolution was contingent on violence even in the Erie Canal hinterland. The Loomises' market revolution was not a struggle for legitimacy between old and new visions of a moral economy, nor was it a struggle for preeminence in the outer borderlands of capitalism. Instead, it was a radical claim about the boundaries of acceptability in the new economy, a claim that clashed directly with the limits being drawn by their more anxious neighbors. And this clash could be resolved only by the old-fashioned methods of murder, lynching, arson, and eventual banishment.

This tale of competing economic visions in central New York begins with the contrasting lives led by a brother and a sister, Amos and Abigail Osborn, born three years apart to a long-established family in Trumbull, Connecticut, in the 1760s. Like many New Englanders of his generation, Amos Osborn left home to try his luck on the frontier of upstate New York. He arrived in Sangerfield in 1802, just a decade after the township's first Anglo-American settlers, and found immediate success as a distiller. Amos quickly became a shining example of young New Englanders' ability to get ahead on the New York frontier. Within a decade, he had married, acquired a propitiously located farm, and started a family of five children. Indicative of his market savvy, he "was one of the few men who had money to let" in the early decades, although he "was sure to have only good security, and exact but lawful interest and punctual payments."[5] His material success was reflected by his public embrace of his generation's ideals of manly morality; one late nineteenth-century local historian remembered him as "a man of industry and integrity, which with frugal living and wise management of affairs brought him a handsome competence later in life."[6] A local newspaper writer similarly remembered him as "strong-minded, honest, and of excellent judgment," while his wife was thought to be "a kind, frugal and benevolent woman, taking great pride in her children, who proved worthy of her care, and became a blessing to their parents."[7] By the time he died in 1848, Amos was one of the longest-established and most prosperous inhabitants of the booming village of Waterville, the population center of the township.

Despite this later sentimentalization, Amos Osborn's success was not entirely a result of his superior work ethic and business sense; he was also in the right place at the right time. The opening of the Erie Canal in 1825 heralded a boom in wheat and dairy agriculture along its route, and Sangerfield was advantageously located close to the economically vibrant canal port at Utica. Indeed, it did not take long for Sangerfield to become even more closely integrated into the national transportation network. The Chenango Canal, which opened in 1837, skirted the boundary of Sangerfield and gave its farmers and merchants easy access to the Erie Canal at Utica and to the growing Pennsylvania canal system at Binghamton. In 1848, the Waterville and Utica Plank Road opened further access to the regional metropolis, and by the late 1860s a branch of the Delaware, Lackawanna and Western Railroad passed through the township. During this period, inhabitants of the agricultural hinterland of Utica took advantage of its climate and its excellent market integration to turn the area into the epicenter of hop cultivation in the United States. In 1840, New York was already the leading hop-producing state, and by 1850, it grew almost three times more hops than all other states combined. By 1860, New York produced nearly 90 percent of the nation's hops. Oneida County, which included the township of Sangerfield, dominated this market, along with three or four of its neighboring counties. Central New York's preeminence in hop production lasted for the rest of the nineteenth century, only to be ended by crop diseases, western competition, and eventually, Prohibition. Like many forms of market agriculture, hop cultivation was subject to wild boom-and-bust cycles, but nevertheless, it made many of Sangerfield's farmers quite wealthy. Amos Osborn, who became prosperous because he worked hard and played by the rules during a particularly fortuitous moment in central New York's economic history, was one of them.[8]

Amos's children, particularly his fourth son, Amos O. Osborn, inherited his wealth and his local prominence. Indeed, it was this second generation of Sangerfield Osborns that most fully embodied conventional notions of success in midcentury central New York. Amos O. capitalized on his father's "handsome competence," obtaining a sound education at a local academy and a couple of years at Yale, followed by legal training in the chambers of a judge in Utica. In 1839, he opened a law practice in Waterville, where he quickly assumed multiple positions of business and civic leadership. No doubt influenced by his father's informal moneylending business, he became the director of the Bank of Waterville, a position that he held for forty-five years.

Amos O. was also a prominent participant in the civic life of his community. He was a founder, lay leader, and financial supporter of Grace Episcopal Church. He served as the first and longtime president of the Waterville Cemetery Association, incorporated to bring the moral and aesthetic values of the nineteenth-century rural cemetery movement to citizens of Sangerfield. He belonged to the Sons of Temperance and the Waterville Grange. He was a prominent local historian who wrote about and lectured on the history of Sangerfield and Oneida County, an amateur naturalist who had a locally discovered fossil named in his honor, and a member of several national scientific organizations. Amos O.'s personality matched his long list of public roles. Remembered as a man with a "genial smile and cordial manner," he was lauded for "his generous aid in case of need, his quick response of sympathy in joy or sorrow, his unvarying interest in the welfare of the public as well as its individual members, [and] his public spirit always manifest in everything promising progress or improvement." As this breathless list of achievements, affiliations, and temperamental qualities demonstrates, Amos O. had the carefully constructed persona and résumé of a progressive, upwardly mobile, middle-class man of business. He derived his financial success from Sangerfield's increasing integration into statewide, national, and international business networks, and he used his prominent position to engage in a public project of self-refinement and community betterment. He was rewarded with "the respect and esteem of the public in the community which gave him birth and which has strengthened and grown with his advancing years."[9]

Amos O. Osborn was very much a man of his time and place, a man of the conventional market revolution. Sangerfield lay within what Carol Sheriff has called "the Erie Canal corridor," the line of rapidly developing cities that was strung across upstate New York, situated within equally prosperous hinterlands. The Erie Canal corridor was populated by a polyglot mixture of yeoman farmers and immigrant laborers who found their livings in market agriculture and, increasingly, industrial production. It largely overlapped with what Whitney R. Cross has called the "burned-over district" because during the mid-nineteenth century it was torn by waves of fiery evangelical religion. The region's emerging political and economic leaders were firmly committed to "progress" and "improvement," by which they meant that "men and women were taking an active role in realizing a divinely sanctioned movement toward the perfectibility of the natural and human worlds."[10] Like his peers, Amos O. was politically and ideologically committed to the kind of "improvement" that had brought his family prosperity and prominence. He was active in the Whig Party in the 1840s and 1850s, serving as a town supervisor, as a justice of the peace, and ultimately as a two-term member of the New York State Assembly beginning in 1853. During this period, the Whigs, particularly in upstate New York, "claimed to be the party of improvement," which meant they sought to use government to promote public morals and economic development.[11] But as Amos O.'s biographer explained, his commitment to the developing mechanics of the market economy went deeper than his political service. Like a good member of the midcentury middle class, Amos O. was not only "untiring in self-development" but also "greatly interested in the development of Sangerfield, especially earnest in his views of right and law that should govern corporations and municipalities as well as individuals."[12] At least according to this biographer, Amos O.'s deepest commitment was to the construction of the political and legal structures, economic institutions, and moral creeds necessary for the integration of his hometown into the market-driven mainstream of nineteenth-century American life, a movement he would have no doubt described as justifiable "progress."[13]

If the two generations of Amos Osborns represented the prosperous, aggressive, and self-congratulatory mainstream of nineteenth-century Sangerfield, then the descendants of the senior Amos's younger sister Abigail offer a sharply contrasting story. While still in Connecticut, Abigail married Zachariah Mallett, and sometime around 1802 the couple followed Amos to Sangerfield so that Zachariah could enter into the distillery business with his brother-in-law. Yet sometime before 1815, the stories of the Osborns and the Malletts diverged. Zachariah was everything that Amos was not; he quickly gained a criminal record for counterfeiting and created a scandal in the frontier settlement by conducting a public affair with a married woman. The adultery brought him infamy and the counterfeiting brought him an extended prison sentence, neither of which was conducive to the establishment of a prominent lineage of Sangerfield Malletts. Indeed, only one child of Zachariah and Abigail appears in the local histories that spilled so much ink over the Osborns' exemplary lives. Their daughter Rhoda Mallett, who was probably born in Connecticut in the 1790s and came to Sangerfield with her parents as a girl, also became a prominent local figure like her first cousin Amos O. But as we shall see, Rhoda would make economic choices that flouted the legal and moral strictures to which her cousin Amos devoted his life.[14]

Like the Osborn siblings, George Washington Loomis arrived in Sangerfield from New England in 1802. Also like the Osborns, George was attracted to the area by a family connection to other early migrants; his sister had come a few years before and had already established herself as the wife of the community's first and leading doctor. According to local legend, George arrived with his saddlebags filled with three thousand dollars in gold, the profits of a brief and dramatic career as a horse thief in Vermont. Regardless of the truth of that story, he was able to purchase a sizable and well-located farm in 1806, and by 1825, he was successful enough to build a large, "sightly and commodious" new "mansion" on his extensive and valuable property. This early and apparent success attracted the attention of Rhoda Mallett, and the two were married soon after George returned from military service at Sacketts Harbor in the War of 1812.[15]

George and Rhoda had twelve children between 1815 and 1838, ten of whom lived to adulthood. Like their cousins the Osborns, the Loomises were well positioned to achieve prosperity in the booming economy of their time and place. By all accounts, their farm was large, productive, and ideally situated for the market-oriented hop agriculture that was making some of their neighbors wealthy. They had access to the capital necessary to engage in large-scale commercial farming. Even if George's gold-filled saddlebags were apocryphal, the family's ties to the banking Osborns could have given them the credit they needed. The Loomis farm lay close to the transportation infrastructure that allowed Sangerfield easy access to state, national, and international markets. It was only six miles from the Chenango Canal, and an extended plank road ran almost from the Loomises' doorstep to the bustling city of Utica by the late 1840s. During the final decade of the Loomises' dominance, a branch of the Delaware, Lackawanna and Western Railroad was being extended down the valley where they lived (see Figure 1.1). In short, the Loomises had the land, the family connections, the growing market access, and the capital—whether ill-gotten or not—to achieve success in the booming hop market in central New York, if they had so chosen.[16]

Indeed, evidence suggests that their farm was profitable on its own terms, but George and Rhoda did not limit themselves to growing cash crops for the market. After all, they had both tasted the danger and the potential profit of illicit activity before settling down together on their new farm. When their children were young, from 1815 to the 1830s, George and Rhoda limited their nonfarm enterprises to those in which they had experience—dealing in stolen horses and counterfeit currency. Having learned his lesson from his early brushes with the law in Vermont, George apparently stopped stealing horses himself, and instead developed a fencing operation, using the wandering paths and secret clearings of nearby Nine Mile Swamp to hide his activities. Rhoda evidently inherited an interest in counterfeiting from her father, and the passing of forged notes remained a lucrative business for her family across several generations. Thus, in the early years of southern Oneida County's market boom, the Loomises' farming activity was not dissimilar to that of their more honest neighbors, and the family's criminal activity followed neatly in the tracks that had been established as early as the turn of the century.[17]

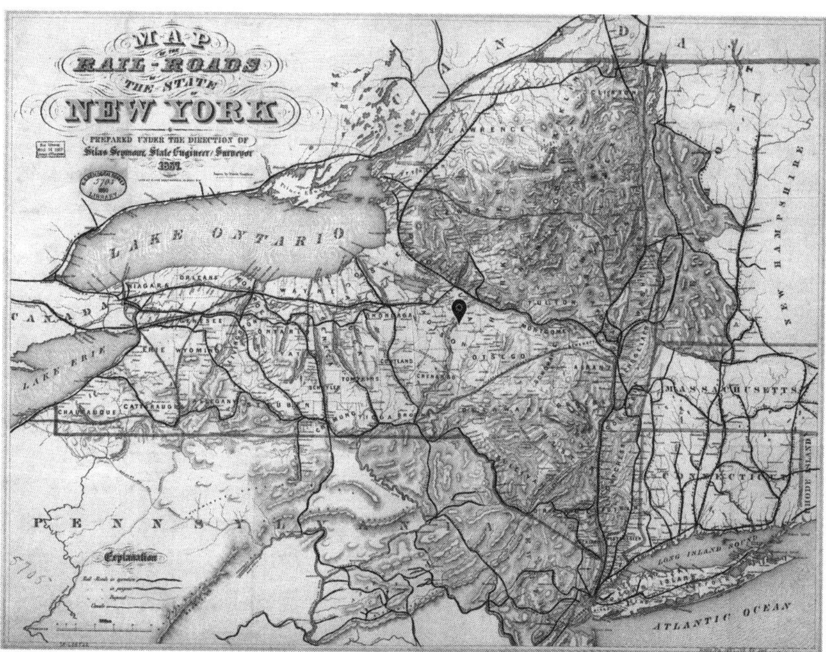

Figure 1.1. The Loomis farm, marked by the black pin, was surrounded by roads, canals, and railroads by the late 1850s; indeed, it was thoroughly enmeshed in the lineaments of the market revolution in central New York State. The members of the Loomis Gang took advantage of this location to divide their fields of operation into organizational territories that enabled the rapid redistribution of stolen goods and helped them to avoid detection by agents of the law. "Map of the Rail-Roads of the State of New York, Prepared Under the Direction of Silas Seymour, State Engineer Surveyor" (Albany, NY: Lith[.] of C. Van Benthuysen, 1857). Courtesy of the Library of Congress, Geography and Map Division.

As George and Rhoda's children came of age in the 1840s, however, the family began to supplement their core business in horse thieving and counterfeiting with petty larceny and dealing in stolen goods. Acting under Rhoda's tutelage and encouragement, the children embarked on criminal careers that generated both numerous anecdotes for local historians as well as occasional legal troubles for themselves. For example, in 1844, Wash, George and Rhoda's second son, was convicted for stealing money from a store in a nearby village. Wash appealed his conviction all the way to the New York State Supreme Court, which overturned it on a technicality. In 1847, Wash and his older brother Bill were indicted for "taking 'with force and arms' seven buffalo robes valued at five dollars each from a store" in another nearby village; in this case, the brothers forfeited their bail and the charges were dropped.[18] Cornelia, one of the younger Loomis daughters, made a name for herself by stealing women's fur muffs from cloakrooms at social functions and inns. Her preferred method was to pull the muffs on over her legs, underneath her skirt, and then nonchalantly leave the premises. Although she was caught in the act, she was never prosecuted, because the victims and witnesses of her thefts were apparently too intimidated to press charges. As the younger generation grew into maturity, the family grew more innovative in their activities.[19]

It was at this moment, in the mid-1840s, that the Loomises' market revolution emerged as a distinct model of social and economic life. If the Osborns embodied the prosperous middle-class mainstream during the market revolution in central New York, the Loomises pushed their vision of economy and society up to and even beyond its logical conclusion. For example, Rhoda arranged her domestic life in ways that were at once familiar and strange. We know a great deal about the relationship between economic development and changes in the family in Oneida County in this period, thanks to Mary Ryan's *Cradle of the Middle Class*. As the region became more deeply integrated into the market and industrial economies, ideal gender roles within the family became more sharply bifurcated, between the masculine "breadwinner" husband who earned a living in the new economy and the pious, pure, domestic wife who exercised moral and practical authority over domestic space. According to Ryan, adherence to this evolving ideology of the family quickly became one of the cornerstones of membership in the emerging middle class—the main beneficiaries of the market revolution—in places like Oneida County.[20] In their own way, the Loomises considered themselves part of central New York's elite, so it is perhaps unsurprising that their family arrangements reflect Ryan's findings, albeit with a twist.

In the emerging middle-class families of Oneida County, the relationship between mother and children quickly emerged as the "central place in the constellation of family affection."[21] Like her more conventional neighbors, Rhoda Loomis believed that a woman's highest calling was to physically and morally nurture her children and to prepare them for success in the modern world. But she had a profoundly different understanding of the "modern world" and a correspondingly different idea of what "nurture" and "success" meant. Fuller Torrey, a local historian, recounted Wash's childhood memories of Rhoda's maternal style, which taught commercial acumen, if not commercial morality. "We sometimes traded little things like boys do, and learned quickly to deceive and cheat," Wash apparently recalled. "Mother smiled approval when she learned of what we did and told us not to get caught nor to allow anyone to get the better of us. We were always supposed to seize the advantage. When we stole things, Mother approved. As long as we were not caught she said it was all right. If we got caught we got licked."[22] The precise yet stilted nature of this recollection suggests that it is at least apocryphal if not wholly fabricated, but nevertheless it conveys something of the odd hybridity of Rhoda's gender performance, revealed in the confrontational stare she offered the camera (see Figure 1.2).

Wash's memory of a nurturing mother, focused on teaching life lessons to her children, is a stock set piece from the "cult of true womanhood." Even the phrase "Mother smiled approval" sounds as though it was ripped directly out of a sentimental novel from the 1840s. To use a more proximate example, Wash's memories ring in the same emotional register as the biographers' descriptions of the wives and mothers of the Osborn family. But rather than using her "natural" feminine skills to nurture a brood of upright businessmen and pious housewives, Rhoda created a generation of clever, fearless criminals. She shepherded her children's intellectual and moral development, just as her gender and class position required, even if the content of her morality fell well outside the mainstream.

In fact, schooling youth in criminality seemed to be one of Rhoda's special skills. In a retrospective piece published a dozen years after the Loomis Gang's fall, the *New York Sun* described the Loomises' recruiting practice as "inciting young visitors to petty peculations and crimes." The newspaper's correspondent cast Rhoda herself as the central figure in this criminal seduction:

> If they were licentious, the attraction was blooming girls who had been brought to the mansion as servants on promises of good wages, and started upon an infamous career. If they were given to drink, the best liquors were set before them. . . . The young fellows were on the road to crime before they knew it. When they were about to leave the house, the old lady [Rhoda] would place her hand on their arms and say: "Now, don't come back without stealing something, if it's nothing but a jackknife." . . . Their dexterity was praised and the fruits of their marauding were placed upon the table.[23]

In both of these instances, Rhoda's place as the moral and emotional center of her family may have made her even more effective at teaching her young

Figure 1.2. This photograph of Rhoda Loomis, taken late in her life, reveals the forceful personality and hybrid gender performance that contemporaries attributed to her. Image courtesy of the Waterville Historical Society, Waterville, New York.

charges to steal and to prostitute themselves.[24] Her notion of motherhood was the inverse of the dominant middle-class ideology of motherhood promulgated by her more conventional contemporaries, like the famous author and educator Catharine Beecher. Rather than instilling sobriety and prudence, she taught absolute obedience to the emerging middle-class "sacramental belief in the universal beneficence of profits."[25] Indeed, Rhoda's vision of an economic world characterized by unfettered competition, in which profit and gain were the only measures of success, was at the cutting edge of her generation's economic thought. In many ways, she was a thoroughly conventional middle-class mother, except that she took her maternal lessons about the competitiveness of the market to their logical, if criminal, conclusion.

Rhoda was evidently successful in putting her mode of maternal nurturing to work, because by the late 1840s Wash's outstanding indictments for larceny had become numerous and serious enough that he elected to join the '49ers in California. He stayed there for two years, returning just as his father was dying in early 1851. Wash was by all accounts the smartest and most levelheaded of the Loomis children, and his parents sought to develop his capabilities by sending him to study law with a judge in a nearby village. The parallel to Rhoda's cousin Amos O. Osborn is striking: although Amos O.'s training was more prestigious and put to very different purposes than Wash's, both young men understood that legal acuity would be critical to success in the market. Wash's personality, skills, and experience allowed him to assume leadership of the family's criminal activities in his father's stead upon his return from California.

Indeed, under his leadership, the Loomises' market revolution sped apace. As the farmers of southern Oneida County increasingly grew cash crops for sale in distant entrepôts and as small-town businessmen increasingly bridged local and national markets through the Erie Canal and the railroads, so too did the Loomis Gang evolve from a local, family-centered operation into an organized and disciplined criminal operation that bridged multiple markets and attracted local and even international coverage. No longer was this a loose confederation of family and a few friends who engaged in counterfeiting, horse theft, and petty larceny when the opportunity arose. Rather, the enterprise grew into a large, hierarchically structured gang with regional operations around New York State and in Pennsylvania, New England, and Canada. Their expanded scope gave them the flexibility to move their products around according to market conditions. They invested in the legal knowledge necessary to influence the justice system and the political process in ways that were advantageous to their business. In other words, the growth of their criminal enterprises paralleled the evolution of their neighbors' businesses.[26]

With Wash in charge, the Loomis Gang's activities were formally organized by region. Bill, the eldest Loomis son, oversaw the gang's northern arm from his farm in Hastings Center, some forty miles north of Sangerfield. He coordinated a group of horse thieves that ranged over northern Oneida, Oswego, and Lewis counties, and he took charge of the gang's sales channel into Canada. Bill and his associates drove stolen horses through Sacketts Harbor into Ontario and Quebec, selling them as far away as Montreal. Grove, another son, ran a similar network to the south, in Otsego, Delaware, Sullivan, Chenango, Broome, and Cortland counties and in northeastern Pennsylvania. Like Bill's team, Grove's associates both stole horses from local farmers and distributed stolen horses from other regions. With the relative proximity of the Pennsylvania state line, Grove had the added responsibility of spiriting fugitive members of the gang out of the state when conditions got too hot. A family associate named Big Bill Rockwell handled operations to the west around Syracuse and throughout the Finger Lakes area. Wash himself took charge of the eastern region, including Herkimer, Fulton, Montgomery, Schoharie, and Albany counties. His personal supervision of the east was critical because it covered two of the gang's most important markets. George's longstanding connections in Vermont made it lucrative sales territory, and the state capital of Albany was both a significant market and an important source of political influence. As market development organized the business activity of central New York into larger units and tied it more closely to the statewide, national, and international markets, the Loomis Gang followed suit.[27]

These regional operations were coordinated from the Loomis farm in Sangerfield. Individual horse thieves functioned as independent operators who delivered their contraband to Sangerfield in return for a flat payment of twenty-five dollars, with another fifteen dollars payable upon the horse's final sale.[28] In earlier decades, George had found private clearings in the tangled wilds of the adjacent Nine Mile Swamp in which to pasture stolen horses, dye them, and otherwise change their appearance for resale. Wash built upon this natural advantage by scaling up the transport and processing operation in the swamp, where horses had their identifying markings removed and were forwarded for sale in distant counties. Derived from amateur oral histories conducted in the early twentieth century, these monetary figures suggest that this clearinghouse operation was highly profitable for the Loomises. At the time, the price of good horses regularly exceeded one hundred dollars and would approach twice that amount in 1863 and 1864, when the demands of the Union army inflated prices.[29] As one late nineteenth-century critic put it, the Loomises "operated an 'underground railroad' of their own, but not for the purpose of assisting vagabond negroes."[30]

As this rough sketch makes clear, the Loomis Gang at its peak in the 1850s and 1860s was a well-organized and disciplined enterprise, with a sophisticated understanding of the market for stolen goods and a centralized structure that managed both supply and demand for maximum profit and minimum government interference. Their practices mirrored those of the most aggressive and forward-thinking of their commercially oriented contemporaries, and they grew equally prosperous as a result. New York was the first state to pass a general incorporation law in 1811, and by the 1830s many of the features of a modern corporate business system were thriving in the state, including banks, stock and commodity exchanges, brokerages, and financial information clearinghouses. In the 1850s and 1860s, railroads emerged as the "first full private, large-scale, socially capitalized business corporations," capable of marshaling enormous investments, extending themselves across large territories, and influencing government policy.[31] The purpose of incorporation was to use the tools of financial, bureaucratic, and technological organization to enlarge businessmen's reach and the scale of their potential profits and to limit government interference with their operations.[32] Indeed, it was precisely these types of businesses that Amos O. Osborn hoped to encourage in his political, legal, and banking careers. Short of legally incorporating and listing themselves on the nascent New York Stock Exchange, the Loomises deployed all of these modern techniques to ensure the long-term profitability of their operations.

Contemporary observers of events in southern Oneida County acknowledged the superlative organization and increasing market sophistication of the Loomis Gang. The Prison Association of New York, a private organization empowered to observe and report on the conditions in the state's prisons, included a lengthy and scathing description of the Loomis Gang's activities in their annual report for 1866. The association reached beyond its narrow purview to comment on the state of crime in New York generally. "A survey of the State this year shows that there is a strong and increasing tendency of crime to crystallize," they wrote, "into aggregates and masses." Criminals in New York no longer worked alone, the association claimed. They formed themselves into a variety of small and large gangs, and even local gangs showed a tendency "to affiliate with and reciprocally assist and receive assistance from all the others in the State, . . . [and t]hrough the agency of these affiliated societies of thieves property once stolen is passed rapidly from hand to hand, until it becomes almost impossible to trace it; or, if it is discovered, the original depredators cannot be ascertained, and therefore go unwhipped of justice." This increasing organization and sophistication were visible both in New York City and in the rural parts of upstate New York. "If this tendency to aggregation and organisation continues to increase for the future as it has done for the few years past," the association moaned, "we shall have organised bands of associated depredators in all the counties of the State, whose members . . . will mutually assist each other in disposing of their plunder, in baffling arrest, in escaping from jail, or in procuring bail, which will effect their release from custody."[33]

And whom did the Prison Association choose as the primary exemplar of this phenomenon? "A family residing in Oneida County who, according to common fame, have followed the profession of thieving for nearly twenty years . . . [and who] have grown rich by their unlawful practices." The report detailed the criminal activities of the Loomis Gang's "well-trained confederates" spread over much of the state. It also devoted considerable space to the Loomises' ability to control the legal and political processes in the counties in which they operated. "Substantial farmers" were always ready to post bail for gang members, and constables and judges who pursued the Loomises too vigorously found their barns burned, mortgages foreclosed, and professional reputations ruined. The association even recounted examples of the Loomises' using their control over the legal system to wrongfully imprison their innocent enemies. "We do not suppose that any of the gangs of thieves and robbers in other counties are as well organized or as successful as this," the Prison Association conceded, "but the defects in our criminal administration are tending to this result. The tendency to operate in bands is greater than ever before; and there is reason to fear that each year will add to the perfection of their organization, and consequently to the success of their schemes of depredation."[34] As this report shows, contemporary observers of the Loomis Gang noticed their tendency to apply the organizational and business techniques of the market revolution to their criminal enterprises, and for those who were concerned with the prevalence of crime in New York, the prospect was frightening indeed.

This concern about the Loomises' market revolution even percolated into the debates at the New York State Constitutional Convention in 1867 and 1868. Under the Constitution of 1821, the district attorneys for each of the state's counties were appointed by the judges before whom they served.

However, under the democratizing Constitution of 1846, district attorneys were elected by the voters of each county. During the debates for a proposed new state constitution twenty years later, John Gould, a delegate from Columbia County, proposed returning to the old system of appointment from the Constitution of 1821. After all, he pointed out, "it is exceedingly undesirable to make this officer, who is intended for the protection of society and the punishment of crime, to be nominated by political convention." His argument against election hinged on the increasing organization of "bands of thieves" and the attendant influence they could exert over local elections through "a very perfect combination of effort in all matters connected with their profession." The example that he used to support his argument was the Loomis Gang, whose members Gould described to his fellow delegates as "having their center of operations, in the county of Oneida; they are known to be energetic politicians; their ramifications are known to extend into Madison, and as far south as the county of Sullivan, and they are exceedingly active in those counties when the subject of district attorney is brought up for discussion."[35] Gould fundamentally doubted the capacity of the legal system to distinguish between legitimate and illegitimate influence when it could be controlled by groups like the Loomis Gang, whose members so effectively blurred the lines. This argument for returning to the appointment system persuaded the convention, and they accepted his proposed amendment.[36]

The Loomises' star turn at the Constitutional Convention shows how powerful their reputation had become by the late 1860s. It also shows that they had learned an important lesson about how essential political influence was to business success in a market economy. The Loomises sought to control the areas of government that directly affected their enterprise, just like their law-abiding neighbors. The prosperous farmers of central New York put considerable pressure on politicians to address the matter of protective tariffs for wool and hops, and the local and statewide mercantile interests that linked the region to the larger national and international economy exerted heavy influence over the state's canal and railroad policies. The Loomises used the means at their disposal to control the elections of the district attorneys that affected them most directly—in the counties in which they operated. Like the other developing market-oriented business enterprises that surrounded them, the Loomises used their economic power to affect political change in their favor. That they did so in pursuit of a criminal agenda was profoundly unsettling to statewide leaders like John Gould, even if it was less of a concern to the more democratically inclined statewide electorate.

These high-level discussions of the market implications of the Loomis Gang came at the apex of the gang's career. Their horse-stealing operations had been growing in size and scope since the 1850s and reached their pinnacle during the Civil War, when the Union army's insatiable need for artillery and cavalry horses drove both demand and prices up sharply. Under Quartermaster General Montgomery C. Meigs, the government purchased tens of thousands of horses a year, and although the price varied widely depending on the type of horse and local market conditions, it averaged over a hundred dollars a head and could approach twice that amount. Although Meigs attempted to rationalize the acquisitions system and control price and quality by building on the prewar system of government contractors who could supply horses in large numbers, the army's needs could not always be met in a timely fashion by this cumbersome and bureaucratic system. Especially late in the war, local supply depots increasingly cut out the middlemen and bought horses in small quantities directly from local farmers.[37] For example, in July 1864 the Albany depot reported buying forty horses from eighteen different sellers, none of whom sold more than five horses apiece. Although none of these small sellers can be definitively tied to the Loomises given the limited extant records of the sales, the disorganized and information-poor market in which they participated was precisely the kind the gang was best positioned to capitalize on.[38] Individual government buyers were more interested in the quality of the horses than their provenance, they were under time pressure to make purchases, and they communicated more with the central office in Washington than with other agents in New York. It is highly likely, then, that the Loomises, given their practiced ability to move horses to profitable and anonymous markets through their far-flung network of allies, were called upon to make sales to the army and thrived in the chaotic environment of wartime.

The war years were profitable for the Loomises, but their success heightened tensions between them and their neighbors and hardened local resistance in ways that the family, despite their skills and connections, were not able to control. The family was politically out of step with the moment, as they sought to capitalize on a conflict that was demanding real sacrifice from the small farmers that were the Loomises' most common victims. Support for the war was very strong along the Erie Canal corridor, and Oneida County alone sent around ten thousand soldiers to the Union army, about 10 percent of the county's entire population.[39] As most of Sangerfield mobilized for war, the Loomises ramped up their operations, especially as mounting prices made horse stealing increasingly profitable in 1863 and 1864. The gang grew in some measure by absorbing deserters, who found shelter from the law and gainful employment with the Loomises and their associates.[40] The growing scope and intensity of their wartime operations, increasingly carried out by unpopular deserters in a region that had sent many loyal husbands and sons off to die, meant that the people of southern Oneida County were growing much less tolerant of the Loomises' depredations.

Since the gang's organization and structure had rendered them largely immune from legal prosecution, exasperated neighbors and local law enforcement officials turned to extralegal measures to fight back. Pressure began to mount in October 1864, when a Madison County courthouse caught fire the night before several Loomis indictments were scheduled to be heard, and the local fire company dispatched to fight the blaze found that their hoses had been cut with an ax. The brazenness of this arson put pressure on local politicians like Roscoe Conkling (who was busily building a national reputation for himself as a Republican power broker) to more effectively prosecute such outlaws. The local press began to openly call for a California solution, so called because of the dominance of private vigilance committees in contemporary San Francisco.[41] The editor of the *Waterville Times* suggested to the community, "Give [the Loomises] so many hours in which to leave the State and if not gone at the end of the time, specify a judicious lynching."[42] This open acknowledgment of local hostility suggested that the balance of power had finally shifted against the once powerful gang.

During the summer of 1865, a local constable named Jim Filkins, one of the Loomises' most tenacious opponents, organized the Sangerfield Vigilance Committee. On its face, the formation of such a committee was not unusual in nineteenth-century rural America. Private, locally oriented anticrime societies had been a feature of rural northeastern life since the 1780s, operating as "protective societies," "vigilance committees," and "detecting societies." Although some had broader aims, most were focused on catching and prosecuting horse thieves. Members of these societies were generally more interested in enhancing the state's power to catch, prosecute, and punish criminals than in replacing it with a separate, private form of justice. Of course, "detecting" was not the problem that the Oneida County authorities faced; the Loomises' guilt was common knowledge. The family's control over the legal system meant that the members of the Sangerfield Vigilance Committee could not follow the usual pattern of "assisting 'the arm of justice'"; instead, they had to administer their own. And in doing so, they went well beyond the prevailing norms of private law enforcement.[43]

The committee's plans were put into effect on Halloween night, 1865, when a band of men broke into the Loomises' house. With a passion and force driven by years of accumulated resentment, they beat Grove and lit him on fire. Other gang members quickly extinguished the blaze, but while they attended to Grove they realized Wash was missing, and upon searching they found him beneath the woodshed, covered in blood from mortal head wounds. He died the next afternoon. Within a week Filkins was arrested for Wash's murder, and although the prosecution held overwhelming evidence against the constable, his willingness to stand up to the Loomises earned him a good deal of public support in Oneida County, and more importantly, it brought Roscoe Conkling into the courtroom on his behalf. Home on break from his service in the House of Representatives and on the brink of an appointment to the Senate, the ambitious politician saw an opportunity to burnish his credentials as a defender of middle-class market morality. With Conkling's legal skill and growing national political power on his side, Filkins spent only four days in jail before being released on bail.[44]

The Loomises quickly found themselves on the defensive, an unfamiliar place for them. Enraged, vengeful, and without Wash's steady leadership, the gang struck closer to home and with escalating violence, culminating in the brutal murder of a neighboring farmer in December and the nonfatal shooting of Filkins in May. At last, on June 16, 1866, a crowd of over one hundred people gathered at the nearby Morrisville Hotel, armed with firearms and rope, determined to eradicate the Loomises from Sangerfield for good. The dogs were poisoned and then, shortly before dawn on June 17, the mob proceeded to the farm. A number of local sheriffs joined the crowd, and although they first attempted to serve warrants on Grove and his brother Plumb, the situation quickly spiraled out of control. The mob set the house alight and lynched Plumb and family associate John Stoner. Each man was strung up several times while being interrogated about multiple arsons and the shooting of Filkins. Neither was killed—although the mob came close to murdering Plumb—but in the course of the lynching both Plumb and Grove confessed to all of the charges against them. Satisfied, the crowd released them and, after torching the remaining barns and outbuildings, warned the family to leave the area within thirty days if they did not want a repeat of the night's events. According to a local newspaper, "the family, after the occurrence, were sitting at the roadside on the fences with scarcely anything left but [the clothes] they had upon them."[45]

A California solution indeed; the Loomises' market revolution lay in shambles. With the hanging of Plumb Loomis and John Stoner, the Loomis farm destroyed, and local hostility at a peak, Rhoda and most of her remaining children retreated to Bill's farm in Hastings Center, forty miles away. The Loomises did not suddenly become model citizens; there is evidence that Bill in particular carried on the family business through his involvement with the curiously named "H. W. M. H. T. and C. C. Union" gang of horse thieves, which "grew out of" the Loomis Gang in 1867 and operated "from Augusta, M[ain]e., to central Indiana and spreading through New York, Pennsylvania, and Ohio" by 1880.[46] But the Loomis Gang, at least in its original form and with its original leadership, ceased to exist. The family was no longer a threat to the respectable farmers and merchants of Sangerfield.

Although lynching was doubtless a solution to Sangerfield's Loomis problem, it was not exactly a California solution, given that the term framed it as a practice of another place, a phenomenon of the barbarous, lawless West. Rather, such a lynching was not a particularly unusual resolution of a fatal clash between competing visions of the limits of moral behavior in a market economy. As Joshua Rothman has argued about a similar lynching of professional gamblers in Vicksburg, Mississippi, in 1835, the mob's action was "a vital means of defining the boundary between legitimate and illegitimate kinds of economic striving."[47] By acting collectively, with the support of both legal and extralegal authority, the residents of Sangerfield sought not only to draw a sharp line between their own economic activity and that of the Loomises but also to enforce it. Viewed in that light, lynching was as much a central New York solution as it was a California solution.

But members of the Sangerfield Vigilance Committee embraced a central New York solution in another sense, too. Their choice of enforcement mechanism was profoundly influenced by market thinking: with their direct action, they privatized justice. Indeed, this is precisely the conclusion drawn by the Prison Association of New York. "What can we expect, throughout the State, when such organisations shall have been everywhere formed and perfected?" its 1866 report asked. "Since like causes produce like effects, can we doubt that the inhabitants of other counties will resort to the same remedy of private vengeance which we have seen in Oneida and Madison? The very foundation of society will be broken up, law will be despised, and, as with the Ishmaelites of old; 'Every man's hand will be against his neighbour.'"[48] The Prison Association definitely did not endorse such privatization of justice; indeed, the association thought it heralded the return to a turbulent Old Testament world rather than the continued construction of a modern political economy in which the state held a monopoly on violence. Nevertheless, the association acknowledged that lynching was an attempt to fight fire with fire; if the Loomises could organize, so could their opponents. Roscoe Conkling exploited this argument in 1867: now a senator, he returned to Oneida County to defend Filkins at his trial for Wash's murder. Conkling won his client's acquittal by arguing that Filkins had succeeded where public justice had failed, and that the county's judicial system could preserve its reputation only by providing its tacit approval of Filkins's brutal measures.[49] Filkins and the Sangerfield Vigilance Committee took care of the Loomises, but ironically they ended up reinforcing the Loomises' might-makes-right vision of morality in a market economy.

What conclusions can we draw from the Loomis Gang's market revolution? To begin with, this story offers vivid support to the overall argument of this volume, which is that the line between the legitimate and the illegitimate economy was distinctly fuzzy in nineteenth-century America. But it was more than just fuzzy; the story of the Loomises demonstrates that in the hurly-burly world of the nineteenth-century economy, the boundaries between legitimate and illegitimate were drawn contextually and tactically, in order to consolidate political and economic power in the hands of certain people and to exclude it from others. This is not to say that horse thieving had ever been considered acceptable; the way the Loomises made their living had always been deemed outside the bounds of legitimate activity. But so too were lynching, arson, and murder, which became the only tools by which Loomis opponents could break the family's power in Sangerfield. The Loomises borrowed liberally from the emerging organizational strategies of nineteenth-century business, and in return the surrounding farmers and shopkeepers borrowed liberally from the Loomises' outlaw lexicon in order to break their power. But Rhoda and her children lived out their days in infamy, whereas their leading opponent, Jim Filkins, was remembered as a "brave and shrewd deputy sheriff," and his powerful ally Roscoe Conkling became a respected and well-connected national political leader.[50] In the end, the mantle of market legitimacy was draped on the Loomises' bourgeois neighbors, consigning the family and their antics to the dustbin of historical oddity.

CHAPTER 2

The Promiscuous Economy

Cultural and Commercial Geographies of Secondhand in the Antebellum City

ROBERT J. GAMBLE

Few streetscapes captured the enticing qualities of early nineteenth-century capitalism better than Philadelphia's Chestnut Street. Visitors to the city's most famous commercial street in the 1840s and 1850s, like Englishman William Chambers, observed "the thronging of well-dressed people" and its "large stores shewing a long vista of elegant counters, shelving, and glass-cases, such as may be seen in the better parts of London and Paris." The window displays of the street's jewelry establishments, George Foster wrote in 1848, "would have brought tears to the eyes of Benvenuto Cellini himself." Another English sightseer similarly was dazzled by the "hundreds of omnibuses . . . constantly in motion in every direction."[1] Frenetic as all of this commercial movement was, Chestnut Street and its shoppers maintained a veneer of order and self-control, with "elegant throng[s]" of men and women arranging themselves in "regiments" and "coolly inspecting every stranger they meet." The retail innovations that unfolded on Chestnut Street, beginning with the Philadelphia Arcade that went up in the late 1820s and continuing with the dry goods palaces that flourished in the late 1840s and 1850s, contributed to that decorous order. These emporiums, along with the numerous perfumeries, cigar shops, booksellers, photographers, jewelers, and specialized retailers that dotted the streetscape, catered to the sensibilities of an increasingly self-aware upper-middle class. By the 1850s, when the *North American* designated Chestnut Street as the focal point of the metropolis's "great vortex of business," commercial establishments paid to be included in pictorial directories published by Julio Rae and George Baxter that advertised not only individual stores but also an orderly, fashionable experience.[2]

South Street, running parallel to Chestnut Street a half-mile away, also served as literary inspiration for observers seeking to understand the city and its commercial life. In 1844, the *Public Ledger* proclaimed South Street as the city's preeminent "emporium of cheap merchandise" and as arguably "the most remarkable thoroughfare" in the nation from the perspective of trade. Between its intersections with Front and Second Streets, the columnist observed, "the traveller encounters cheap dry goods stores, millinery shops, second hand furniture warerooms, interspersed here and there with cellars for the purchase and sale of old iron." The latter stores overflowed with "shovel and tongs, andirons, bolts, bars, pots, pans, griddles, saws, knives, and every imaginable implement . . . scattered in confusion on the display stands."[3] As the writer moved westward, there emerged a clearer sense of spatial organization and commercial specialization. Dry goods and millinery shops congregated between Second and Third Streets, while the block from Third to Fourth Street was "the great depository of second hand furniture." Beyond Fifth Street lay the pawnshops and fripperies, where—his tone shading cynical—"the traveller . . . unacquainted with a peculiar kind of poverty, will wonder how the tradesmen can find customers for the old looking, tattered and dirty garment, which he will observe swinging from the doors."[4]

Propelled by a century-long revolution in the production and consumption of household goods, commodities inundated the homes, streets, wharves, shops, and market houses of cities in the Early Republic. The flow of commodities transformed the urban landscape, as pedestrians vied with farmers and their produce on their way to market, stevedores prepped ship cargoes, drays hauled merchandise from warehouses to storefronts, shopkeepers used sidewalks as temporary storage spaces, and hucksters erected stalls every morning. The spectacle of goods in transit was impressive. Visitors abroad marveled at the modern docks and warehouses of Liverpool and London, spaces where the orchestrated transshipment of global commodities underscored "the sublimity of rationalized capitalism," as Tamara Plakins Thornton writes.[5] By the 1820s and 1830s, canals and railroads inspired many Americans to celebrate the remarkable velocity with which commodities could make it from Atlantic ports to the shelves of general stores in the Ohio Valley. With increasing insistence in the 1840s and 1850s, retailers promoted a narrative of orderly commercial abundance in their lithograph advertisements, labor management, product arrangement, and one-price policies that stressed uniformity among goods and consumers.[6]

For many antebellum observers, however, there was nothing inherently rational or orderly about the city's assemblage of goods. To give readers a sense of the "medley of merchandize and eatables exposed for sale in the market houses of this city," a Philadelphia writer proposed to inventory all the things he found in High Street Market one Saturday morning in 1829: "Beef, butter, and black lead; wooden spoons, peaches, and brickdust; cows' horns, hominy, and carpets; toys, cow hides, and tongues; pork, mushrooms, and hobbyhorses." He juxtaposed the quotidian (buttermilk, tooth brushes, and old hats), the unusual (cures for dyspepsia, murderers' confessions, and mouse traps), the political (biographies of George Washington and Andrew Jackson and a bust of Lafayette), and the suspect (lottery tickets, dirks, and fighting cocks). The list of 242 articles revealed the "comfort and convenience" these goods promoted at the same time that it evinced a certain degree of wariness. His jumbled inventory reflected not only the sheer volume and variety of consumer goods but also the impossibility of categorizing them or assessing their myriad values.[7] Antebellum consumers needed not venture to the public market to witness this spectacle, for they could simply scan the dizzying array of goods advertised in newspapers.

Moreover, plebeian commercial activities—in South Street, market houses, street corners, and countless other spaces around the city—defied the fiction of order and rationality promoted by the champions of Chestnut Street. The *Public Ledger*'s determined focus on block-by-block specialization in its 1844 description of South Street could not obscure the myriad ways that secondhand was a flashpoint for contests over the shape of the commercial city, the consumer practices of the urban poor, and the legitimacy of economic transactions in these spaces. Plebeian economic activities quite often straddled these shifting cultural and legal boundaries, facilitating an insecure but potentially profitable economic landscape for men and women with ambition and resourcefulness, if not resources. Studying secondhand consumption, in particular, reveals a range of ways in which the working poor enacted discretionary choice and elective consumption, concepts usually reserved for middle- or upper-class consumers. To counter abstract forces beyond their control and the vagaries of daily life, poor men and women collaborated in shopping networks, pooled resources, bartered, negotiated, and exercised creativity in ways that blurred neat categories of legitimate and illegitimate consumption.[8] In rapidly expanding port cities like Philadelphia and Baltimore—two of the three largest cities in the country—promiscuity, not stability, characterized the urban consumer economy of most residents.[9]

Ordinary people's promiscuous secondhand economies also raised questions about the meanings of goods, which social and political authorities attempted to control through formal and informal mechanisms of policing. Commodities took many routes to becoming secondhand: they were alternately borrowed, donated, inherited, pawned, recycled, or auctioned. In the eyes of many authorities, the expansive trade in secondhand articles further complicated efforts to police theft and other illicit activities. Indeed, an article's transformation from firsthand to secondhand never went uncontested, whether its value was negotiated, its character disputed, its ownership debated, or its provenance investigated. Scholarship on the "social life" of commodities offers fruitful questions to ask of these secondhand goods. The circulation of commodities is an inherently political process not only because it illustrates the dynamics of privilege and social control, as Arjun Appadurai contends, but also because commodities persistently breach frameworks (of price, bargaining, and so forth) established by those in power to contain the flow of goods.[10] Circulating through both informal and formal marketplaces, commodities—like the people who consumed them—resisted easy distinctions as licit and illicit items. Secondhand goods illustrate how antebellum capitalism did not operate under its own power. Rather, it was a system shaped by numerous, visible hands that moved goods rapidly and sometimes surreptitiously, refashioning and contesting their meanings and value in every transaction along the way.[11]

The proliferation of goods, beginning with the eighteenth century's consumer revolution, enabled the inventive responses to scarcity in the nineteenth century. Household commodities, in particular, possessed three characteristics that facilitated an expansive secondhand marketplace: they were fungible, mobile, and mutable. The rise of cheap, ready-made clothing, for instance, did not dampen the trade in used clothing but instead provided new outlets for buying it and new opportunities for those selling it, particularly Jewish Americans and African Americans. In 1830, one observer declared that "the sale of cast off clothes, as now opened in cellars by the blacks, is quite a modern affair."[12] Buying and selling secondhand clothing or furnishings comprised one of numerous temporary or permanent strategies for working-class families to make ends meet, accompanied by taking in boarders, scavenging, and vending homespun articles in the city's marketplaces. Such makeshift economies were not foolproof, especially when uncontrollable forces made paying for rent, fuel, and food often difficult and at times impossible.[13]

When patching together precious resources proved untenable, city residents learned to navigate a labyrinthine system of public and private charities. Voluntary associations took up the material concerns of the poor in the Early Republic, accumulating and distributing infants' clothing, coats, fuel, home furnishings, and food to individuals whom reformers deemed worthy. Many beneficiaries recognized the value they could add to their meager alms by reselling donations in the secondhand marketplace. Men and women like Hugh O'Hara, officials complained, arrived at the almshouse "in a very wretched condition, with disease & Rags, Winter'd here got cured & cloathed, and went off in the Spring . . . & immediately Sold most of his Clothing and soon drank the whole they produced."[14] The act of donation ostensibly removed these used articles from the marketplace, formally decommoditizing them and labeling them as items of charity. And yet many of these donated goods quickly found their way back into the secondhand consumer economy, to the chagrin of relief associations. It is revealing, though, that associations frequently reported donations, which were already secondhand, in terms of the monetary value of the goods received. By obscuring and redefining the value of used or donated goods and controlling access to them, charitable associations exerted power over the commodities and consumers of the promiscuous economy.[15] Despite authorities' efforts to restrict the value and circulation of donated clothing, however, participants in secondhand economies evaluated the meaning and worth of goods on their own terms.[16]

Charitable associations were among a wide range of urban entities asserting authority over the consumer habits of the laboring classes. While poorer men and women articulated a consumer economy out of secondhand, reformers from across the class spectrum critiqued their gratuitous and imprudent spending of precious resources. Labor advocate William Heighton decried working-class consumers as "the dupes of the indolent, the interested, and the knavish," purchasing "a scanty portion of the coarsest and meanest of their own productions."[17] In an 1832 broadside titled "Advice and Suggestions to Increase the Comforts of Persons in Humble Circumstances," political economist Mathew Carey cautioned the poor to "avoid all unnecessary expenses, however small." This meant eating a meal of "mush and molasses" for breakfast but not drinking tea or coffee, where there was "no nourishment," in addition to avoiding "all species of gambling, whether in lottery tickets, or otherwise." He encouraged the poor to purchase "good, cheap, strong, lasting [clothing] . . . made up plainly" as well as other necessaries with cash, which would curb frivolous spending as well as allow buyers to "procure better terms."[18]

Procuring liquid capital itself could be a challenge, however, leading many to rely on pawnshops and secondhand stores for access to goods. Moral authorities like Philadelphia physician James Mease emphasized the sentimental value of the articles that were loaned for cash—whether family Bibles or clothes—to sharpen their critique of the avarice of pawnbrokers and the shortsightedness of pledgers.[19] In 1817, the Pennsylvania Society for the Promotion of Public Economy proclaimed the propagation of "clothes-sellers," lotteries, and pawnbrokers in neighborhoods like Southwark to be "a most serious and growing evil" that was "certainly instrumental in reducing many persons to want."[20] While social betters argued that pawnshops and other secondhand outlets preyed on the poor, Wendy Woloson suggests that the brisk business done by these shops is perhaps better understood in the context of working-class consumers "exercising a great deal of personal agency over what they bought."[21] This agency hinged on the decisions of countless men and women to treat commodities as currency, viewing their fungible everyday possessions as a far more stable receptacle of value than paper or coin in an era when banks failed weekly.

When it came to basic provisioning, consumer strategies hinged not only on the availability of secondhand food but also on the mobility of buyers and sellers. This was yet another aspect of the daily life of the poor that provoked intense scrutiny from police and invited additional control by moral authorities. Lacking the means to buy and store produce in bulk from grocers and butchers, laboring families relied most heavily on the public markets that honeycombed Baltimore's and Philadelphia's built landscapes. Public markets, like the one in South Second Street that linked Chestnut and South Streets in Philadelphia, were the cities' most regulated spaces and their most kaleidoscopic and plebeian. Many market vendors stayed late on Saturday evenings "to accommodate mechanics paid on Saturday afternoon," but in general laws served to hinder working-class access to public markets. In early national Philadelphia and Baltimore, property owners successfully waged protests against the holding of markets on Sunday, laborers' lone day off, claiming not religious motives but rather that the spaces were becoming "the resort of idle and dissolute persons."[22] Moreover, working-class consumers in neighborhoods like Southwark or Old Town had to walk a half-mile or more to the cities' better-stocked central market houses. This reflected the ability of property owners to convince municipal leaders to erect marketplaces in their neighborhoods, anchoring asymmetries of access to fresh food—"food deserts," in modern parlance—in the built environment.

Itinerant hucksters purchased fruit and vegetables from farmers on roads leading from the countryside and resold it in city streets, forming the connective tissue of the urban food economy. Hucksters not only provided consumers with more flexible and convenient purchasing arrangements, sometimes going door-to-door and often taking payment in kind, but also offered cheaper comestibles than those that might be found in public markets.[23] But cheapness came at the price of freshness. Meat and produce spoiled easily in the market's open-air stalls, particularly during the summer and in spite of farmers' efforts to transport their goods at night when it was cooler.[24] If a farmer or vendor was unable to sell items on market day, hucksters bought up the unsold articles in bulk. Thus fruit and vegetables cycled through the city's public markets until they were eventually purchased. Food that traveled farther and passed through many hands was most likely to be consumed by the poor. All but the most spoiled produce, meat, and fish found a consumer, even if that consumer was one of the pigs or goats raised in working-class neighborhoods.[25]

Middle-class commentators remained anxious about the increasingly mediated nature of the urban food supply and the hucksters who made it so. They alleged that street vendors defrauded their poor customers. Some likened hucksters to alchemists, manipulating both price and quality. Butter, the Baltimore *Sun* alleged in 1839, lent itself to easy adulteration by market women who "work up ransid butter with their begrimed hands, stamp it, rent the use of a countryman's cart, and vend it for a fresh article."[26] The produce and prepared foods that hucksters sold, including pepper-pot soup, peaches, and watermelons, acquired reputations for being prone to "vile deception," captured vividly in the sobriquet for watermelons: "cholera bombshells."[27] As with the debates surrounding mock auctions, observers who denounced unscrupulous street vendors also blamed customers for exercising poor judgment or being easily deceived. Others recognized that a lack of money, time, and storage facilities—essentials enjoyed by the middle and upper classes—fundamentally shaped the consumer practices of the urban poor. Hucksters made butter, cheese, meat, and other articles more readily available to those of limited means by cutting them into smaller pieces. Petitioning to have their license fee reduced in 1824, a group of cut bacon vendors reminded Baltimore lawmakers that their product "is sold only to the poor class which is very numerous and in proportion as the competition is reduced so will the cut pieces raise [prices on the] poor."[28] Fresh or prepared food was only one of several services hucksters provided to their urban clientele, who also purchased smaller portions of wood, soap, candles, cotton, pins, toothbrushes, and tinware from these mobile groceries.

Hucksters were among a wide range of commercial agents who forged linkages in this promiscuous economy with their physical mobility. One of the signal features of this economy was that participants, be they hucksters, counterfeiters, hack drivers, merchants, or pawnbrokers, benefited and gained knowledge from their access to both the formal and informal marketplace. They leveraged their ability to mediate between buyers and sellers, producers and consumers, to make a profit that not everyone believed was legitimately earned. A frequent charge leveled against hucksters was that they acted in concert to manipulate popular knowledge about the prices and availability of food, an ancient concern that reemerged in nineteenth-century urban America. In eastern cities, hucksters served as a human-scale target for mounting concerns about western cattle speculators and monopolization of the nation's food supply in the late 1830s and 1840s.[29]

Hucksters were not the only urban itinerants who attracted growing scrutiny as Americans attempted to navigate the fluid distinction between legitimate and illegitimate commerce. Men, women, and children scavenged for cast-off produce, cotton, hardware, and piping, selling them to an array of retailers and producers, including manufacturers, junk dealers, and hucksters.[30] Because some of these articles inevitably had owners, scavengers blurred the meanings of theft in a society in which goods were discarded more rapidly than ever before. Junk and scrap dealers proliferated in antebellum cities to provide quick means and secure places to transform not only luxury goods but also copper pipes and lead plate into commodities devoid of any characteristics that might direct authorities or previous owners to them. Baltimoreans complained in 1824 of "minions and slave negroes" stealing house keys one at a time and supplying them to "old Iron petty dealers" or, worse, "vagabond thieves." While these outlets undoubtedly permitted people to convert stolen goods into marketable assets, they were also essential for the thousands of ragpickers who earned a legal, if marginal, livelihood in antebellum cities.[31]

In a highly transient society, the physical mobility of commercial itinerants also raised moral alarm. The quandary of movement was most pronounced in the case of prostitution, a commercial activity transacted in the same public markets, streets and courts, wharves, boardinghouses, and taverns that served as venues for the transactions of hucksters and junk dealers. An 1838 grand jury charge intimated that there was a link between vending fruit and vending sex when it called for the better policing of "hordes of beggars—of unlicensed pedlars and hawkers—of prostitutes who nocturnally swarm in some of our frequented streets and public walks."[32] Book peddlers and newsboys perambulated the city selling didactic literature alongside erotica. The newsboys' mobility heightened fears of the spread of licentiousness, for their familiarity with the city was seen as a stepping-stone to a life of vice as pickpockets or worse.[33]

For the promiscuous economy's critics, the potential for fraud necessitated the policing of mobility. Carters and draymen, charged with the task of conveying commodities and passengers throughout the early nineteenth-century city, capitalized on their extensive grasp of urban space and both its visible and invisible linkages. What made common carriers so effective in greasing the wheels of the urban economy—their intimate knowledge of the city, its streets and alleys, wharves and buildings—also made them potential threats to the public good. Like the hucksters who monopolized fruit and vegetables arriving from the countryside, carters and draymen closely guarded entry into their profession and vigorously fought legislative efforts to banish them from high-traffic areas of the city.[34] In 1817, Baltimore mayor George Stiles bemoaned the hack drivers who charged strangers "unwarrantable" fees and took them on circuitous routes. He requested that the council hire more watchmen to police a city whose population exceeded 60,000 residents, hoping to establish order through surveillance of the promiscuous economy's main players and purveyors.[35]

Because police forces were small before the 1850s, licensing remained the most commonly used means of checking the mobility of commercial itinerants. When Mayor Robert Wharton drew up a list of ten improvements and submitted them to Philadelphia's city council in 1810, first on the list was his call for "Hackney coaches, carts and drays [to] be numbered and licensed" and "owners of such carriages [to] give bond for the good behaviour of their hirelings."[36] Meanwhile, Pennsylvania and Maryland required petitions for peddlers' licenses to include the signatures of several "respectable" members of the community. In mandating that an annual fee be paid at local court offices, that sureties (often wealthier members of society) pay the bonds of licensees, and that itinerants display their licenses in a conspicuous place, license laws enmeshed mobile individuals within well-defined relationships of power.[37]

Participants in the promiscuous economy faced the most intense surveillance or suppression when their knowledge of urban space intersected with other perceived dangers to social order. In antebellum Baltimore and Philadelphia, few groups were as routinely singled out for their supposedly unregulated movements as free persons of color. African Americans engaged in trades dependent on mobility, such as carting, huckstering, and chimney sweeping (occupations in which a considerable number of free blacks worked in the two port cities), were special subjects of attention for the authorities.[38] At its most benign, interest in the widespread presence of African American vendors and laborers in city streets was registered in visual and written descriptions of urban life. Books such as *Cries of Philadelphia* (1810) and *City Characters* (1851) drew sentimental "portraits" of itinerant black workers that identified them as dependable and inoffensive fixtures in the urban tableau.[39] Artists depicted black street vendors in order to explore several themes, particularly surveillance and promiscuity. For John Lewis Krimmel, scenes of hucksters and oystermen and their customers provided a lens through which to view the intimacy and heterogeneity of antebellum Philadelphia street life (see Figure 2.1). Others, including Edward Clay in his "Life in Philadelphia" series, drew sensationalized and racist illustrations that captured urban northerners' fears of the social and geographic mobility of free persons of color.[40]

State and local laws hewed closer to Clay's interpretation of blacks' mobility as inherently transgressive and in need of vigilant and occasionally extralegal policing. Again officials used licensing as an instrument to regulate the economic activities and range of movement of free and enslaved blacks, particularly in southern towns and cities. Proslavery newspapers frequently portrayed unlicensed tippling houses as spaces in which "assaults and batteries, riots, affrays, homicides, trading with slaves, and receiving stolen goods" occurred. Another columnist tried to rouse slave owners into assisting "a revision of the license laws," exclaiming that "neighborhoods are again infested with grog-shops, where men grow rich notoriously by corrupting slaves and receiving stolen goods."[41] The laws in Maryland, like those of most other slave states, required free blacks to take out a license to engage in the trade of any agricultural products. Significantly, these laws also made the purchase of these goods from an unlicensed African American trader punishable under laws prohibiting the receipt of stolen goods. In concert with other legal instruments like vagrancy and apprenticeship laws, license laws stymied free blacks' pursuit of economic independence, which rested upon their ability to pass from country to city and back again.[42]

Figure 2.1. At night in the Early Republic, a medley of mobile laborers and consumers transformed patrician thoroughfares such as Philadelphia's Chestnut Street into plebeian spaces where food and other goods circulated promiscuously. John Lewis Krimmel, *Nightlife in Philadelphia—an Oyster Barrow in front of the Chestnut Street Theater*, ca. 1811–1813. Metropolitan Museum of Art, 42.95.18.

The promiscuous mobility of secondhand goods drew particular scrutiny to used clothing dealers and pawnshops. Municipal laws required owners to keep ledgers and allow for their frequent inspection, and exacted strict licensing requirements for these businesses because they reputedly served as clearinghouses for stolen goods.[43] While a majority of the secondhand trade was legitimate, the relatively few dealers who fenced goods on the side loomed large in popular and legal constructions of secondhand. The fact that poor, black, and immigrant men and women often ran these establishments only sharpened prejudices toward the secondhand trade. A Philadelphia grand jury articulated these elite attitudes when it called for the crackdown on "Pawn Broker's Offices, Shops for the sale of old Clothes, and petty Auction Stores, which now lamentably abound."[44] Others feared the customers of such businesses. In 1824, a group of Baltimoreans complained that the recent arrival of a number of itinerant vendors of "old cloathing" had turned the west side of Harrison Street into "a mere harbour for drunken disorderly persons."[45] Yet in spite of authorities' efforts to produce knowledge about the goods that such establishments displayed for sale and the people who bought and sold them, commodities that were fungible, mobile, and mutable continued to pass from owner to owner, destabilizing categories of meaning and value in the process.

Ultimately, what was threatening about mobile commercial actors was their ability to forge expansive commercial networks that were invisible, illegible, and impenetrable to authorities. Just as America was becoming a society of strangers, the value of commodities and currency needed to be ascertained and was simultaneously uncertain. In 1838, in the midst of the controversy over unregulated paper money following the Panic of 1837, a newspaper story reprinted in the Baltimore *Sun* titled "Autobiography of a Fip Shin-Plaster" offered readers a primer for the promiscuous economy's interconnectedness, its sundry participants, and its debates about value. The fipenny bit described its origins: "fresh from the hands of the Corporation Clerk . . . I was received by a green grocer, as part of the exchange for a five dollar bill. He tied my companions and myself together in a greasy pocket-book, and laid us carefully in his money-drawer." After being "consigned to the custody of a prim old maid," it was regularly cleaned and ironed until "times grew hard" and its "kind mistress" was forced to pay it over to a butcher: "From this day I date my fall. I became unctious [*sic*] in the hands of such an owner, and began to look as oily as a whaler." Passing back and forth between men and women who were wealthy and impoverished, wholesome and unhygienic, the shinplaster kept promiscuous company.[46] Sullied and mired in the cash nexus, the shinplaster's circulation through the city brought to life the vagaries of the economy. From the butcher, it passed on to "a rosy cheeked girl" visiting the public market on a whim, who in turn gave it to "an old beggar." He exchanged it with a baker for a loaf of bread, bringing the fip "into bad company again." From there it passed through the hands of a miller, tavernkeeper, and chambermaid, who used it to buy "a narrow blue ribband." A store clerk attempted to slip the fip into his waistcoat but was caught midtheft, leaving the shinplaster torn and forgotten. Prevailing cultural assumptions about gender roles and class hierarchies saturated the piece: images of women "ironing me out smooth and nicely," urban artisans and their uncouth behavior, the beggar desperately and graciously kissing the fip, and the chambermaid spending her meager earnings on an item of personal adornment. Moreover, each recipient interpreted or valued the fip differently—as an object of sentimental value; as a blessing; or as an object to be hoarded, exchanged, burned, or spirited away. The shinplaster's downward trajectory, from its origins in a clean, uncut sheet of bills (of questionable value) to its last days as a soiled rag, may also be read as an allegory of the debasing effects of the urban economy.[47]

The writer, by anthropomorphizing the shinplaster, traced the arbitrary relationships produced through economic transactions and highlighted what the nineteenth-century urban economy was. The shinplaster story dramatized the fact that certain kinds of commodities could travel more swiftly and surreptitiously than individuals or information, posing considerable limits to the policing of the economy. City leaders struggled to establish order over the circulation of goods that, like the shinplaster, passed promiscuously from one owner to another, resisted ready calculations of their value, and muddied the distinction between licit and illicit exchange.[48] Elites may have wanted to make an idealized, respectable Chestnut Street the operative vision for urban capitalist society, where people and goods were in perpetual, but orderly, motion. Yet there was no escaping the fact that disheveled South Street, the home of inferior, cast-off, and recycled things and the people who found inventive ways to recirculate them, more accurately represented the economy as a whole.

Nevertheless, a variety of observers set their sights on illuminating the city's less visible economies. The remainder of this essay will explore these issues from the perspectives of two Philadelphians who attempted to do so in the late 1820s. Joseph Watson, the city's mayor from 1824 to 1828, was most invested in tracking the activities of interstate networks of counterfeiters, horse thieves, confidence men, and kidnappers. His efforts to cobble together a piecemeal system of surveillance and information sharing underscore the broader challenges men like Watson faced in establishing control over the networks of promiscuous commerce that crisscrossed the mid-Atlantic. Meanwhile, from 1828 to 1830, an anonymous contributor to the *Mechanics' Free Press*, writing under the nom de plume Night Hawk, countered Watson and others' official geographies of the city in a series of essays that explored the nocturnal city. Over the course of sixty-one essays, he exploded the distinctions that members of the "good society" of Chestnut Street drew between themselves and the laboring classes of South Street by revealing the promiscuous economy of all urban streets.[49]

While Watson and the Night Hawk had different purposes for charting the geography of the city's subaltern economies, a number of features unite them. Both dwelled on how goods and people could be transformed as they moved through spaces that were themselves mutable. Watson was concerned with how quickly criminals could adopt new identities and find markets for their stolen goods and counterfeit money. The Night Hawk, meanwhile, examined a series of conversions: how nighttime awakened the city, how fashion distorted men and women, and how power corrupted people. Relatedly, both were invested in questions of authority in the market: who wielded it, how was it exerted, and to what ends? As Watson sought to expand the presence of municipal police on the ground, the Night Hawk mocked watchmen and constables as lazy, incompetent, and shifty. Finally, although neither directly acknowledged the role of secondhand goods in the urban consumer economy, both approached the question of secondhand in other ways. As seen above, municipal officials like Watson tended to conflate, or at least assume, an innate link between secondhand and illicit commerce. Secondhand performed a more political function for the Night Hawk, who castigated "idle accumulators" for interposing themselves, like hucksters, between laborers and the value of their work.

Cultivating networks of knowledge about participants in the city's economy constituted a major aspect of Watson's role in administering the police and criminal court. He was in constant communication with the leaders of Baltimore, New York, and other major cities, as well as nearby towns like Lancaster, whose mayor asked Watson to examine his "Black list" and pass along any information that would "be of assistance in detecting rogues."[50]

Watson reached out personally to many of his informants. On one occasion, he mailed the cashier of the State Bank of Georgia a counterfeit twenty-dollar bill, explaining that he was "not at liberty to say how this sample came into [his] possession," but sent it with the aim of opening further dialogue.[51] His reputation for having an "invincible hatred of crime" led many citizens and officials to bring evidence to him rather than to local sheriffs or judges.[52] One correspondent, Charles Williams, looked to translate his self-declared expertise on illicit mobility into a city job: "My situation as an agent for Steam Boats & stages for the last 7 years has made me acquainted with a host of villains composed of Counterfeiters, Gamblers, thieves, etc." He requested an appointment as a special constable so he could "cleanse this city of some confirmed scoundrels who now infest it." While hucksters and carters required regulation because of their unique knowledge of how goods and people circulated, others stood to gain from their familiarity with these markets in the form of pardons or employment.[53]

In almost every case, however, the information passed between Watson and his network was time-sensitive, verging on obsolete by the time it reached the right set of hands. The mutability of goods and the people who used them—qualities of the secondhand trade more generally—complicated his efforts. Thieves and runaways could don a new set of clothes, adopt new aliases and personal histories, and remove themselves from the neighborhoods in which they were most likely to be discovered. Watson and his associates succeeded in capturing participants when men or women failed to do one or more of these things. When Robert Anderson made his way from Detroit to Philadelphia by stage with $1,000 of stolen watches in tow, fellow travelers noticed that he wore the same thin coat and dusty hat every day, despite the cold, the length of the trip, and what appeared to be a heavy suitcase in his possession. Calling himself Robert Henderson, he became highly agitated when someone accidentally called him Anderson, thus betraying his true identity.[54] Clothing also betrayed William Francis Thomas, who was caught in Lancaster wearing the same "blue frock coat with velvet collar, one blue vest, one shirt &c." he had stolen from a Philadelphia man over three weeks earlier. Both Anderson and Thomas failed to repurpose their clothing as often or as well as other participants in the promiscuous economy, making them stand out in a society in which changed appearance was the norm.[55]

The velocity with which articles could travel and be transformed raised particular issues about ownership. Even with stolen goods that could not be recycled or repurposed, the farther they traveled from their owners, the less likely they would be recovered. The question of complicity in such illicit exchanges was an important but convoluted one, for in most cases stolen goods were not found with the individual who had perpetrated the theft. The penalties for receivers of goods who "knew them to be stolen" were stiff, though more stringent punishments were meted out to those convicted of larceny and robbery. But what did it mean to "know" that an article had been stolen? As with counterfeit currency, there was a certain degree of willful ignorance on the part of customers who recognized that, at one point in the social life of the coat they were buying, it may have been considered stolen. Involving the police could mean not only losing the value of the stolen coat or counterfeit bill by having to return it but also implicating oneself in a crime.[56] The participation of authorities only muddled this issue further, as sheriffs auctioned off stolen goods that went unclaimed by owners, generating a reward for the constable who retrieved the stolen article and legitimating its entrance back into the secondhand economy.

Mayor Watson, in charting the movement of people and goods through the region, concentrated his efforts on the city's northwest suburbs, a sparsely settled neighborhood with virtually no police presence. A meeting of residents of Penn Township and Germantown in the late 1820s directed Watson's attention to the activities of felons recently released from prison who would "sally out into the surrounding country in search of plunder . . . [succeeding] with very little risk of detection in consequence of the lonely and scattered situations of the inhabitants, cut off as they are by the intervening districts from the active interference of the police of the City." Limited transportation options and poor roads contributed to their isolation, but the residents viewed the problem as systemic. Decrying the "present loose system of police regulation, and want of concentrated information, to carry their good intentions into effect," they looked to the day when "a permanent prompt energetick system of police should be established in the different incorporated districts around the City, taking the city as a nucleus, or centre." Vigilantism filled the vacuum of law enforcement in Philadelphia's hinterlands, serving only to attenuate the networks of surveillance and information that Watson attempted to establish.[57]

In 1828, aldermen voted to replace Watson with George Mifflin Dallas, whose entrance into office coincided not only with the ascendancy of Democrats in the city but also with a new era of working-class politics. Dallas and other elites encountered an increasingly alienated and articulate class of mechanics who believed that the paternalism of lawmakers and capitalists, which had governed social relations in the city, was now being turned toward new political and commercial ends. William Heighton, the most prominent voice in Philadelphia's labor movement and profoundly influenced by Ricardian political economy, sought to educate laborers about the intrinsic value of their labor, to be wary of commercial intermediaries who profited from the products of labor, and to distrust political and moral authorities whose interests nearly always aligned with those of the commercial class.[58]

One of his main venues for advancing these ideas was the *Mechanics' Free Press*, the first newspaper in the nation both edited by and published for mechanics. Its success was marked by a circulation of over 1,000 and an even larger readership.[59] The Night Hawk, judging by the length of the column's run and its many imitators and offshoots, struck a chord with the paper's readers. The essays were particularly innovative in form and represent one of the earliest sustained forays into urban-sensationalist journalism in America (nearly two decades before George Foster, George Lippard, Ned Buntline, and others set out to expose the "mysteries and miseries" of the nocturnal city).[60] The Night Hawk, along with later authors who created the subterranean city in the popular imagination, fashioned the gaslight economy into a print-culture commodity that blended melodrama and social critique.[61]

The conceit of the Night Hawk, an avian author who could pass undetected through the night skies, was at times clumsy; the author slipped in and out of human form and was variously visible and invisible, an active participant and a passive onlooker. Nevertheless, he explored Philadelphia's shadows as few others had in America, tracing people and their complicated motivations for engaging in the nocturnal economy. His "preface" promised readers he would "soar in [the city's] gloomy regions, regardless of the shafts of men to bring him down; he is a night demon, one whose passage through life has been of romance." The Night Hawk established his credentials as a proto-flâneur whose anonymity accentuated his—and it was a masculine activity—powers of observation. He asserted, "My knowledge of lanes and alleys, dark intricate and deep, have gave [*sic*] me the means of escape, when necessity urged my ability in that way; in thus *eluding* I have *deluded*, and rendered myself an object of terror to the watchmen."[62] Later, he reminded his audience, "*I am every where and in every place*; not exactly *omnipresent*, but a transient visitor, to every public house."[63] Like the hucksters and carters, the Night Hawk's alternative, even subversive, knowledge of the city's visible and invisible spaces trespassed against the official geography of the city defined by lawmakers and patrolled by policemen.

The Night Hawk, in the process of traversing and connecting these ephemeral and opaque spaces for his readers, revealed the disparities of power in the city. Foremost among his characters were municipal officials, particularly watchmen, whom he described as corrupt, inept, or powerless. The Night Hawk suggested that constables, whose duty it was to furnish the courts with a list of licensed and unlicensed tippling shops, took their "bribe money out in *small glasses*," and that instead of going to the police office, anyone needing the attention of an officer should "go to the tavern, and there, lolling on a settee, drinking, smoking, or sleeping, you [will] find our active and efficient police!!"[64] When Dallas became mayor in 1828, he instituted a new policy for watchmen regarding public drunkenness. Previously, the Night Hawk wrote, "all drunkards and young frolicking blades [were] forcibly dragged to the watch house" and taken before the mayor the following morning, with the watchman "acting on the same principle as Dog-catchers" and receiving "fifty cents per head" for their exertions. Now, Dallas called on watchmen instead to take these men to their homes. With no financial incentive in place, "wretched females and houseless blacks . . . made the streets their home" with the full complicity of watchmen.[65] When authorities meted out justice, they were more lenient to those from respectable backgrounds than to those of the working class, so long as the wealthy transgressor paid a heftier fine.

Like the author of "Autobiography of a Fip Shin-Plaster," the Night Hawk provided a variegated, if highly stylized, portrait of the city's commercial geography. The likely suspects for nocturnal surveillance—oyster cellars, gambling dens, and brothels—were present in his peregrinations, but so too were intelligence offices, pawnshops, fortune telling establishments, millinery shops, boarding houses, public markets, lottery ticket offices, and fancy charity balls. Spaces that served one set of functions during the day were repurposed and virtually unrecognizable after dark: market houses, for instance, were converted into holding pens for vagrants by night watchmen. Although working-class neighborhoods like Southwark figured prominently in his rambles, the Night Hawk readily ventured into wealthier neighborhoods to expose the vices of the wealthy—he made much of his ability to pass in both plebeian and patrician spaces. But he also endorsed the view that certain neighborhoods were especially degraded. Following a sojourn to the Northern Liberties to explore its dance halls and oyster cellars, the Night Hawk compared the area to "the meanest part of London," a refuge for "Sailors, Raftsmen, Coalmen, and cut down Dandies." He concluded that Vine Street not only divided the city from the Northern Liberties but also delineated "two separate and distinct classes of people, whose manners, actions and conduct differ as much as the English differ from our Cherokee Indians."[66]

Yet, if moral and political authorities drew boundaries around neighborhoods like the Northern Liberties to call for their reform, the Night Hawk's purpose was more ambivalent. Like later nineteenth-century slumming narratives, the Night Hawk's warning about these "dens of iniquity" was also calculated to stimulate curiosity. Looking past his moralizing rhetoric, readers could employ his geography of vice as a guide to Philadelphia's various forms of lurid entertainment, a precursor to the sporting men's guides to brothels that were published in the 1840s and 1850s. Shippen Street, for instance, was "noted for its immorality, and its receptacles of vice in all its forms." On Race Street could be found "a gambling house for *apprentices* and *dishonest* clerks from *Market street*."[67] Considering that the Night Hawk's audience consisted mostly of working-class or lower middle-class young men, such as apprentices and clerks, his indictments of spaces defined by low sociability were in no way straightforward, because he understood that these venues and the people who frequented them were mutable.[68]

Like Watson's efforts to distinguish thieves who assumed new names and new visages, the Night Hawk dwelled on the artifice of fashion in a society in which people and goods slipped in and out of sight. "Our city abounds with temptations," he sighed; "the baits are so nicely laid, that few escape the snare." Even young Quakers kept "an extra suit of clothes" in the city for their sojourns to oyster cellars, "and, caterpillar like . . . change their form" in their "hankering for pleasure." Changing out of their "mode of dress . . . which unites neatness with convenience," the "young puritans" were immediately transmogrified.[69] Another essayist in the *Mechanics' Free Press*, "Paul," expanded the Night Hawk's case into an argument about purchasing goods of foreign production. "The fascinating allurements of foreign commerce, *on which foreign fashions are predicated*, when not kept under wholesome restraint by the government," he wrote, "has ever tended to hurry, not only its immediate votaries, but the nation thus licensing its sway, to the pinnacle of imaginary wealth." Suggesting that "a glittering show of tinselled toys has dazzled the understandings of the people," Paul summarized the views of Heighton and the Night Hawk: "That which is of intrinsic value, has been disregarded and neglected, until the whole nation has sunk beneath the ponderous weight of expense, which is ever attendant on this most irrational vice."[70]

Temptation derived not only from promiscuous sociability and exchange, the Night Hawk and Paul contended, but the debasing effects of consumption in a promiscuous economy.

To this more traditional republican critique of fashion the Night Hawk added a stinging rebuke against the moralizing and self-aggrandizing attempts of individuals like Mathew Carey and James Mease and voluntary associations like the Society for Public Economy to instill bourgeois notions of thrift in the working classes. His critique of fashion and authority culminated in his fortieth essay, in which the Night Hawk visited a charity fair held at the Masonic Temple on Chestnut Street. Social elites appropriated the fair, "originally intended for the benefit of the ingenious artizan and practical farmer . . . for no other purpose, seemingly, than to injure those for whom they were originally intended as a benefit." Obtaining articles normally produced and sold by "poor and distressed widows," the "rich and affluent missionaries" in charge of the fair proceeded to buy and sell these goods at artificially high prices: "ten dollars for a gingercake . . . one dollar for a two-penny pin-cushion!!!" He noted wryly, "The generous customers seemed over anxious to part with their money, as speedily as possible. One little woman, whose father never gave a cent to a poor person in his life, gave $5 for a basket made of fancy beads." Asking whether "these persons [would] so freely give half that sum to aid a suffering family in this city," or "purchase a bunch of matches from a poor, wretched, half-naked child in our streets," or buy "an apple, or cake, from a poor widow with five or six children dependent on her for support," he answered with a resounding "No!"[71]

This charity fair represented an opportunity for elites to co-opt the secondhand economy and establish order in place of the promiscuity that marked the secondhand trades in food, clothing, and household goods. Instead of purchasing creature comforts from the producers themselves on streets throughout the city, wealthy men and women paid admission and money for goods at a charity bazaar. They pitted laborers in competition against each other to lower the cost of goods, only to bid up the prices of those goods as if they were eager consumers at an auction in order to benefit church charities instead of poor widows. And yet, these wealthy men and women could not quite obscure poor people's production or consumption, the motive forces behind the fair, behind the promiscuous secondhand economy, and behind capitalism—that secondhand economy writ large.[72]

Thirty years after the Night Hawk last returned to his nest and a half-century after Krimmel documented the itineracy and promiscuity of the urban

Figure 2.2. An advertisement for the street's businesses, Baxter's panorama presented Chestnut Street as a space of order and self-governed shoppers, the continuation of a half-century-long project to remove or compartmentalize signs of promiscuity from the city's burgeoning commercial landscape. De Witt C. Baxter, *Chestnut Street, from Seventh to Eighth, (south side)* (Philadelphia: D. W. C. Baxter and Co., 1859). Library Company of Philadelphia, P.2006.1.15a&b.

economy in *Nightlife in Philadelphia*, De Witt C. Baxter provided a different gloss on the cultural landscape of Chestnut Street (see Figure 2.2). Published from 1857 to 1880, *The Baxter Panoramic Directory* endorsed a refined and gentrified vision of the street that appealed to the sensibilities of businessmen and property holders, whose investments Baxter courted. In contrast with other lithographs depicting the late antebellum commercial landscape, Baxter's scenes removed all signs of the hucksters, carters, and poor Philadelphians who employed the street for commercial uses other than genteel shopping. As Dell Upton and others have shown, images like these provided a crucial idiom for articulating ideas about commerce, urban space, and social taxonomies at a time when the meaning of terms like "capitalism" was amorphous.[73] Just as the commercial landscape meant different things to different people, so too did secondhand invoke a range of ideas about used goods and the people who sold, mediated, or consumed them. The only significant difference between Chestnut and South Streets, then, was the fact that the latter resisted efforts, from above or below, to define it as a static and harmonized space.

The Night Hawk's pointillist approach provides a useful way of thinking about capitalism. While the merchants of Chestnut Street operated within complex, transatlantic trading relationships, recording their activities in ledgers and diaries, the commercial networks of South Street were just as dense, if mostly invisible to the historian. Battles over the knowledge of this alternative geography of consumption took shape in the courts, correspondence, the streets, and the press. Ultimately, the circulation of secondhand goods through the antebellum city exposed a sharpening tension in American society over the democratization of consumption, the meaning of goods, the best means to appraise their value, and which social and political authorities should govern these practices. A focus on the promiscuous circulation of commodities can yield new insights about the contested terrains of class, gender, race, and consumerism in antebellum America, recasting elite anxieties regarding the consumer habits of the poor.

CHAPTER 3

The Era of Shinplasters

Making Sense of Unregulated Paper Money

JOSHUA R. GREENBERG

In March 1837, Illinois governor Joseph Duncan approved legislation incorporating the Dixon Hotel Company in Dixon's Ferry.[1] There was no bank in the new and expanding frontier town, so the company also asked for the right to issue paper money, but legislators struck out that part of the bill and passed it without such permission. The partial victory did not dissuade John Dixon and the members of the hotel company from printing their own shinplasters, including some featuring the misleading explanation "Chartered by the State of Illinois in 1837" in big letters across the top. While capital funds for the hotel building dried up almost immediately and the structure known as the Nachusa House was not completed until 1853, "The Dixon Hotel Company" or "The Dixon" issued several rounds of one-dollar, two-dollar, three-dollar, and five-dollar paper currency over the next decade.[2] The bills promised to be payable "on demand at their office in Dixon's Ferry." Visually, they looked like any legal bank notes of the era, featuring vignettes of cherubs, steamships, western-bound wagons, Native Americans with horses, and topless maidens in agricultural settings printed both by Durand and Company and the New England Bank Note Company.

Despite these attempts to inspire confidence in the notes' appearance, it is hard to know just how well or widely they circulated. The fact that a sizable group of the extant notes from 1837 and 1838 seems to be made out to "N. Biddle or bearer" also complicates the story a bit. Were they satirically inscribed as a subtle poke at the former director of the Bank of the United States, a wink to

Figure 3.1. One of the numerous illegal Dixon Hotel notes made out to N. Biddle. Obsolete Currency: Illinois Dixon's Ferry, The Dixon Hotel Company, $3, Uniface. Printed by the New England Bank Note Company, December 25, 1838. Massachusetts Historical Society.

the public that something was a bit off with the notes, or simply notes actually paid out to someone named N. Biddle (see Figure 3.1)?[3] By the early 1840s, the reputation of people who accepted Dixon Hotel money was open to public mockery in Chicago, where one newspaper commenting on a new run of the bills noted that "some people have been fools enough to take them, *but they lived in New York*."[4]

The story of Dixon Hotel Company shinplasters raises some important questions about the way market conditions affected Americans' currency choices and how they actually used paper money in the nineteenth century. Why would someone agree to take paper money from an unregulated, nonbank institution issuing illegal notes? And if such questionable currency could circulate, often with relative ease, then what does that tell us about Americans' understanding of the law and of the currency system? This essay argues that especially during economic downturns or when state regulations prohibited legal bank notes from circulating (at face value or at a discount), Americans turned to paper bills from unregulated, nonbank institutions. They did not embrace these notes enthusiastically or promiscuously, but with care and with as much control as their knowledge of local money markets allowed. Because Americans had to use paper currency to make purchases and pay debts on a daily basis, they utilized both legal notes (when they could) and, reluctantly, dubious shinplasters when better currency options were not available. However, such practices ultimately increased the circulation of various notes of questionable value and undermined Americans' confidence in all paper currency.

Paper money was the connective tissue of the market revolution and proliferated extensively in the mid-nineteenth century. Yet its wide use did not necessarily provide certainty or engender confidence in the market. In addition to the vast quantities of illegal counterfeits, some bills flowed from chartered, solvent banks backed by specie in their vaults, and others were issued in great amounts by legal but barely regulated institutions that could never hope to redeem a fraction of their notes.[5] A separate category of paper money—alternatively called shinplasters, scrip, bastard paper currency, private money, and unaccounted currency—was issued by merchants, businesses, and municipalities and operated on the fringe of the law. The term "shinplaster" came into wide use in the 1830s, so named according to one account because the bills were printed on such poor-quality paper that they resembled the bandages used to treat the shins of men in the eighteenth century who wore knee breeches and rapidly moved from cold horsebacks to warm fires. The alternating temperatures and mostly exposed lower legs resulted in tender shins that needed to be covered with "salves, ointments, and plasters."[6] George Morris told a more colorful version of this origin story after the Panic of 1837. A Revolutionary War soldier, injured in the leg at Bunker Hill, was paid in heavily depreciated continental notes by the government. The veteran, "believing that the money was printed upon paper of an *adhesive* quality, and knowing it to be good for nothing else, . . . was in the habit of dressing his wound with the rags, and calling them 'shin plasters'; hence the name, which will always stick to them to the end of the world."[7] Aside from the convenient connection to the nation's revolutionary past, what is especially notable about this tale is not only the inherently poor quality of shinplasters but also the fact that they represented a broken promise—whether by the government or any other issuing body.

Early Republic Americans' relationship with paper money was shaped by a conundrum: they needed more currency to enable market transactions yet lacked faith in the value of the paper money in circulation. At particular moments when the nation's economy declined or when state legislatures altered monetary laws, shinplasters issued by unregulated sources could alleviate the shortage of available money. Shinplasters, rendered suspicious because of their questionable legality, nevertheless did often manage to sustain local market exchanges through difficult economic periods. Yet in the process, they also ironically shook Americans' confidence in paper money of all sorts. Democratic and Whig spokesmen quickly seized on these public anxieties to seek political advantage and push their state and national banking (or antibanking) agendas. In the years following the Panic of 1837, day-to-day currency matters were used to wage larger battles about political economy. Tellingly, people increasingly used the term "shinplaster" to characterize not only unregulated, illegal private bills but also legal bank notes of poor quality. The antebellum period became an Era of Shinplasters in which all paper was suspect, based not on its legal status but primarily on its ability to convince others that it was a good note that they should invest with confidence.

Shinplasters—a term I use here to refer to paper money that was neither regulated by a state government nor a counterfeit version of a state-regulated bill—have largely slipped through the cracks of Early Republic scholarship. Local histories provide a wealth of information about shinplasters as examples of how frontier communities made do in the years before a national currency, but these are largely anecdotal rather than systematic accounts.[8] Likewise, numismatists have published several books on the existence of what they label scrip, with the intent of formally categorizing each monetary instrument. But their desire for accuracy in terms of the legal status and provenance of paper money obscures how Americans in the Early Republic actually used and discussed such paper money.[9] Economic historians, on the other hand, do not usually include shinplasters in their studies of banking and currency because of their focus on institution building and the effects of economic policy on the formal (and calculable) money supply. One of the few articles that deals explicitly with shinplasters even refers to them as "unaccounted currencies," because most scholars have failed to include them in calculations of the nineteenth-century monetary flow.[10] Sidestepping such econometric questions, this essay focuses on the features of the economy that allowed shinplasters to develop and probes some of the wider implications of a capitalist system maintained both by a potentially dangerous combination of bank bills that failed to satisfy demand or inspire confidence and by unregulated notes of questionable legality.

The American population faced a profound shortage of cash during the antebellum and Civil War eras, and to fill the void merchants, nonbank institutions, and municipalities printed their own shinplasters for local or regional markets. There were specific reasons for the lack of money: a chronic shortage of gold and silver coins for change, laws in some states that restricted banks of issuance, laws passed occasionally and in almost every state prohibiting the circulation of small-denomination bank notes under five dollars, cyclical financial crises that forced banks to stop redeeming their notes for specie, or simply frontier geographies that placed communities far away from busy currency markets. Not all of these conditions had to be in place simultaneously, but collectively they made it difficult for many people to get what they needed from regulated, lawful sources. Importantly, the persistent lack of currency did not cause Americans to retreat from adopting cash, but rather led to greater risk-taking in receiving questionable forms of paper money. If anything, the widespread circulation of merchant and corporate shinplasters in the first fifteen years of the nineteenth century demonstrated how currency transactions of any form had become an essential aspect of market relations for a vast number of individuals. Whether it was their ease of use in comparison with older models of book debt or just their familiarity, given how many pieces of paper money circulated in the new nation in the Revolutionary and Confederation eras, Early Republic Americans preferred dealing with cash for small transactions.[11] So, when new regulations or other economic circumstances curtailed the flow of legal bank notes, they used whatever medium of exchange they could.[12] As one account simply stated about shinplasters, people "took them, knowing them to be worthless, because there was no other currency."[13] While there is not the space here to detail the full range of shinplasters that developed to deal with these systematic currency shortages, it is useful to examine briefly the ways some communities adapted to the problem.

The five-year period between the dissolution of the first Bank of the United States in 1811 and the creation of the Second Bank of the United States in 1816 was one of the first moments when federal banking and monetary policy caused ripples in local currency patterns. Without a national institution overseeing state-level credit and currency production decisions, local banks overextended their circulations. When the events of the War of 1812 (specifically the British invasion of Washington in 1814) led individuals to hoard as much specie as possible, the banks suspended redemption of their notes and shinplasters multiplied alongside the unbacked bank notes.[14]

The title character in an 1815 satirical piece, *The History of a Little Frenchman and His Bank Notes. "Rags! Rags! Rags!,"* gets caught in this trap of bad, confusing money as he travels from Savannah to Boston and is swindled time and again.[15] Because the Frenchman is a traveling foreigner who does not know how to negotiate a variety of paper money rather than a single, stable currency, he does not have any of the local monetary information necessary to make discerning decisions about currency. In a typical scene, the naif attempts to pay for a drink in a Bristol, Pennsylvania, tavern with a shinplaster issued by the landlord of a Philadelphia hotel where he had recently stayed. The narrator says that the hotelier, "in order to be in fashion, had also commenced Banker among the rest. This note his brother landlord at Bristol refused to receive in payment."[16] In another example the Frenchman tries to use a twenty-five-cent note he received from a steamship captain to pay a turnpike gate toll as he travels in a carriage. He is rebuffed by the driver, who "pointed his whip to a little brook about three hundred yards behind, and mentioned they did not pass beyond that, northward."[17] The shinplasters confounded the traveler, not only in their bewildering variety but also in the way distance and his own movements seemed to affect the value of his notes and whether they would pass. This fungibility marked a real difference between bank notes and shinplasters. Bank issues that decreased in value the further they traveled from their home institutions could be bought low in one place and sold high in another, creating thriving and somewhat rational money markets. Because they were conceived for local use, shinplasters, however, actually lost their function as workable financial instruments when they moved outside their more intimate region of circulation.

The Frenchman's lack of information put him at a disadvantage in his transactions with merchants who themselves were caught in a national currency crisis playing out within local exchanges. Often, state regulations created the conditions that pushed merchants to issue their own cash and ensure enough small change in the market. In these moments government controls actually resulted in the generation of even more dubious notes that circulated ever more widely. One of the earliest state-level restrictions against small-denomination bills came from Massachusetts, which passed a 1799 law prohibiting bank notes under five dollars and restricting private banking companies from issuing notes without the consent of the legislature.[18] The theory behind such denominational limitations was that while there was no harm in allowing merchants to use large bank notes to transact their business, ordinary workers and farmers would lose out to inflation and devalued currency if easily printed, unlimited paper money replaced their hard money coins. The result of the 1799 law, however, was that specie became harder to find in Boston, so some city merchants helped supplement the need for small change by printing their own shinplasters.[19] The regions of the commonwealth that had little specie and few banks scrambled for alternatives.

This was particularly the case in Maine, where only one bank, the Portland Bank (established in 1799), existed. By 1804, locals' currency needs far outstripped supply, and so Portland Quaker merchants John Taber and Daniel Taber began issuing one-, two-, three-, and four-dollar notes, payable to the bearer in silver on demand. The good reputation of the merchants helped "Taber's bills" circulate widely in Portland; officials and the local population seemed to have no qualms about sidestepping the small-note regulations. Whether the Tabers saw their printing of shinplasters as a well-intentioned service to the community or merely a cynical ploy to make money is hard to say. The notes themselves (which were technically illegal) seemed to reflect this ambiguity, featuring as they did the Latin phrase "Quid Leges Sine Moribus," which roughly translates to "Laws without character are worthless."

The public clearly felt torn between their desire to follow monetary laws and their daily currency needs, resulting in a tenuous relationship with shinplasters. They countenanced Taber's bills only as long as they really needed them, and when given the opportunity to follow the law, they complied. When Massachusetts repealed its small-bill prohibition in 1805, competition from other institutions and eventually the toll from the Embargo of 1807 pushed John Taber and Son into bankruptcy. Making the situation worse, Daniel Taber had been filling out new batches of bills in order to supply himself with extra cash without his father's knowledge. After the collapse of his business, John Taber went to see fellow Quaker merchant Samuel F. Hussey to collect an outstanding debt. Hussey reportedly grabbed sixty dollars in Taber's shinplasters that he had been stuck with and handed them over. According to one account, Taber nervously said, "this money is not good now," to which Hussey replied, "Well, well, that is not my fault. Thee ought to have made it better."[20] While amusing, the anecdote also speaks to the very serious matter of people's fragile relationship with shinplasters. The notes had no real legal standing and circulated only when the community decided to extend its goodwill to the notes and their producer. When citizens' confidence abandoned the issuer, the notes lost their value.

While small-denomination prohibitions like the 1799 Massachusetts law passed through most of the nation at different times before the Civil War, some states took more dramatic steps to banish paper money from circulation. Iowa's Democrats, their territory having recovered from the prolonged economic downturn following the Panic of 1837, crafted their new state constitution in 1846 in a way that championed hard money policies and prohibited banks that issued paper money.[21] Bank bills nevertheless pushed their way into the state's economy. Several institutions, such as the Bank of Florence and the Fontanelle Bank of Bellevue, both incorporated in Nebraska, printed notes that were then "floated" out of nonbank exchange offices in Cedar Rapids, Des Moines, Sioux City, and a half dozen other Iowa towns.[22]

The decision to eliminate legal bank notes and the subsequent influx of Nebraska bills dramatically altered Iowa's economy. A resident of Burlington, Iowa, bragged that during the Panic of 1837 Iowans fared well on currency matters, exclaiming, "We have not been cursed with that 'bastard trash,' i.e., 'shinplasters.' A silver dollar can't be seen in the East—they jingle here."[23] However, bound by the new rules, most of the Nebraska-Iowa banks faltered during the Panic of 1857 and the population wound up clinging to whatever local unregulated notes they could trade, turning "bastard trash" into coveted currency. A Chicago paper even ran an article titled "The Shinplaster Era" that mentioned that Burlington currency had earlier been made up of "Nebraska bills and orders on the city treasury [municipal shinplasters]. When the Nebraska banks went the way of all wildcats, the city orders only were left."[24] A story recounted by a man from Dubuque in these years also colorfully characterized the proliferation of local shinplasters: "[He had] a very distinct recollection of seeing [this business man] carrying in his [high silk] hat whole printed sheets resembling bank bills [and in] his vest pocket a pair of scissors, so that whenever and where-ever he was met on the street or other place, he was prepared to pay in this currency for wheat or pork or any other legal claims by simply extracting from his capacious hat a sheet of what he called money and with his scissors cutting off the necessary sum to liquidate the claim!"[25] Without a usable legal paper currency, Iowa was highly susceptible to fluctuations in the specie market, and when it dried up during the Panic of 1857, people made do with anything that passed as money, even if it was not being issued with care or forethought. It was simultaneously valueless, valued, and valuable (see figure 3.2). As the case of Iowa demonstrates, numerous state and federal laws and local decisions to issue shinplasters all affected currency supply and demand and ensured that the money markets in no two locales operated in exactly the same way. Yet, it also reflects in many ways the resiliency and know-how of people to make their own highly local and variable market work.

As the case of Burlington, Iowa, demonstrates, in addition to merchants and other businesses, municipal corporations issued shinplasters in great numbers when they surmised that local markets could not support them-

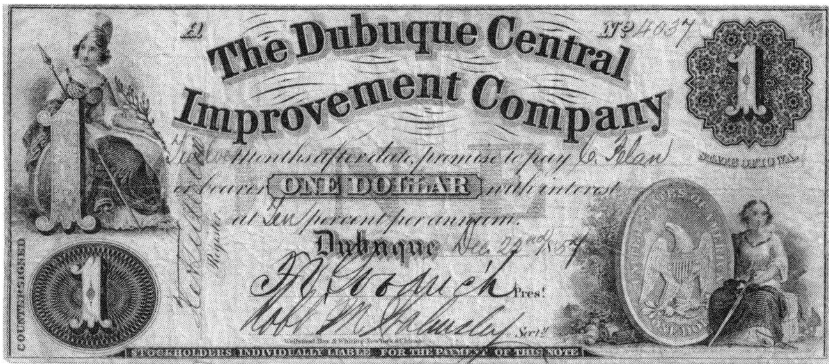

Figure 3.2. Several corporations in Iowa issued notes to skirt the state's constitutional prohibition on bank notes. The Dubuque Central Improvement Company, Dubuque, IA, $1, December 22, 1857. Author's collection.

selves with the current money supply. Usually surfacing during financial downturns when banks failed to circulate their notes or redeem them for specie, municipal shinplasters functioned like other forms of paper money and varied in quality, legality, and how much confidence they could inspire at various points in their life cycles. The number of municipal note issuances was surprisingly large. In one study, John Muscalus found that almost a dozen different kinds of shinplasters under two dollars from towns in Georgia entered local circulation between 1816 and 1840.[26] He also located more than eighty notes from boroughs and cities in Pennsylvania in just the 1830s and 1840s alone.[27] However, the large number of these city-issued shinplasters did not mean that they were always well received. In New Orleans, for instance, the poor quality of the paper used to make Second Municipality notes became a running joke around town, serving as a symbol of the poor quality of the bills supposedly pledged on the faith of the local government. One satirical piece played on the fact that the cheap, nearly translucent paper used to print the bills often tore and needed to be repaired with sticky paste made from water and wheat flour. When one such note was placed in the drawer at a local French restaurant, the paste attracted bugs that devoured the shinplaster and the good notes that were stuck to it. The account also included some anti-French humor for good measure.[28]

Many Americans were unhappy about the increasing monetary supply, even as they also recognized its necessity. They were generally willing to trust notes issued by governments more than they were willing to attribute value to the shinplasters of merchants trying to make a profit in these dire moments. In the public's never-ending quest for good money, the stability of a town or county seemed to offer more reassurance than a retailer or proprietor. One New York commentator noted that "Shin-Plasters are overspreading the land like the frogs of Egypt," but even in such a plague, he acknowledged that the public should be discriminating and that "notes of city and other amply responsible corporations may barely answer for change where they are issued; but individual and oyster-house promises to pay should be kept or driven out of circulation."[29] On some level it makes sense that town governments should have had the power to step in when currency supplies contracted so much that they threatened the viability of the local economy, and as the previous writer made clear, this seemed like a better option than allowing just anyone to pass worthless bills. However, in most cases, municipal corporations had no more legal authority to issue shinplasters than a random oyster seller.

Although shinplasters issued by merchants and municipalities circulated in great numbers during the early nineteenth century in violation of the law, there is little evidence that any individuals or officials were held responsible for the infractions. It is also quite clear that those who issued and circulated the bills knew the law. State regulations regarding banking could be confusing and filled with jargon, but sections concerning paper money clearly defined what categories of notes could pass legally. A typical law from Massachusetts, passed in 1836, declared, "If any person shall issue or pass any note, bill, order, or check, other than foreign bills of exchange, the notes or bills of some bank, incorporated by the laws of this Commonwealth, or by the laws of the United States, or of some one of the United States, or by the laws of either of the British Provinces in North America, with the intent that the same shall be circulated as currency, he shall forfeit for every such offense the sum of fifty dollars."[30] A similar law passed in Kentucky in 1834 dealt with institutional and municipal shinplasters: "no corporation shall presume to issue and circulate promissory notes, bills or checks, of the character and currency of bank notes, or to exercise any of the powers and privileges of banking, under any general provisions of its charter; and no charter shall be construed to confer such powers and privileges, without a grant thereof in express terms."[31] Such laws named a wide range of institutions, foreign and domestic, that could circulate legal notes in this economy, but they placed limitations on paper bills. Individuals and corporations could issue notes only if they had a state charter to do so, and most people who printed shinplasters did not. However, given the lax enforcement of such regulations,

Figure 3.3. Transportation corporations in Pennsylvania printed large numbers of bills during the years of currency shortage between the First and Second Banks of the United States. Easton and Wilkesbarre Turnpike Company, Wilkesbarre, PA, $1, March 16, 1816. Author's collection.

significant potential fines for illegally circulating shinplasters seemed to function more as idle threats than real punishments.

Staying current with such regulations was vital to both merchants and consumers who wanted as much monetary information as they could accumulate and as they made choices between conducting their businesses within the bounds of the law and utilizing whatever paper money they could muster to complete a transaction. Aiding Americans in staying abreast of even minor fluctuations in state regulations, local newspapers made sure to publicize the smallest of changes in currency policy. The *Luzerne County Gleaner*, for example, reported that in consequence of a new 1817 Pennsylvania law, "Bridge and Turnpike notes can no longer be received at the bank" in Wilkes-Barre, but they were "still current and are received at all the stores and taverns &c. and paid by the Treasurers, of those institutions" (see Figure 3.3).[32] While still allowing shinplasters to circulate person to person and in payment to local merchants, the Pennsylvania law limited the uses of shinplasters to specific places and contexts. Some institutions, like the Wilkes-Barre Academy, made it known to their students that "No money will be taken in payment of school bills, except such as will be taken at the bank in this place."[33] So, while the finer points of currency law constantly shifted, a steady supply of information regarding those changes found its way to the public.

Of course, not all consumers had equal access to information about these alterations in currency legislation or the means to use that information to change the way they handled the shinplasters in their possession. Frederick

W. Seward's recollections of his boyhood in a wealthy political family included a memory of being taught about shinplasters during a financial panic. Accustomed to keeping copper cents or Spanish sixpence pieces in his "money-box," he noticed that during the summer of 1837 "nobody had any 'change'" but that there began to "appear in use little square tickets of paper, like those of the circus or the baker or milkman. On these was printed, 'Good for 5 cents,' or [']Good for sixpence,' or 'Good for 1 shilling,' and they bore the name of some merchant or tavern-keeper." He was told by older family members that the notes were called "shinplasters" and that they "seemed to pass from hand to hand as easily as other money," so he thought to put one in his box for safe keeping. He was then warned not to do so, "as it might prove worthless any day. The only thing to do was to get rid of it as speedily as possible,—which was always easy at the candy store and toy shop. Then later I was told that some of the men who issued them were 'calling them in' and burning up whole handfuls of them, which seemed a great waste of good money."[34] It is no surprise that young Frederick would have received such guidance from his family. His father, William Henry Seward, led Whig opposition to the New York State law, passed in 1835, that banned bank notes under five dollars. Blaming the "odious" law for unleashing a "flood of 'shinplasters,'" he pushed for its repeal in 1838 as part of his successful gubernatorial campaign.[35]

This anecdote clearly illustrates that people considered shinplasters flimsy pieces of paper indistinguishable from circus tickets and at the same time thought them extremely useful financial instruments that were highly time sensitive and location specific. Seward's recollections also express something of how information about (and hence confidence in) shinplasters influenced their movement from person to person (or parent to child): in the game of hot potato being played in the currency market, even an acceptable shinplaster should be passed into someone else's hands as quickly as possible. The production, circulation, and destruction of notes detailed by Seward did not mention anything about their legality, just that they seemed to pass as well as anything else during the short term of the financial panic. In the long term, shinplasters could not even elicit the small amount of confidence generated by often questionable, albeit legal, bank notes. They were literally not worth the paper they were printed on.

As a young lad, Frederick Seward learned from others about the rules of using currency and reacted to their counsel in his own experience. Adult consumers were more proactive in their attempts to master banking laws and their implications, remain within the bounds of law, and use shinplasters to make a profit. As shown in the case of Taber's Bills in Portland, Maine, a restriction on small bank notes under five dollars in Massachusetts after 1799 resulted in various merchants and private bankers filling the void with printed shinplasters. As the commonwealth moved to ease those restrictions, it simultaneously sought to end the circulation of the small-denomination shinplasters that had flourished under the previous regulations. A March 1805 act, set to go into effect on April 10, prohibited any entity other than a regulated bank from issuing "private notes, bills, orders and checks under five dollars" under penalty of a fifty-dollar fine.[36] The law was of particular interest to Dr. Nathaniel Ames of Dedham, who kept a vigilant watch on his paper money finances and on numerous occasions enumerated in his diary the notes that he held (usually after a bank collapse) or commented about the current bank note rates in southern Massachusetts.[37] He was also a self-righteous justice of the peace and former court clerk who chose to follow the new regulations down to the letter of the law. He wrote in his daybook on April 10, 1805, that he sent four dollar bills to "Boston to get changed this being the last day of their legal currency as money."[38] It may be hard to imagine every holder of shinplasters (or private notes and bills as they were described in the 1805 law) ensuring their proper redemption by the deadline, but Ames's insistence on doing so shows his awareness of the law and his intention to follow it.

If Nathaniel Ames was keen on using shinplasters only in a legal manner, those issuing the unregulated notes and most consumers did not often follow the same standards. Given the changing state regulations on currency over time and space, not all shinplasters technically violated the law, but those that did were not hidden from the public or authorities; they circulated freely and openly, but not promiscuously, since their circumstances were highly circumscribed. Building on David Henkin's chapter on bank notes, titled, "Promiscuous Circulation," Robert Gamble's essay in this volume describes a fip shinplaster's unrestrained movements around the urban economy where anybody could potentially utilize it as cash when needed.[39] However, it is vital to separate the experience of individual consumers from that of the bills themselves. Americans exercised care and a degree of control in their own dealings with shinplasters and knew enough not to take the questionable currency when other options presented themselves. Unfortunately, during financial panics like the one that provides the context for Gamble's anecdote and other moments when money markets dried up—like when Nathaniel Ames utilized privately issued bills—other good options did not exist and shinplasters filled the gap.

It was during these precarious moments in local money markets when even illegal shinplasters could move throughout the economy. Richard Timberlake argues that most issuers of illegal notes understood their legal transgressions but managed to avoid prosecution by issuing shinplasters that were "customarily confined to local use and limited in quantity so that the laws prohibiting them would not be enforced."[40] Another way that merchants downplayed the legal gray area they entered by issuing their shinplasters was to evade it or at least put suspicious parties at ease with disclaimers on the notes themselves. It is not clear that printing "This is not intended as a circulating medium" or "this is a memorandum only, and to use when we have no change" on notes convinced anyone that they were legal.[41] It is just as unclear whether such statements made those who were worried about how much confidence to invest in a note any more likely to accept them. From a legal standpoint, such caveats did offer an easy defense in case issuers or users of shinplasters were ever accused of violating a state law curbing the notes' circulation.

But did such cases take place? Even if shinplaster issuers tried to obscure the legality of their notes, state officials could take steps to warn the public about those who broke the law. The Ohio Bank commissioners' report of 1840, for example, included a list of paper bills in "illegal circulation" that highlighted shinplasters issued by such sources as the Ohio Railroad Company, the Orphan's Institute, the Washington Social Library Society, and the Franklin Silk Company (see Figure 3.4). However, the same document explained that bank commissioners in the state had little jurisdiction over the circulation of shinplasters and that to date, no one had complained to local authorities.[42] So state officials knew about illegal shinplasters, but they did little about them. On the rare occasions when they chose to act, warnings and threats seemed to come easier than investigations and prosecutions.

In the 1830s, the Louisville Hotel Company began printing what looked like bank notes with vignettes of George Washington and the Marquis de Lafayette and made payable on demand at the Louisville Savings Institution. The notes promoted the company's $200,000 capitalization and noted the hotel's charter year of 1833. Like the Dixon Hotel in Illinois, the Louisville Hotel's charter did not allow it to issue shinplasters, and the Kentucky legislature soon became aware of the misconduct. The legislators issued a statement warning that they would hold the Hotel Company's president and

Figure 3.4. The Franklin Silk Company never managed to produce silk, but it did produce thousands of notes which continued to circulate illegally even years after the company folded. "Franklin Silk Company," Franklin, OH, $2, 183-. Author's collection.

secretary liable for each note they signed "to the holder, with costs and nine times the amount thereof, as a fine and penalty, for the violation of the corporate powers of said company, recoverable before any justice of the peace." They further declared that if the hotel continued to print notes, their "corporate powers are to be abolished, and the plates which the company have caused to be engraved, are to be delivered up and destroyed."[43] It is unclear when, or if, the hotel stopped issuing its notes, but there did not seem to be any actual fine levied against the hotel, which thrived for decades. It is also interesting to consider how politics might have been involved in the legislature's decision to give some leeway to the hotel for operating outside of its charter. Antimonopoly Democrats in the 1830s certainly had no wish to uphold what they saw as restrictive charters and might have been more accommodating.[44] However, allowing institutions to break existing charters, even in the short term, sent a clear message to the public that it was possible to disregard currency regulations without serious repercussions.

Although operating outside the law, merchants issuing shinplasters could avoid prosecution if their notes circulated at the more intimate local level, because by managing a community's currency shortage, they were seen as providing an essential service. Geographic proximity and knowledge of the issuers created trust among a community that enabled shinplasters to be effective for the short time and in the exact place they were needed, quite different from the way bank notes, with their national circulations, worked. In

Dayton, Ohio, shinplasters began to flow in the aftermath of the Panic of 1837, when a wave of bank closures led to a lack of currency. These notes included bills printed by local builder Thomas Morrison, but when an 1838 Ohio law prohibiting the use of shinplasters seemed to coincide with Morrison's preparing to skip town, he posted a public notice about his intentions and motivations. Titled "Shin-plasters in Danger!," Morrison told readers with regret that he was going to leave Dayton and move to Greenville, about forty miles away,

> because the law prohibiting the circulation of shin-plasters is soon to take effect. I wish to satisfy my fellow citizens that I am not the man under any circumstances to take advantage of a law by which the State allows me to act the rascal. I intend to redeem every note I have put into circulation, and that as soon as I return, and will do it with pleasure and satisfaction. I desire my fellow citizens and all who have confidence in my word of honor not to refuse to take them until my return, when every cent shall be paid with the addition of six per cent. interest. On my return I will give public notice so that holders of my notes may call.[45]

The promise of face value plus interest seemed to satisfy the public, as there were no attempts to hold Morrison accountable for the notes while he was in Greenville. Morrison later returned to Dayton, and at least one source indicates that he did make good on his promise to fully redeem his shinplasters.[46]

Thomas Morrison's public statement to the city of Dayton referenced potential lawbreaking and mass fraud but also argued that his promises ensured the essential stability of his bills' value. However, at least one Ohioan who held Morrison's bills disagreed with the issuer about the value of shinplasters. The back of an extant 12½-cent Morrison bill includes the following rant against shinplasters: "Ever since Van Buren has been president the Country has been infested with this trash. Jackson tinkered with the currency so much it robed the people of a metalig kind that they had and these damd rags was nec[ess]ary to be printed. huza for democracy. Signed A holder."[47] While the statement is fascinating for the way it called out Democratic politicians for not pursuing hard money policies strongly enough, it is more important for what it highlighted about the relationship between shinplasters and the often disgruntled public during the panic era. Agitated by Morrison and his shinplasters, the note's author chose to express his anger through politically motivated graffiti rather than to pursue legal action or contact the authorities. Maybe Daytonians seemed less concerned with upholding the newly passed law because like other Americans at the time, their confidence in all paper currency was so low that whatever value they got from what they were holding sufficed.

Several cases involving the theft of shinplasters also point to the public's confusion about and ambivalence toward the notes. Even judges who prosecuted the use of notes they knew to be illegal found their tasks difficult, for shinplasters' immediate exchange value vanished when taken out of their local market context. In Delaware County, Pennsylvania, in 1838, for instance, "A man was arraigned for stealing a pocket book containing two fifty cent notes. He was convicted of stealing the book, and a verdict of not guilty was rendered as to the notes, it being decided that as they were issued in violation of law, it was not an offence against the law to take and carry them away."[48] This verdict demonstrated a few interesting points about how Americans interacted with and thought about shinplasters in the late 1830s: first, certain laws defining what could and could not be paper currency (in this case a state law prohibiting small note denominations under $5 from circulating) created bills that were illegal by nature but were considered to be part of a crime only when they circulated; second, illegal notes seemed common enough to the court and the public that rather than shock about their existence, there was but mild curiosity about how the judicial system would handle them; and third, people acknowledged they were at once essential mediums of exchange in specie-strapped economies and such worthless pieces of paper that they could not even be "stolen."

One upshot of this case was the recognition that the populace had become so used to dealing with shinplasters as a necessary outgrowth of a broken currency system that it did not see the mere possession of illegal money as evidence of a crime. Another case from 1838 dealt specifically with stolen municipal shinplasters. A man in Batavia, New York, was arrested for stealing a "two dollar Rochester shin-plaster" and was arraigned for the theft. Everyone associated with the case acknowledged that he had stolen the note, but at trial his defense argued that since the corporation of Rochester issued its notes in violation of a state regulation, "they were void from their inception, and not collectable by law." The judge in effect agreed, declaring that the prisoner stole "nothing," so he "was discharged."[49] Such cases demonstrate the murky legal standing of shinplasters in American society, especially in the midst of a financial downturn. Demand prompted the creation of the notes, and there was little desire to prevent them from circulating, as they served an indispensable service to the local community who invested them with value. However, even when they were explicitly illegal, possessing them did not result in a penalty, because outside of the local market context where they circulated, they had no inherent value.

In fact, the few times when newspapers or pamphlets called for shinplasters to be investigated because of their questionable legality, the accusation turned on local partisan political conflicts in which one side hoped to gain advantage over the other. In a typical case from Detroit, an article in the *Democratic Free Press* titled "Our Whig Shin Plaster Corporation" pointed out that the "issuing of shin-plasters by our Whig common council is a violation of law" that needed to be stopped. The Detroit notes had been legal in Michigan during a short period in late 1837 and early 1838 when the banks stopped redeeming their notes, but when that moment ended, people were supposed to stop circulating the notes. To drive the point home, the article also included the text of "An Act to prevent the circulation of bills or tickets of a less denomination than one dollar," which was the law being violated by the continued use of the Detroit notes.[50] Calculated more to attack Whig politicians than to prevent lawbreaking, Detroit's Democratic newspaper later chastised the Whig mayor for failing to properly redeem the city's shinplasters and refusing to issue more when there was demand.[51]

Another politicized case came from the grand jury for the Ross County, Ohio, Court of Common Pleas, which investigated shinplasters issued by the town of Chillicothe. The jury concluded its inquest by handing down a statement that the notes qualified as a "common and public nuisance."[52] Aimed mainly at local Whig politicians, the ruling exploited technical language in the town's 1838 incorporation act that specifically provided that Chillicothe's council could not "issue any printed notes or tickets, to be issued under their authority, or under the authority of said city, as a circulating medium of trade, or exchange, or in any way or manner, either directly or indirectly, engage in the business of banking."[53] The jury's pronouncement also included a complaint that the poor-quality notes circulated for so long that they "have become so worn and defaced as to become nearly illegible." Of course, this part of the complaint failed to mention that the shinplasters stayed in circulation for such extended periods because currency problems in Chillicothe created a great public demand for the notes. The indictment against the Whig leadership in Chillicothe also seemed to parrot Democratic talking points about specie, declaring that "we have at present very little, if any, depreciated paper money in circulation; and there can be no doubt whatever that, if the 'shinplasters' were withdrawn, their place would immediately be supplied by small coin."[54] Even within this highly political proceeding, the jury seemed to acknowledge that the town should have some flexibility in issuing shinplasters.[55] Its main objection stemmed mostly from reissuing notes that had already come back for redemption, while they seemed less concerned with the original circulation.

There did not seem to be much public support for these Democratic legal cases against municipal shinplasters, but that did not stop Whigs from realizing that they too could use aspects of the shinplaster issue as a political cudgel to hit their opponents about the nation's currency problems. *Sober Second Thoughts*, a political cartoon printed by Whig supporter Henry Robinson in 1838, tried to blame the poor economy on Jackson and Van Buren's supposed antibanking and antipaper monetary policies by appealing to working men who may have previously backed the Democrats (see Figure 3.5). The bricklayer in the center of the image seemed to echo Whig objections to small note prohibitions while making a distinction between good and bad money when he said, "We are in favor of Bank Bills under Five Dollars, but want no Shinplasters."[56] Political cartoons naturally avoid subtlety, and the Whig message here could not be clearer: it was not the paper money system as a whole that was hurting working men; it was poor-quality, worthless paper money supported by Democrats.

Using central Ohio as a case study shows how neatly political rhetoric dovetailed with pronouncements about currency policy and shinplasters in the partisan press. The *Scioto Gazette* (Whig) and the *Chillicothe Advertiser* (Democratic) traded rhetorical blows over politics and banking and debated whether there had been an increase in worthless "paper money, under Locofoco legislation" or whether the Whigs supported the careless "creation of more banks" that would fail to redeem their notes.[57] Another series of articles in Chillicothe, Columbus, and Cleveland newspapers in the early 1840s under the title "The Better Currency" likewise debated the utility of putting new shinplasters into circulation and whether this was a "villany" or a "necessary expedient" to meet the area's currency problems.[58] The editorials even sometimes reprinted images of the questionable shinplasters and highlighted some of their visual or textual features. One article displayed a Corporation of Lancaster one-dollar post note from March 1841 that promised to pay in current Ohio bank notes, but only in December 1842 (if a reader could hold it for that long).

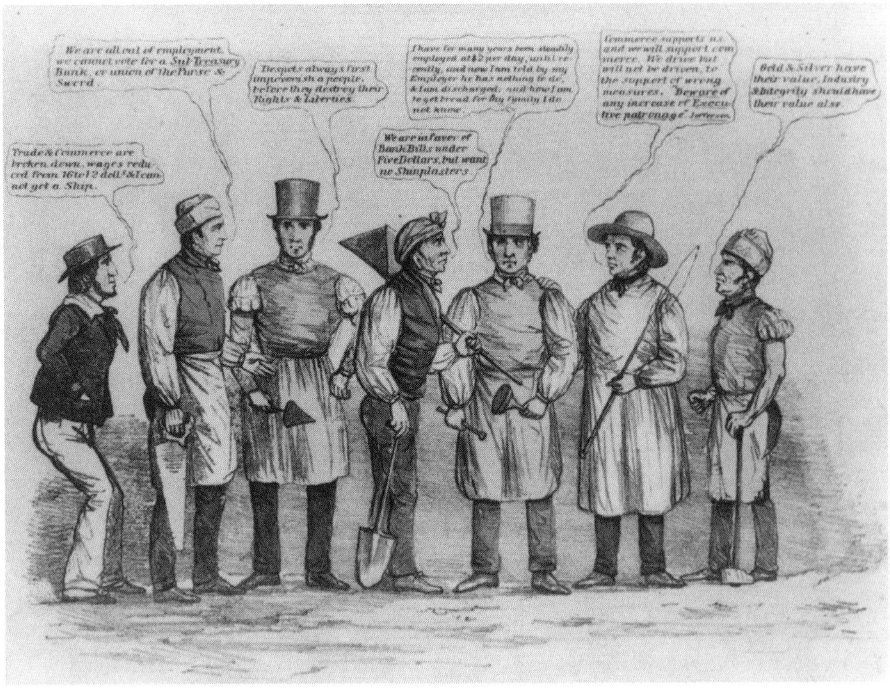

Figure 3.5. This Whig political cartoon featured artisans and laborers regretting their support for Democratic hard money policies that in turn led to currency shortages and indirectly encouraged more shinplasters. Henry Dacre, *Sober Second Thoughts* (New York: Henry Robinson, 1838). Library of Congress.

The battle reached its height in the summer of 1843, when anti-shinplaster sentiment swept central Ohio and community groups held protest meetings to take action against the questionable paper. Reported as far away as Brooklyn, New York, merchants from Mount Vernon declared shinplasters to be a "public nuisance" and signed a pledge "not to pay out any more shinplasters; and after the 4th of July [marking their independence from bad money], not to take a less sum than five dollars, and then only for the purpose of sending them home."[59] Just a few weeks later they were joined by Chillicothe merchants who publicly announced that it was "inexpedient to continue in circulation small bills or 'shinplasters'" and that they would be taking steps to "arrest this evil." Signed by more than fifty merchant houses and businesses, the statement said that after July 20, they would no longer receive the notes "in payment for debts or merchandise."[60]

Especially following the currency woes of the Panic of 1837, a tension developed between those Americans who wanted to entirely eliminate paper money (like in the 1846 Iowa Constitution), regulate paper money by supporting legislation to curtail small-denomination notes, or alter the system by removing the barriers to opening new banks and dramatically increasing the money supply. The problem was that none of these approaches could ensure that enough good currency, whether paper or metallic, would flow through the economy or that the economy would not simply be burdened by additional forms of bad paper. More than half of all states chose to legislate new rules for establishing banks. Starting with Michigan's in 1837, eighteen legislatures around the nation passed so-called free banking laws in the antebellum years. Meant to ease monopoly charters and democratize the financial sector, the laws led to an explosion of new, undercapitalized institutions that increased the number of bank notes by over 200 percent in states like New York and Vermont.[61] Many of these new bank notes inspired no more confidence than locally circulating shinplasters of questionable legality.

The result of all of these failed monetary regulations was an evolution in the meaning and use of the term "shinplaster" in the years following the extended economic downturn of the late 1830s and early 1840s. Confidence replaced legality as the primary criterion in determining what was and was not labeled a shinplaster. Once reserved for unregulated notes issued by nonbank entities, the term "shinplaster" now also referred to legal bank notes of poor standing. Inundated with poor-quality bank notes, Americans came to see themselves as living in an "era of shinplasters" in which all of the paper money they came into contact with was suspect; notes issued by legitimate banks were considered no better than the illegal, unregulated notes printed by merchants or municipalities.[62] Experience had taught citizens of the Early Republic to warily accept shinplasters and try to accumulate as much information as they could about their quality before bestowing them with confidence—a task made easier by their local circulation. However, in the years following the Panic of 1837, even discerning consumers could not easily evaluate the quality of increased quantities of paper money printed by a growing multitude of issuers. Most consumers came to accept that as long as they could find a use for the paper in their hands and pay their bills (with bills), legality hardly mattered.

By the 1850s, the term "shinplaster" was used to define any bad paper money that lacked confidence. The *Brooklyn Eagle*, for instance, used the specific, traditional definition when it thanked local citizens for resisting a recent attempt to circulate "those obnoxious abominations, the shin plasters,"

Figure 3.6. One of the many merchant or business shinplasters tied to a particular shop that was payable in dry goods or groceries rather than specie or current bank notes. "The Store at Alleghany Furnace," Alleghany Furnace, PA, 5¢, January 1, 1856. Author's collection.

which would have been "payable in groceries, in bread, in 'refreshments,' and in current bank bills when presented in sums of one dollar and up" (see Figure 3.6).[63] However, other uses of the term during this time were just as common. The *Chicago Daily Tribune* argued that the Middle West had weathered the beginning of the Panic of 1857, but in 1858 was under assault from a wave of notes from bad southern banks. In dismissing their quality and their ability to hold value, it alternatively used the phrases "Georgia wild-cat," "Georgia rag-money," and "Georgia shin-plasters," while questioning whether "there is a man in Illinois so stupid as to believe that the confidence of the public in this stuff could have been maintained for a month."[64] This was the key issue in the evolution of the term "shinplaster." The article explicitly discussed paper money issued from legal albeit poorly run and regulated banks in Georgia, but was free to equate those depreciated bills with illegal shinplasters because of the lack of public confidence. A bill was useful if it could inspire confidence enough to pass and its legal status was not a main component of that calculation.

Illegal shinplasters were not necessarily more acceptable to the public than legal bills, but when bank notes from lawful institutions repeatedly lost some or all of their value, they did not seem, nor were they, much better than shinplasters of dubious legality. One last example shows the place of shinplasters in this currency conundrum. Even though it looked like a standard bank note of the era, including vignettes of a steaming locomotive and a dog's head labeled "Fidelity," an 1858 bill worth five dollars in merchandise from the

Bridgeton Glass Works was an illegal shinplaster. If confidence was solely based on the law, the note might not have inspired much confidence from the residents of Bridgeton, New Jersey. However, in the aftermath of the Panic of 1857, the note compared favorably to other currency options. Bridgeton had only one bank in those years (the Cumberland Bank), and much of its circulating paper money came from remote states at depreciated value.[65] Conversely, the glass works had been founded in Bridgeton in 1836 and operated as a dominant business and employer in the area during much of the nineteenth century.[66] Given the choice between an illegal shinplaster from an easily accessible and known business with strong local ties and a legal note from a distant bank of questionable reputation, the choice remained clear. The problem for Americans in the era of shinplasters was that their currency options often limited these choices. With tight monetary supplies, bank notes and shinplasters did not circulate promiscuously. Rather, consumers were presented with a plethora of bad options and did not have the opportunity to be discerning consumers and carefully use the knowledge they had accumulated about local money markets.

CHAPTER 4

The Rag Race

Jewish Secondhand Clothing Dealers in England and America

ADAM MENDELSOHN

"New York," wrote James Fenimore Cooper in 1846, was a "Rag-Fair sort of place." By the time he penned these words, the city had secured its position as the mercantile and financial capital of the United States. For all of its commercial glories, the city, with its "hobble-dehoy look," reminded Cooper of Rag Fair, the tattered clothing mart centered on Petticoat Lane in London whose infamous reputation had been exported abroad. Despite ballooning almost 750 percent in size since the beginning of the century, the metropolis retained the "country air" of a much smaller town—and a neglected town at that. Cooper's recurrent complaint about "wretched pavements" suggests an annoyance borne of stumbles in the rutted roadways of the city. Other visitors, awed by the marble palaces of Broadway and the city's hive-like intensity, recalled tatterdemalion Rag Fair only when they ventured into the filthy thoroughfares—roadways crusted with refuse rolled flat by passing wagons and trampled underfoot by pedestrians—around Chatham Street on the outskirts of the clapboard slums of the Five Points district.[1] Chatham Street reminded visitors of Rag Fair for two additional reasons. If Petticoat Lane became synonymous with the street trade in old clothes in London in the mid-nineteenth century, Chatham Street was its New York counterpart. Observers were also quick to note that, as in London, this business was dominated by Jews. Starting in the 1830s, residents and visitors to the city

Figure 4.1. A father and son fitted up by a Chatham Street clothier. Even the youngest salesman offers the silver-tongued assurances that the public came to associate with the street and its salesmen. In the doorway another salesman accosts potential customers, two of whom appear to be sailors. "Chatham Street, New York," *Harper's Weekly*, December 18, 1875. Image courtesy of the author.

began to complain about the volubility and vigor of Jewish salesmen who waylaid and wheedled passing pedestrians. Visitors protested that, as in Petticoat Lane, passersby could "hardly walk Chatham-street, New York, without being asked to purchase, or else being taken by the arm, and half-coaxed, half-forced into one of their shops to make a purchase."[2] "No thank you," Ragged Dick replied politely in a Horatio Alger tale to an invitation from a Chatham clothier to peruse the clothing in his store, "as the fly said to the spider" (see Figure 4.1).[3]

For the next few decades, muddy and littered Chatham Street and its dingy storefronts, persistent proprietors, and overhang of flopping frock-coats and pantaloons featured prominently in depictions of New York by journalists, travelers, and belletrists. The thoroughfare fostered equal parts fascination and repulsion.[4] For some of its critics, it served as little more than a source of indignation, a nefarious place controlled by an ethnically marginal and untrustworthy people. While worrying, the excesses of Chatham Street and the secondhand trade could be tamed. But for others, it was a manifestation of a deeper malaise. Was New York, with all of its commercial pretensions, little more than a second-rate knockoff of Europe, as Cooper seemed to suggest? And was the city's economic system, and that of America itself, being built upon the kinds of trickery and shoddy merchandise associated with Chatham Street?

Those who sought to understand New York, or capitalism, through a perusal of the antic activity of Chatham Street found no shortage of parallels across the Atlantic. As in New York, the collection and resale of secondhand clothes in London was a staple occupation of the Jewish underclass. The ethnic niche had older roots in Albion; Jewish ragmen were a fixture of street life in London from at least the 1780s. The old clothes man, with his echoing chant of "old clo'," hoarsely competed for attention within the urban cacophony of London with vendors and hawkers demanding notice: "Pine apples, a penny a slice," "kearots," "sparrowgrass," "milk ho!," "butcher!," "baker!"[5] At the height of the trade, perhaps one to two thousand Jewish collectors of clothing and rags walked the streets of the British capital.[6] To the eye of the outsider, they wandered at random. In reality, there is evidence that collectors walked a regular beat, trudging familiar streets with a pack or basket, proffering flowers, trinkets, crockery, and jewelry in exchange for worn garments, and converging in the afternoon at Rag Fair—a boisterous open-air market in Rosemary Lane (Old Mint Street) close to the Thames and near Tower Hill—with their daily harvest of cast-off clothing.

The rag collectors were slaves to fashion, lugging to market cast-offs abandoned by the middle and upper classes (or bartered by their servants) as outmoded or threadbare. Few of these itinerant collectors were women, although the latter were involved in the sale of used clothing and prominent among clothes dealers. As with many dimensions of the petty forms of capitalism, the intricacies and operation of this market in both London and New York were shrouded in mystery to most observers. By what alchemy, many wondered, were ragmen able to transmute tattered cast-offs into profits? What exactly was the value of repaired clothing and how could it be determined? These uncertainties shadowed the trade and its practitioners. Surely, most assumed, the only means to extract profit from this marginal trade was through dishonest means. The reputation of the secondhand trade was already in decline as consumers gained access to ready-made clothing; its association with Jews did its standing few favors, and vice versa.

In both England and America, a sack of cast-offs and stack of rumpled hats—the commodities traded on Petticoat Lane and Chatham Street—

became convenient shorthand for the Jew. Despite the prominence of Jews, the secondhand garment trade has been largely absent from studies of the Jewish immigrant experience. This is particularly the case for the United States.[7] This neglect at least partly reflects the stigma once associated with used clothing dealers and their wares. Although doing substantial business, those who dealt in used clothes were seen as marginal participants within the larger economy.[8] Well beyond the nineteenth century the "old clo'" dealer was often a figure of fun and a source of embarrassment. His reputation was bespattered by the taint of criminality, the stain of poverty, and a whiff of the Old World. He was believed to inhabit a shadowy zone with murky morals: many found it difficult to define exactly what he did or precisely who he was.

Additionally, the trade was (incorrectly) viewed by some as a vestige of a best-forgotten past. Ragmen and street-sellers raucously hawked and bartered in ways that seemed to some to be increasingly out of step with the new commercial norms of the middle classes. Instead of setting a fixed price, they seemed to relish haggling. Instead of operating from fixed premises, they bought and sold wherever they could accost potential customers.[9] Customers knew full well that secondhand dealers profited from the dubious, uncertain, and contested value of their goods—garments rarely matched the exaggerated claims made on their behalf—knowledge that evoked anxiety and distrust. To some journalists and writers who described the secondhand trade to a broader audience, Chatham Street in New York and Petticoat Lane in London served as stages for a morality play in which debates about the boundaries of the developing capitalist system were acted out with Jewish ragmen, auctioneers, pawnbrokers, labor brokers, and sweatshop owners as protagonists. Jews were not necessarily singled out because of their numerical predominance (they were often outnumbered by others) or because of the distinctiveness of their economic behavior (often no different from that of their competitors) but, to borrow Claude Lévi Strauss's felicitous phrase, because they were "good to think [with]."[10] For native-born Americans, Chatham Street, old clothes, and Jews were useful pegs on which to hang their arguments and anxieties about the evolution of American capitalism. Yet as we will see, all the attention lavished by contemporaries on the Jews of Chatham Street distracted from another marginal and misunderstood niche that proved to be of far greater consequence for this ethnic group. If those who study American Jewish history have largely ignored the secondhand trade, historians of the antebellum United States have, until recently, done little better in analyzing the racial and ethnic dimensions of capitalism's economic niches. Despite its scale and significance, scholars have been as reticent about secondhand markets and other less visible forms of capitalism as they have about ethnic business networks during this same period.[11]

There was good reason to specialize in the collection and sale of cast-off clothing. A would-be secondhand trader required relatively little capital to open a stall or store, and none at all if he chose to begin by scouring the streets for discarded garments. Although exhausting, the work required little skill and only the most basic proficiency in English. For many it was a temporary or transitional occupation performed until a more promising alternative appeared. To eke out a living, collectors relied on the value that clothing retained once it had been discarded by its original owners. Tailored garments remained beyond the means of much of the population well into the nineteenth century. There was no shortage of purchasers. Cast-off clothing was widely worn even after mass-manufactured garments became affordable to wage workers. Paradoxically, the growing number of people able to purchase new ready-made clothing ensured that the secondary market was well supplied with discarded garments.[12]

Because of the low barriers to entering the business, several groups tried their hand at the trade. Poverty rather than skill or prior experience made the trade tenable. In Boston, a city that attracted relatively few Jews before the Civil War, the sale of secondhand clothing was dominated by African Americans who operated a cluster of stores on Brattle Street.[13] In California, Jews and Chinese competed, sometimes hotly.[14] In London, the hold that Jews had established over the petty trading of a variety of goods was loosened by a swelling population of Irish seasonal and permanent migrants in the 1830s and 1840s. The children of Erin rapidly took over the hawking of nuts and oranges from the children of Aaron. Unsurprisingly, this process involved occasional skirmishes in the streets. The collection and resale of used clothing was contested by the wives and daughters of Irish laborers who worked on the docks that bordered the Thames.[15] While Irish migrants came to dominate the down-at-the-heel market for preworn shoes (first "translating"—renovating—old shoes and boots and then reselling them at markets at Seven Dials and elsewhere), Jews seem to have continued to dominate the more capital-intensive business of wholesale dealing in old clothes.[16]

There is some evidence that Jewish used clothing dealers in London seeded the wind for their coreligionists in America. At least some of the earliest dealers in used clothing in Chatham Street emigrated from England and set up shop on American shores in the late 1820s. Of the 500 Jews who lived in

New York—a city of 166,000—in 1825, only a handful were involved in the clothing business. This changed rapidly as the city began to attract large numbers of Jewish immigrants from Europe. By 1830, a handful of English and Dutch Jewish immigrants to New York began to cluster in the clothing trade. Of the six Jewish clothiers residing in New York in 1830 whose birthplace is recorded in census returns, three were Dutch and three English. A similar pattern held true in Baltimore, New Orleans, Philadelphia, and Charleston.[17] This propensity might partly be explained by familiarity with the trade acquired across the Atlantic. Certainly in Mobile, Alabama, Solomon I. Jones, a "Renovator, from London" announced to the readers of the Mobile *Register* in October 1830 that he was opening a store to pursue the "business of Dyeing and Scouring of clothing."[18] Others may have benefited from access to shipments of used clothing dispatched by dealers in London. By the 1840s, far larger numbers of Jews had begun to cluster in Chatham Street.

Even as the exoticism of Chatham Street and its denizens attracted thrill-seeking tourists, its storekeepers benefited from a tide of visitors, temporary sojourners, and new residents who settled in the city. New York was brimful of newcomers. Some were on their way to other destinations—69 percent of all immigrants who made their way to the United States in the four decades prior to the Civil War entered via its ports—and others were the sons and daughters of farmers from the countryside who flocked to the city in search of work and excitement. New York's population more than doubled between 1820 and 1835 as the opening of the Erie Canal secured its position as the new republic's greatest trading emporium. Over the next few decades, railways, river barges, and ever more sailing and steam ships expanded the reach of its merchants and manufacturers westward and southward. By 1855, the city had more than doubled again in size, exceeding 600,000 residents, over half of whom were immigrants. In 1825, the city began to peter out at Fourteenth Street; within four decades, homes, offices, and shops swept as far north as 42nd Street and beyond.[19] The traders of Chatham Street benefited from the constant traffic of transients, travelers, and newcomers. There was a kernel of truth to an oft-repeated stereotype that Chatham Street's hucksters targeted gullible greenhorns. Yet while some may have been unscrupulous, honest money could be made in transforming a newcomer whose duds marked him as different into someone who could pass as a New Yorker. Each new arrival who strolled down Chatham Street with dollars in his pocket was a prospective customer. As late as 1860 an observer noted that clothes dealers were especially attentive to "countrymen, sailors, foreigners, [and] men in

California hats."[20] Secondhand clothes moved beyond Chatham Street on the backs of customers who traveled elsewhere. An economy that some tried to marginalize continued to be central because of the promiscuity of goods and the activities of shoppers, as well as the best efforts of dealers.

The bustling neighborhood around Chatham Street was a patchwork of slops-sellers, pawnbrokers, hawkers, and secondhand dealers catering to a working-class clientele. A quarter of the city's clothiers who specialized in ready-made garments were located in the vicinity during the 1840s.[21] The proximity of pawnbrokers to petty retailers was not accidental. As Beverly Lemire and Wendy Woloson have demonstrated, garments played an essential role in the household economy of the poor, serving as an alternative currency system and as a savings mechanism. Clothing was redeemable for cash or kind, maintained a steady value, and was easy to pawn.[22] The poor often assessed new clothing for its pawnability, seeing it as a strategic reserve against hard times. Solomon Solomons, the part owner of a large pawn-brokerage toured by a journalist in 1859, reported an average of 250 transactions a day, with clothing the most common item put up as security. He sold unredeemed pledges at auction.[23] Other pawnbrokers sold unclaimed clothing to dealers or dabbled in the clothing trade themselves by mending, cleaning, and then reselling forfeited garments. As in England, these interrelated occupations became closely associated in the public mind with criminality, particularly the fencing of stolen property and the staging of mock auctions that gulled bidders into purchasing baubles whose value was vastly inflated by the puffery of an auctioneer or by collusion with confederates in the audience. The police also thought that secondhand dealers kept bad company. Officers in the municipal police force created in the city in 1844 were tasked with reporting "all suspicious persons, all bawdy houses, receiving shops, pawn brokers' shops, junk shops, second-hand dealers, gaming houses, and all places where idlers, tipplers, gamblers and other disorderly suspicious persons may congregate." In some cases their suspicions were not misplaced.[24]

Commerce in Chatham Street subverted a variety of other emerging middle-class social conventions. In a city of newcomers where clothing might otherwise provide a measure of differentiation between social classes, the garments sold by Chatham Street dealers gave the poor access to the fashions of their supposed social superiors. How was one to tell who was a respectable member of the city's bourgeoisie when a frayed frock coat repaired to its former glory or ready-made clothing that reproduced modish styles at modest prices could speed a parvenu's progress?[25] In the hands of a skilled tailor, a threadbare suit could be made to look new by cutting and resewing, or by the strategic application of bootblack and other tricks of the trade. Chatham Street clothing dealers also blurred the boundaries between new and old. Some of those who sold cheap ready-made apparel also purchased worn garments to refurbish and sell as "fresh goods." Others may have objected to refurbished clothing for a very different reason. Re-dyed and repaired clothing often still looked shabby, presenting a direct affront to proud and egalitarian-minded Americans like Horace Greeley who liked to say that you could not tell the mechanic from the boss or the clerk from the merchant. Some members of the elite, on the other hand, worried not just about promiscuous social movement between classes and the circulation of ill-gotten objects but about the unrestrained flow of "hordes of beggars—of unlicensed pedlars and hawkers—of prostitutes who nocturnally swarm in some [of] our frequented streets and public walks—and disorderly assemblages of youths" through the city. Those who sought to impose order on a cityscape they perceived to be anomic often grouped clothing dealers and pawnbrokers with those they regarded as troublesome lawbreakers.[26]

The American trade in used clothes followed a similar pattern to that in England. Itinerant collectors bought, begged, and bartered for old garments, sometimes swapping china and glassware for cast-off clothing. As in England, few of the clothing collectors were women. Once acquired, clothing was cleaned and "made over, some made smaller, some turned, some changed in form" within the household economy, or sold to dealers who arranged for repair and resale. This process was labor intensive; the final product was profitable only if stitched and sewn by an unpaid or low-wage workforce of wives, daughters, and impecunious immigrants. One female store owner interviewed by the social reformer Virginia Penny described employing two girls and three men to make over worn clothes for her store; she paid her female employees thirty-one cents a day for twelve hours of work. (This rate of pay was comparable to that of seamstresses, but unfavorable when compared with a variety of other occupations identified by Penny).[27] As in London, this labor system would later be reoriented to the piecework production of new clothing. Repurposed articles—boys' cloth caps and women's shoes made of old coats and pants "so worn in parts as to be unsalable," coats "made of cloaks, bonnets of aprons, &c."—were sold in stores located in poor neighborhoods or at informal markets like the one near Penn Square, where Philadelphians could see "ranged, on an open space, a large quantity of second-hand clothes, shoes, dresses, &c., for sale."[28]

Once reconditioned, the clothes found eager buyers. One storekeeper described the diversity of his clientele—"French, Irish, and negroes"—but noted that "Germans do not like to buy second-hand clothes."[29] Some dealers advertised their wares in the press and encouraged those who were hard up to sell their wardrobes for cash. At least thirty-eight such dealers plied their trade in New York City in 1845 and one hundred by 1863. Some purchased used clothing for the local market, while others shipped it in bales to buyers in the South and West.[30] Although Philadelphia, Baltimore, Boston, Charleston, and Chicago also had streets tightly packed with Jewish secondhand clothing dealers, the old clo' dealers of Chatham Street became embedded in the popular imagination. This reputation was exported overseas. In the 1860s and 1870s, foreigners in Canton, China, referred to a street of old clothes sellers as the "Chatham Street" of the city.[31]

Despite similarities between the raucous clothing markets in Petticoat Lane and Chatham Street (and Harrison Street in Baltimore, South Street in Philadelphia, and several other clusters), in America the used clothing trade did not acquire the scale and sophistication before the Civil War that it did in England. By the early 1840s, the center of the trade in London began to shift to enclosed marts in Houndsditch that could serve a combined capacity of around six thousand customers.[32] The creation of these marts initiated a process of consolidation within the used clothing business. Each began to act as a clothing bourse, facilitating new levels of specialization and sophistication within the market. The Clothes Exchange was the largest of the marts. Its owners were not particular about the business conducted on their premises—they provided space to dealers in "anything and everything"—as long as they were paid (see Figure 4.2).[33] The Clothes Exchange had space for 500 stalls, most little more than a tarpaulin draped on the ground.[34]

The sellers were a motley mix. Ragmen converged on the market from far and wide, bringing with them cast-off clothing they had gathered during the week. The sacks of clothing they emptied provided the "positively overpowering" stench of which visitors complained.[35] Although some of the clothing they carried was picked over and purchased by members of the public, much of it was claimed by dealers and hawkers who eyed it for salvage. Cast-off clothing bought by petty dealers and street sellers from ragmen one week would reappear in the market or on the streets the following Sunday repaired and ready for resale at inflated prices.[36]

The rival Simmons and Levy's Clothes Exchange focused on the wholesale trade: naval and military stores, portions of auction lots, unsold stock from

Figure 4.2. The frenetic commerce of the Old Clothes Exchange. In the center, a ragman totes a sack of old clothing. The artist has supplied several visual cues that the dealers and many of their customers were Jews. "The Old Clothes Exchange, Phil's-Building, Houndsditch," *Illustrated London News*, January 21, 1882. Image courtesy of the author.

retailers, and unredeemed pledges from pawnbrokers. While the clothes exchange predominantly supplied the local trade, this smaller sibling sent used garments and fabric farther afield. According to one observer, this exchange handled the export of about twelve bales of cast-off clothing and fabric each week, mostly to Ireland and Holland but also to the continent, the United States, and the colonies.[37] By one exaggerated estimate, "half the second hand habiliments of the empire" passed through the two exchanges at some point in their life cycle.[38] The Irish traders who rented rooms close by were part of a cosmopolitan clientele that included buyers from France, Holland, Germany, Greece, Switzerland, and North Africa. One observer noted that each group specialized in a particular segment of the market: purchasing great coats and police uniforms for export to Ireland, the scarlet tunics of British infantry to Holland, children's clothing in bulk, or garments from hospitals.[39]

The continuous tide of clothing that flowed into the marts was quickly channeled into a sophisticated distribution system that aggregated, repaired, and then dispatched these items. According to the journalist George Augustus Sala, three types of old clothing were collected and sorted. "First class" clothes were good enough to be either "revivered, tricked, polished, teased, renapped, and sold" in secondhand stores or pawned for as much as they would fetch. "Second class" clothing was exported in "great quantities" to the colonies, Ireland, the "South American Republics," and the United States (the import of second-class secondhand clothing into America could not have pleased those who feared that the United States risked becoming a second-rate imitation of Europe). "Third class" clothing—"utterly tattered and torn"—was destined for the shredder and eventual refabrication for use in "plate-glass-shops, middlemen, sweaters, cheap clothes, and nasty."[40] This centrifugal system sent garments in bulk to distant markets or to the pavements outside the marketplace, often to be distributed and sold by coethnics.

The London marts provided important economies of scale. In the absence of a sophisticated alternative distribution system, some manufacturers and wholesalers of new clothing and footwear brought their wares to the market to tap into these distribution channels. Some clothiers visited the market daily to purchase stock.[41] By comparison, Jewish clothing dealers in America established only a rudimentary system of agglomeration and regional distribution (junk and scrap dealers, by contrast, were more successful in doing so for their favored wares); there were no grand marts to rival the clothing exchanges of London. Several factors worked against the systemization of the used clothing trade in antebellum America. Secondhand garments were probably in shorter supply in New York than in London. For a viable trade in used garments, ragmen needed ready access to a reliable harvest of quality cast-offs that could be purchased cheaply, refurbished, and sold at a profit. As Michael Zakim has demonstrated, in the Early Republic, homespun clothing filled the ideological and practical needs of many consumers. This rougher clothing was less likely to sustain its longevity and value when recycled than the tailored finery that was discarded by the upper classes of London society.[42] Although there was a lot of secondhand clothing in circulation, there may not have been sufficient surplus to reliably supply markets outside New York. Jews were also less well prepared to create an elaborate recycling system in America. Whereas in London Jews had dominated the trade in secondhand clothing since the late eighteenth century, if not earlier, in the United States the ethnic niche was of much more recent origin. London had long had a large Jewish population—between 15,000 and 20,000 strong in 1800—the majority of whom, as part of the city's underclass, engaged in a variety of forms of petty commerce.[43]

While in London Jews created an elaborate and efficient system for accumulating, sorting, repairing, and distributing secondhand clothing over the decades—and then made the leap to centralizing the trade in marts only after encountering considerable pressure from the city constabulary—in America Jews were less well positioned to do so. Prior to 1820, most members of New York's small Jewish community were merchants and artisans.[44] The English and Dutch Jewish immigrants to the United States who began to corner the trade in cast-off clothing in the 1830s lacked coethnic precursors with a substantial presence in the secondhand economy on American soil. The structure of the market for used clothing also differed in England and America. Dealers in London benefited from the scale of the metropolitan market—which supplied collectors with ample stock and buyers aplenty for refurbished clothing—and its strong commercial ties to the provinces, Europe, the United States, and the colonies. It was no accident that the markets in Rag Fair and in Houndsditch were close to the Thames and the docks; bales of clothing could be quickly and cheaply exported or dispatched northward to other domestic destinations. Given its accessibility to dealers in England and elsewhere, London became an entrepôt for secondhand fashions. By contrast, geography worked against the consolidation of the used clothing trade in the United States. No single city dominated the trade as did London. The distance between cities and the expense of transportation militated against the shipment of clothing to a single city to be sorted, repaired, and redistributed. Even as other sectors of American business had begun to develop these expansive business networks, consolidate production, and specialize in particular goods, factors distinct to the used clothing trade may have made this less profitable. The supply of cast-offs was likely tighter in American cities—perhaps a consequence of the influx of immigrants outstripping supply and a relatively smaller middle- and upper-class parting with proportionately fewer garments—making the economies of scale achieved by centralization in England more difficult to attain and less cost effective.[45]

Many of the Jews who began to experiment with new methods of manufacturing and selling new clothing in London in the 1840s were schooled in the art of dealing in rags, cast-offs, and slops. Whereas in England the vitality, scale, and sophistication of the secondhand trade provided an advantageous platform for those inclined to experiment with new modes of producing and marketing clothing, in America collecting and reselling used clothing on aggregate promised dimmer prospects for advancement within the trade. Given the limitations of the secondhand market for clothing in the United States relative to that in England, it was more challenging for the ragmen and dealers of Chatham Street to graduate from the insalubrious underside of the clothing business to its more respectable twin than it was for their kinsmen in Petticoat Lane.

If not by cast-offs, how then did Jews enter the business of making and selling new clothing in the United States? Fortuitously for the future of American Jewry, dealers in cast-off clothing in New York, Baltimore, and Philadelphia who hoped to recruit a corps of collectors encountered another challenge less familiar to their counterparts in London—competition. Whereas in London the persistence of poverty within the Jewish community ensured that there was no shortage of rumpled foot soldiers willing to carry the collector's sack, in America most Jewish immigrants who arrived prior to the Civil War preferred an alternative, readily available source of employment. The peddling of fancy goods, notions, and clothing to rural customers became a rite of passage for a generation of Jewish immigrants from central Europe.[46] This too was a marginal occupation that took on a strong ethnic coloration as Jews came to dominate the ranks of peddlers. And it too has largely been left out of the larger story of American economic history.

Peddling offered several allures to young men hoping to sink roots in American soil: independence and self-employment, the prospect of advancement through hard work, and the promise of eventually owning a store. It was an entrepreneurial niche made possible by the market and transportation revolutions—peddlers sold mass-produced cheap merchandise to farmers who fell within the interstices of an expanding railroad, canal, and road network. The arrival of a Jewish peddler often coincided with that of canals, roads, and railways that hitched a town to the regional and national economy. To entrenched commercial rivals who had enjoyed a period protected from competition by the difficulty and expense of transportation, the Jewish peddler was the physical manifestation of the coming of a geographically expansive market that cared little for cozy arrangements between local retailers and producers. Although peddling carried a smaller social stigma than collecting garments discarded by others, it was also viewed by some with suspicion. Shopkeepers and other commercial rivals, fearing for their livelihoods, cultivated this suspicion, but it also extended to some potential consumers who projected their anxieties onto the itinerant traders. Some consumers, particularly in the South, developed an equivocal attitude toward peddlers. On the one hand, a peddler who unpacked his goods before a spellbound audience—a performance that could take an hour as each item was displayed to best effect—conjured up the excitement of a far-off city. On the other hand, the outsiders speaking with English accents who carried northern goods across the thresholds of southern homes exemplified the concerns that generated so much heat and thunder in the South before and after the Civil War. A lone itinerant trader seemingly presented little threat, but together with armies of others he was seen as the cutting edge of a campaign by northern manufacturers, merchants, and bankers to drain the South of specie, undercut local industry, and render the South's inhabitants perpetually dependent. The occupation rewarded those adept at the art of selling, a skill viewed with suspicion in Jacksonian America and even with unease by some Yankees who carried a peddler's pack.[47] Yankee peddlers, who had dominated the ranks of peddlers before the period of Jewish migration, gained a reputation as urban tricksters and dishonest salesmen. These tropes were easily transferred to Jews, as American prejudices against itinerant traders intermixed with older ideas about Jewish commercial practices.[48]

While some peddlers may have sold used clothing—there is some evidence that slaves were eager purchasers of inexpensive and brightly colored garments carried by some peddlers in the South—peddling broadened Jewish participation in the trade of goods both old and new.[49] Many rural and poor urban customers had little access to ready money, but they did own plenty of items that an enterprising traveling salesman could resell for profit in a market in which such goods were scarcer. Frederick Law Olmsted, traveling in the Mississippi backcountry a few years before the Civil War, met a peddler from Düsseldorf who described this arbitrage in action:

> All poor folks, dam poor; got no money; oh, no; but I say, "dat too bad, I don't like to balk you, my friend; may be so, you got some egg, some fedder, some cheeken, some rag, some sass, or some skin vot you kill." I take dem dings vot dey have, and ven I gets my load I cums to Natchez back and sells dem, always dwo or dree times as much as dey coss me; and den I buys some more goods. Not bad beesnes—no. Oh, dese poor people dey deenk me is von fool ven I buy some dime deir rag vat dey bin vear; dey calls me "de ole Dutch cuss." But dey don't know nottin' vot it is vorth. I deenk dey never see no money; may be dey geev all de cheeken vot dey been got for a

> leetle breastpin vot cost me not so much as von beet. Sometime dey all be dam crazy fool; dey know not how do make de count at all. Yes, I makes some money, a heap.[50]

Rags constituted a central part of this barter economy. In nineteenth-century America, rags were collected in greater quantities than brass, lead, rubber, glass, and any other domestic recyclable. In many households, women gathered rags, interacted directly with the peddler, and often controlled the spending of "rag-money."[51] Rags and old clothing served not only as a currency for the peddler and his customers but also as a commodity valued by many of the retailers and wholesalers who supplied the peddler with his merchandise. Rather than returning to the depot for resupply with an empty pack or wagon, the peddler carried recyclables that he could trade at a favorable rate of exchange for new stock. Some retailers and wholesalers collected rags directly from peddlers for barter or sale to shoddy mills and paper manufacturers. Others relied on middlemen who aggregated the raw material for bulk sale and shipping.[52] The routine collection of rags and other recyclables ensured that the scrap business too became part of an emerging Jewish ethnic economy. Peddling provided Jewish immigrants with a grounding in mass merchandising, a hard-won familiarity with the vagaries of the market, a network of contacts involved in wholesaling and retailing, and an apprenticeship in sales, inventory management, risk, and credit. Moreover, those who moved from peddling to manufacturing and wholesaling could in turn use Jewish peddlers to distribute their wares cheaply and efficiently, creating an ethnic supply chain that benefited all parties. Although a sense of kinship between Jews seeded an ethnic ecosystem, it was the coursing of money and goods on credit through it that gave it life.

The provision of credit and the promise of mutual benefit fertilized bonds of solidarity, obligation, and reciprocity. For the system to work, it needed to provide advantages to the manufacturers who sat atop the food chain as well as to the peddlers who burrowed for business at the bottom. While a peddler may have returned to the same supplier again and again out of habit and convenience, some storekeepers provided incentives to strengthen these relationships. Those who extended favorable terms to peddlers or supplied goods on credit likely did so with the understanding that it would generate repeat custom and perhaps even long-term loyalty. A peddler who owed money would need to return to repay his debts and replenish his stock. Some wholesalers recruited and financed newly arrived Jewish immigrants as peddlers to extend the reach of their businesses and increase the volume of their sales, offering a share of the profits on every article sold. Other suppliers fronted goods to recent immigrants with the understanding that the outlay would be recouped with interest or paid to peddlers as a set monthly wage.[53] A peddler who faithfully returned to a supplier week after week could be useful in other ways too, supplying reliable information about the shifting preferences of customers and local economic conditions that might, in aggregate, be beneficial to a storekeeper seeking to judge demand in an otherwise unpredictable market. Peddling ultimately served as a springboard for Jews in America, propelling them out of the ranks of petty hawkers and into the business of producing, wholesaling, and mass retailing inexpensive garments. Several of the largest clothing firms operating in the country in the 1870s and 1880s were built on the backs of men who peddled decades before.

Even though the Jewish ethnic economies built around the clothing trade took shape differently on both sides of the Atlantic, the ultimate outcome by the 1870s and 1880s was not dissimilar. In England a wave of Jewish used clothing dealers deployed skills learned in repairing, distributing, and selling old garments to begin manufacturing and retailing new clothing in the 1840s and 1850s. The concentration of Jews in the secondhand trade ensured that even if few secondhand dealers successfully transitioned to manufacturing, a substantial proportion of the earliest manufacturers were Jewish. Although those who traded cast-off clothing in the streets and alleys of the East End of London competed against one another, they formed a mutually beneficial cluster of expertise in clobbering and cheap retailing. Putting out and piecework were strategies already employed by slopsellers and used clothing dealers who found it profitable to subcontract to others to clean and repair worn and damaged clothing for resale. Such methods were easily transferable to the sewing of new clothing, particularly since early manufacturers could draw upon a pool of local contractors and workers familiar with this system. It was a short stretch to scale up a system already in place for clobbering of old clothing to mass manufacture. These innovations in production preceded the introduction of reliable sewing machines in the mid-1850s.

In America peddling provided a better preparation for this transition. Although Jews came to control much of the collection and resale of secondhand garments in several antebellum American cities—and created a profitable niche around the commodification of used clothing—peddling provided a surer pathway into the ranks of the clothing manufacturers and retailers. The secondhand trade achieved a much lower level of sophistication and consolidation before the Civil War than it did in England. In America toting a backbreaking peddler's pack to rural customers provided an essential apprenticeship far more advantageous to Jews than collecting and hawking cast-off clothing. It was no accident that in the decades before and after the Civil War, many of the Jews who opened garment factories came not from the ranks of used clothing dealers or skilled tailors—who would have had to abandon their traditional craft to do so—but from men who had begun their careers as peddlers.

By the 1880s, the retailing and manufacturing of new clothing had displaced peddling and dealing in used clothing from the center of the Jewish ethnic economies of England and the United States. Although neither occupation disappeared as options for immigrants, the move into mass manufacture transformed a staple industry of the Jewish working class. The arrival of hundreds of thousands of poor Jewish immigrants from eastern Europe with basic tailoring skills—many of whom would likely have otherwise started as ragmen or peddlers—provided an easily exploitable labor pool for the expansion of the subcontracting system. Whereas once many of the poor and recent immigrants found employment in the various branches of the used clothing trade, now they became the poorly paid sewers and cutters who underpinned the piecework system. Without earlier Jewish dominance of the used clothing business, however, this outcome would have been unlikely.

This shift within the ethnic economy occasioned change in the representation of Jews and Jewish economic life in popular culture. Over time, the popular tropes that associated Jews with Chatham Street were displaced by a changing commercial reality in New York and other cities. By the 1880s, Jewish clothing and dry goods firms, many owned and operated by former peddlers and their sons, were far more prominent on Broadway than on Chatham Street. And the clothing trade had also moved on. Although many poor consumers continued to rely on secondhand clothing, inexpensive ready-mades were plentiful and commanded much more attention. Though Chatham Street no longer played the same role in the secondhand economy as it once had, Jews remained a useful focus for anxieties about American capitalism. These concerns, however, now reflected anxieties about mass production. The Jewish sweatshop owner, a putative exploiter of immigrant workers, was demonized for undermining craftsmen and bastardizing honest labor. Even as one set of stereotypes declined, another rose to take its place.

CHAPTER 5

Lickspittles and Land Sharks

The Immigrant Exploitation Business in Antebellum New York

BRENDAN P. O'MALLEY

In August 1844, William Brown, a clothier from Leeds, sailed from Liverpool to New York with his family in a second-class cabin aboard the packet ship *Oxford* of the Black Ball Line. The vessel carried roughly three hundred Irish passengers in steerage. As the ship glided across New York's Upper Bay at the end of the journey, Brown admired the "splendid city" coming into view. He noted "the steeples of numerous churches" that were "glittering in the sun like gold and silver." Brown posited that from this vantage point, a weary traveler arriving in the "Empire City" for the first time might be led to believe that "if a paradise exists in the sublunary world, it is here."[1]

But at the moment the ship moored at the pier, a ferocious clamor burst Brown's reverie. "A gang of 300 or 400 ruffians, calling themselves runners, jump[ed] on board, [and] beg[a]n, very much in the style of plunderers or pirates, seizing hold of the passengers' baggage, and endeavoring to persuade them to go to some inn or lodging house which they represent." Competing runners denounced each other, assuring a newcomer that if he went with a rival, "you certainly will be robbed and perhaps have your throat cut if you entrust yourself and baggage into his hands." Brown lamented that "the swearing and fighting of these runners, the shouts of the passengers, the crying of the women and children, make as great a confusion as ever was heard at Babel."[2]

Up close, Brown found the appearance of the runners "the most disgusting possible." They dressed "without coats, without cravats, with shirt necks flying open," and held a "large roll of tobacco in each cheek, the juice from which exuded down the corners of their mouths." They appeared to him "a mongrel breed, half Indian and half Irish," and probably because of their tanned visages, he likened their physiognomy to that of gypsies in England. According to Brown, runners made their living by luring travelers to "lodging-houses and grog shops" where the proprietors would pay a small fee for each traveler brought in. Innkeepers would then charge exponentially higher rates than the runner had promised for room, board, and luggage storage, holding baggage hostage until the bill was paid. Brown claimed that runners would augment their income by stealing passengers' trunks outright, stating that twenty-seven trunks owned by the *Oxford*'s steerage passengers vanished in this way. He declared this state of affairs "a disgrace to the police of the city to allow passengers to be robbed by such a race; but there has been no effectual stop put to their depredations, although every vessel with passengers suffers by them."[3]

Brown was far from the only writer to depict the waterfront predations of the "emigrant runner." By the 1840s, the runner had earned a place among other mythic archetypes in the city's pantheon of entrepreneurial lowlifes, joining the "sporting man" who gambled to support himself, the prostitute and brothel keeper, the "Peter Funk" mock auctioneer, the pick-pocket, and the shoulder-hitter on the politician's payroll. A broad spectrum of publications related the activities of these underworld figures, starting with the "penny press" of the 1830s, the even more lurid but short-lived weekly "flash press" of the early 1840s, and the American version of the "mysteries of the city" genre pioneered by Ned Buntline and George Foster a few years later.[4] The figure of the runner also played into a developing conceit that Edwin Burrows and Mike Wallace claim is reflected in the "Primal Deal" of the mythical $24 purchase of Manhattan by the Dutch: "New Yorkers love yarns about city slickers scamming rural suckers."[5] Even reporters for the respectable metropolitan dailies knew runners made good copy. Such writers not only condemned the immigrant exploiters and demanded greater government oversight but also delighted in lavishing vivid monikers on these rogues: crimps, harpies, land-pirates, land-sharks, man-catchers, sharpers, touts, "boarding-house black-legs, leeches, or lickspittles," and "hordes of soulless vampyres."[6]

Writers and policymakers returned again and again to the figure of the runner since he was one of the most visible workers within the emerging commercial system of mass transatlantic migration. The inner workings of this system remained opaque to the outside observer, but its results were plain to anyone witnessing the fresh arrivals who disembarked on the city's piers every day. The annual number of newcomers in the United States first broke the 50,000 mark in 1832 and hit 100,000 a decade later; by 1846 the number topped 150,000 and then doubled to 300,000 in 1849. They came in the wake of the Irish famine and political, economic, and social upheaval on the European continent, and it was the Port of New York where the great majority of these newcomers landed.[7] Between 1840 and 1860, customs officials recorded about three million "alien passengers" entering the United States by sea, and roughly 75 percent of these passed through lower Manhattan's congested waterfront.[8] The "respectable" businessmen who profited from this system—shipowners, railroad investors, and owners of canal boat lines among them—operated at a significant remove from it and were thus hard to hold accountable for conditions within it. Ships involved in the steerage trade, for example, were rarely owned by one individual. Multiple shareholders, rather, pooled their resources to minimize any one individual's risk and responsibility.[9] Government efforts to regulate and reform this system, therefore, proved exceedingly difficult because it was often nearly impossible to identify and punish a responsible party.

The runner, unlike the behind-the-scenes commercial investor in transportation companies who may or may not have engaged in predatory practices, *was* visible on ship decks, wharves, and streets, an embodiment of the moral qualms and anxieties Americans had about the business of mass migration. Indeed, outrage generated by runners' exploits drove the rallying cry for reform. In 1847, the New York State Board of Commissioners of Emigration was established as the first government body designed to protect immigrant welfare and regulate immigrant transportation in the United States.[10] The board struggled for several years to establish its legitimacy as the exploiters sought to undermine it at every turn. The commissioners did not make much progress in their war against runners and their ilk until they secured a beachhead at Castle Garden, the War of 1812-era fort-turned-theater in Battery Park. In the summer of 1855, the board converted the structure into the world's first immigrant landing station, at last putting vulnerable newcomers behind thick sandstone walls, out of the reach of the land sharks.

Runners and their constituent businesses proved so difficult to regulate because they occupied an economic and legal "in-between" space in a new transatlantic mass commerce in humanity and could represent themselves as legitimate businessmen when they needed to do so. Well-intentioned laws and government authorities lagged behind new developments in mass migration, ill-equipped to deal with the reality before them, much like the ways governments now struggle to regulate Internet commerce. Contrary to the persistent myth that the antebellum United States was a nearly stateless, laissez-faire, free-market utopia, legal historian William Novak has argued that local and state governments occupied a robust place in people's lives.[11] And yet, the intensely local nature of most regulatory regimes made them woefully inadequate to deal with the new mass circulation of goods and people that accompanied the economic "revolutions" of the 1830s and 1840s. Immigration was a prime example of this state of affairs, especially in the nation's busiest port. Before 1847, the city and state of New York still employed local, eighteenth-century strategies, based on English poor law tradition, to cope with the onslaught of "strangers." These mechanisms, including the requirement that shippers post a bond or pay a fee to city authorities for each steerage passenger in case he or she became a public charge, proved incapable of providing for the needs of the large volume of people flowing through and being stranded in the city. The bonding system, for example, was more effective at giving city officials opportunities for corruption than providing meaningful support for immigrants.

Most observers agreed that runners' abuses needed to be curbed, but opinions about the transatlantic immigration business as a whole varied greatly. Defenders of immigration, like one 1836 editorialist, saw it as "the main source of our prosperity," noting that immigrants had "cleared the forest, dug the canals, and built the cities of our country."[12] Yet many Americans viewed mass migration as an almost existential threat to their society, political system, and economy. In the 1830s and 1840s, they struggled to define what constituted economic independence in an environment in which wage labor was becoming more prevalent, and since many newcomers were seeking jobs that paid wages, their presence fed these anxieties. Not a few American thinkers and policymakers, like Maine Free Soiler George Weston, feared that European "pauper labor" might infect and degrade "free" American workers.[13] These anxieties were reflected in Americans' belief that, after England's Parliament passed Poor Law reform legislation in 1834, English and other European municipalities were paying the transatlantic passage fare of workhouse and prison inmates to "dump" them on the young Republic.[14] Although evidence suggests that the practice was rare, the figure of the "foreign pauper" served as effective political cover for immigrant exploiters: many Americans did not care whether or not an immigrant's impoverishment happened before or after landing; what mattered was that almshouses in the major port cities were filling up with the foreign-born and creating a significant public burden.[15]

The image of the steerage passage business was also tainted by the fact that it bore more than a passing resemblance to the ways unfree laborers had been introduced into the country in the not-so-distant past. The legal Atlantic slave trade shut down in 1808 and the indentured servant trade had collapsed by 1820, but for decades afterward, the steerage trade could not shake its associations with bonded labor.[16] For some Americans, the possibility that certain shippers were profiting from the importation of those likely to be economic dependents cast a shadow on the immigrant passenger business. Most white northerners opposed both slavery and abolition because they believed that African Americans threatened their own freedom and well-being, and many saw immigration in similar terms. Immigrants who scraped together $15 to $25 for steerage fare from Liverpool to New York had not passed a bar high enough to assuage anxieties about disease, immorality, and threat to the social order in the way that cabin passengers—people of independent means who could afford $80 to $100 for first-class passage—did. Poverty, low moral character, and susceptibility to infectious disease remained firmly linked in the minds of middling and elite Americans, although advances in public health were beginning to challenge these linkages.[17]

Carrying steerage passengers was a lucrative business, and New York's wealthiest and most influential merchants enjoyed substantial earnings from it. Through influential bodies like the New York Chamber of Commerce, they took an active interest in shaping legislation, making sure it would not impinge on the trade's profitability.[18] In the 1840s, the city's merchants owned most of the packet lines that dominated not just the immigrant trade but nearly all commerce between New York and its chief transatlantic partner, Liverpool. New York merchants created the Black Ball Line in 1817, the first service with a fixed schedule of transatlantic departures. Before this time, almost all transatlantic ships delayed departure until their holds were full. Packets initially carried fine freight and first-class cabin passengers, leaving steerage passengers to transient vessels that did not sail on fixed schedules. But as steamships in the late 1830s and early 1840s began to steal away lucrative first-class cabin passengers and fine freight, packet owners increasingly turned to steerage passengers to fill their vessels on the return trip to New York.[19] While visiting London in 1848, Robert B. Minturn, one of New York's preeminent "merchant princes," testified before a parliamentary committee on emigration, stating that "the amounts paid for the passage of emigrants go very far towards paying the expense of [the] voyage of ships from America to Europe and back."[20] When the decision was made to carry migrants instead of freight in steerage, carpenters hastily erected pinewood bunks, "knocked together with coarse planks" and looking "more like dog-kennels than any thing else," according to the narrator of Herman Melville's 1850 novel, *Redburn*.[21]

Respectable shipping firms kept their distance from the rough-and-tumble business of recruiting steerage passengers. They turned this task over to the middlemen of the transatlantic system: the "passenger broker." By the 1850s, there were over fifty such brokerages in Liverpool, some viewed as respectable, and others not.[22] In that city on the Mersey, brokers and boardinghouse keepers would employ runners in a manner that mirrored the system in New York. Some passenger brokers would send runners far out into the Irish countryside, luring many to emigrate by promising high wages and easy living across the Atlantic and bargaining fare prices that would not be honored in Liverpool, earning them the sobriquet "man-catchers." Some Liverpool brokers followed British restrictions on the number of passengers a ship could carry per its tonnage, but others employed a variety of tactics to evade such restrictions, like manipulating the passenger lists submitted to the naval officer in charge of enforcing the passenger laws. Most often, brokers would contract an entire steerage deck of a ship, enabling them to pack it as densely as they could while still evading scrutiny. Some were also boardinghouse keepers and sellers of victuals, and they would bribe captains to delay departure of transient vessels to squeeze out a few more nights of room and board. Several brokerages were situated along Goree Plaza, where Britain's most prominent slave traders had headquartered before 1807, drawing out inevitable comparisons between slave and steerage trades.[23]

Having survived the treachery of Liverpool's shady runners and passenger brokers and the crossing of the turbulent North Atlantic, new arrivals had to run the gauntlet yet again upon entering the Port of New York. The process usually began when an immigrant ship anchored in the Narrows between Staten Island and what is now Brooklyn so that a state health inspector could board the vessel. At this point, if passengers were deemed healthy and not detained at Quarantine, the ship could continue across the bay to

Manhattan. Runners used this moment to their advantage, bribing captains or using force to come aboard the vessel. This "head start" was a significant competitive advantage, because once the vessel carrying passengers landed at a Manhattan dock, the total chaos that William Brown had observed would ensue. As the gangplank lowered to the dock, a new wave of predators rushed on board.[24]

Most runners appear to have been Irish or German immigrants themselves who used exaggerated promises and other modes of verbal persuasion in native tongues to convince the newcomers to engage their services. But if runners' words failed to elicit trust, they would "take charge of [the immigrants'] luggage, and take it to some boarding house for safe keeping, and generally under the assertion that they will charge nothing for carriage hire or storage."[25] Cartmen and "baggage smashers"—adolescents who would carry bags for an exorbitant fee—would also use this tactic to secure custom.

Runners in New York were usually of two distinct types: those who corralled their charges into boardinghouses and those who solicited business for establishments selling tickets for inland transportation, often called "forwarding offices" or "express offices." Boardinghouse runners often shepherded newcomers to Washington Street, which parallels the North River waterfront and in the 1840s was lined with inns catering to immigrants. Keepers of these establishments paid the most productive runners on a monthly salary, while others received a per-head piece rate.[26] A reporter for the *Brooklyn Eagle* strolling down Washington Street in June 1846 observed, "From the Battery up to Courtland [*sic*] street is a series of the most squalid habitations, each one being fitted out in the lower story as a low groggery. These places were teeming with newly arrived immigrants, in all manner of costumes, and speaking all manner of dialects, from the ancient Erse and Teutonic, to the modern low Dutch."[27] For room and board, proprietors would charge immigrants "three or four times as much as they agreed or expected to pay, and exorbitant prices for storing their luggage, and in the case of their inability to pay, their luggage is detained as security."[28]

While boardinghouse runners worked within a local circuit, those representing passenger forwarding offices operated within more geographically expansive networks that shadowed those established by operators of packet lines between New York and Liverpool or railroads between Albany and Buffalo. Forwarders in New York frequently coordinated scams with agents in Albany and other transfer points along the route to the Great Lakes and shared the profits. One common tactic was for a runner to represent a ticket to Albany as one for Buffalo and charge an immigrant the full passage price to the city on Lake Erie. As 1847 testimony to a New York state legislature committee tasked with investigating immigrant exploitation explained, "A pretence is also often set up for not honoring these tickets, that the freight is not paid, or at least not enough has been paid upon the luggage, and the emigrant is either detained at Albany, or compelled to pay additional charges."[29] The worst scammers in this category were impostor ticket agents who collected fares and left to "go back to the office" to fetch the tickets, never to return. A reporter for the *New York Herald* noted in June 1845 that this practice was "quite common, yet the rogues are hardly ever detected."[30]

Ticket brokers and passenger forwarders could also make considerable profits by funneling immigrant passengers into upstate transportation networks. In the 1840s, canal boats remained dominant modes of carrying immigrants across upstate New York. Passengers could choose either an express "packet" or a slower "line" boat along the canal system. If they were willing to pay more, they could use some combination of canal boats and short rail lines to quicken the pace. By 1851, two cross-state rail lines had been completed: the Erie Railroad across the state's Southern Tier, and several small lines that together comprised an Albany-to-Buffalo link. Canal boats gradually began to lose favor to these faster conveyances.[31]

By 1848, a hard-nosed steamboat proprietor named Isaac Newton and his forwarding firm of Newton, Wolf and Ruschmuller had gained a monopoly over transporting immigrant passengers to railroad connections along the Hudson River. In May of that year, an independent passenger forwarder named "R. Schoyer" wrote to Erastus Corning, the industrialist, railroad investor, and former mayor of Albany, knowing that Corning had considerable influence over several railroads, including the Utica and Schenectady and the Michigan Central. Corning would also soon preside over the consolidation of the New York Central Railroad in 1853.[32] Schoyer tried to convince Corning to rethink Newton's monopoly, arguing that he could carry passengers more cheaply and that competition would be advantageous to the railroad: "it is a question of great importance for the R.R. Co. to decide whether it is best to give one person a monopoly or to place all forwarders on a footing and thus make it the interest of all to work for the R.R."[33]

Schoyer claimed that he would have 10,000 to 15,000 immigrants from Europe consigned to him that season, but seemed aware that Corning might have some suspicions about his respectability. To assuage Corning's fears,

Schoyer offered to send along his account books to show that he had not overcharged passengers in the past: "I am pleased to have the opportunity to do away with the mischievous reports you had of me." Schoyer further built his case for respectability by noting that he removed his trade from the canal the previous year because he viewed those who controlled access to it at Albany as thuggish fraudsters who used intimidation and tampering with luggage scales to enable overcharging. And he claims to have done so despite the possibility of harm to himself. "I was the first and only one in this city who withdrew the business from that chanal at the risk of being *killed* by a *slug shot* from one of their *Bullies*."[34] Fighting his less-than-sterling reputation, Schoyer depicted himself as unwilling to engage in fraud and violence like the Albany canal forwarders. By cultivating the appearance of an honest businessman, perhaps Schoyer was casting his lot with the future direction of the business, in which the canal forwarders' brutish practices would no longer be acceptable after respectable men like Corning had gained control.

Runners of all sorts were successful in ways that other commercial entrepreneurs were successful, by developing influential local and regional contacts, understanding the possibilities provided by transportation systems, and marshaling information about the movement of people that their customers did not have. They possessed qualities that accorded with the ascendant free-market ethos of the day—ambition, persistence, and the perpetual seeking of competitive advantage—but to a grotesque extent. Their ready use of violence and intimidation marked their position outside the boundaries of respectability upheld by wealthy and powerful merchants and professionals. Runners had not forged their business practices within the genteel environment of the countinghouses, but rather in the context of the rough, hypermasculine, working-class culture that emerged in American cities in the decades before the Civil War. The antibourgeois "sporting man" celebrated violence in the boxing ring, political arena, and saloon.[35] In this milieu of "shoulder hitters" and prizefighters, being good with one's fists made a man influential and respected.

So when runners' business contacts, their access to transportation and information, and their ability to persuade immigrants failed them, they resorted to the violent means that Schoyer condemned. The vulnerable political, economic, and legal standing of immigrants in tandem with the weak state of law enforcement in the city helped them get away with it. Even after a semimodern police department replaced New York's antiquated sheriff and night watch system in 1844, the initial legislation limited its size to 800 men, a tiny force for a city whose population would reach over 500,000 by 1850. Moreover, the force was scattered across the city, far more likely to be deployed in "respectable" neighborhoods than the waterfront. An 1853 letter writer to the *Tribune* noted, "It is a fact that on the docks where immigrants land, no other law exists than that of the fist. There is downright robbery. Few emigrants, even if they have the assistance of some friends residing here, can escape being plundered by baggage smashers, runners, and car[t]men." The writer observed that immigrants rarely pressed complaints in the courts against their victimizers, since "most of them don't stay in the City; justice is too slow; they don't know anything about our laws, and are glad to get away with their lives."[36]

While violence was a regular feature of antebellum urban working-class life, it was even more common among those who worked in the highly congested space of New York's waterfront. Maritime laborers in antebellum New York, including "sailors, riggers, boatmen, ferrymen, stevedores, and a variety of craftsmen whose work related to the shipping industry" were, according to historian Paul Gilje, "a rough lot. . . . Brawls broke out often. . . . The slightest confrontation could end with drawn knives and murder."[37] Runners operated in this milieu, and the vicious competition for trade between them frequently resulted in runner-on-runner violence. In December 1854, at the Chambers Street Pier on the North River, a runner for the Erie Railroad named Hugh Hagen announced to anyone who would listen that Dennis Carrick, a runner for another line, would overcharge immigrants for carrying their luggage. Carrick responded by swinging a cart rung—a heavy iron spoke that served as the nineteenth-century brawling equivalent of a tire iron—at Hagen's temple. A reporter observed the blow and saw Hagen crumple to the ground, bleeding from a "frightful wound, that will probably result in the loss of the life."[38]

Manhattan's waterfront was not only violent. It was a chaotic, disorganized, and peripheral urban space. Runners used the chaos of the waterfront and the neglect of authorities to their advantage. As historian David Scobey has argued, "The disorganization and blight of the waterfront . . . stood in stark contrast to New York's economic power and the natural endowments of its port. Ships commonly experienced delays of up to a week in landing their cargoes; the growth of trade, combined with an ad hoc method of assigning berth space, made it nearly impossible to obtain dockage without patience or bribery."[39] "Respectable" New Yorkers began to avoid the waterfront, and even Battery Park, once a fashionable promenade in the 1820s and 1830s, had by the 1840s lost this status as elites increasingly moved their residences farther uptown and into the center of the island. The disorganized and dispersed layout of the waterfront itself made policemen's surveillance difficult, thus allowing runners to use intimidation and violence with little fear of intervention by city authorities.

But even if the police did arrest a well-connected land shark, the runner had little to fear because the political and legal system often failed to punish offenders. Runners applied intimidation and violence to commerce in much the same way Tammany applied it to politics; not surprisingly, shoulder-hitters and runners were often one and the same, as was the case with John Morrissey, a runner who later would gain fame as a bare-knuckle boxer and U.S. congressman.[40] Having cultivated political connections, runners often received preferential treatment from elected city judges during criminal proceedings. An 1859 *New York Times* editorial complained that a system that allowed a particular judge "to sentence a poor Irishman . . . to forty years for stealing six cents, and suspend sentence—or, in other words, release—on a shoulder-hitting emigrant runner, guilty of a murderous assault, is almost a caricature on criminal justice."[41] Another exasperated *Times* editorial published around the same time, mockingly titled, "Is Swindling Legal?" complained, "We read, almost daily, statements of persons who have been swindled by Peter Funk auctioneers, by emigrant runners, or by members of the fraternity of thieves, with the addition sometimes that the offender was made to refund the money. But why are these scoundrels let off on such condition? Is there no law to punish them?"[42]

The anarchic and lawless conditions on the waterfront made it difficult for reformers to rein in the immigrant exploitation business, but what made the problems even more intractable was that corrupt government officials charged with regulating immigration frequently profited from the status quo. Municipal authorities of the City of New York administered an antiquated system that in theory provided for the immigrants who became indigent. The state legislature passed the law in 1824, a time when national immigration rarely exceeded 10,000 people. It required shippers to post bonds for every "emigrant passenger" who landed in the state, with each being recorded by the mayor's office. In addition, shippers had to pay a "head tax" to support the Marine Hospital at Quarantine on Staten Island where sick immigrants and sailors were treated. If the newcomer became a public charge within two years after landing, the city's almshouse commissioners called in the bond to pay for that individual's support.[43] Shipowners found the bonds burdensome, especially as the volume of immigration increased in the late 1820s, and pressured city authorities to find another solution. Without any modification to the state law, city officials instituted a "commutation fee" of $1.50 a head in lieu of the bond if the immigrant in question was deemed unlikely to become a charge (for those who seemed likely to become indigent, a bond was still required). The commutation funds in theory would be turned over to the commissioners of the almshouse for the care of immigrants. But it was discovered in 1842 that John Ahern, the city clerk overseeing this process, not only had failed to keep accurate records of the fees collected but had absconded with a sizable portion of the funds. Ahern and other officials entrusted with migrant welfare set the tone for the rampant exploitation of the 1840s, undermining the idea that municipal authorities might play a role in reform.[44]

Merchants and shippers were also complicit in one of the more vicious aspects of the bonding and commuting system that developed in the early 1840s. For a small fee, a shipper could sell an immigrant bond to brokers who were often passenger forwarders as well. In general, bond brokers who had purchased immigrant bonds from shippers did not have enough capital to cover all of their liabilities if they came due and were taking a calculated risk in making this transaction. If city officials tried to collect on bonds that "fly-by-night" firms could not pay, these businessmen would simply shut their doors and re-form under a different name or flee to Europe or California.[45]

More established bond and passenger brokers, like the firm of William and James T. Tapscott Brothers, had an even more pernicious strategy to avoid paying for the care of bonded immigrants. Like several of the bigger forwarding houses, Tapscott Brothers ran a transatlantic business: William operated a passenger brokerage in Liverpool and James maintained the New York bureau and oversaw the bond brokerage. The Tapscotts established their own private hospital and poorhouse to shelter those immigrants unfortunate enough to have had their bonds purchased by the brothers' firm. In 1846, a select committee of the Board of Assistant Aldermen investigated the Tapscotts' private immigrant poorhouse in the town of Williamsburg (now in Brooklyn), and found its inmates sickly and starving. The committee judged the premises unfit for human habitation and the food rotten.[46] Curiously, the scandal seemed to have little effect on the brothers' reputation as businessmen. Five years later, a credit agency reporter called them a very responsible house that did a good business selling passage through their "Emigration Office" and distilling camphene and alcohol used for lanterns on ships. The reporter noted that the Tapscotts were rich, honorable in business dealings, prompt in payment, and possessing abundant capital.[47] The example of the

Tapscotts demonstrates not only the difficulties in trying to regulate the immigrant trade but also the near impossibility of drawing a clear line between respectable and illicit practices within it.

In 1845, the Common Council, acknowledging runners' rampant exploitation, passed a law requiring them to have licenses in an attempt to establish order on the chaotic waterfront. "No person shall exercise the vocation of runner," the law read, "to solicit custom for boarding-houses, forwarding or transportation lines, without the Mayor's license, for which he shall pay the sum of twenty dollars per annum." In addition, the licensed runner had to give "satisfactory bonds" to the Mayor for $300 as security for his good behavior and wear "a label or plate with the words, 'Licensed Runner'" that indicated his license number. An unlicensed runner would pay a fine of $25 for the first offense and $100 for additional ones.[48] This new system, however, did little to bring the problems under control; if anything, the official plaques made runners appear trustworthy while doing nothing to change their practices.

During the 1846 sailing season, the extensive abuses perpetrated by runners and their employers in combination with the first wave of the Irish famine migration galvanized reformers. In December 1846, the radical Democratic politician and journalist Mike Walsh published two editorials in his paper, the *Subterranean*, that reflected a widely shared disgust with the status quo. In the first, he expressed astonishment that the top runners made $75 to $100 per month, a lordly sum for individuals "distinguished for nothing but the most unblushing effrontery, hopeless depravity, and brutal demeanor." Furthermore, Walsh thought it unseemly that "the most mercenary and thievish portion of [the exploiters] hold office too under the government."[49] In his second editorial, published a week later, Walsh noted that several prominent citizens had contacted him in support of his condemnation of the runners. He expanded his critique, arguing that nearly everyone who came into contact with incoming immigrants was complicit in the system of exploitation: the Quarantine doctor and his staff on Staten Island who charged unnecessary fees, ship captains and officers who accepted bribes, city officials like John Ahern, former mayor Robert Morris, boardinghouse keepers, operators of "fictitious transportation companies," and "that most graceless, heartless and abandoned horde of hirelings and ruffian pilferers known by the now degraded appellation of 'runners.'" Even officers of various protective immigrant societies came under fire for having entered "into villainous speculations" similar to "those connected with the swindling transportation companies." In Walsh's opinion, the worst was the president of the Board of Alderman, Oliver Charlick, who owned a stake in a fraudulent passenger forwarding business. Walsh called him the "Leader of the Coenties Slip clam boys" and "Friendly skinner of Emigrant passengers."[50] For Walsh, those who passed laws or ran benevolent societies that supposedly protected immigrants but who in fact were using their position to profit personally from exploitation operated on a moral plane even lower than that of the runners themselves. To Walsh, runners were merely the rotten extremity of a gangrenous body politic.

Two months earlier, in October 1846, city Democrats had conducted "a large and influential meeting" at Tammany Hall to decide upon methods to reform "the present outrageous system" of landing steerage passengers that left them so vulnerable to predators.[51] By January 1847, a bill to reform the system was working its way through the state legislature at Albany. The initial proposal was that the reformed system would remain in control of city authorities, despite their miserable track record in limiting runners' abuses. But upstate legislators, driven by the increase in the foreign poor in their own county almshouses, pushed to create a statewide immigrant welfare agency, the New York State Board of the Commissioners of Emigration, which would distribute commutation funds to support foreigners in county almshouses across the state. Governor John Young signed the bill that enacted the board into law on May 5, 1847. On that occasion, an editorialist for the *Albany Evening Journal* expressed his hopes for what the new agency might accomplish: "This Law takes the Stranger out of the hands and out of reach of those who lie in wait to prey upon him. It provides Guardians for the Immigrant, who, instead of plundering them, will take them by the hand, give them needed information, cheapen their expenses, and facilitate their movements."[52] It quickly became evident that the board had considerable work to do before it could give any credence to those words.

In its first years, the new authority made headway in creating a statewide welfare system for sick and indigent immigrants, building new hospitals and an "Emigrants' Refuge" on Ward's Island in the East River.[53] But it failed to check the rampant exploitation of immigrants until it opened its Castle Garden Emigrant Depot on August 1, 1855, after several previous failures to secure a dedicated landing place. Runners knew an enclosed and protected space for immigrants to land posed a threat to their livelihoods, and they protested vehemently in the initial days of the depot's operation. On the evening of August 6, 1855, they even organized an "indignation meeting" in Battery Park against the commissioners, whom they referred to as "those men

Figure 5.1. "Emigrants at Castle Garden—Runners and Crimps at Work—a Characteristic Group." *Frank Leslie's Illustrated Newspaper*, October 24, 1868. Picture Collection, the New York Public Library, Astor, Lenox, and Tilden Foundations.

who would erect a Charnel House in our midst, in spite of our most urgent wishes, and regardless of the health, prosperity and interest of the lower wards of the City." The runners' rhetoric tried to reignite long-held fears about immigration introducing even more disease, pauperism, and vice into the heart of the city. The raucous crowd marched defiantly in front of the Castle Garden walls and shot fireworks at the structure, perhaps with the intention of setting it ablaze.[54]

Castle Garden did curb some of the worst abuses, but the immigrant exploitation business in New York persisted and in certain ways became more sophisticated and institutionalized. Some operators, finding their opportunities more limited in the city, moved overseas. In 1858, one author claimed that Castle Garden "effectually broke up the system by which emigrants had so long been shamefully defrauded in the city of New York, but only led to the transfer of the seat of depredations from that port to the port of embarkation."[55] More American passenger forwarders opened up shop in European ports, selling fraudulent or overpriced tickets for inland transportation to destinations in the U.S. interior. Like other commercial men, exploiters continued to adjust and seek new competitive advantages as regulatory conditions changed, creating new networks that spanned the Atlantic Ocean. But as the illustration published in 1868 in *Frank Leslie's Illustrated Newspaper* shows, some small-time operators still lingered around Battery Park, looking to take advantage of a green newcomer, a state of affairs that persisted at least until the closure of the Castle Garden Depot in 1890 (see Figure 5.1).[56]

In the decades following its establishment, the Castle Garden regime itself struggled to maintain its legitimacy as an authority to regulate the immigrant trade, and often faced well-founded charges of corruption and abuse. The accusations that immigrants were overcharged for railroad fares purchased at the concession within Castle Garden were constant: suspicions pointed to payoffs made to board employees by the railroad corporations in exchange for access to Castle Garden.[57] A near death-blow to the board's legitimacy came in 1870 when the Tweed Ring, empowered by a Democratic majority in both chambers of the state legislature for the first time in sixteen years, reorganized the board as a vehicle for Tammany Hall sinecures and patronage opportunities.[58] While the board was restored to its original form after the ring's fall, the episode nevertheless demonstrated the frailty and inherent instability of the city's and the state's regulatory authority. But by the 1870s, the systematic corruption and fraud of the great railroad corporations and the Tweed Ring had dwarfed the misdeeds perpetrated by the emigrant runner. In the decades before the Civil War, the land shark had been a particularly despised cog in the matrix of economic fraud and political corruption that shaped immigrants' experiences and cultural debates about the regulation of urban space and the legitimacy of commercial endeavor. By contrast, the postbellum runner was a quaint rogue whom Horatio Alger nostalgically rendered as a safe fictional protagonist.[59]

CHAPTER 6

"The World Is But One Vast Mock Auction"

Fraud and Capitalism in Nineteenth-Century America

COREY GOETTSCH

In July 1845, the *New York Herald* printed a story about a swindle that was commonplace in antebellum New York City: the mock auction. The article recounts the story of "John Brown," a "verdant youth" from the "wild woods of New Hampshire." He was walking down Chatham Street when his "attention was arrested by the cries of an auctioneer—'going, going, for only $5.00.'" He entered a mock auction store and was bedazzled by an array of beautiful watches, jewelry, pistols, and other items. Drawing on both the man's sympathy and impulse for a good bargain, the auctioneer told him that the lot of goods had been the property of a "poor widow, and must be sold." Brown could not resist: he entered the bidding with an offer of ten dollars. Little did he know that the people bidding against him had no intention of buying any goods, but were in fact coconspirators of the auctioneer. Almost immediately, the hammer went down—Brown was the winner! He entered the back room to pay and discovered that the glittering silver he thought he purchased was in fact "a lot of rings, breastpins, and worthless articles." He was also informed that he owed fifty dollars, not ten. At this point, "Brown expostulated, but to no purpose; there were the goods, and his ten dollars were already in the possession of the knaves who insisted upon his paying the balance." In the nick of time, "Our hero's Yankee spirit" came to the rescue.

An enraged Brown "seiz[ed] the auctioneer by the throat, . . . took his money from his hand, and after a violent struggle, made his escape from the den of thieves."[1]

Unlike most stories about mock auctions, the one involving John Brown had a happy, albeit violent, ending. By the time the story was printed in 1845, the popular press had familiarized nineteenth-century Americans with the mock auction swindles of New York City, even if they had never visited the metropolis. Mock auctioneers modeled their scams on regular auctions, using deceptive measures to entice victims into buying shoddy goods at inflated prices. "Peter Funk," the accomplice of the auctioneer, acted as a fake bidder—one newspaper described him as the "most miserable specimen of the human family" who acted as a "hired decoy duck. A fellow who is paid to attend the swindling mock auction, as if he were a stranger, and either by making mock purchases himself or else by lauding the articles under the hammer to induce the innocent and unsuspecting to purchase worthless trash for five times its value."[2] As "sales held for the sole benefit of inexperienced countrymen, at which more or less worthless articles, imitation jewelry, watches of gilt copper and the like, are offered," they were particularly designed to take advantage of those who were inexperienced in the market.[3]

Mock auctioneers and Peter Funks, shrewd businessmen who used creative but unethical business practices to make money, were central figures in the nineteenth-century imagination and yet are marginal ones in the historiography. Mock auctions appear as subjects in hundreds of primary sources, including newspapers, story papers, magazines, novels, guidebooks, poems, and broadsides. And yet, traditional histories of the American economy have ignored the entrepreneurship of these petty criminals, choosing to focus instead on the activities of elite capitalists and industrious members of commercial firms.[4]

Far from being insignificant, the innovative but predatory business practices of mock auctioneers and other swindlers played critical roles in the debate that defined the rules of commercial engagement in the nineteenth-century United States. Stories about mock auctions appealed to readers because they helped illuminate the complex moral quandaries that capitalism posed. By the time mock auctions appeared in popular periodicals, Americans had been debating for decades whether legitimate auctions were fraudulent, monopolistic, and distorters of true market value.[5] Mock auctions forced readers to take up the debate again, puzzling over the ways they unsettled their notions about the ethical issues involved in making economic transactions. The

John Brown story cited above, for example, draws on two conflicting stereotypes: on the one hand, the mark was a naïve countryman preyed upon by vicious city swindlers; on the other hand, he was a shrewd Yankee on the hunt for a good deal.[6] The story mentions that the goods came from a "poor widow." However, the reader likely inferred that the countryman knew that this was not so—it was likely they had been stolen. The reader would certainly also note that this story constituted a modern fable in which the countryman was punished for his hubris: Brown was presented with a bill much larger than he expected for goods that he discovered were "worthless." The reader might laugh at the man's misfortune. But the story contained one more compelling element. The Yankee escaped from the clutches of the mock auctioneer, perhaps to the delight of readers. Stories about mock auctions played an important part in the discourse used to establish the legitimacy of some transactions and the illegitimacy of others, enabling Americans to better understand and influence the prevailing market values and practices.[7] Stories of mock auctions were about sharp swindles: as modern parables, they forced Americans to consider the role of trickery and the contours of proper behavior in *all* business dealings.

Efforts undertaken by New York City authorities to suppress mock auctions thrust them into the center of debates about the role of deception in the market. In 1846 and in 1853, the municipal government mobilized its resources to quash the business of mock auctions: the first effort involved the employment of men who walked up and down the street with placards warning citizens against mock auctions, while the second effort criminalized them through a new law that threatened fines and imprisonment for those who engaged in auction fraud. Both efforts failed to stop mock auction swindling, however. As the efforts to suppress mock auctions demonstrate, criminals like mock auctioneers helped clarify the boundaries of economic activity by brazenly pushing at those boundaries. Criminals' innovations constantly pushed the limits of legality in pursuit of profit. The authorities were forced to play a game of catch up, passing laws and devising methods to curtail the opportunities for profit available to mock auctioneers. The source of innovation is clear: criminals were always one step ahead of the authorities. Mock auctioneers were ultimately agents of creative destruction who left scores of victims penniless and laws governing commerce ineffectual in their wake.[8]

The focus on mock auctions in discussions of business trickery led to the exoneration of New York's leading capitalists. By focusing on mock auctioneers, the misdeeds of so-called legitimate businessmen fell from view. Mock auctioneers and other petty swindlers like them became the scapegoats of commercial misbehavior, permitting elite capitalists to distance themselves and their business practices from the unambiguously predatory tactics of the mock auctions. Peter Funk became a label assigned to any fraudulent and immoral man of business, and other capitalists were able to claim respectability by contrast.[9] While mock auctions opened up an avenue to discuss trickery in business, the debate about them played a crucial role in the bifurcation of American capitalism into two distinct worlds: the respectable "sunlight" capitalism of America's famous businessmen and the shady underworld of "gaslight" capitalism discussed in this volume. Yet the debate ultimately could not obscure the ways these worlds intersected with and depended upon each other.

The origins of the debate about mock auctions began in 1814 with the rise of dry goods auctions and the movement to suppress them. In the early nineteenth century, New York City emerged as the nation's commercial and financial capital, and auctioneering played a crucial role in this growth.[10] English businessmen helped to produce this commercial boom, "dumping" goods in the city following the War of 1812. English manufacturers and exporters circumvented American importers and wholesalers and consigned their goods cheaply to American auctioneers. As a result, retailers were often able to purchase goods for lower prices at auctions than from wholesalers or importers.[11] Because of these advantages, most imported goods in New York were sold at auction during the late 1820s and early 1830s.[12] Importers and wholesalers did not regain their economic standing until just before the calamitous Panic of 1837 that plunged the nation into an economic depression.[13]

Threatened by the stiff competition of the auction houses, wholesale merchants and artisans waged a bitter anti-auction campaign in the 1810s and 1820s. It was during this period that auctions became a mechanism through which merchants, city elders, and the public discussed larger issues about the market. Anti-auction critics blamed auctions for just about any conceivable ill that might be associated with the economy. Jacksonian Democrats asserted that auctions represented a great evil because they fostered monopoly and were "destructive" to both manufacturing and importing interests.[14] According to one anti-auction critic, business was entirely transparent before auctions rose to prominence: "Goods were of a uniform quality, and were what they appeared to be." When auctions became more prevalent, however, "the floodgates of fraud [had] been thrown open, and the old barriers of honesty [were] swept away."[15] Auctions, according to their critics, had tainted capitalism with dishonesty and greed. Yet their critique can be read as a sour-grapes lamentation about the competition at the heart of capitalism. It is worth noting that anti-auction commentators were anything but disinterested citizens performing their civic duty. Quite to the contrary, auctions directly threatened their livelihoods, and one ought to read their complaints with a skeptical eye. It seems unlikely that capitalism, in the "halcyon" days before auctions, was an economic system defined entirely by transparency and benevolence.

The debates about auctions raised issues that would continue to resonate when mock auctions emerged and began to stake out the boundary between legitimate and illegitimate economic practice. To Americans who believed that goods had intrinsic value, the dramatic price fluctuations of auctions raised eyebrows. One anti-auction pamphleteer claimed, "Every article . . . comes to the purchaser in such a rapid fluctuation of prices as to destroy all notions of its comparative importance and intrinsic value."[16] Critics also argued that auctioneers employed particularly deceptive and predatory business practices. According to one anti-auction circular, "The frauds of auctions have become proverbial. The practice of selling defective and damaged goods, under deceptive circumstances, is so common, that remarks upon it have become trite as the existence of the practice is undeniable."[17] Auctioneers, claimed one critic, "pick up innumerable articles that are damaged, and many that are absolutely worthless, . . . [yet] these are offered for sale by indescribable arts of displaying excellencies and concealing defects."[18] Opponents claimed, moreover, that auction houses used fictitious bidders to drive up prices. According to one such critic, "AUCTIONS *produce, from their very nature,* THE GROSS FRAUD OF FICTITIOUS BIDDINGS."[19]

While auctions were taking their place as highly contested venues that represented the crisis of legitimacy plaguing the broader economy, they were also distinct places in which particular types of transactions occurred.[20] Auction sales were especially public and noticeable, and therefore unlike deals that were struck in intimate retail spaces. The sales were loud, group experiences in which people dramatically competed against one another for goods, and the auctioneer kept the audience engaged with his distinctive chant. Auctions laid bare the antagonistic nature of market exchange, as bidders competed with one another to get the lowest price possible and as the auctioneer pitted participants against one another to raise the price.[21] More than any other kind of transaction, auctions blurred the line between entertainment and commerce, since the auction was a public spectacle that even nonpurchasers could enjoy, and the auctioneer, who bore more than a passing resemblance to an actor, played to the passions of the purchasers through his rapid-fire speech.[22]

Ironically and perhaps not coincidentally, regular auction houses were in a state of decline at the same time that mock auction stores began to appear, around the Panic of 1837. And the importance of auctions to public debates on the role and place of misrepresentation in trade only grew more pronounced with their appearance. Surfacing in 1836 in New York, mock auctions took aspects of auctions that Americans already found questionable or controversial and presented them in a highly exaggerated form, thus making them especially useful for discussing the rules of commerce in the larger marketplace. Mock auctions traded solely in low-quality goods whose value was deceptively inflated, and auctioneers used predatory selling practices, including the introduction of fake customers to puff the goods on display and bid up their prices when they arrived on the auction block.

As the opening vignette reveals, the mock auction functioned by masquerading as a legitimate auction. A *New York Herald* exposé explained the general mode of swindling practiced at mock auctions: "These 'mock auctions' are got up by a sort of confederacy, composed of half a dozen individuals, termed Peter Funks. One becomes the auctioneer—another officiates as clerk and the remainder constitute the audience." Mock auctions were highly orchestrated yet criminal versions of the normal auction, with a fake audience loudly bidding on goods going for outrageously cheap prices. Passersby could not help but be drawn to the commotion. The unwary, it seems, could have the bargain of a lifetime—for instance, a lot of high-quality jewelry for cheap. The trap was set for "some Connecticut or eastern man" to enter the store. When he arrived, a by-bidder offered a mere cent for the "lot" of goods, which had "been judiciously exhibited." The Yankee, "elated by the prospect of a glorious bargain," bid two cents and won the lot. When it was time for him to pay up, however, the mock auctioneer told him he owed two cents for "every article on the whole lot and if he refuse[d] to pay," he would be "at once pounced upon and plundered of the cash in his possession."[23] Dozens of stories corroborated the *Herald*'s account.[24]

One of many contemporary periodicals to depict mock auction scenes, *Frank Leslie's Budget of Fun* captured the essence of how the swindle drew victims in by generating excitement and trading on appearances of legitimacy. As Figure 6.1 illustrates, the gold watch for sale appeared to be real, and the store was full of individuals appearing to be customers. The apparent commotion was intended to draw attention from passersby, and this auditory element is represented in the caption. The auctioneer loudly recounted a narrative of the watch that would surely have gotten the attention of potential gulls: he announced that it was "the identical watch of Prince Albert, which the Queen Victoria, the gal he married, gave him on the wedding day . . . [,] jewelled with the famous Koh-i-noor—the one in Windsor Castle being an excellent imitation!"[25] This far-fetched and inaccurate story lured customers into the store. The prospect of acquiring a gold watch with such an alleged provenance for cheap was too good to pass up. The auctioneer's intent of getting the attention of potential marks in the store succeeded. The urgency of the bidding war encouraged passersby to set aside their reservations and jump into the fray: "Eight dollars—nine dollars—ten dollars! Another dollar—say another? Eleven dollars!—It [could be] yours—Koh-i-noor and all!"[26] Bidders believed that they had to act fast, lest the opportunity—and the gold watch—be lost. The auctioneer and the by-bidders worked in perfect coordination, drumming up interest in the goods for sale and then driving up the price. The mock auctioneer paid careful attention to the psychology of buyers and used powerful visual and auditory cues to entice bids.

Savvy manipulators of their customers' confidence, mock auctioneers and their employees were shrewd businessmen who used deceptive tactics to make money. Every aspect of the mock auction, down to the subtlest detail, was carefully calculated to deceive the mark, from the dress of the accomplices to the arrangement of the goods and the pace of bidding. The testimony of myriad bidders recorded in the indictment records for New York City not only confirms the sales techniques described in newspaper accounts but reveals just how successful mock auctioneers were in capitalizing on people's desire to navigate a market they often did not quite understand—all to make a good bargain. For example, one gentleman named Jacob Joseph Adolphus testified against mock auctioneers who swindled him on May 8, 1837. He was "attracted by the selling of Watches, Jewellry, &c., by auction," he told the court. After he "had been there a short time he had fifty six dollars for a Watch which was then offered for sale & was knocked down to him at that price." He also bid on a box "which contained various Articles, such as a Watch, Pencil Cases, Rings, Breast pins, &c., which were warranted to be gold." He was presented with two bills: "one for the Gold Watch for fifty six Dollars, and the other for One Hundred and Five Pieces of Jewellry at fifty cents each." The auctioneer Elias Aaron and Adolphus disagreed about the

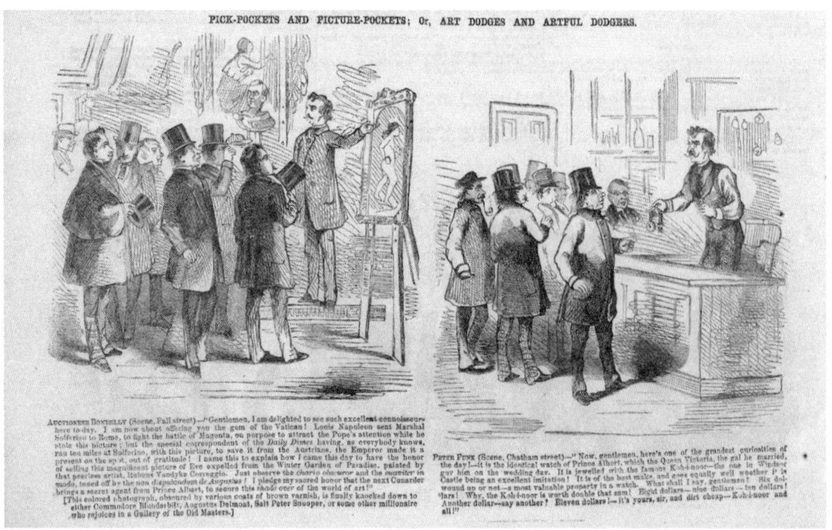

Figure 6.1. A Mock Auction in Progress. "Pick-Pockets and Picture Pockets; or, Art Dodges and Artful Dodges," *Frank Leslie's Budget of Fun*, April 1, 1860. Courtesy Library Company of Philadelphia.

number of pieces in the box. Neither trusted the other's count, so each took stock of the items. Adolphus counted ninety-three, while Aaron counted 216 pieces. Aaron threatened to prosecute Adolphus if he did not pay for all 216 items. And contrary to Aaron's claims, Adolphus found that none of the items in the box were gold except "for a Watch and a . . . pencil case."[27] Another plaintiff, Joanna Shaw, accused mock auctioneer Phineas Alden of fraud for selling to her "pieces of jewelry [that] were not Gold or Silver but were of some metal . . . of very little value or no value."[28] Mock auctioneers' methods fostered potential bidders' attraction to the goods and to the process by which they were sold. These same methods gave bidders little time to determine whether the goods they purchased had value or not.

In addition to by-bidding and charging by the piece instead of the lot, mock auctioneers employed other novel entrepreneurial strategies. One such method was for one of the Peter Funks to offer to purchase half of the goods, splitting the cost of the lot with the mark. John K. Barton, a Yankee from Vermont, entered the mock auction store of Pliny E. Davis in 1838. He encountered a "Peter Funk, dressed in the guise of a countryman" who drew Barton into a transaction by "offering to share the purchase if it was knocked down to him, and when the moment of reckoning came, the sham countryman was minus the requisite amount of funds, and Barton had to foot the bill."[29] A. H. H. Lummis of New Haven, Connecticut, fell victim to a similar tactic when one half of the lot was offered to be taken "by Mr. Williams (a Peter Funk)."[30] Mr. Williams, of course, did not pay his share. Another dupe, Mr. Richard Shields of Baltimore, was told by a Peter Funk masquerading as the "watch inspector of the city" that he had just purchased a worthless watch. Charging three dollars for his "advice," the Peter Funk recommended Shields sell the watch at another auction. It appears that Shields, having once fallen victim to a mock auction, became a Peter Funk by auctioning off the watch he had just bought to unaware bidders at another mock auction. Sadly for him, he acquired another "galvanized watch" at the second establishment that was as worthless as the first one.[31]

Mock auctioneers also preyed upon victims by capitalizing on the courtesies, expectations, and transaction records established and used in other commercial venues. For instance, they sometimes offered to buy back certain goods, pretending to be motivated by goodwill. A man who charged John Crowe with mock auction theft claimed that a Peter Funk offered to "give [me] ten dollars for said Ear Rings and Breast Pins."[32] However, when it came time to pay, the other man was shoved out of the way. The plaintiff in this case believed that "said person was hired there as an under bidder and that shoving him back and preventing his entrance was only done for effect."[33] Mock auctioneers even manipulated receipts to prevent the victim from seeking recourse. One anonymous victim appealed to the authorities that his watch was not gold. "The auctioneers, however, had made out his bill so carefully that he could obtain no relief."[34] As Michael Zakim has argued, bookkeeping did not merely reflect which transactions were made in the market; it fundamentally shaped their form and helped men establish the economy's parameters.[35] The power of commercial paper to define the accuracy of accounts worked for fraudulent as well as honest men.

Mock auctioneers also leveraged the widespread anxiety about the circulation of counterfeit bills and the anonymity of the urban marketplace. A citizen of Buffalo, New York, who visited a Chatham Street mock auction house bid four dollars for the goods and "handed a $5 bill in payment, which the clerk of the store took possession of, and then asked him, had he not any other $5, as the first one looked suspicious." The clerk snatched the bill and promptly told the visitor that the lot of goods he purchased cost $33 rather than the $4 dollars he had bid. At this moment, a Peter Funk of "respectable appearance" approached him and "whispered to him by all means to pay for the goods." This Peter Funk offered to pay for half of the goods and asked the victim to accompany him to his store. Upon finding that he had no money in his store, the Peter Funk offered to take the victim to another auction house to sell the goods. "The auctioneer immediately took the goods, put them up for sale, and after receiving three or four bids, knocked them down for $9, and the purchaser paid for them and walked away."[36] The Peter Funk feigned surprise and told him to make the best of a bad bargain.

Stories about mock auctions were staples in popular print in part because the authors of these stories situated mock auctions within dominant tropes about the market and then challenged readers to undertake the difficult task of delineating the boundaries between legitimate and illegitimate economic behavior and practice. As the cases of Shields and the citizen from Buffalo reveal, one such trope was the shrewd but simultaneously naïve mark on the lookout for a bargain. Readers could relate to, laugh at, and critique the grasping but inexperienced bidders who tried desperately to make transactions that were shaped by accounts that remained illegible and inaccessible to them: paper and goods whose value they could not trust; smooth-talking, respectable-looking men whose true identities and trustworthiness could not be discerned; and their own willingness to cross the legal and moral lines of legitimate practice. While Barton and Shields both hailed from cities, many newspapers tried to shoehorn mock auction marks into the stereotype of the rural Yankee. As one *New York Morning News* story related, "Joseph King, of Herkimer county, N. Y., took the honorary degree of A. S. S. . . . at the institution of St. Peter, 116 Broadway, on Saturday last."[37] A *New York Herald* exposé wryly noted that "it is somewhat strange that nine out of ten [victims] are from that region of our country that claims, and is genuinely reported to be, the birthplace of the cunning and the shrewd."[38] Much like the story of John Brown that opened this chapter, some, although certainly not all, of the accounts on mock auctions describe the victim as a Yankee—sometimes using the phrase "'cute Yankee."[39] The Yankee stock character highlighted some of the ambiguities of rural Americans' participation in the marketplace. On the one hand, the popular press portrayed them as simple fools who lacked basic skills in market transactions. On the other, Yankees were also considered drivers of hard bargains—acute and shrewd businessmen.[40] Readers would have ridiculed this figure, who was simultaneously sharp and credulous and would have gotten his due for being too greedy. Stories about mock auctions forced readers to question how far bargain hunting should go and examine how people—auctioneers, bidders, and readers—could work the market to their own ends through bad dealings.

While some stories about mock auctions asked readers to examine their own greed, others identified mock auctioneers and Peter Funks as scapegoats who took the blame for bad behavior in the market. Associated with shady business practices writ large, Peter Funks were portrayed in many guises, including ethnic stereotypes that readers might recognize. Sometimes Peter Funk appeared as a Jew, tapping into popular discourses about Jews as market outsiders and participants in shady business practices. One newspaper exposé featured a Peter Funk who spoke in the accent of German Jews: "Such a bargain—I vishes I had the means."[41] The *New York Atlas*, limning profiles of different characters in American life, drew a Peter Funk with a stereotypical hooked nose (see Figure 6.2).

The author explained, "We have selected a Jew Peter Funk for our portrait, because a thorough Jew rogue is of all rogues the most cunning."[42] Jews in New York tended to cluster in occupations like pawnbroking, auctioneering, and secondhand clothes dealing and were often portrayed as commercial outsiders who took profiteering too far.[43] American readers would have been aware of the association of Jews with immoral business practices when they read about mock auctions.[44] Peter Funk, a symbol of market trickery, was more comprehensible when linked to a familiar stereotype, and the stereotype in turn strengthened the popular assumption that the mock auctioneer was one of capitalism's odious bogeymen, a figure to blame for the unfairness and greed on display in the market.

These tales not only helped readers comprehend the moral quandaries of the market, evidently populated by " 'cute" Yankees and swindling Shylocks, but also allowed readers to learn about customers who fought the injustice of the transaction. Sometimes in these tales, auction bidders triumphed, overcoming both their own and the mock auctioneers' greed. After getting their just reward, the bidders in these stories then eluded the grasp of the mock auctioneer, turning a tale of woe into a harmless joke. For example, in the opening vignette, John Brown found the courage and strength to escape the clutches of the mock auctioneer. Another Yankee brought a gang of friends to the mock auction shop after he was swindled, and threatened to stuff the auctioneer into a sack and hang it from the ceiling. Threatened with violence, the mock auctioneer refunded the bill.[45] In another account, a swindled

Figure 6.2. Peter Funk as a German Jew. "The Peter Funk," *New York Morning Atlas*, Supplemental "*Atlas* Picture Gallery" Issue (1840). Library of Congress, Serial and Government Publications Division.

Spanish sailor returned with fellow "Jack Tars" who "made the Peter Funks return the money."[46] The New Orleans *Daily Picayune* told readers of one savvy countryman who got to keep a gold watch for a bargain he made in New York. When an auctioneer offered to "clean" a gold watch he had just hammered down to a Yankee bidder, the buyer wisely fled the store with his purchase rather than let the auctioneer switch the gold watch with a spurious one made of copper.[47] These stories about nefarious deals and dealers not only aimed to frighten and entertain readers but also suggested that violence was permissible when perpetrated against bad market actors.[48]

Yet despite tales of victims triumphant, mock auctions continued to cause anxiety, not only because they were shady businesses run by untrustworthy characters but also because they seemed to be spreading throughout the city. By the 1840s, public outrage against mock auctions reached a fever pitch. Newspaper reports of the spread of mock auctions beyond Chatham Street—a thoroughfare also associated with secondhand clothes dealing and Jewish merchants—outraged New Yorkers and made the mock auction swindle seem all the more dangerous as it encroached into Broadway and Wall Street, loci of respectable business.[49]

As mock auctioneers pushed against the boundaries of custom and law, they forced officials to take action and clarify the meaning of licit and illicit through legislation and criminal enforcement. The *New York Herald* demanded, "If there is no law against them to protect the ignorant from being duped by these fellows, let one be enacted immediately."[50] Another article argued in favor of new laws because victims had little recourse available beyond bribing the police: "we have no remedy—there is no law to cover these offences—but you can employ a police officer who may possibly recover back a part of your money, if you pay him well for his trouble."[51]

Police officers, it should be said, were not always so expensive. Purchasers of goods at mock auctions, if they felt cheated, often resorted to the law for assistance in reclaiming their money. New York City policeman William H. Bell came to the aid of several beleaguered countrymen who fell victim to mock auction swindling in the 1850s. On one occasion, Bell "went to a mock auction store in Chatham Street and got a countryman's money back . . . for a watch they had stuck on him."[52] Sometimes, mock auctioneers would not forfeit their winnings without the policeman resorting to threats. In another entry, Bell described saving a "man from Albany who bought a Watch at [Warren] Gilbert's Mock Auction store in Chatham St. yesterday for $20." He "Went and saw Gilbert," who "refused to give the money back when some persons who was in company with the man was going to turn the *Crib up* and he *forked over*."[53] Evidently, Gilbert's accomplices demanded that Gilbert pay up so that they would not suffer legal reprisal.

Policemen, despite their willingness to help, could not curtail thc mock auction scourge on their own. The mayor of New York responded with a public campaign of new laws and regulations to end mock auctions. In 1843, police officers had been legally authorized "to caution strangers and others against . . . pick pockets, watch stuffers, mock auctions, &c."[54] In August 1845, Mayor Andrew Havemeyer used this law to hire men to stand outside mock auction stores with "large placards" that bore the warning, "Beware of Mock Auctions."[55] The strategy appears to have been quite effective—at least initially. Within a week of the placards' display, the mock auctions along Chatham Street and Broadway began closing.[56] By the end of September, the *Herald* was convinced that "Mayor Havemeyer has destroyed the brilliant prospects which these worthies entertained of making fortunes of . . . gullible strangers."[57] In the long run, however, the campaign did not end the mock auction swindle. Run by petty criminals keen to evade law enforcement and able to find new ways to profit on the fringes of the market, they tenaciously persevered.

Commentators were captivated by the "Beware of Mock Auction" phenomenon almost immediately after the placards appeared. It allowed them to explore the connections between mock auctions and the economy as a whole. It would be hard to overstate the novelty of the appearance of the "Beware of Mock Auction" signs in Manhattan's cityscape. In antebellum New York, signs were primarily commercial in nature. It was not until the Civil War era that they had any regulatory function, such as directing traffic.[58] Numerous writers highlighted the visibility and originality of the placard campaign: Charles Haswell, recollecting the scene over half a century later in 1896, distinctly remembered how "one of our Mayors conceived the effective method of employing a man with two large canvas placards . . . on which were emblazoned in large letters 'Beware of Mock Auctions.' "[59] The placard campaign provided a space in which the mock auction could be openly compared to other businesses. For example, Mike Walsh, editor of the *Subterranean*, saw an opportunity to point out the irony of the campaign against mock auctions: if trickery shaped economic transactions, then how should consumers be warned against all of the deceits they would encounter in the marketplace? After Havemeyer's campaign had begun, Walsh wrote, "Two years and more ago I suggested the idea of sending chaps with sign boards or muslin banners to parade in front of swindling establishments, with cautionary instructions on them." According to Walsh, his original idea was to use the placards against not only mock auctions but also other shady establishments: "I insist on the full carrying out of my suggestion. Let another be stationed in Centre-street, immediately in front of the Tombs, with '*Beware of Shysters, Stool-pigeons and False Witnesses!*'; and in Wall-street with 'Beware of Usurers, Bank Swindlers, and bullet-eyed Brokers.' "[60] In another editorial, Walsh suggested that mock auction trickery was small potatoes compared to the frauds that took place in other parts of the city: "we . . . hope they'll go right to work and haul up the *big* Mock Auction men down in Wall street, Front street, and adjacent places."[61]

Other Americans agreed. According to *Yankee Doodle*, if the mayor's campaign were used against all types of deceit in capitalism, "The *street would be impassable, being blocked up by an army with placards*."[62] The placard campaign and its visibility enabled critics to argue that all areas of economic activity, and not just mock auctions, deserved warnings: trickery was a characteristic of capitalism itself—a few men with anti-auction placards were surely not enough to manage the myriad swindles in the marketplace.

In the *Knickerbocker*, Charles Briggs, who used the pseudonym "Harry Franco," gave the mock auctioneer his say about the placard campaign and the economy more generally. Like Walsh and other critics, the mock auctioneer found the public warning to be a suitable device for addressing the injustices at the heart of capitalism.[63] Walking down Broadway, the protagonist notices "a man stationed opposite a store, which had a small red flag hanging at the door, with a large muslin banner" stating "BEWARE OF MOCK AUCTIONS!" The narrator enters the store and strikes up a conversation with Peter Funk. Emphasizing his honesty as a merchant, "Mr. Funk assured me that he was amenable to the laws, like any other merchant, and that he would'nt [*sic*] grumble at paying the penalty of any crime of which he might be convicted." Funk claims, "My legal advisor . . . tells me I can recover immense damages from the mayor, for injury to my business." However, he seeks retribution not through restitution but through a slanderous placard campaign: "'Here's my programmy,' said Mr. Funk. I am getting up some 'Bewares' myself, and a most immense sensation I'll produce with them, I'll assure you. First, I will have a large banner carried by a Kentucky giant opposite the City Hall, with this inscription in bloody red letters: 'BEWARE OF LAWYERS!' Opposite Trinity Church, at the head of Wall-street, I will station another, . . . with this inscription in gilt letters: 'BEWARE OF FANCY STOCKS!'"[64]

Peter Funk produced a small list of other "Beware" signs: "LADIES, BEWARE OF FRENCH MILLINERY AND FANCY GOODS!" for afternoon shoppers; "TO READERS: BEWARE OF TRASH!" for the publishing houses; and "BEWARE OF HUMBUGS!" for five hundred other businesses that the author refused to name.[65] Briggs's message was clear: if the municipal government was allowed to put a halt to one type of swindle, it ought to campaign against all of them, and there were many. Where should (and how could) Americans draw the line between right and wrong in economic affairs?

Mock auctioneers fought efforts to regulate them out of business. In September 1846, Warren Gilbert, the owner of a mock auction house, filed a lawsuit against Havemeyer's successor, Andrew Mickle. He argued that the placards were libelous and sought $10,000 in damages. In response, the court temporarily suspended the mayor's ability to use the anti–mock auction placards.[66] The suit was decided in the mayor's favor when in November the New York Court of Chancery ruled that the court had the jurisdiction to restrain a private nuisance by injunction and that placards warning of mock auctions could be construed as libelous. But since the mayor of New York was authorized by law to warn strangers against entering mock auctions, the court could not use its power of injunction against him. The mock auctioneers' recourse was to seek a change in the laws. Gilbert, if his 1850 run-in with Police Officer Bell was any indication, doubled down on swindling after moving his auction rooms from well-appointed Broadway to dilapidated Chatham Street.[67]

Popular opposition to their shops precluded mock auctioneers from marshaling any concerted opposition to the signs. Yet, despite the court ruling, the signs did not put mock auctions wholly out of business. In July 1847, the chief of police reported that there were "11 mock auction shops, 215 junk shops, and 115 second hand clothing stores" in the city and "all [were] receivers of stolen goods."[68] In the years after the debates about "Beware of Mock Auction" placards, commentators continued to compare other businesses to mock auctions. For example, George G. Foster offered a sweeping indictment of consumer capitalism in his assessment of mock auctions: "While passing these mock-auction establishments and wondering for the hundred-thousandth time at the gullibility of human nature, we have sometimes asked ourselves what would be the result if all the mock auctions in the community were at once to be exposed?" The evils worth illuminating included "the mercenary editor selling his columns to the interest . . . that would pay him best . . . [and] the financier originating falsehoods to facilitate his extensive operations and swell his profits. . . . [A]fter contemplating it should we not be ready to exclaim, 'The whole world is but one vast Mock Auction!' "[69] But however cynical Foster may have seemed about the myriad ways people took advantage in the capitalist system, he profited from selling lurid stories of New York's underworld. Writing about mock auctions was big business—one from which Foster earned a great deal of money. And Foster was convicted for forging checks: he, too, was a Peter Funk in the broader, stereotypical sense.[70]

Mock auctions became the swindle against which the city's myriad other confidence games—whether finessed at the stock exchange, in the church, within government offices, or inside retail stores—were defined. Others agreed with Foster: capitalism was one big mock auction. In an article bemoaning the prevalence of fraud in retailing, the *New York Morning News* held up mock auctions as the most well-known version of consumer fraud: "The public mind has been attracted to the numberless frauds upon the trading public which are continually multiplying. The various modes of buying goods under false pretenses have been discovered, and the abominable frauds practised by the mock auctions have frequently irritated the public mind."[71] An article in the *New York Herald* claimed that "Wall street has been turned into a vast mock auction, . . . [and] many commodities which are dealt in there—in the shape of a railroad and other stocks—are no more valuable than pinchbeck watches of the Chatham street auctioneers are gold."[72] The *American Review* referred to the sales of land in imaginary villages as "mock auctions," explaining that "one conspirator would buy of another and sell to a third, at rising prices of course[,] . . . [in order to] effect a sale of a whole 'village' to a speculating company from abroad."[73] The *Advocate of Moral Reform* wondered, "is it really more important that strangers who enter the city should meet, as they do, a sentinel on the public walks, holding a print before him in flaming capitals, 'Beware of mock Auctions' than they should meet through a like agency . . . BEWARE OF INTELLIGENCE OFFICES kept by the unprincipled[?]"[74]

Despite efforts to suppress them, mock auction swindles continued to thrive in midcentury New York, when newspaper articles chronicled the frequent swindling of "verdant" countrymen at mock auctions.[75] The *New York Herald* complained in 1848 that "the old haunts are again made the theatre for operation, and the eternal chattering of those who decoy the unwary and unsuspecting, assails the ears of passersby" and wondered, as had many observers before, "Surely it ought not be difficult to put into operation a law for effectually crushing such marts of crime as the mock auction stores."[76] It was not until 1853 that New York City finally passed such a law, mandating imprisonment for up to three years or a fine of $1,000 for auction fraud. Furthermore, it required that "every auctioneer shall take out a license, and file a bond of $5,000, which license can be cancelled by the Mayor."[77] Several arrests were made under the law, and the newspapers rejoiced.[78]

The bliss was short-lived, however. One newspaper in October 1853 lamented that "these swindling-shops are in full blast."[79] According to one estimate from the summer of 1855, "There are about sixteen mock auction shops now open throughout the City."[80] In attempting to explain why there were actually *more* mock auction stores in 1853 than there were in 1847, the article found that the anti–mock auction law was just not being enforced: mock auctioneers, "when brought up to answer a charge of swindling, managed to escape justice through some flaw of the law, or on the payment of the sum fraudulently obtained, and are allowed to depart."[81] In 1859, statistics released by the police of New York revealed that there were about "212 arrests for mock auction swindling" in 1858 and noted that "the parties were compelled to remand the money and permitted to go and victimize others."[82]

Mock auctions, the efforts to suppress them, and the debates surrounding them tell us a great deal about the process through which the rules of capitalism were negotiated. Courtrooms were not the only arena in which the boundary between fraudulent and permissible business practices was debated. Popular culture was also an important site for the negotiation of business ethics. The anxiety caused by mock auctions suggests that the rules governing transactions in the marketplace were not self-evident. It was not clear to Americans when deception in business dealings went too far.

And mock auctioneers and other petty swindlers were not inconsequential to the larger history of American capitalism. As the movement to end mock auctions makes clear, petty street confidence games caused such anxiety among American consumers that the mayor of New York was forced to adopt novel means to shut them down. Mock auctions, a seemingly insignificant swindle in New York City, proved to be an important part of nineteenth-century debates about the morality of the market. Mock auctions and the stories told about them alternately widened and narrowed Americans' conception of capitalism. These shops seemed to proliferate everywhere, but they also seemed to be isolated. Their proprietors seemed to be like every businessman and also seemed to be stereotypical outsiders. Their customers were like other ordinary Americans and also caricatures delineated for laughs. The expansive and contracted views that mock auction narratives provided made it difficult for Americans to think deeply about what capitalism as a process was doing to their society. It became easier to create a bogeyman than destroy the entire system. For all of the ruckus raised against mock auctions and their similarity to other capitalist enterprises, Peter Funk became capitalism's misfit, diverting attention from the ways elite capitalists manipulated markets and perpetrated fraud. Peter Funk, an archcapitalist who took the antagonistic logic of market exchange to its natural conclusions, ironically became the anticapitalist scapegoat for all commercial misbehavior. As Americans denounced mock auctioneers' bad business, elite capitalists became less reprehensible by contrast. Perhaps mock auctions' greatest contribution to the history of American capitalism is the ironic way in which they distanced other capitalists from association with criminality.

CHAPTER 7

Underground on the High Seas

Commerce, Character, and Complicity in the Illegal Slave Trade

CRAIG B. HOLLANDER

The United States banned Americans from participating in the transatlantic slave trade through a series of state and federal laws, culminating in the 1807 Slave Trade Act.[1] The market for African slaves was far from closed, however. With foreign planters in the Caribbean and Brazil offering enormous sums for new slaves, numerous American merchants attempted to outfit illicit slaving voyages. Other Americans worked on slave ships, transporting Africans to the Americas in exchange for higher wages than sailors who served on vessels trading other African commodities. Slave traffickers were better compensated for the risks associated with breaking the 1807 act. And those risks were real, although historians have long argued that federal authorities turned a blind eye to the continuation of the slave trade. In fact, the American Navy, backed by the support of the federal government, contributed to the failure of many slave voyages. For instance, in 1819, President James Monroe instructed U.S. naval vessels to seize any American slavers they encountered.[2] The U.S.S. *Cyane* sailed for Africa in 1820 to implement Monroe's orders and sent four alleged slave ships to the United States for adjudication.

It is thanks largely to such efforts to suppress the illegal slave trade that historians have had opportunities to learn about the clandestine traffic.[3] As this essay will describe, the detailed judicial inquiries into two of the *Cyane*'s prizes, the *Science* of New York and the *Plattsburgh* of Baltimore, documented otherwise obscure aspects of the illegal voyages. The sources associated with these two inquiries reveal that by 1820, America's transatlantic slave trade had already transitioned from a relatively open form of commerce into an underground smuggling operation. It is also evident that the slave traders took seriously the threat of capture and prosecution, even though the United States had outlawed slave trading only twelve years earlier. As a result, they employed innovative techniques to mask their crimes, ensure their anonymity, and cover their tracks. These precautions were complicated, time consuming, and costly. But those involved in the two voyages were convinced that their crimes would be considered serious legal and moral transgressions, even worthy of murder to keep secret.

At the time, most Americans did, indeed, feel that the transatlantic slave trade was a grave crime against humanity, although slavery and the domestic slave trade were still perfectly legal in the United States.[4] They assumed, therefore, that those participating in the slave trade were villainous seafaring mercenaries, not unlike pirates. In that sense, the criminalization of the transatlantic slave trade had created more than a new type of human traffic. It had also created a new type of human trafficker—brazen enough to break the law, ruthless enough to commit the heinous acts, and effective enough to warrant military surveillance. It is, then, no wonder that the United States elevated slave trading to the level of piracy, making it, just a few weeks after the capture of the *Science* and *Plattsburgh*, a capital crime punishable by death.

And yet, cases like the *Science* and the *Plattsburgh* helped to expose and publicize an uncomfortable reality for Americans of the Early Republic: the "piratical" business of the illegal slave trade depended upon the ambition and desperation of many commercial and laboring men who were seemingly virtuous and upright citizens. In particular, the captains of the two slave ships, Adolphe Lacoste of the *Science* and Joseph F. Smith of the *Plattsburgh*, did not conform to the pirate archetype. Of course, they committed their crimes for financial gain, like most other lawbreakers. But Lacoste and Smith were reluctant first-time offenders, as opposed to career criminals. Moreover, they participated in the illegal slave trade to provide for their impoverished families during the Panic of 1819. In that regard, Lacoste and Smith aspired to be men of good character. In fact, the merchants who hired Lacoste and Smith to serve as slaver captains did so because they appeared to be responsible, trustworthy, and honorable. Eventually, President Monroe came to believe in their decency, too. He pardoned Lacoste and Smith, implying that their participation in the slave trade was a lapse in judgment instead of a mortal sin. This essay is, then, intended to reveal that perhaps the most nefarious criminal enterprise of the Early Republic was conducted by men who spoke the increasingly intertwined languages of character and the market. These men were therefore able to manipulate the cultural scripts of ambition, honor, and virtue to make themselves—rather than their African victims—the objects of pity.

It is difficult to comprehend how quickly the United States transformed the transatlantic slave trade from an open, though quasi-legal, form of commerce into an underground traffic. Although Americans were not legally permitted to transport slaves between foreign ports after 1800, they participated rather openly in the foreign slave trade between 1800 and 1808, dispatching more than 400 slave voyages from American ports in those eight years alone.[5] American slave traders were still willing to risk breaking the law to take advantage of the burgeoning markets for slaves following the federal government's ban of the slave trade in 1808. But they took increasingly greater pains to disguise their illegal activities. Slave traffickers relied even more heavily on such techniques after Congress passed three supplementary slave trade acts that enhanced the federal government's ability to capture and prosecute slave traders.

Cuba was the primary market for the American slave trade of the Early Republic. The Spanish colony was a late-blooming sugar producer, owing much of its meteoric rise to the sudden collapse of Saint Domingue's plantation economy during the Haitian Revolution. But as the Cuban plantation economy flourished, Spain, under British diplomatic pressure, announced in 1815 that it would abolish the slave trade within eight years.[6] In both Cuba and Puerto Rico, Spanish planters stockpiled slaves before the deadline, which, after several delays, was set for December 1820. The Spanish authorities did not curb this elevated demand. Rather, they limited price controls and import duties on Africans.[7] According to Cuba's 1817 census, 314,202 persons of color resided on the island, including 124,324 slaves. Cubans then imported 25,976 African slaves in 1817; approximately 17,000 in 1818; and 14,668 in 1819.[8] A British subject in Havana, Robert Jameson, estimated that slave traders reaped 150 percent returns in Cuba toward the end of the legal period. "The value of slaves in the island rose prodigiously," he noted, adding that "the articles usually required in trafficking for them on the African coast, fell, as the anticipation of the demand soon ceasing, caused the holders to throw them plentifully on the market. Thus negroes were *purchased*, probably, *a third cheaper*, in Africa, and sold *three times higher* in the Havana."[9]

Under the circumstances, Jameson did not believe that "any other traffic in the world . . . holds out such strong inducements to illicit endeavors as that in slaves."[10]

Americans were susceptible to these "inducements." In New York City, a naturalized American citizen from Spain named Eugene Malibran outfitted his schooner *Science* for the slave trade in the fall of 1819. He provided his accomplices with instructions for each length of their impending journey around the Atlantic.[11] According to these guidelines, the *Science* was to travel from New York to San Juan, Puerto Rico, where it would be "sold" to Malibran's brother, Pedro Malibran, a resident of Trinidad, Cuba. Once the Spanish flag flew deceptively over the *Science*, a Spanish citizen named Juan Termison was to be "acknowledged as her . . . *Capitan de Papel* (nominal Captain)."[12] Malibran anticipated that his authentic captain would have to discharge the (law-abiding) American crew members, "excepting those who shall wish to pursue the voyage." Considering the nature of this voyage, his final instruction for his captain was critically important: "On your arrival at Porto Rico, you must procure about 50 shackles; in the barrel that you have on board the *Science*, there are only 4 pair, and 50 pair hand cuffs."[13]

Baltimore's merchants, not New York's, earned a reputation during the Early Republic for being the most willing to break the slave trade laws. "What city has of her own accord, become the grand depot of a horde of pirates and robbers . . . ?," asked the *Mirror* of Hartford, Connecticut, in 1819. "Is it not Baltimore?"[14] It was, indeed, no surprise that the "Sodom of America"—as the *Mirror* referred to Baltimore—made the most concerted effort to capitalize on the spike in demand for slaves in Cuba. The city developed such a notorious reputation for slave trading that, when a slaver from New York was caught, a Baltimore newspaper chimed, "We are glad to hear that Baltimore is not obliged to father all the disgrace of slave trading."[15]

Many citizens of Baltimore found their community's disreputable role in the illegal slave trade rather distressing. In 1816, a writer for the *Christian Herald* called out the city's "traffickers in human flesh," explaining, "You send off your vessels—you tell the public that [the vessels] are sold in the West-Indies—that they are the property of foreigners, while in reality, they are traversing the ocean as your own property, from Havana to Africa, and from Africa back to Havana. From thence *your* profits are transmitted to Baltimore." This author vowed to release "fatal evidence" about the slavers if they did not reform. "I know you all," he declared. "Your punishment is swiftly advancing. The time will soon be, when the fruits of your iniquity will be considered as dross and dung, in comparison with the happiness which you have lost."[16]

But for several merchants in Baltimore, the potential for bonanza profits in the slave trade outweighed any fear of punishment. As the *Christian Herald* alleged, these men operated under the assumption that, once their vessels acquired the trappings of foreign ownership, they could deny any involvement in the crime. Their personal assets would therefore remain safe, even if the authorities seized their vessels as a consequence of engaging in the illegal traffic.[17] And, with credit still available to them, the financiers could live to profit another day. Or so thought Thomas Sheppard, a prominent merchant, politician, and former privateer owner who, like Malibran, decided in 1819 to become a financier of the slave trade to the Spanish colonies.[18] That year, he agreed to pay $6,000 over an extended period to the merchants John D'Arcy and Henry Didier, Jr., for their shares of the *Plattsburgh*, a schooner that the three merchants had purchased together in October 1817.[19] Sheppard planned to turn the vessel into a slave ship.

Sheppard's coconspirator in the voyage was George Stark. The two made an agreement with the privateer captain Thomas Boyle to use Boyle's brig *Eros* as the *Plattsburgh*'s auxiliary in the crime.[20] To fool prying customs inspectors, Sheppard and Stark would split up suspicious components of the cargo between the two vessels, including a cache of weapons, materials for assembling additional water casks, and planks for constructing the slave deck. The *Plattsburgh* and the *Eros* would then set sail, supposedly for different destinations. Once the customs officials were safely in their wake, the *Plattsburgh* would anchor in the Chesapeake Bay, where the crew would load it with articles for the slave trade. The *Plattsburgh* and *Eros* would rendezvous and sail together for Santiago de Cuba, where Stark would "sell" the *Plattsburgh* to a Spanish accomplice and outfit the vessel for transporting slaves. Meanwhile, the *Eros* would return to Baltimore with any American crew members from the *Plattsburgh* who refused to participate in the voyage. Sheppard and Stark assumed that in Cuba there would be no shortage of foreign sailors to hire for the slave trade, much as Malibran expected in Puerto Rico.

Even though Malibran, Sheppard, and Stark hoped to staff their vessels with foreign crew members, they refused to entrust their ships and the outcome of their voyages to strangers. Slave trading was a complicated business, not to mention a criminal enterprise. And so, as in any complicated business, these slave trade financiers looked for trustworthy men of character to serve as their de facto supervisors. For these merchants, trustworthy men were those familiar to them who possessed experience and could be expected to return to the United States with the proceeds from the voyages. But such men also had to be daring and desperate, as well. If the authorities caught an American captain in the act of slave trading, he would not enjoy the same invisibility as the financiers. Instead, he would face the penalties outlined in the new Slave Trade Act of 1818: imprisonment for three to seven years and a fine of between one thousand and five thousand dollars, a tremendous sum for a sailor. A conviction would come at a social cost, too, as respectable merchants and tradesmen would likely steer clear of doing business with someone who had committed a crime widely considered to be among the very worst.

Given the potential legal and social penalties, it is worth asking what sort of person would agree to serve at the helm of a slaver in 1819. Who would risk his own freedom to make money by forcibly separating hundreds of enslaved Africans from their homelands and families? Historians of the slave trade have avoided such questions, suggesting that the answers are obvious: slaver captains ranged between heartless scoundrels and deranged sociopaths, naturally untroubled by the suffering of others. The slave trade, writes Emma Christopher, "rendered the captain singularly powerful, the vessel being something of a kingdom of which they were king."[21] She adds that "the cruelty exercised by captains on captive Africans, and the universal degradation of the trade as a whole, created an environment where stark violence appeared to have no consequences for the [captain as the] persecutor, and where the squandering of human life appeared mundane."[22] That characterization echoed the popular image of slave ship captains during the Early Republic. They were "unfeeling" and "*monsters* capable of this foulest of murders."[23] It was this widespread belief in the essential wickedness of slave traders that impelled the federal government in May 1820 to make slave trading a capital crime.

In actuality, though, many American slave traders seemed quite ordinary. As the political philosopher Laurence Thomas states, "it must be acknowledged that evil can be perpetrated by individuals who were once ordinary people, that is, morally decent people."[24] The captains of the *Science* and the *Plattsburgh* appear to have been such people—that is to say, they were not hardened criminals, let alone "monsters" who were thought to be "capable of this foulest of murders." And, ultimately, it was the ordinariness of the two captains that would be their saving grace, as it enabled others to empathize with their predicaments. But who were these men?

Malibran recruited a twenty-one-year-old French national named Adolphe Lacoste to serve as the captain of the *Science*.[25] Little is known about

Lacoste's upbringing on "one of the French West-India Islands," except that he was "a descendent of a once affluent family" and "twice a prisoner of war to the English, and left penniless on both occasions."[26] It is even unclear when Lacoste's family emigrated to the United States. The family was not listed in the U.S. Census of 1810, though Lacoste's mother, a widow named Eleanor Florence Lacoste, appeared in the 1816 directory for Charleston, South Carolina.[27] In all likelihood, though, Lacoste did not spend much time in South Carolina, because his mother remarked that he was in the "habitual employment [of] foreign vessels."[28] As further evidence of Lacoste's travels, the French Consul in New York claimed that he had known Lacoste for several years. This official described Lacoste as "a very good character, young, & possessing to the highest degree filial and sisterly love."[29] Lacoste would not have quarreled with this characterization, unabashedly referring to himself—probably through a mediator—as "a young man . . . who from his early infancy has had unconcealed in his Bosom the true principles both of a Christian and man."[30] Most Americans of the Early Republic would have scoffed at the notion that a slave ship captain could ever possess the "true principles both of a Christian and man." But the financiers of the illegal slave trade relied on sailors like Lacoste who considered themselves honorable, despite their willingness to break the law and subject hundreds of Africans to the horrors of the Middle Passage. It is, then, no surprise that Malibran thought highly of Lacoste, writing to him that, "for the transaction of all this operation, I refer myself absolutely to you, well persuaded as I am, that you can correspond to the confidence which I repose in you—I doubt not but you deserve it."[31]

Nevertheless, slave trade financiers could not rely just on the character of their charges, for their good intentions might lead to poor business decisions in distant places. Character, in other words, was still no substitute for experience and commercial knowledge. Only when supplied with the latter could young men of character serve the interests of their employers. In Malibran's view, then, the "government" of the *Science*, as well as the slave trading process, had to be highly orchestrated. For that reason, the correspondence between Malibran and Lacoste resembled the correspondence of ordinary commercial proprietors and their subordinates. "I cannot recommend it to you too much the choice of the cargo which you go to seek," Malibran stressed, "and I beg of you to give all your attention to it and to act agreeably to my separate instructions relative to the manner of trading in the countries where you are going. These instructions are given by a very experienced person, and it is important to follow them as much as will be possible for you." Malibran ordered Lacoste, "You will manage so as to obtain [in Africa] a superb cargo in exchange for the merchandise which you have on board the *Science*, and which I consider much more considerable than is necessary for a single cargo, for I know of expeditions of the same kind, which have doubled the number [of slaves] that you can carry, and which had not more merchandise than you have." He gave Lacoste even more specific directions regarding some transactions: "I forward to you in a small box . . . 48 watches of English manufacture, double case, which I authorize you to exchange at the place where you are to take your cargo, either for Gold dust or for Elephants' teeth of handsome quality." He admonished Lacoste: "You must consider that those watches cost $10 each, and you must regulate yourself consequently to make in exchange of them which may be advantageous to me." Regarding the rest of the *Science*'s cargo, Malibran anticipated that Lacoste would have a surplus of goods that could be used for a second slaving voyage. He told his captain, "In case then that there should remain to you some merchandise (which I much hope) after having obtained a handsome and heavy cargo, you will bring it back to Trinidad, in Cuba, and it will serve for a second voyage."[32]

To lead the *Plattsburgh*, Sheppard and Stark hired Joseph Findley Smith, who was about twenty-seven years old in 1819. In nearly the same way that Lacoste considered himself "a young man but on the threshold of life," Smith, too, described himself as "not yet on the threshold of manhood."[33] Although the 1817–1818 Baltimore city directory listed Smith's residence at 34 Bond Street in the district of Fells Point, his home could have been described more aptly as the high seas.[34] In his youth, Smith had served as an apprentice on the *Sidney*. Under the tutelage of Captain Hugh E. Davey, he sailed to faraway lands, probably including Batavia in Dutch Indonesia, Canton in China, and Montevideo in Spanish Uruguay. During the War of 1812, Davey made Smith the third lieutenant on his privateer *Pike*. The *Pike* feasted on British merchant vessels, seizing over $50,000 worth of goods.[35] Smith served with distinction in the war, rising to the rank of first lieutenant. But on August 25, 1814, the British brig-of-war *Dotterell* cornered the *Pike* near Savannah, Georgia, and ran her aground on Tybee Beach. Smith was the only officer to remain with the wreckage, attempting to save his wounded comrades.[36] The British took him prisoner, preventing him "from serving his country which was his great desire."[37] After the war, Smith served as a mate on the ship *Augustus*, which sailed from New York to Buenos Aires and then on to Surinam. A passenger on the *Augustus* described Smith as "an honest, poor, hard working American sailor . . . in almost every respect a good example of an American man—plain, un-boasting, unobtrusive, a manly thoroughbred seaman."[38] He could have added devoted husband, son, and brother to his list of Smith's admirable qualities.

On September 1, 1819, Smith married "a decent but poor girl" named Dorcas Franklin. Although the newlyweds lived in "a very small house," they were, it seems from their letters, very happy with one another.[39] When a friend offered in a letter to look after Dorcas while Smith was incarcerated, Smith asserted in a postscript: "In your letter you say that Mrs. Smith's honor will be safe with you. I have proof enouf without that observation. Thair is nothing in this world that I vallue so mutch as my wife & I am willing to trust her with you without a note of hand."[40] Perhaps Smith expressed his love for his wife and faith in matrimonial fidelity in an overtly commercial language from force of habit. However, it was surely meaningful for a sea captain to assign "mutch" "vallue" to anything in a world that depended on corroborating "note[s] of hand." For her part, Dorcas rarely referred to Joseph in her letters without adding that he was her "dear" or her "only hope and stay."[41] In all likelihood, the two would have remained among Baltimore's anonymous working class were it not for Smith's decision in November 1819 to serve as the *Plattsburgh*'s captain. On the one hand, it is easy to understand why Sheppard and Stark were drawn to Smith, who, like Lacoste, seemed responsible, trustworthy, and honorable. On the other hand, it is not clear why Lacoste ("a very good character") and Smith ("a good example of an American man") would become human traffickers, not to mention outlaws.

It is easier to speculate about the rationalizations of Lacoste, who hid behind his French nationality as an excuse for his participation in the slave trade.[42] It is also possible that both Lacoste and Smith were conditioned to the cruelties of slavery, and thought little of adding Africans to the slave population of Cuba. After all, slavery was deeply entrenched in their respective hometowns of Charleston and Baltimore. Slave sales were held routinely throughout the towns—at auction houses, in taverns, and at various civic centers.[43] Frederick Douglass, who lived as a slave near Smith's residence in Fells Point, remembered watching "the slave ships in the Basin, anchored from the shore, with their cargoes of human flesh, waiting for favorable winds to waft them down the Chesapeake."[44] The fact that the *Plattsburgh* was outfitted near ships involved openly in the domestic slave trade could have helped justify Smith's decision to serve in the transatlantic slave trade. At least William G. D. Worthington, a Maryland statesman, thought so. In a letter to John Quincy Adams, he remarked, "for horribly as I, from my soul[,] view this dealing in human flesh—many of our country men don't seem so to regard it [like I do]—Smith too, was born & bred in a slave holding state—[but] I say no excuse for it."[45]

What may be surprising, however, is that most Americans of the Early Republic did not believe that the existence of slavery justified the continuation of the transatlantic slave trade. Abolitionists would begin to emphasize the similarities of the domestic and foreign forms of human trafficking later in the antebellum period. In the meantime, though, Lacoste and Smith did not attempt to excuse their participation in the illegal slave trade by highlighting the legality of slavery or slave trafficking within the United States. The two slaver captains and their advocates implicitly conceded that the transatlantic slave trade was very different from domestic slavery. In fact, they all professed to support the ban on transatlantic slave trading. For instance, Smith once condemned the slave trade as an "infernal traffic which both 'the law of God & man forbid.'"[46]

As his reason for agreeing to become Sheppard and Stark's accomplice in crime, Smith admitted that he was lured by the prospect of reaping a large financial windfall. He explained, "The conditions which Sheppard & Stark made to me for the intended voyage to the *coast* of Africa, were that I should have $100 [per] month, five dollars [per] slave, and two slaves gratis."[47] According to Smith, the financiers "supposed that the *Plattsburgh* would carry about 500 slaves." Considering the vessel's modest size, this number was unrealistic. Nevertheless, at the outset, Smith believed that he would earn at least $4,500—more than ten times what an ordinary seaman earned in a year.[48] "The idea of obtaining an independent fortune in the space of eight or ten months," he acknowledged, "were too great inducements for me not to yield."[49] Indeed, Sheppard and Stark may well have identified Smith as an attractive candidate to take such a risky venture because they knew he might not be able to resist the financial temptation. They also realized that he would consider participating in the slave trade as a means of living up to powerful cultural imperatives that put ambition, independence, and honor above the law.

For Smith, then, the decision to engage in the illegal slave trade was a perverse (though probably not uncommon) way to preserve his character as a provider for his family, even if it meant risking his reputation as a law-abiding citizen. However, his interest in becoming a slaver captain also reflected his financial desperation, perhaps even more than his greed. In the best of times, Baltimore's working class suffered from chronic shortages of food, fuel, and employment. And the latter part of 1819 was hardly the best of times, especially for those involved in overseas trade. The post-War of 1812 economic boom had come to an end during the previous summer, when commodity prices plummeted, real estate values shrunk, and credit evaporated. "We have been truly sowing the wind, and are now reaping the whirlwind," wrote Thomas Jefferson to Richard Rush in June 1819. "At present all is confusion, uncertainty and panic."[50] In all likelihood, it was this financial panic that prompted Smith to consider breaking the law in the first place. He needed to support a widowed mother, two sisters, and a wife. But sailors in Baltimore could not find work during the crisis, his wife later recalled. Smith therefore decided to commit perhaps the worst form of theft—that of robbing other human beings of their freedom.

Unlike Smith, Lacoste did not explain why he became a slave ship captain. But Lacoste's family was encountering the same financial woes as Smith's. An outsider noted that Lacoste "is and has constantly been the only support of a helpless mother who is a widow and of his two sisters."[51] Given his family's pecuniary distress, Lacoste probably came to the same conclusion as Smith: the slave trade offered his best chance to collect a hefty payday for one voyage. In that regard, Malibran offered Lacoste comparable terms to Smith's, assuring that he "must have reason to be satisfied with them." Malibran wrote to Lacoste: "I allow you $45 per month, to be reckoned from the day on which you have taken command of the *Science* until your arrival, and during your stay at Porto Rico." He then guaranteed Lacoste $60 per month for the riskier length of the voyage, which would "be reckoned from the day of your departure from Porto Rico, until your arrival at Trinidad in Cuba." Finally, as an additional incentive, Malibran offered Lacoste performance bonuses, much like the ones that Sheppard and Stark offered to Smith. Dropping his euphemisms for slave trading, Malibran gave Lacoste "a privilege of four *Heads*, which I authorize you to buy with part of the cargo at your disposal; moreover three dollars per head delivered at Trinidad in Cuba."[52] Lacoste must have been "satisfied" with Malibran's terms; the *Science* departed New York on New Year's Day, 1820. On January 15, the vessel arrived at San Juan, where Lacoste "sold" it to one of Malibran's accomplices.

Smith was not onboard the schooner *Plattsburgh* when the vessel cleared for St. Thomas on December 4, 1819. He was likely creating an alibi for himself in case a U.S. customs collector detained the vessel for engaging in the illegal slave trade. It was a prudent decision. Despite the poor reputation of Baltimore's federal officials—President Monroe called the city "as rotten as corruption can make it"—a collector detained the *Plattsburgh*'s auxiliary, the *Eros*, on the suspicion that it was bound for the slave trade.[53] The collector even confiscated a cache of guns from the *Eros* before finally letting her set sail on December 6. If the crew members of the *Eros* had brought with them the latest edition of the *Baltimore Patriot and Mercantile Advertiser*, they could have read a letter published from an American residing in their destination of Santiago de Cuba. The author inveighed against the town's flourishing slave trade. "Several vessels have arrived here with slaves from the Coast of Africa," he wrote despondently. "This traffic is abominable, and should be broken up. It is a source of much regret that many Americans are engaged in this barbarous trade, to which I hope a speedy stop may be put by our government."[54]

But the ordinary seamen aboard the *Plattsburgh* and the *Eros* did not realize initially that they were engaged in the transatlantic slave trade. Most learned the truth about their voyages only en route to Cuba. At that point, they, too, were forced to make decisions about their level of involvement in the illegal traffic. According to a crew member named John Fervor, a thirty-year-old from London, after clearing from Baltimore the *Plattsburgh* sailed about fifteen miles south of the city and anchored at Long Point, Maryland. Late that night, a boat loaded with grape, round, and canister shot came alongside. Under cover of darkness, Fervor helped bring the projectiles aboard the *Plattsburgh*. As he worked, Fervor "moved a barrel & observing that it was very heavy he asked the steward what it contained. . . . On [his] repeating the question the steward said the barrel contained irons."[55] The seaman William Flowers, a freeborn African American from Norfolk, Virginia, had a similar moment of realization. While working below deck, he also "saw a quantity of hard irons or shackles stowed away in the run."[56]

The *Plattsburgh* remained at Long Point for three days, allowing Smith to come aboard. Smith then ordered the *Plattsburgh* to sail to New Point Comfort, Virginia, where the vessel anchored for ten days. The crew became confused, because the wind was "generally favorable for her to have sailed."[57] However, the *Eros* soon arrived, along with George Stark, who was received as the *Plattsburgh*'s supercargo. On that day, the two vessels sailed for Cuba. The destination came as a surprise to the crew of the *Plattsburgh*, which had cleared for St. Thomas. It would not be the last change of plans. The officers soon informed some crew members what many of them had already begun to suspect—the *Plattsburgh* was going to sail from Cuba to Africa for slaves. But while Stark maintained his faith in the dependability and commercial knowledge of the crews as the foundation for the success of the venture, Smith began to grapple with the ways complicity in illegal and immoral commerce corrupted personal integrity.

Indeed, Smith supposedly had second thoughts about committing the impending crime. "On my passage to St. Jago," he later claimed in a plea for pardon, "I reflected on the impropriety of my conduct, & was resolute to retract my word when once in St. Jago."[58] Smith included this claim to stress that he had not desired to be a slave trafficker. On the contrary, he had resolved to break his agreement, even if it meant sacrificing his family's financial well-being and ruining his credibility among Baltimore's tightly integrated merchant community. In that sense, Smith was attempting to show that he was a morally decent person, someone who knew right from wrong. But he was also weak. Smith was, then, depicting his participation in the illegal slave trade as a temporary abdication of good character in the face of financial temptation. Presumably, he hoped that this portrayal would resonate with others who were worried about the susceptibility of character to the corrupting influences of illegal and immoral commerce.

Despite the equivocation of its captain, the *Plattsburgh* arrived at Santiago de Cuba on Christmas Day, 1819, and the *Eros* followed a few days later. On January 5, 1820, the *Plattsburgh*'s crew finished unloading the vessel's cargo of flour, tobacco, rice, beef, pork, butter, cheese, and liquor. Using planks from Baltimore, the crew then constructed a berth deck to receive the cargo that would be taken to Africa. This cargo consisted of tobacco, rice, calicoes, dry goods, iron pots, looking glasses, small arms, and Spanish brandy, all typical commodities for slaving voyages. In the meantime, the crew of the *Eros* discharged from its hold about 100 barrels of flour, 20 hogsheads of tobacco, some cases of umbrellas, and shooks, which coopers used to assemble water casks.[59] The crew of the *Eros* also moved 300 casks of gunpowder from the *Eros* to the local magazine, where they were stored safely until the *Plattsburgh* was ready for them to be brought aboard. Once the water casks and powder were transferred to the *Plattsburgh*, the crews disassembled the *Plattsburgh*'s berth deck and mounted on the vessel two twelve-pound carronades and an eighteen pounder—added protection for traversing the Gulf of Guinea. With their tasks complete, the two crews were discharged.

But the *Plattsburgh*'s stopover in Cuba required far more work than outfitting the vessel for the slave trade. After all, slave trading was only one phase in a series of transnational commercial transactions. The *Plattsburgh*'s voyage therefore required the same multilevel coordination and business expertise as legal commercial voyages. This business was conducted through the counting house of William B. Wanton. An American expatriate clerk named Frederick J. Rapp reported that Wanton was an Irishman by birth, but a Spaniard by citizenship. "Wanton had all the privileges of a native born Spaniard," Rapp said. "He could clear out a vessel which is the highest privilege." Moreover, Wanton's nationality enabled him to become an "actionist" for the *Plattsburgh*'s voyage to Africa. As Rapp defined the term, an actionist was an investor who held a share (the action) in a slaving voyage. However, according to Rapp, the names of the various actionists "never appear upon the vessel's papers nor are [the actionists] considered as owners of any part of the vessel or cargo but only [recipients] to a share [in] the ultimate profits of the voyage according to the amount of the action or actions which they hold." The system was, Rapp believed, "particular to the Spanish law & to Africa slave voyages."[60]

But Wanton was more than just an actionist for the *Plattsburgh*'s voyage to Africa. He also served as the local broker for selling the cargo that the *Plattsburgh* and *Eros* had transported from Baltimore to Cuba. "Stark could not have done the business himself," Rapp explained. "A Spanish house must be used." Much of the cargo belonged to merchants with seemingly no interest in the ensuing slave voyage, involving in the slave trade honest merchants who either did not know or did not care about the illegal venture to Africa. Unlike Smith, they probably did not think that these legal dealings made them complicit in the illegal ones. For instance, Peter Saverwine owned fifty barrels of flour; John Reese owned two hundred barrels of flour, beef, and pork; and Talbot Jones and Daniel Hoffman each owned two hundred barrels of flour in the cargoes of the ships. Wanton exchanged most of these commodities for coffee and sugar.[61] These proceeds were then remitted to the merchants on the *Eros*, which sailed for Baltimore on February 12, 1820.

The business of the illegal slave trade proceeded apace, buoyed by these legitimate transactions. In addition to serving as a broker, Wanton helped Stark arrange the sham sale of the *Plattsburgh* to a Spanish citizen named Juan Marino and the hire of another Spanish citizen, Manuel Gonzalez, to serve as the vessel's titular captain for the voyage to Africa. On January 12, 1820, Marino paid $12,500 for the *Plattsburgh*. Following this "sale," Wanton became the ship's husband. The *Plattsburgh* was also renamed the *Maria Gertrudes*, reflecting the vessel's new Spanish identity. Marino then posted a bond in exchange for a royal passport for the *Plattsburgh* to engage in the slave trade. Rapp did not know whether any American citizens had an interest in the vessel or its cargo. However, he verified that the *Plattsburgh*'s two American mates and either six or eight of its seamen from Baltimore chose to reship with the vessel because he paid them wages in advance. Rapp noted, "It is usual to get American officers on board of vessels going to the African coast *especially the Baltimore Schooners* as they understood them better." Not surprisingly, Stark also planned to sail to Africa. Rapp was under the impression that Stark was in the process of becoming a Spanish citizen. But because Stark was still an American, he needed a plausible excuse for his presence onboard the *Plattsburgh*, just in case the authorities intercepted the vessel. Toward that end, Wanton drew up a phony contract that depicted Stark as an employee of his firm and granted him permission to sail onboard the *Maria Gertrudes*.[62]

Although Smith was not privy to all the business details, he also later verified that, once "the *Plattsburgh* arrived at St. Jago, her cargo was immediately discharged, a sham sale took place, and she was then called *Spanish property*."[63] Throughout this process, Smith claimed that he battled his conscience, as well as a case of yellow fever, which precluded him from opting to return to Baltimore on the *Eros*. "Two days befor[e] the *Eros* sailed for Baltimore," he wrote, "I was attacked by the yallow [*sic*] fever a[nd] when the *Eros* sailed I was not in a situation to go on board & consequently I was left behind."[64] During his convalescence, Smith continued to contemplate whether he could stomach the slave trade. "When the [*Plattsburgh*] was fitting out," he recalled, "I was asked by Mr. Wanton of St. Jago, then acting ship's husband, whether I intended proceeding with her, I gave him no positive reply to this interrogation, but merely said I would think about it." Struggling to justify his role in the voyage, Smith decided to explore the local slave pen to test his fortitude. He recollected, "When in company with Captain McCoy [from the *Eros*] curiosity actuated us to direct our steps towards the establishment in which the newly imported slaves were kept for sale." Smith was appalled, remembering, "I there beheld a sight that melted my heart within me so much, that my face assumed a death-like paleness, which attracted the attention of Captain McCoy, who requested to know that occasion of this sudden alteration." Feeling overwhelmed, Smith "could say no more, but let us leave this dismal scene." Smith then told McCoy that he "could not reconcile [his] feelings & conscience to such a trade; & therefore had no wish of making the voyage on board of the *Plattsburgh*."[65]

Smith's visit to the slave pen reaffirmed his conception of himself as a man of virtuous character, someone who would refuse to participate in an abhorrent crime like the slave trade. But Stark believed that every man had his price. First, he raised Smith's bonus from five to eight dollars per slave, in essence reminding his captain that he was only a round-trip voyage away from achieving financial security. Second, Stark sought to convince Smith that slave trading was morally acceptable, offering him "advices" and "examples" of "*priests* that were actually engaged in this traffic, which as they pretended was neither against the laws of God, or man, for certainly these holy men otherwise would not be concerned in it." As a result, Smith found it increasingly difficult to maintain his belief in the immorality of the slave trade. Eventually, he "yielded" to the extra financial "temptation added to the vile *persuasions* & *exhortations*."[66]

Because he was an American, Smith's presence onboard the "Spanish" slave ship *Maria Gertrudes* required yet more coordination, subterfuge, and fraud. Like Stark, Smith would pose as Wanton's employee on the voyage, supposedly traveling to Africa on the merchant's behalf to scout the "goald dust and ivory traid."[67] "My name," he wrote, "was in none of [the vessel's] papers. I intended to appear as a passenger whenever circumstances required it. This duplicity was for my own safety."[68] On February 23, Wanton sent his instructions to the *Plattsburgh*. Although the letter was intentionally misaddressed to the phony captain, Manuel Gonzalez, its substance was unambiguous: "I have the satisfaction of placing under your command and direction the Spanish schooner *Maria Gertrudes*, in order that you may proceed with her to the free ports on the coast of Africa and traffic for . . . at least four hundred or four hundred and fifty negroes."[69] Despite all the misdirection, though, Smith was simultaneously too careless and too careful to avoid creating a paper trail for his involvement in the criminal conspiracy. That day, for instance, he wrote an order to a mate with various instructions for the crew.[70] And, when the *Plattsburgh* set sail from Santiago de Cuba three days later, Smith began keeping a logbook in English—probably one of the only such logs remaining from an illegal American slaving voyage. Smith's naïve endeavor to be a responsible captain would soon lead to his undoing.

According to Smith's log, the *Plattsburgh* reached Fogo in the Cape Verde Islands on March 30. Slavers often planned to arrive on the African coast between March and June to ensure that they would have enough time to deliver their slaves to the West Indies before the December sugar harvest.[71] Sailing east from Fogo, the *Plattsburgh* arrived at the Manna River in the British colony of Sierra Leone on April 6. But the *Plattsburgh* was not the only American vessel in the vicinity. In early 1820, Monroe had ordered the U.S.S. *Cyane*, a twenty-four-gun corvette, to escort the American Colonization Society's ship

Elizabeth to Africa and then seize "all vessels navigated under [the American] flag engaged in that trade, and to bring them in to be proceeded against in the manner prescribed by the law." The president "hoped that these vigorous measures, supported by like acts by other nations, will soon terminate a commerce so disgraceful to the civilized world."[72] And so, after visiting Sierra Leone in late March, the crew of the *Cyane* turned its attention to stopping any Americans from engaging in the illicit trade of Africans.

And there was much work to be done in that regard. "The slave trade is carried on briskly in this neighborhood," wrote Samuel Bacon, the federal government's attaché to the American Colonization Society, upon his arrival in Africa. "Had I authority so to do, I could take a vessel lying within the floating of one tide, say 25 miles from us . . . under American colors, taking in a cargo of slaves." It did not take long for the Americans to gather their own intelligence about how the slave traffickers operated amid the British cruisers. As Bacon explained, they "come with a cargo of goods suited to the market, deliver it to a slave factor on shore, and contract for slaves. They then lay at anchor in the river, or stand out to sea for a specified number of days, till the slaves are all procured and brought to the beach, and placed under a hovel or shed prepared for the purpose, all chained two and two. At the appointed time, or on a concerted signal, the vessel comes in and takes her slaves on board, and is off in an hour."[73]

To outrun the British cruisers, traffickers used smaller and faster vessels. This practice added to the cruelties of the Middle Passage, as it required packing slaves more tightly and leaving less room for food and water. To illustrate this point, Bacon told the Secretary of the Navy that he had purchased "a vessel of 104 tons, a swift sailor, [which] was intended to take a cargo of 100; she has a [galley] fitted to boil rice. . . . Slaves receive one pint each per day."[74]

After nine days in Sierra Leone, Captain Edward Trenchard of the *Cyane* decided to take the offensive against "several vessels of suspicious character" that were reportedly hovering off the Gallinas River.[75] Early in the morning of April 5, the *Cyane* spotted one brig and six topsail schooners and managed to detain six of them. The crew of the *Cyane* was shocked and appalled to learn that the captain of one of the captured slave ships was an active U.S. Navy midshipman named Alexander McKim Andrews of Baltimore, who had intended to carry 500 slaves.[76]

On April 10, Trenchard ordered his second officer, Lieutenant Silas H. Stingham, to take a boat from the *Cyane* and inspect several schooners sailing toward Cape Mount on the African coast. Stingham's crew consisted of eighteen sailors. As he approached the schooners, one of the vessels, the *Plattsburgh*, fired its cannon, narrowly missing the boat. Stingham ordered his men to hoist the American flag. He then warned the schooners to desist. The first vessel that Stingham boarded was the *Science*. Stingham asked the captain of the *Science*—Adolphe Lacoste—about the vessel that fired on his boat. Lacoste had no information to offer about the *Plattsburgh*. Stingham hailed the vessel but did not get a reply. Fearing another barrage, Stingham admonished the crew of the *Plattsburgh* that "if they resisted [when he boarded their vessel] he would put every man to death on board." Smith responded that Stingham should "keep off."[77] But Stingham reiterated his threat and ordered his sailors to row toward the *Plattsburgh*. In a panic, Stark ordered the crew of the *Plattsburgh* to load the eighteen-pound gun and sink the oncoming boat. The crew filled the cannon with thirty-six pounds of musket balls. Writing after the fact, Smith claimed that he had reached another moral turning point. Before the crew could fire, he appealed to them in the language of manly and patriotic honor, protesting "that the boat was an American a[nd] that I would not see my countrymen murdered & staited [*sic*] the impropriety of such a [deed]."[78] As Smith recalled in another letter, "I solemnly told my men if any one of them attempted to fire without my orders, I would blow his brains out."[79]

Thanks to what Smith considered a form of "persuasion"—sea captains were hardly averse to threatening their crews with acts of violence—Stingham and his men were able to board the *Plattsburgh* without further resistance.[80] While boarding, Stingham heard Stark mutter that "it was Smith's fault the schooner was taken, he ought to have blown the boat out of water and that if [he] had known they would have been detained [he] would have done it."[81] Smith met Stingham at the gangway. When Stingham asked Smith his name, Smith replied that "his name was *Joseph Parker* and that he was merely a passenger" from Spain.[82] Stingham asked to see the captain and the ship's papers. Smith informed Stingham that Gonzalez was the captain. After examining the ship's papers, Stingham remanded Smith to the *Cyane* under the pretense that Smith was bilingual and returned to the *Science* and the *Plattsburgh* to investigate.

There was little doubt that the *Science* and the *Plattsburgh* were slavers. An officer on the *Cyane* determined that the *Science*—despite being a former pilot boat—was contracted to carry more than 100 slaves. Meanwhile, Stingham found on board the *Plattsburgh* "forty or fifty pairs of handcuffs and fifteen or twenty long bolts such as he understood are used to secure slaves on board of vessels."[83] But were these vessels American? While searching the *Plattsburgh*, Stingham found in a trunk the letter that Smith wrote to his mate in Santiago de Cuba on February 23, 1820, signed "J. F. Smith." The letter was in English and gave orders "just as might be expected to be given in course of business from a master to a mate."[84] Upon being informed by the steward that the trunk belonged to Captain Smith and that Smith "was the gentleman who you had at first taken on board the *Cyane*," Stingham returned to the *Cyane* and asked Smith why he "dare[d] tell him such a lie."[85] Smith did not prevaricate again. He admitted to writing the letter and confessed his real name. Trenchard placed both Lacoste and Smith under arrest.

Sailors from the *Cyane* escorted seamen from the captured vessels to New York, but Lacoste and Smith were taken to Boston. Newspapers urged the authorities to prosecute the two men to the full extent of the law. The *Boston Daily Advertiser* commented that it was "necessary for the security of society, that they should be held responsible who are guilty of the overt act."[86] The president was in full agreement. "I hope," Monroe wrote, "that the offenders [of the slave trade laws] will be made an example of." He reasoned, "There will be no security . . . for the suppression of this nefarious practice without a rigorous execution of the law."[87] As they advocated for harsh punishment of the slaver captains, most Americans continued to disassociate the transatlantic slave trade from the institution of slavery, including the domestic slave trade. "The question of slavery," wrote one essayist, "may have opponents of mixed feelings—motives of interest and of policy may supersede principles of humanity. . . . [But] what is there in that portion of creation, that can justify seizing and selling [Africans] to slavery?" This author added, "The question, whether slaves born in our country, shall be permitted to move from one state to another, which is adjoining is not one that can bear comparison, or has affinity to trading, capturing, and bringing slaves from the coast of Africa;—they are distinct. . . . [a]nd I hope, that every vessel engaged in this inhuman traffic, may be captured and sent in for condemnation."[88]

Lacoste and Smith were jailed, lacking the $6,000 necessary to post bail. Indicted for violating the Slave Trade Act of 1818, they entered pleas of not guilty. Joseph Story, an associate justice on the U.S. Supreme Court, and John Davis, a district court judge, presided over the two trials. One jury found Smith guilty on November 2, 1820, while the other convicted Lacoste a day later. On January 12, 1821, the attorneys for Lacoste and Smith entered motions on behalf of their clients, alleging numerous defects in the indictments.[89]

They demanded retrials, but the judges denied their motions. On January 25, Lacoste and Smith were sentenced to five years in jail and each was ordered to pay a $3,000 fine, nearly the maximum penalty.[90]

The convictions of Lacoste and Smith made headlines throughout the United States. Newspapers noted that the two should have considered themselves fortunate for being caught before May 15, 1820, when another slave trade act took effect and would have made their crimes punishable by death. However, their cases were not closed. Even in captivity, Smith and Lacoste possessed something that they never would have afforded their captives: the ability to contact allies and rally them for help. Despite the popular image of slave traders as faceless "monsters," Smith and Lacoste did not emerge from a vacuum; they came from tight-knit communities where they had families, friends, and elected representatives. From prison, in early 1821, Smith and Lacoste began writing to their contacts, pleading for assistance in obtaining pardons.[91]

Ultimately, Lacoste's advocates—including several in the French consulate—persuaded the Monroe administration to pardon the convicted French national. On March 9, 1822, the Secretary of State, John Quincy Adams, forwarded to Boston a presidential pardon for Lacoste, including a remission of his $3,000 fine. The marshal discharged the twenty-two-year-old from prison on March 15 after he had served twenty-two months.[92] Monroe later explained that he pardoned Lacoste because he was merely "a sailor & a minor," as opposed to being a captain.[93] Others, too, were ready to forgive Lacoste, even though he had, in fact, been the captain of the *Science*. Undoubtedly, the pitiful situation of the Lacoste family tugged at many heartstrings, especially among those facing similarly tough times. Prefacing an editorial with the disclaimer that "no one will suppose us to be the vindicators [of the slave trade]," the *National Intelligencer* argued that Monroe was justified in showing "clemency" to the slave trader. The newspaper commented, "When we take into consideration the extreme youth of Lacoste[,] . . . his exemplary conduct up to that [time of his crime], having, for a long time previous, contributed to the support of his aged mother and his sisters; the punishment he had already undergone . . . and the sincere repentance he always expressed for having been engaged in a disgraceful and illegal traffic, we cannot but think" that he deserved the president's forgiveness and pardon.[94]

Suffice it to say, such sentiments were an about-face from 1820, when newspapers lamented how the *Science* was captured before the law provided "the punishment of Death" for convicted slave traders.[95] Lacoste was now commended for his desire to support his family, rather than being condemned as a monster "capable of this foulest of murders."[96] It was a forgivable offense, even though Lacoste had committed a supposedly unforgivable crime.

Smith took a different approach than Lacoste. He divulged his transgressions and offered an apology in 1822. Smith freely admitted his involvement and confirmed the prosecution's case in a letter to Monroe. He apologized for his misconduct, stating, "If sorrow & repentance will be considered by your Excellency, as an expiation of my crime . . . I sincerely experience them from the bottom of my heart." Begging for absolution, Smith wrote, "I most humbly entreat forgiveness for this my first heinous guilt against my God & country."[97] And yet, Smith was eager in this confession to explain away his complicity in the slave trade—note that he asked forgiveness because this offense was his "first." He was not a roguish repeat offender. Smith also tailored his words to fit the narrative of familial sacrifice that Lacoste had used. "Compunction," Smith wrote, "added to my insupportable misery, & the distressing & forlorn state to which my unlucky conduct has reduced my young, innocent & helpless wife, induces me to make you a full & free acknowledgment of my crime; a statement of the causes which led to commit it; the names of my owners, humbly hoping & praying that my long & protracted sufferings & punishment may, at length, find their termination through your clemency."[98]

Smith shifted some of the blame from himself to the financiers of the slave trade—the "artful men"—whom he accused of luring desperate mariners like himself into the illegal business.[99] He asked the president for a pardon and promised to "substantiate the facts of [his] statement" against Sheppard and Stark. To Monroe, Smith's confession and contrition were secondary to whether Smith, as the captain, had an ownership stake in the slave voyage. From prison, Smith scrambled to gather witnesses attesting to his poverty. For instance, he reached out to William G. D. Worthington, a fellow Marylander and former federal official, who happened to be a passenger on his voyage to Buenos Aires in 1817. Worthington complied with Smith's request for help. "I will offer my humble recommendation of [Smith]," he wrote to the Monroe administration, adding that "[Smith] neither owned [an interest] in the vessel, nor is worth ten dollars in the world."[100] Eventually, Monroe was convinced that Smith did not have any ownership in the *Plattsburgh*. Consequently, he rewarded him for providing the federal authorities with the names of the slave ship's owners. On August 30, 1822, Smith was released from jail. He returned to Baltimore, completing his thirty-three-month Atlantic odyssey.

Lacoste and Smith exited the public spotlight as quickly as they entered it. Although little is known about the remainder of their lives, the legacies of the two captains is now clear: the American public's eagerness to punish slave traffickers began to dissipate when pitiful sailors trying to support impoverished families—as men of character were supposed to do—were among those first convicted for slave trading.[101] Some voiced concern that the pardons would set a bad precedent for the suppression of the slave trade. "It will be recollected," the *Arkansas Gazette* predicted, "that the first person found guilty under the act for preventing the slave trade, was pardoned." "How then," the newspaper wondered, "can others be executed with justice?"[102] Others wished to focus on punishing the financiers of the slave trade, rather than the traffickers. The *National Intelligencer*, for instance, argued in June 1820 that the United States "will have achieved little by shedding the blood of a few men who are merely the desperate instruments of more guilty but more cunning and imposing contrivers and instigators of the crime."[103]

The federal government did pursue—to some degree of success—its cases against the owners of the *Science* and the *Plattsburgh*. The authorities auctioned the two ships for the benefit of the captors and the federal government. In 1821, a grand jury in New York indicted Malibran on charges relating to the slave trade, but he somehow skirted punishment until 1828, when he was retried, convicted, and fined $2,000.[104] Meanwhile, the *Plattsburgh*'s "pretended" Spanish owner, Juan Marino, appealed the forfeiture of the vessel to the U.S. Supreme Court (no doubt on behalf of the vessel's real owner, Thomas Sheppard). He claimed that the voyage had originated in Cuba, rather than in the United States, making it beyond the purview of federal laws against the slave trade. Marino also argued that the *Plattsburgh* had not been outfitted for the slave trade when it departed from Baltimore because the incriminating cargo was shipped on the *Eros*. He received no sympathy from Justice Story, who was already familiar with the case from Smith's trial. Story upheld the forfeiture in 1825.[105]

In general, though, the authorities were rarely able to bring such perpetrators to justice. As the various sources stemming from the cases of the *Science* and the *Plattsburgh* reveal, the "contrivers and instigators" of the illegal slave trade knew how to disguise their voyages and then cover their tracks. And on the rare occasions when they did confront law enforcement officials, they, too, skillfully manipulated cultural narratives about character, the household, and the market to justify their illegal activities. For instance, after a merchant in Baltimore named John Gooding was caught financing a slave voyage in 1822, several "very respectable citizens" personally implored John Quincy Adams to make the prosecution enter a *nolle prosequi* in the case. Gooding, they pleaded, "had once been in flourishing circumstances . . . but was now ruined, and had a wife and eleven children dependent upon him for bread."[106] The financiers of the illegal transatlantic slave trade were also able to make complicit in their illegal ventures a large number of people, making it all the more difficult for the authorities to assign clear blame to any one person or group. It is therefore impossible to determine with any certainty how many Americans participated in the illegal slave trade, but the lure of bonanza profits coupled with dire economic circumstances motivated many individuals to assume and then explain away—as Smith phrased it in his confession—this "heinous guilt" against their "God & country."

CHAPTER 8

"Some Rascally Business"

Thieving Slaves, Unscrupulous Whites, and Charleston's Illicit Waterfront Trade

MICHAEL D. THOMPSON

On August 21, 1835, a master cooper in Charleston, South Carolina, named Jacob Schirmer recorded in his diary that "Lynch Law was exhibited this morning on the person of a Mr. Carroll, who has been carrying on the business of a Barber, but who has attended more to the purchase of Stolen cotton."[1] The *Charleston Courier* explained that R. W. Carroll—actually an alias employed by Richard Wood—had used his shop at 4 Queen Street near East Bay Street and the Cooper River wharves to receive "stolen goods, from negroes" and to export "about 60 bales of cotton annually."[2] Wood had been prosecuted many times for carrying out this illicit trade, but had been "shielded . . . from *legal* punishment" as a result of unspecified technicalities of the law. The "Lynch Club"—turning a blind eye to those in the port's mercantile community who bought the bundles and profited from their reintroduction in the cotton market—had advised Wood to leave the city by August 20, but he greeted such warnings with "contempt and defiance" and persisted in "his dishonest traffic." Taking matters into their own hands, a number of citizens assembled on August 21 and removed the culprit from his shop. According to the *Courier*, Wood "was immediately marched down to Price's wharf, tied to a post, and there received about twenty lashes on his bare back; a tub of tar was then emptied upon his head, in such a manner as to cause it to extend over his whole body; and the *gentleman* was properly decorated with a covering of loose cotton, the principal material in which he had carried on his illicit traffic, with much advantage to his purse." After being "tarred and Stuck with Cotton," Richard Wood was escorted up East Bay Street and marched through the market and other public thoroughfares "in order that others guilty of the like practices should take warning by his fate." Afterward, Wood was lodged in the city jail for his own protection before being "put on board of a vessel & sent to New York."[3]

The theft and pilferage of cotton, rice, and other valuable commercial goods from Charleston's waterfront was rife during the antebellum period. Though blacks and whites alike were the perpetrators of these crimes, white masters and employers concluded that blacks were inherent thieves and defined the "thieving" bondsman as "one who stole much more than the average."[4] As state jurist John Belton O'Neall put it in 1839, "Occasional thefts among the tolerably good slaves may be expected."[5] But white Charlestonians, unwilling to acknowledge that slave theft contradicted proslavery claims that the South's bondsmen were contented, docile, and mastered, rationalized that thieving slaves simply did not know any better. Despite punishing guilty slaves—whether by sending them to the work house, relocating them from the city to a more isolated and constricted rural plantation, or selling them—slaveholders believed black offenders were manipulated, passive victims of "unscrupulous" whites. Shopkeepers like Richard Wood, they felt, depraved the city's slaves and enabled their theft and pilferage by providing a market for their purloined goods. "It is sincerely to be hoped that this exhibition of the popular feeling," declared the *Courier* in the wake of Wood's lynching, "will operate as an effectual warning to all engaged in the nefarious practice of corrupting our colored population, by purchasing stolen property from them, to desist from their illegal and dishonest course," adding that it was "the fixed determination of the inhabitants of Charleston no longer to submit quietly to such a system of spoliation and robbery." Frustrated by the law's failure to rein in a particularly egregious offender who had identified and exploited the system's loopholes and acted "in perfect defiance of the community," one group of Charlestonians turned to extralegal and summary justice.[6]

In an antebellum southern economy built upon the ownership and employment of valuable slave labor, the specter of debased and thieving bondsmen acting in concert with whites provoked much apprehension. "How long are we to submit to these worse than abolitionist enemies?" asked Charleston's grand jurors in May 1851, warning state legislators of the "disastrous effects" local white abettors were having upon slaves, slave owners, and the entire institution of slavery.[7] Despite reports that Richard Wood had arrived in Charleston from Alexandria, Virginia, where his wife and children still resided, the Lynch Club shipped its victim to New York City in an effort to rid the entire region of a man who destabilized slavery.[8] Not coincidentally, anxious white Charlestonians recently had seized and publicly burned thousands of abolitionist pamphlets mailed to Charleston from New York by members of the American Anti-Slavery Society.[9] Concerned about white men who resorted to the "disreputable mode of gaining a livelihood" by trafficking liquor to bondsmen, the 1851 grand jury complained that such degraded men "induce the slave to drink drugged beverages, which speedily destroy his health and encourage him to pilfer as a means to pay for the poison."[10] Similarly decrying those "unprincipled white men" who seduced slaves "into crimes and practices, calculated to destroy them, and despoil their owners," yet another grand jury insisted that if laws prohibiting the receipt of stolen goods were not enforced, "we shall soon be overrun by a lazy, drunken, and pilfering set of slaves."[11]

Illicit trading with slaves was not a new problem. The 1740 Negro Act passed in response to the Stono Rebellion was the first to prohibit slaves in Charleston from buying, selling, or trading any goods on their own accounts, or on behalf of their masters without first obtaining a ticket granting permission to do so. But only offending slaves and not the white shopkeepers who traded with them were punished under this colonial law. Therefore, a 1796 state act sought "more effectually to prevent slaves without tickets from dealing with shop-keepers, traders and others," and another in 1817 "increase[d] the penalties which are now by law inflicted on persons who deal or trade with negro slaves, without a license or ticket from their master or owner." An 1806 city ordinance, meanwhile, declared, "No negro or other slave . . . shall on his or her own account, buy, sell, barter, trade, traffic or deal in any goods, wares, provisions, grains, or commodities, of any kind whatsoever, upon pain of forfeiting the same." Similarly, slaves "with or without a written license or ticket" who sold or offered for sale many enumerated commodities had to surrender such articles "to any person or persons seizing the same."[12] A typical notice appearing in the *Charleston Mercury* in 1839 accordingly read, "Brought to the Guard House by a person unconnected with the Guard, a quantity of CORN, said to be offered for sale by Negroes on Mays [Mey's] wharf. Any person claiming said Corn will call, and verify the same on or before Thursday next, otherwise it will be disposed of according to Law."[13]

Such a system invited whites to contest slaves' commercial activities and coerce from them trade goods that were honestly and painstakingly produced or obtained, but to which bondsmen held no official right of possession or protection under the law. But if the confiscated merchandise indeed proved to be stolen, the mere return of the property to its rightful owner was not an effective deterrent to enslaved thieves. Throughout much of the antebellum period, slave pilferers took advantage of such vague and weakly enforced laws to steal and sell massive quantities of cotton and other commercial goods from the wharves.

Scholars have vigorously debated the extent to which slavery was an economically rational and profitable institution and whether slave owners were capitalists.[14] They also have carefully examined the international and domestic slave trades, as well as the mutually beneficial economic relations between southern planters and northern and foreign industrialists.[15] Likewise, historians have illuminated the extent to which the impoverished, the enslaved, the marginalized, and the dispossessed also regularly engaged in the economy, in sometimes sophisticated (though not always open or lawful) ways.[16] Seeking to define and then police the terms of such commercial exchange, contemporary authorities made clear distinctions between those who were white and black, free and enslaved, propertied and dispossessed, virtuous and corrupt, honorable and dishonorable, scrupulous and unscrupulous, legitimate and illegitimate, lawful and unlawful. Maintaining and enforcing such an ideologically contrived framework was nearly impossible, however, given the public's awareness that free white men also crossed the threshold into unsupervised and disorderly local economies. With the boundaries of commercial conduct and propriety so contestable and the "rules of the game" so pliable, merchants and miscreants, lawmakers and lawbreakers, masters and malefactors jostled continuously for control over community property and mores.

Slaves, of course, exercised far more autonomy and agency than the white master class was willing to acknowledge. Fully conscious of their actions—and of the widely held perception that they were simply passive figures whose actions were influenced by whites—bondsmen willfully engaged in the illicit traffic of waterfront commodities not only as a means of subsistence and survival but also as a form of protest, resisting their enslavement and taking their share as partial redress for expropriated freedom, wages, and other grievances.[17] Situated on the western rim of the Atlantic world—in what might be characterized as an amphibious or littoral borderland—slaves laboring on the wharves of Charleston and other southern waterfronts were afforded ample occasion not only to steal or pilfer valuable commercial goods but also to interact with northern and foreign mariners, stow away in dockside vessels, and abscond to northern ports.[18] These labor and life experiences were in many ways unique. Because of the nature of their indispensable labor, enslaved dock workers in coastal ports like Charleston were daily subject to outside influences and presented with remarkable opportunities and enticements not available to most plantation slaves, or even to other urban bondsmen not employed along the water's edge. State and municipal authorities—who usually were also local slave owners and employers—responded by regularly passing laws and implementing policies designed to control the entrepôt's most vital laborers and curb their most subversive actions. Aimed primarily at blacks, such efforts ranged from requiring slave badges and hiring stands to fixing wages, censuring work songs, regulating free black sailors, and enacting ship inspection laws. Authorities further tried to combat waterfront theft and pilferage with street lamps and surveillance, padlocks and policemen. Yet these restrictions often were unsuccessful. Striving to preserve their long-held customary rights as urban wage earners, enslaved dock hands resisted these controls with daily and sometimes clever and intrepid circumvention.

Part and parcel of this struggle for dignity and dominion on antebellum southern docks was a contest over the limits and meanings of slaves' market activities within the nation's dynamic nineteenth-century economy. Enslaved pilferers, their white abettors, and those who tried to police their activities all shaped both the urban market in staple goods and slaves' ideas about and opportunities for establishing limited autonomy within urban slavery. Though their agency paled in comparison to that of white commercial proprietors, the slaves who took cotton and the "unprincipled" white men who laundered it back into circulation helped to determine what the contours of the cotton market were, handful by handful, bag by bag.[19] Though city slaves rarely were able to cultivate plantation-style garden plots, those who toiled along the seaboard often treated the wharves and warehouses as urban "provision grounds" from which to harvest marketable merchandise.[20] By covertly stealing, concealing, transporting, and trafficking commercial goods, bondsmen exhibited not only a remarkable capacity for survival but also a penchant for opportunistic risk taking, resourcefulness, and avarice. Slaves, in other words, were just as enterprising, ambitious, and acquisitive as the white shopkeepers who peddled their stolen goods and the white merchants whose warehouses they raided. All played essential roles in establishing the connections by which staple commodities flowed through the broader commercial economy.

Throughout the eighteenth and nineteenth centuries, large quantities of commercial goods were stored uncovered and unprotected on Charleston's open wharves. Not just subject to the elements of nature, merchandise piled on the waterfront also was accessible to thieves, a fact—and an opportunity—that was widely known. As early as 1740, merchant Robert Pringle advised John Erving of Boston that bricks were "the worst Commodity a Ship Can bring here" since "There is always a very great Breakage on them & as they Lye expos'd on our Common Wharfs after Landing are Lyable to be Stolen and Embezell'd by all Comers." Planter and wharf owner William Smith, Jr., testified on December 1, 1808, that "two barrells of tar of the value of seven dollars, were on this morning feloniously stolen, taken and carried away from his wharf," by a white man named Joseph Daniel who, though a perennial rabble-rouser, ultimately was acquitted. In June 1823, fifteen barrels of flour, valued at $108.75 and belonging to bakers James and William Maynard, were stolen from the wharves. Unsure of whom to blame for the theft, chamber of commerce arbitrators concluded "that it must have been carried off by some person or persons, who had no right to the said flour."[21] Aside from the difficulty of policing an expansive public space, authorities' prosecutorial efforts often were met with much uncertainty and frustration.

While goods lay on wharves, ripe for the picking, thieves also targeted waterfront stores and warehouses. Entering at night either through a window or the roof, an unknown culprit plundered five hundred pounds of bacon from Samuel Davenport's store on Elliott Street in July 1822. Ensnared within a racialized conception of illicit market deportment, local jurists conjectured that the purloined article "might have been stolen & sold by a negro" to a dubious white shopkeeper named Francis Deignan. Unable to identify the thief or prove the guilt of the accused beyond a reasonable doubt, however, the court acquitted Deignan. The *Charleston Courier* reported in May 1830 that someone burgled two bags of coffee from a store on Depau's Range near Chisolm's Wharf. On the evening of August 22, 1833, a thief broke into the store of J. C. and C. Burckmyer and Company at 140 East Bay Street, stealing two barrels of flour. The barrels soon were recovered from a boat at Magwood's Wharf, and two of the vessel's crewmen were found guilty of the crime and sentenced to twenty-five lashes in the city market. According to the cooper Jacob Schirmer, these men purchased the flour from a slave owned by David B. Lafar, another cooper on Magwood's Wharf.[22]

In one major case of waterfront storehouse pilferage, wharf owner and merchant Otis Mills was informed on November 3, 1857, that commission merchants Cay, Montaner and Company intended to hold him responsible for the disappearance of sugar "occasioned since [its] deposit in your warehouses" on Atlantic Wharves. Hauled before chamber of commerce arbitrators, Mills acknowledged that his company owned the warehouse that was storing 148 hogsheads of sugar belonging to Cay, Montaner and Company. Neither admitting nor denying "that several of [the] said hogsheads have been robbed of their contents while in [the] said store, as alleged," Mills rejected the charge that he was liable for any missing sugar. Cay, Montaner and Company, on the other hand, contended that between September 11, 1857, when the sugar was deposited in Otis Mills and Company's warehouse, and December 18, "divers quantities were at divers times abstracted from the warehouse, (by what means it is not for us to enquire)." But Cay and Montaner averred that "due diligence was not used" by Mills and Company, since "the locks to the doors of the warehouse were not secure, and the windows not properly fastened." After the discovery of the pilferage, "the insecure condition of the warehouse was brought to the attention of [the] respondents by Mr. Gordon, a Custom House inspector, and soon after the locks were changed for others, and further measures of precaution taken by [the] Respondents." But despite such preventative measures, Cay, Montaner and Company claimed that the equivalent of five hogsheads worth of sugar valued at five hundred dollars was missing. Otis Mills and Company owned and employed numerous slaves on Atlantic Wharves, most or all of whom had access to the company's warehouses where this sugar was stored and ample occasions to embezzle it.[23]

The relative seclusion of ships' holds likewise afforded slave laborers abundant opportunities and temptations—not only to stow away, engage with northern and foreign seamen, procure abolitionist literature, and even plot insurrection but also to pilfer cargo. In February 1857, John Fraser and Company paid East Bay Street grocer James Bancroft, Jr., $11.38 to cover the cost of a cask containing seven dozen pints of porter "Short delivered" or missing from the vessel *Gondar*. Two and a half years later, the agents of the *Ann and Susan* paid Bancroft 84 cents "for 6 Bottles Ale taken out of one of the casks," which was a portion of the 114 bottles purchased by the storekeeper.[24] All manner of merchandise and cargo remaining at the bottom of the hold or dropped on the wharf also routinely made its way into the pockets of stevedores, dock hands, draymen, and other people who gleaned the waterfront to make ends meet.[25]

Laborers employed many other tactics to capitalize on dockside bounties. Whether black or white, enslaved or free, workers sometimes intentionally damaged goods and broke open barrels to gain access and enable pilferage. The logbook of the fittingly named ship *Robin Hood* recorded that on February 9, 1833, the vessel's crew and four local hired slaves were discharging ballast and loading 1,790 bushels of rough rice. Tasked with stowing the rice in the ship's hold, the enslaved wharf hands "broached 1 barrel of pork."[26] In 1853 Charleston grocer John H. Graver sued the agents of the steamer *Palmetto* because only four of the five barrels of bacon shipped from Baltimore and consigned to Graver were delivered. The *Palmetto*'s agents averred that when the barrel at issue was unloaded it "was found to be so badly broken, as not to be able to hold the Bacon." The defendants went on to explain that all of the bacon was taken out of the broken barrel, packed into a new cask, and delivered to the consignee Mr. Graver. But upon receiving this fifth barrel, Graver protested that the bacon lacked the proper marks and was "ranced and bad, inferior in quality, and of a smaller sized flitch than that in the other four casks." Though possible that the barrel of bacon was damaged in transit, it is equally feasible that stevedores and dock hands engaged in discharging this tasty commodity from the hold broke open the cask and pilfered a portion of the meat. Graver pointed out, after all, that some of the bacon seemed to be missing from the barrel in question.[27]

Draymen and carters too broke into cargo and pilfered waterfront articles. "The slave Gadsden," for instance, "was hired as a drayman by . . . the agent of a line of vessels between New York and Charleston, to transport goods and merchandise from the vessels to the Rail Road depot." Unmoored from a fixed hiring stand and entrusted with the conveyance of valuable articles through the city's streets and alleys, Gadsden seized on this opportunity to supplement his income. According to court records, "He broke open two boxes of hats and carried part of the contents" to a white grocer named Tiedeman. One of the "unscrupulous" corruptors of ostensibly faithful slaves, Tiedeman was found guilty in January 1850 of receiving the stolen goods.[28] Largely unsupervised, draymen and carters also joined their fellow waterfront laborers in helping themselves to fistfuls of readily concealable commodities. Coal, for instance, was an easy target for pilfering workers seeking fuel for cooking or to warm an ill-constructed dwelling on a cold night.

Afforded such prodigious opportunities and enticements for unlawful behavior, bondsmen like David Lafar's dock hand, Otis Mills's warehousemen, and the drayman Gadsden played important roles in the illicit commerce of the waterfront and often worked in collusion with whites to steal merchandise from the wharves. On October 2, 1823, for instance, Charleston merchant Michael Lazarus claimed that someone stole ten barrels of his rice branded with the marking "RV" from Prioleau's Wharf. Between 8 and 9 o'clock that morning, a white man named Charles Smally had arrived with a dray at the corner of Meeting Street and South Bay Street and pointed out the targeted rice barrels to an enslaved drayman. Because few whites labored on the city's waterfront in the early decades of the nineteenth century, Smally reasoned that a black conveyor would garner neither attention nor suspicion. Having noticed that he was being watched by a group of white men, however, Smally began to walk away from the scene. But "believing that [Smally] was concerned in Stealing the Rice," several of these men followed him and seized him for questioning. Asked if he had come to the waterfront for the rice, Smally "answered no, that he came to Take a Load from on board the Steam Boat." After a Mr. Murden interjected "that there was no Load on board the Steam boat," Smally changed his story, explaining that he had come to get a berth on board the vessel. But when "he was then ask'd what he wanted with a dray with him, [Smally] made no answer."[29] Despite hedging his bets against detection by engaging with a black thief, Charles Smally and his white co-conspirators acted too conspicuously and carelessly to escape the notice of fellow white Charlestonians.

That same morning a grocer named Thomas Ryan who was on South Bay at the end of Meeting Street "saw a niger fellow Take Two Barrells of Rice marked RV." Ryan followed this black drayman and his load to the residence of James Davis at 3 Swintons Lane, where the rice was emptied onto a carpet and the barrel heads with the markings were thrown into a fire. Ryan also observed "Two other Barrells with the Same Marks" delivered to Davis's house. Maria Davis (presumably the wife of James Davis) claimed that "a man named Jack came to her house No. 3 in Swintons Lane with a dray with Two Barrells of Rice and ordered them to be Roled in," and that afterward Charles Smally hastily arrived with two additional barrels. Mrs. Davis also confirmed that "Two of the Barrells were Emptied on a carpet in the yard," and that she saw the barrel headings in the fire. After a state constable found four of Lazarus's stolen barrels of rice—worth fifty dollars—at Davis's house, Charles Smally was charged with grand larceny and James Davis with receiving stolen goods. On October 15, 1823, both were found guilty and sentenced to be branded on the left hand with the letter T (for Thief) and imprisoned for one month.[30]

It is unclear whether the black draymen in this case knowingly abetted the theft of Michael Lazarus's rice from Prioleau's Wharf. But enslaved workers implicated in such crimes did not necessarily get off scot-free, even if they were considered unknowing participants. In February 1826 a parcel of three hundred new bricks belonging to builders Henry and John Horlbeck went missing from Mey's Wharf. The Horlbecks "had frequently lost Bricks at divers times which they were unable to find out," so upon learning that some of their stolen materials were in the yard of Patrick O'Connor's store at the corner of Hard Alley and East Bay Street, the brothers at once went to confront O'Connor. Henry Horlbeck testified that upon entering the door of the shop, O'Connor immediately approached him and pointed out the bricks, stating that "they were [brought] here by your Carter a Black man." The bricks, which the Horlbecks examined and confirmed to be their property, "were laying in a heap in the yard as if just dropped from a Cart," and "the Gate into the yard was large enough for a Cart to drive in." A young woman named Judy Cumming who frequented O'Connor's store swore that she "never knew [him] to buy Bricks from any person whatever." But she recalled being alone at O'Connor's one day in February when "two Black men came to the Shop Door—and soon after heard the Noise of some Bricks falling out of a Cart in the yard." Cross-examined by O'Connor's attorney, Horlbeck identified the "Negro Carter" who took the bricks from Mey's Wharf that day as "Abraham," and attested that "he was punished on the Tread Mill [at the work house] for a month, or Six Weeks, till he got Sick when he was taken out of Confinement." But not letting O'Connor off the hook, the Horlbecks also obtained a warrant and had him "taken up for the offence of receiving their stolen property." Despite O'Connor's claims that he did not know the bricks were stolen and that he did not purchase the bricks, the jury found him guilty of a misdemeanor.[31] Enslaved thieves and the "manipulative" white shopkeepers who received their stolen goods all stood to benefit from commercial opportunities born of the chaos and uncertainty of the waterfront—when they could get away with it. But when caught, the private punishments meted out to "manipulated" bondsmen often proved far more severe than those publicly dispensed to whites under the protections of citizenship and the law.

Because cotton was the king of Charleston's export economy, it was, not surprisingly, the primary target of waterfront theft and pilferage. The transportation and market revolutions in the first half of the nineteenth century—highlighted in South Carolina first by the opening in 1800 of the Santee Canal connecting the upcountry to the lowcountry, then by the completion of the South Carolina Railroad linking the plantations along the Savannah River to Charleston in 1833—facilitated an upsurge of cotton arriving in the port.[32] In 1825 approximately 159,327 bales of cotton were shipped from Charleston; one decade later 204,119 bales were exported, and in 1840 the number had risen to 307,679.[33] As more and more cotton piled on the docks of the city's waterfront, more and more of it disappeared—stolen and resold.

So sizable and indiscreet were some of the attempted cotton thefts that, like Charles Smally and James Davis's rice-stealing scheme, authorities could not help but notice and act. On the evening of January 10, 1830, Ezekiel Hartley was at the residence of Captain John Todd at 16 Market Street along with Enias Prin and a free black man named Richard Thompson. Between 9 and 10 o'clock "a free mulatto man" named William Simpson came into the house and proposed to Prin and Thompson "to go on some Wharf and roll away a bale of cotton, sell it for Six dollars and share the profits." Hartley claimed that he had "warned Prin not to go, saying it was some rascally business, & he would get himself into trouble." Prin, a white man, nevertheless accompanied Thompson and Simpson across the street to Fitzsimons's Wharf and "in about a half-hour they returned with a bale of cotton"—with city guardsmen in pursuit. But when Prin ran into the house, Hartley claimed to have "collared him & delivered him over to the Guard saying he was the man that stole the cotton." William Patton, the wharfinger (wharf manager) and factor on Fitzsimons's Wharf, testified that the stolen bale of short staple cotton was the property of merchants William Montgomery and George Platt and "was lying on Fitzsimons Wharf last night." Believing that Prin, Thompson, and Simpson had stolen the bale, estimated to be worth thirty dollars, Patton called for them to be "prosecuted according to law." Thompson and Simpson were tried and convicted by a Court of Magistrates and Freeholders, which heard the cases of free blacks and slaves. Despite the damning testimony of Hartley, Patton, and Todd, the Court of General Sessions acquitted Enias Prin on January 20.[34] Though disparaged as "rascally" and as much a threat to community stability and conventions as "nefarious" and "unscrupulous" white buyers like Richard Wood, Prin eluded legal justice while the two free black culprits were held to account.

Stealing entire bales of cotton was exceptional; more common was the embezzlement and sale of smaller amounts because of the comparative ease of concealment, transport, and exchange. Cotton pilferage was ubiquitous among dockworkers. Draymen and carters, warehousemen and pressers, weighers and wharf hands all had ample occasion to swipe loose cotton. Employed to stuff protruding strands back into bales before sewing up the torn bagging, cotton menders found it especially easy to pocket handfuls of the article from each bundle.[35] Much cotton vanished from the waterfront in this manner, prompting merchants to acknowledge that "after the Cotton is weighed and before it is shipped the weights have fallen short . . . repeatedly."[36] Noted in the account book of factors Ker Boyce and Company in January 1837 was a remarkable instance of "125 lbs. cotton Robbed from 1 B[ale] C[otton]."[37] At seventeen cents per pound, this purloined cotton afforded the thieves with as much as $21.25 worth of cash or trade goods. For a hired-out slave collecting ten or twelve dollars a month—most of which had to be turned over to his or her master—this sum often equaled the net earnings of an entire year. But most transactions of illicit cotton were small-scale and far below market price. On May 9, 1835, for example, a slave named Lewis sold an eight-pound bag of cotton to Elizabeth Mills for only eight cents, roughly 6 percent of the commodity's prevailing value on the legal market.[38] For the purchasers of this purloined cotton, such relatively small and less noticeable parcels could add up to a substantial and gainful traffic, even if resold considerably under the going rate. For enslaved suppliers like Lewis, these modest gains, measured by the penny, nevertheless augmented paltry and garnished wages. Those in desperate circumstances—whether black or white, slave or free—developed their own distinct sense of an illicit article's fair value, and negotiated mutually acceptable terms of exchange with one another within this market.

Despite the risks of detection and punishment, such enterprising but needy Charlestonians continued to steal great quantities of cotton. Waterfront plunder became so pervasive, in fact, that during the 1830s over forty wharf owners, wharfingers, and merchants petitioned the South Carolina Senate. "The evil has at length gone so far that Your Memorialists . . . are now induced to come before your Honourable Body for [the] relief and protection . . . of the Cotton and Rice lying upon the Wharves of Charleston," they explained. The petitioners stated, "Cotton especially, from the immense quantities received, and the little injury it sustains from exposure to the weather, is frequently not Stored [in warehouses], and is always in large quantities lying upon the wharves."[39] Thus exposed, the unstored bales were "liable to continual depredations by Slaves and free persons of Colour who frequent" the waterfront, and in this way "Rice, and Cotton especially, to an immense amount, are plundered upon our wharves."[40] Despite the thieving of white men like Joseph Daniel, Charles Smally, and Enias Prin, the assumption remained that blacks alone—often dock workers—stole the valuable commodities from the waterfront.

But holding dishonest white receivers responsible, the wharf owners claimed the "startling" fact that Charleston's storekeepers knowingly purchased the equivalent of at least five hundred bales of cotton each year from opportunistic and thieving blacks.[41] Since state law prohibited slaves—who were themselves chattel—from owning property, the petitioners posited that when bondsmen sold commodities such as cotton and rice "the presumption is in fact, and ought to be in law, that they are Stolen." Aside from the connivance of greedy shopkeepers like Richard Wood or impecunious dealers such as Elizabeth Mills, the wharf owners blamed the extensive plunder on the widespread forging of slaves' trading passes or tickets and ineffective laws proscribing traffic with blacks: "the Laws as they exist against trafficking with Slaves, admit of such easy expedients for evading their applications," the petitioners argued, "that they are equivalent to no laws at all."[42]

Though disregarding the wharf owners' impractical call to prohibit all commercial exchange with slaves and free blacks, the general assembly in 1834 decreed it "sufficient for the conviction" of storekeepers who unlawfully traded with slaves to prove that a bondsman entered a shop with an article and then left without the same item.[43] Reluctant to infringe upon the legal and commercial rights of upstanding whites, legislators still allowed storekeepers to trade with slaves bearing tickets purportedly signed by their masters; but by significantly lowering the burden of proof in illicit trading cases, the new law facilitated legal proceedings against unscrupulous white buyers. On May 5, 1835, E. W. Walker swore "that John R. Daniels and his wife named Mary Daniels . . . did on Friday last, (they being traders residing on State Street in the City of Charleston) then and there purchase from three negro men slaves divers parcels of Cotton contrary to the law of the land." The Danielses accordingly were indicted for purchasing a parcel of cotton worth one dollar from a slave named Trim. Despite the proceedings against them, they were not dissuaded from their illicit dealings in the lucrative staple crop. In an affidavit taken on July 1, 1835, James Hector swore that he lived next door to Mary Daniels and that the night before Mrs. Daniels had "received into her premises eight, ten, or twelve negroes, carrying with them each parcels of cotton, [and] that the said negroes came out without the cotton." Nor was this an isolated incident, since "the same practises are carrying on, and have been so for some months past," and were even repeated that morning. Then, state constable Moses Levy deposed on July 31 "that on yesterday evening between the hours of seven and eight, he saw three negroes carry cotton in parcels of twenty or thirty pounds each into the house or shop of John Daniels in State Street." Like James Hector, Levy swore that the slaves exited the property without the cotton and that "John Daniels is a trader in cotton, and he has no doubt that the said Daniels purchased the said cotton contrary to law."[44]

Utilizing the new provision under the 1834 act, authorities indicted John and Mary Daniels for as many as fifteen counts of purchasing cotton from dozens of slaves between May 1 and August 14, 1835. The individual parcels of stolen cotton were estimated to be worth anywhere from fifty cents to five dollars, and in most cases were purchased from male slaves owned by "a person and name unknown," and "having no written permit of his guardian to sell" the cotton. In one instance, however, "a Slave supposed to be the property of John Fraser"—a wharf owner and factor who employed slaves as dock hands—sold a bag of cotton weighing about twenty pounds and worth four dollars to John Daniels.[45] The Danielses pled guilty in October 1835, served three months in jail, and paid a one-hundred dollar fine.[46] During the same month, the court also found fellow and aforementioned illicit cotton buyer Elizabeth Mills guilty of "Negro Trading"—a pregnant phrase perhaps employed to associate "immoral" Charlestonians such as Mills and the Danielses with the Old South's much-maligned and scapegoated white slave traders.[47]

Despite an increase in the prosecution and conviction of white cotton dealers after the passage of the 1834 act, the legislation did not stop all illegal trading. It was in August 1835, after all, that members of the Lynch Club resorted to extralegal punishment after Richard Wood repeatedly dodged the administration of official justice and spurned community mores. Acknowledging the intractability of the problem, the city's wharf owners and merchants turned again to legislative action. In 1836 approximately forty petitioners asked members of the state senate to pass an act permanently closing Mitchell's Alley in Charleston. Running three hundred feet in length from East Bay Street to Bedon's Alley, Mitchell's Alley was said to be a "receptacle of much filth and trash of every description," and thus was "frequently a nuisance." Only eight feet wide at one end and five feet in width at the other, the "Alley is too narrow to admit the passage of any carriage or cart, and is, in fact, of no advantage to the public, as it is not used by the citizens generally who live in the neighborhood of [the] said alley as a passage way." But most importantly, the memorial declared "That [the] said Alley being little frequented, and, at night, very dark, is the resort of negroes and disorderly white persons, and it has not infrequently facilitated the escape of negroes who have been detected in Stealing from the wharves." Blacks—often dock workers—again were the presumed perpetrators of waterfront theft, with "disorderly" and dishonorable whites serving as corrosive conduits and consumers of the purloined goods. In December 1836 legislators in Columbia authorized the Charleston City Council "to cause Mitchells' alley . . . to be permanently closed up at that end . . . which terminates at Bedon's alley," and in February 1837 the city council formed a committee "to adopt such measures as might be deemed expedient for shutting up Mitchell's Alley." By the end of the year this waterfront escape route was eliminated.[48]

The crackdown on the illicit cotton trade initiated in the mid-1830s curtailed theft of the cash crop from the wharves. But failing complete eradication, Charleston's mercantile community relentlessly endeavored to further master and control waterfront larceny—and the alleged black thieves and their "unscrupulous" white enablers—during the 1840s and 1850s. Some owners of waterfront property sought to slow down plunderers with barriers, whereas others employed night watchmen.[49] But authorities also dispensed public funds to defend private property, encourage commercial prosperity, and maintain community order. Wharf owners and merchants convinced the city council to add more street lamps on the waterfront and "organize an efficient Wharf Watch."[50] In 1845 the city spent $220 for "the temporary increase of the City Guard for special duty on the wharves, during the accumulation and pending the shipment of Cotton."[51] A special committee reported to the city council in February 1847 that the protection of the property piled on the open wharves "required seven men of the guard detailed specially for this duty," costing the city an additional $1,300 annually.[52]

Despite increased security and surveillance, the theft of cotton and other valuable commercial goods from the wharves did not cease entirely. In fact, the stealthy and habitual theft of small quantities of goods by those laboring on the waterfront defiantly persisted as it had for decades. Just as waterfront workers flouted badge laws and fixed wages, sang vociferous and indecent work songs, exchanged seditious communications, and escaped bondage by hiding aboard northern-bound vessels, warehousemen, cotton weighers, and other wharf hands had only to slip a handful of loose cotton into their pockets while merchants, factors, and wharfingers were preoccupied or busy elsewhere. In doing so, these otherwise marginal workers were boldly asserting their roles as consequential urban marketers, shaping the local exchange of cotton and forcing authorities to react.

In yet another effort to eliminate cotton theft, the city council passed an ordinance in 1849 deeming it illegal "to pack, bale up, or otherwise prepare for sale" loose cotton without having received a license, or for anyone (whether licensed or not) to transport loose cotton to any location west of East Bay Street "unless the same be in original packages, or has been packed at a licensed press." Indicative of the severity of the pilferage problem, wrongdoers could be fined $1,000 for each violation. Furthermore, "If any person or persons, within the City, shall steal loose Cotton, or shall buy or receive stolen loose Cotton, knowing the same to be stolen," the offender—if white or a free person of color—was to be fined $250, whereas slaves were to be apprehended and either tried and punished by a Court of Magistrates and Freeholders or turned over to their masters for private correction. Finally, licensed cotton presses were to place a brand and number on every bale of cotton, with a one-hundred dollar fine to be doled out to anyone caught altering, erasing, or obliterating such identifying marks.[53]

Legislation ratified by the city council in September 1855 sought to remedy the routine pilferage of cotton menders. Entitled "An Ordinance to Prevent Depredations upon Cotton," this law explicitly decreed that "it shall not be lawful for any mender or menders of cotton bags or cotton bales, to carry with him, her or them, any basket, bag or other vehicle, for the purpose of taking away . . . any sample or samples of cotton, or any loose cotton, from any bags or bales they may be employed to mend." The measure went on to outlaw menders from taking or pulling out cotton from any bag or bale, unless the cotton was damaged and the owner of the cotton directed the mender to pick it out. Targeting illicit buyers as well, the ordinance declared it illegal for licensed cotton packers to purchase loose or sample cotton from anyone other than a factor, a shipping merchant, or the head clerk or salesmen of such persons.[54]

"For the purpose of detecting and reporting offenders," Charleston's mayor was to assign a police officer "who shall keep watch on and along the wharves of the city, at least three hours each day," from October 1 through June 1. So savvy were menders and other pilfering dock hands that the officer was to "change his hours of watch from time to time, for the more effectual enforcement of his duty." White cotton menders caught violating this ordinance faced a fifty-dollar fine. Free black and slave menders were fined only twenty-five dollars but also received at least twenty-five lashes if they failed to pay. This most recent attempt to control pilferage on the wharves paid dividends. For instance, the *Charleston Mercury* reported in February 1856 that "Jim, a colored boy, the property of Mr. Magrath"—an Irish merchant who in 1850 owned four male slaves in Charleston, some or all of whom likely were employed assisting Magrath on the waterfront—"was arrested by Officer Levy, for stealing two large sample baskets of cotton."[55]

Meanwhile, so much imported coal disappeared during the late antebellum years that the city council passed an ordinance in 1848 to reduce the amount pilfered. After being discharged from ships' holds and placed onto carts, each load of coal was to be weighed and then issued a certificate stating its weight (measured in tons) and specifying either the name of the cart owner or the number of the cart. Anyone suspecting the improper removal of coals could demand the reweighing of a vehicle. If ten or more pounds of coal were found to have been taken from the cart, the driver—if a white man—was to pay ten cents for every missing pound and was to be fined twenty dollars. If the offender was a slave, the owner of the cart was to pay these penalties as recompense for his negligence and possible complicity in his driver's illicit actions. When fifty or more pounds of coal were absent, white carters were to pay fifty dollars, lose their license, and be disqualified from receiving a carter license in the future; if a slave, the cart owner again was to suffer the consequences. Municipal officials, in other words, assumed that if coal was missing, especially in relatively small amounts, the waterfront workers who transported it were either pilfering or making illicit exchanges. The weight of a load also could decrease if wet coal dried or if pieces were jolted out on an unpaved and rutted street. But given carters' access and opportunities, they almost certainly were stealing the fuel with impunity. And since the ordinance turned a blind eye if fewer than ten pounds of coal were unaccounted for, it almost behooved laborers to craftily slip handfuls into pockets and pouches for the survival and comfort of themselves and their families.[56]

But as in the case of Richard Wood's 1835 lynching and expulsion to New York, enslaved workers who became too greedy, brazen, and threatening to the stability of the waterfront economy could be placed on the auction block at a discount and removed from Charleston. As one antebellum South Carolina judge explained, slaves' market values were determined by their habits, character, and behavior, and vice could render even the strongest and most skilled bondsmen worthless and dispensable. Much also depended upon "the opportunities [a slave] has to commit crimes, and the temptation to which he is exposed."[57] As with contact with free black seamen and seditious literature or stowing away to freedom, no occupation surpassed the degree of access, opportunities, and enticements to steal as afforded the city's waterfront laborers. In July 1807 wharf owner Christopher Fitzsimons felt compelled to ship an African-born bondsman named Jim to the New Orleans slave market. "He is a very sensible handy fellow and can turn his hand to any work," Fitzsimons explained, "but is a most notorious thief and as I wanted him on the wharf I found he would not answer to that employ."[58]

While Fitzsimons could dispense easily with his human property by making use of a market that stole slaves away from family, friends, and home, he and other white elites found it difficult to square their racism with the fact that enslaved thieves like Jim and shadowy white allies like Richard Wood were crucial participants in the construction of the waterfront economy. These pilferers displayed impressive foresight, commercial acumen, and agency in the ways they circulated goods through new as well as traditional channels to support their efforts to survive in an economy that frequently did not serve their interests. Their existence and persistence, moreover, created the need for a regulatory regime that tried, and often failed, to stem the tide of stolen goods in antebellum Charleston and beyond. The men and women who surreptitiously picked and carried cotton off urban wharves were as influential in shaping the South's economy as the slaves who picked and hauled cotton on rural plantations.

CHAPTER 9

Selling Sex and Intimacy in the City

The Changing Business of Prostitution in Nineteenth-Century Baltimore

KATIE M. HEMPHILL

In the early nineteenth century, Baltimore's deep-water harbor at Fells Point was a booming site of maritime commerce and the gateway through which many visitors entered the city. When young Pennsylvania native William Darlington visited Baltimore late in the summer of 1803, he rode through the streets surrounding the Point's wharves. "I have always been notorious," Darlington wrote in his travel journal, "for gaping about in towns and acting the *haw-buck*—reading all the signs &c." Darlington noted that Fells Point was "a fine place for trade" as well as an amusing place to meander. Its taverns boasted all manner of entertaining and "curious" inscriptions, from a carving of a dove delivering the olive branch to the ark to a sign that read, "Come in Jack, here's the place to sit at your case, and splice the main brace." But the Point had a reputation for offering entertainment of another sort as well. As Darlington put it, "This is a noted place for those carnal lumps of flesh called en francais *Filles de joie.*" Darlington went on to describe a street colloquially known as Oakum Bay, which was filled with women who accepted "rope yarn and old cables" from sailors as payment for sexual services.[1] Fifteen years later, a Wilmingtonian calling himself "Rustic" confirmed Darlington's observations about the neighborhood. Rustic wrote in his travel journal, "It is the rendezvous for all the heavy shipping. . . . There were several fine ships at anchorage: some just arriv'd and others about to embark. But it has the appearance . . . & I was enform'd [it] was a place of great dissipation, prostitution & wickedness."[2]

Darlington's and Rustic's accounts are interesting for what they suggest about the geography and nature of prostitution in early Baltimore, a subject that has remained largely unstudied despite the city's significance to the historiography on capitalism, gender, and labor in the Early Republic. If nineteenth-century Americans tended to characterize prostitution as an expression of moral and sexual depravity, many also acknowledged it as a form of commerce that was deeply embedded in the broader urban economy. In Baltimore as in cities like New York, prostitution developed in tandem with urban commercial and transportation infrastructures. Initially located around the booming port at Fells Point and the areas lining Jones Falls, houses of ill-fame gradually expanded into the western section of the city with the advent of the railroad and the growth of Baltimore's hotel trade. Bawdy houses clustered around public markets and other spaces of economic activity, adding women's bodies to the vast list of commodities sold in the city. Inasmuch as prostitution was regarded legally and socially as an illegitimate form of commerce, it thrived alongside—often literally—the very forms of legitimate commerce and market exchange that drove Baltimore's monumental growth in the early decades of the nineteenth century. The sex trade, then, was neither spatially nor economically marginal in the city.

Over time, the nature of prostitution shifted in accordance with changes in the urban economy. In the early years of Baltimore's development, prostitution was not a specialized form of labor. Most women who sold sex did so on a temporary basis in youth, or sporadically throughout their lives as a means of augmenting other forms of income. Furthermore, they did not typically operate out of spaces specifically designated for commercial sex transactions but rather out of establishments like taverns and boardinghouses that offered patrons a diverse array of services.[3] By the 1840s, however, new establishments in the section of the city to the west of Jones Falls were operating much differently. As the commercial and service sectors of the economy boomed and new transportation infrastructures developed in the central part of the city, brothels followed the paths of other businesses and, like them, became increasingly specialized. Rather than providing men with a variety of domestic services, brothel keepers began to concentrate on offering sexual services and genteel, well-furnished heterosocial spaces in which male clients could interact in ways that modeled the rituals of middle-class sociability and courtship.[4] Such specialization proved a sound economic strategy for prostitutes and madams. By adopting material signifiers and behaviors associated with middle-class gentility, prostitutes in the new model of brothel were able to attract wealthier clients and thus—as one scholar noted—to "increas[e] the value of the commodity they offered for sale."[5]

Yet, even as madams and prostitutes strived to increase the profitability of sexual labor through specialization, their success depended on their ability to conceal their concern with profit. Part of what made high-end brothels appealing to men and tolerated within in a society in which women who aggressively marketed their sexual labor were subjected to derision and violence was their keepers' willingness to downplay their commercial nature. High-end prostitutes and madams projected a genteel, domestic image for their establishments, and in many cases enjoyed tremendous success as a result. Behind that success, however, was a clear irony: the very material goods and trappings brothels required to preserve their genteel image often served to integrate them even further into broader commercial networks of service and retail-based businesses. Brothels' presence in particular neighborhoods bolstered licit commercial ventures, and many restaurant, tavern, and theater owners catered to prostitutes and their clientele as a means of supplementing their income and drumming up business. Additionally, a significant number of Baltimoreans, ranging from wealthy to middling persons, made money by renting spaces to be used as houses of prostitution or assignation. Thus, in a twist that highlights the complicated and ambivalent relationship between capitalism, intimacy, and gentility in nineteenth-century America, commercial sex became an exceedingly profitable sector of the economy in part through the development of establishments that eschewed commercial trappings.

Understanding how and why commercial sex evolved in Baltimore over the course of the early nineteenth century requires knowledge of the city itself. Baltimore's residents were in the habit of referring to it as the "first city" of the Republic because it was, in many senses, born out of the American Revolution.[6] What had been a sleepy port town with a dozen houses in the 1750s had grown into one of the largest cities in the new nation by the turn of the nineteenth century. The deep water harbor at Fells Point made Baltimore an important center for trade in timber, coffee, tobacco, guano, and provisions, and the construction of turnpikes to the West promoted a booming trade in grain and flour.[7] As the city's prosperity and population grew, so too did the service economy, which expanded to meet the demands of sailors, visiting merchants, and other travelers for lodging and board. The number of taverns, grog shops, and public houses in Baltimore rose sharply in the early decades of the nineteenth century, and inns and boarding establishments sprung up in droves along the waterways.[8] Fells Point in particular became a hub of such establishments, with one historian calculating that in the early years of Baltimore's development, Fells Point's Thames and Bond Streets held over half as many inns as existed in the entire city to the west of Jones Falls. West Baltimore, meanwhile, developed establishments that catered to merchants who arrived by land from Virginia and Ohio. Though the number of inns and hotels in that section of the city was small, the establishments themselves were grand; some, including the Indian Queen at the corner of Baltimore and Hanover Streets, "contained each of them a larger number of rooms and beds than all the taverns on Bond Street put together."[9]

The areas in which the inn and tavern business boomed were also the areas in which prostitution was most prevalent in early Baltimore, in part because prostitutes depended on preexisting commercial spaces to ply their trades. In the first decades of the nineteenth century, the term "brothel" was used to refer to an establishment that allowed prostitution to take place on its premises. The type of businesses that later came to be known as brothels—establishments that housed (for days or months at a time) women whose primary occupation was selling sex—were at the time relatively rare. Commercial sex lacked its own specialized spaces, and many arrangements for prostitution were made informally in the streets, in public spaces, or within the context of the service economy more generally.

Boardinghouses, especially those catering to sailors, were particularly common sites for prostitution and other disreputable activities. Fells Point, the city's primary port for shipping, saw frequent influxes of sailors in need of lodging and board. Because seafaring was a homosocial occupation, sailors who were in port after weeks or months on ships were often eager to purchase sex alongside the other domestic services they required.[10] Baltimore's boardinghouse keepers were conscious of the demand, and many offered sexual services in addition to their more standard domestic offerings like room, board, and laundry. The case of "Big" Ann Wilson, one of the most famous and long-operating bawds in Baltimore, was emblematic. Wilson kept a house on Wilk Street (now Eastern Avenue) just east of the Jones Falls bridge. The area, known colloquially as "the Causeway," was lined with numerous houses that, according to one observer, "surpass[ed] the 'Five Points' in the richness of filth and putrid matter." City records document Wilson's involvement in keeping a house of ill-fame in the area at least as early as 1825, though she was rumored to have been in the trade since the first decade of the nineteenth century.[11] While Wilson's business was a notorious sink of vice even by the standards of the Causeway, it also served a "legitimate" economic function: Wilson's brothel was a boardinghouse for sailors that she regularly listed in city directories and ran with the assistance of her son. Sexual services were the most controversial and likely the most profitable of the services her house provided, but they were hardly the only ones.[12]

Like sailors' boardinghouses, the taverns and (later) lager houses so ubiquitous around the waterfront areas in Fells Point and Old Town also proved popular sites for prostitution. Baltimore's flash press noted that East Baltimore was dotted with what appeared to be "well-kept taverns, while in reality they [we]re vile brothels, frequented by the lowest prostitutes."[13] Another commenter complained that a groggery in Pitt Street (later, Fayette Street) drew a crowd that caused the neighbors to be "disgusted and abused, day and night, with the obscene language and drunken orgies of a horde of wretches."[14] The status of taverns and groggeries as heterosocial spaces in hardscrabble neighborhoods in East Baltimore made them ideal spaces in which women looking to sell sex could connect with men looking to purchase it. One mother, who had emigrated to Baltimore from Germany, advertised that her fourteen-year-old daughter had run away. Aware that the young woman was working as a prostitute, she "sought for her in a stew kept by Mary Pearson." Not finding her there, the mother then checked a local tavern, where she found her daughter seated at the bar, apparently trying to attract the attention of men who might be willing to pay for sex.[15] Had the girl succeeded in picking up a customer, she would have found it easy enough to carry out their transaction in the tavern itself. Many establishments had back rooms that their keepers rented out nightly to prostitutes, a practice that was well known to local residents. Another mother of a young woman in Fells Point complained that her daughter had ventured out on the town when she turned eighteen and resorted to "one of those sinks of Iniquity," where she continued to spend "night[s] in riot and debauchery."[16]

Sources detailing the everyday operation of prostitution in early Baltimore are sparse, but scattered accounts suggest that tavern keepers enjoyed a mutually beneficial relationship with women who sold sex, not acquiescing to but rather actively endorsing the presence of prostitutes in their establishments. The relationship between the sale of sex and the sale of liquor tended to be a close one, and the boost in business that accompanied the patronage of bawds and their clients was almost assuredly sufficient to outweigh the fines levied against disorderly and bawdy houses. Many keepers of "rough" taverns were no strangers to the legal system anyway, as their establishments tended to be loci of a variety of illicit and outright illegal commerce (from the fleecing of drunken patrons to the sale of liquor without a license to the fencing of stolen property). Throughout the antebellum period, prostitution thrived alongside these other forms of commerce. By the 1850s, many of the establishments in Fells Point and Old Town came to resemble what William Sanger deemed third- and fourth-class houses of prostitution.[17] Increasingly, husband-and-wife teams ran establishments that, while not wholly centered on selling sex, nevertheless included sexual commerce as an important aspect of their business.

Just as tavern- and boardinghouse keepers used prostitution as a means of supplementing their legitimate income, women who sold sex in East Baltimore took a similar tack. Prostitution as a category encompassed a wide variety of sex work, including acting as a kept mistress, working and boarding in a brothel, and selling sex sporadically and independent of a particular establishment. The sexual labor of the "prostitutes" in East Baltimore often fell into the latter category. Typically, such women were not professional, long-term prostitutes, but opportunistic sex workers. Some were like the German girl who solicited in the tavern: young women who used prostitution as a means of earning a living independent of the restraints of their familial households.[18] Working-class culture tended to be far more forgiving of such exploits than middle-class culture, and it was possible for women to transition into and out of prostitution without long-term damage to their marriage prospects or their familial relationships. Many appear to have done so: a majority of the women who appeared in court records on charges related to prostitution appeared only once, suggesting that sex work was a temporary pursuit for many of those involved.[19]

For others, prostitution proved a longer-term survival strategy but seldom a primary career. Women who worked as seamstresses in Baltimore's garment industry or sold goods at market often had difficulty earning wages sufficient to support themselves, much less their families. Yet, in a maritime-oriented neighborhood like Fells Point, where men could be at sea for months or even years, many women found themselves heading and supporting households. Sporadic forays into sex work could be an important means of making ends meet for these women, whose economic fortunes often depended on their participation in a diverse array of economic activities and transactions. Notably, prostitutes in East Baltimore were likelier than prostitutes in other areas of the city to be older, married or widowed, and living with children. Such women often used prostitution as a means of supplementing other forms of labor or even—as in the instance of the women who allegedly sold sex in return for oakum they could process into rope—gathering the raw materials for that work.

Black and white women alike used prostitution as a survival strategy, and the character of East Baltimore's bawdy culture was decidedly biracial. In some cases, free black women actually rented and ran bawdy houses. Harriet Carroll, for instance, kept a house in Old Town's Salisbury Alley for at least fourteen years, making her one of the more entrenched madams in the city.[20] Cases like hers were rare in the antebellum period, however. Not only did black women have less access on average to the capital necessary to set up houses of prostitution, but the ease with which black women—slave and free alike—could be sexually exploited might have made it difficult for them to promote their own bodies as commodities.[21] Black women who did work as prostitutes tended to sell sex on the streets or in establishments run by white proprietors. Racial mixing was commonplace in many lower-class neighborhoods during the antebellum period, and Fells Point and Old Town were no exception. An 1837 police raid of James Dempsey's house on Fleet Street resulted in the arrest of an "abandoned set of loafers and prostitutes, black and white," one of whom, Wilkey Owings, was apparently a slave.[22] In another instance, an observer noted, "It is possible to enter some [houses] and view the Circassian and sable race beautifully blended together, and their arms intermingled so as to form a lovely contrast between the alabaster whiteness of the one, and the polished blackness of the other." Yet, many saw the racial mixing that occurred in Wilk Street not as a source of eroticism but as an indication of the neighborhood's bad character and a cause for scorn. Other alleys that ran through Old Town and (to a lesser extent) the southern part of the city—Salisbury, Guilford, Brandy, and Diabolic Alleys—provoked similar reactions with their "dens of iniquity" that catered to "the most debased of our black and white population."[23]

Initially, houses of ill fame in West Baltimore adhered to similar commercial geographies as those in the eastern part of the city. Clustered in Park Street, along Howard, and near the public market spaces, such houses catered to locals as well as (in all likelihood) to the farmers and merchants who entered the city via the western turnpikes. Though they lacked the rough maritime clientele of their eastern counterparts, they too were known for being low, unrefined places, associated with criminality. The same commenter who noted the degraded state of the Causeway wrote that "Park Street . . . was once as notorious for its damnable deeds as ever the 'Five Points' was in its Palmiest days."[24]

In the latter decades of the antebellum period, however, commercial sex establishments west of the Jones Falls divide began to distinguish themselves from their eastern predecessors. The commentator who noted that Park Street had once been a place of vice and filth observed "the street has improved of late years." His assessment was accurate. In the decades before the Civil War, Baltimore—and particularly West Baltimore—underwent a transition similar to that of other cities along the eastern seaboard. New commercial and transportation infrastructures boosted the city's status as a center of trade and generated capital, and the nonmanual labor sector of the economy began to expand. The development of the city's commercial core and the emergence of a nascent urban middle class generated demands for new types of housing, and Park Street (with its proximity to the central financial hub of the city) proved an ideal location for the development of a genteel neighborhood.[25] The street became increasingly affluent, and low-end brothels were pushed out of the area, possibly as a result of property owners' refusals to rent or sell to brothel keepers. By 1852, a city guide was referring to the former slum as "the most fashionable part of the City," encouraging visitors to stroll around and to admire its "elegant dwellings."[26]

Yet West Baltimore's shift from a relatively underdeveloped area to the city's center of finance and genteel living did not herald the end of the sex trade in the area. In 1842, Park Street still boasted one brothel "fit for a person to enter": a newly constructed house owned by Eliza Randolph, a woman whom court records reveal had years of experience running brothels. Randolph's establishment was not a rough drinking house or a boarding place for men, but rather a house that boarded an array of young women working primarily as prostitutes. Men who entered Randolph's house could choose from a selection of "about a dozen girls of all sizes, shapes and ages." Other commercially oriented and affluent houses dotted the streets only a few blocks north.[27] What occurred, then, was not the disappearance of prostitution, but a move toward more refined and often affluent forms of brothel prostitution. The shift would be emblematic of one that took place more generally in the western part of the city during the two decades leading up to the Civil War.[28]

When William Darlington and Rustic noted that Fells Point was Baltimore's center of heavy shipping, their remarks highlighted what had been a long-standing problem for the section of the city to the west of Jones Falls: its port was lacking. Whereas Fells Point was a deepwater harbor, the inner harbor was shallow and prone to backing up with debris. Even with frequent dredging, it was unsuitable for large ships, and commercial development in the areas that bordered it lagged behind for much of the eighteenth and early nineteenth centuries. Beginning in the 1820s, however, the western half of the city gradually transformed into Baltimore's hub of finance, commercial exchange, and government. By the 1830s, the blocks surrounding Baltimore (also known as Market) Street housed numerous banks, as well as the new Exchange and Customs House.[29] Urban boosters hoped that these businesses would put Baltimore in a position to challenge New York, Philadelphia, and other major East Coast ports for commercial supremacy. Even as these businesses contributed to Baltimore's economic growth, they also drew established men and young, middling professionals into the central part of the city, creating demographic conditions that enabled commercial sex to flourish.[30]

At the same time, private entrepreneurs and the municipal government coordinated to undertake major internal improvement projects that not only made the city viable as a commercial center and travel destination but also reshaped many of its service industries, including the trade in sexual services. In 1827, a group of prominent citizens secured a charter for the Baltimore and Ohio Railroad Company, and by 1830, the first rail lines opened and began transporting passengers and cargo to and from the city. In the decades that followed, a number of other rail corporations expanded their lines to Baltimore, connecting the city with its western and northern hinterlands as well as to other urban areas along the Atlantic seaboard. While the railroad was touted for its role in promoting trade, it also made Baltimore readily (and rapidly) accessible to travelers and tourists.[31]

New opportunities for mobility increased demand for local accommodations and services. The small inns and hotels that dotted central Baltimore rapidly became outmoded, replaced by "the finer buildings made necessary by the railroad."[32] The most famous of these buildings was the City Hotel, founded in 1826 by David Barnum and George Brown. Built in the center of the city at the corner of Calvert and Fayette Streets, the hotel was a massive structure by the standards of the time, a six-story building spanning the width of an entire city block. It included 172 apartments, a barber shop, a ballroom, retail stores, a bar, a lunchroom, and a reading room in which guests could sit and consult all the major newspapers.[33] *The Fashionable Tour,* a guidebook for travelers in the mid-Atlantic, called Barnum's "the most splendid edifice of its kind in the union, if not in the world."[34] Such was its charm that many of Baltimore's most prominent visitors lodged quite comfortably there, "induced to stay in the city for days and weeks instead of passing rapidly through it."[35] The hotel was so successful that in the 1840s it had to expand to meet increased demand, and it was quickly joined by a number of other large establishments. Among the more notable were Eutaw House, which opened on the corner of Eutaw and Baltimore Streets in 1835, and Guy's Hotel, a 150-room establishment that opened on Monument Square in 1855. The Exchange Hotel, which had opened in 1820 in a wing of the Exchange Building, continued to thrive throughout the antebellum period, despite the eventual failure of the exchange itself.

The commercial sex trade thrived amid the growing bustle of the city center. Enterprising women established a number of houses of ill fame in the area by the 1840s, many "within walking distance of the principal hotels."[36] Such establishments multiplied between 1850 and 1860, no doubt owing in large part to the opening of the Baltimore and Susquehanna Railroad's Calvert Street Station at the corner of Calvert and Franklin Streets. In the 1850 census, which was taken shortly before the completion of the Calvert Street Depot, neighboring Wards 10 and 11 contained a handful of houses that shared demographic resemblances with brothels, three of which housed multiple women who can be identified as prostitutes from criminal dockets and newspaper records. One housed a total of nineteen single women, one married woman and her husband, and two children. By 1860, the number of "bawdy houses" and "houses of ill fame" in Ward 11 alone had risen to eleven establishments with sixty-two total "inmates"—all single women—residing in them. The enumeration for Ward 10 included an additional dwelling in which fifteen women, one of whom had been charged previously with keeping a bawdy house, resided together (see Figure 9.1).[37]

Many of the new brothels were clustered just southwest of the station, in Calvert, North, and Davis Streets. Not coincidentally, these were the same streets visitors were likely to travel in order to reach their hotels or connect with trains leaving from other depots. Newspaper and court records also show that madams opened additional houses of prostitution in the alleys near the Central District watch-house, the Holliday Street Theater, and the Exchange Building; these houses, located in such colorfully named areas as Tripolett's Alley, Watch-House Alley, and Lovely Lane, were also only a short distance from the commercial and hotel districts.[38]

Figure 9.1. This detail of an 1856 map of Baltimore shows the area between the rail station at the corner of Franklin (the street south of Hamilton and north of Bath) and Calvert Streets and the principal hotels and commercial buildings to the south. The area around the intersection of Bath and Holliday Streets, known in the 1830s as "The Meadow," housed several high-end brothels by the 1850s. Base map from *Woods' Baltimore Directory, for 1856 and 1857, Containing a Business Directory, and Engraved Map of the City* (Baltimore: John Woods, 1856), Sheridan Libraries, Johns Hopkins University, digitized version available from JScholarship. Thanks to Jim Gillespie for his help with this source.

The commercial sex establishments that emerged in and at the borders of the central commercial district differed from those that had long thrived in Fells Point and Old Town. While their forerunners incorporated commercial sex into mixed economic spaces (a model of prostitution that predominated into the twentieth century in Fells Point), the new brothels to the west of Jones Falls tended to be high-end, specialized businesses whose character better matched the surrounding commercial geography. In addition to patrons of local hotels, they drew their clientele from a pool of commercial and financial men who boarded and worked in the vicinity. Because they were situated within a network of commercial establishments that provided a variety of domestic and bodily services to visitors and locals alike, new houses of ill fame no longer needed to (or could afford to be) be one-stop shops. Recognizing the advantage of providing a greater number of more specialized services, the keepers of houses of ill fame in and around the central corridors of commerce adopted new business models. Their houses became places of board not for men, but for young women whose primary modes of earning revolved around sexual labor.[39]

As prostitutes who worked in the new model of upscale brothels specialized in sexual labor to a degree their lower-class counterparts seldom did, they also expanded the realm of sexual labor to include intimacy and romance. Low-end prostitutes who worked the streets or taverns could develop cordial and even long-term relationships with particular clients that blurred the boundaries between economic and personal exchange. Such relationships, however, were by no means typical or encouraged by the nature of the trade. Streetwalkers and prostitutes in low establishments often sold sex to multiple men per day to make ends meet, which left them with few incentives and little time to devote to any particular client. The situation in high-end brothels, however, was quite different. Not only were pseudo-and semiromantic relationships between prostitutes and clients common, they were also a central part of the experience that keepers of genteel establishments aimed to sell to men. As commercial sex became increasingly specialized, women who pioneered and labored in first- and second-class establishments sought to attract a new class of customer by catering not just to men's desire for sex, but their desire for sex that was situated in a context of intimacy, sociability, and refinement.

Madams and prostitutes recognized and met a demand when they used intimacy to package sexual services, but the mingling of commercial sex and romance was also part of a larger project on the part of entrepreneurial women to create establishments that would attract genteel men. What gave high-end brothels their status was their keepers' ability to transcend the shady and furtive overtones of other sex establishments. They drew their appeal—and a "better" class of customers—from their ability to project the image of domestic spaces that were havens from the cash nexus. They were places that men could go not only for sex but also for the experience of domestic comforts and heterosocial interactions that imitated middle-class courtship rituals (even as they violated such rituals' central tenets concerning appropriate sexual behavior).[40]

The type of women allowed to "board" and labor in high-end brothels reflected madams' desire to project an image of middle-class respectability that would appeal to their target clientele of clerks, businessmen, and the well-to-do. East Baltimore prostitutes tended to be diverse in terms of both age and race, but that was not the case for women in "genteel" establishments in center city and West Baltimore. The prostitutes who worked out of such brothels were exclusively white, almost always unmarried, and usually in their late teens or early twenties.[41] While some prostitutes did sewing work to give themselves a veneer of occupational legitimacy, to supplement their incomes, or even to make items of clothing for favored clients, few performed the kind of labor required of prostitutes working in poorer neighborhoods. In high-end establishments as in many middle-class households, the strenuous and highly physical domestic labor fell primarily to servants, many of whom were African American women. The presence of servants in brothels exempted the "ladies" of the house from work unbefitting their refined status and allowed them to present an image of respectability that women in lower-class establishments could not attain.

By hiring young women who had many of the hallmarks of respectability, the new class of brothels raised the value of sexual labor in their establishments not just by offering a "better" class of prostitutes but also by creating circumstances in which men could easily project their fantasies onto the women whose services they chose to purchase. Women who worked in high-end brothels were expected to avoid drinking to excess, behave appropriately in the public areas of the house, and otherwise conduct themselves in ways that would not mar their (or the houses') veneer of decorum.[42] Ideally, these prostitutes were expected to play the role of the receptive ingénue, a young woman whose youthful innocence was complemented by her openness to new experience. A description from a male visitor to Eliza Randolph's brothel suggests the ways in which young women in high-end establishments conducted themselves to create the impression of genteel reserve, as well as the effect their comportment had on male clients: "There is one I particularly noted for her extreme youthful appearance and modest deportment; one profane word uttered by any one, would cause a blush to crimson her spotless cheek for very shame. At first sight of her, I knew the sphere she was then filling was not suited to her nature."[43] The seeming modesty of high-end prostitutes not only exempted them from some of the derision heaped on "whores" and other women who aggressively marketed their own sexuality but also made them desirable to men who wished to indulge in the fantasy of despoiling innocence. The appeal of high-end brothels was in part that they allowed men to shop for women who looked like they might be courted rather than sold.

The layout and décor of brothels similarly reflected their madams' desire to create an environment modeled on middle-class domestic standards that would also sublimate the baseness of other forms of sex work. Detailed descriptions of the interiors of commercial sex establishments are rare, but surviving accounts suggest that both bedrooms and common parlor areas were tastefully decorated to evoke the interior of a genteel household. For instance, Hannah Smithson's assignation house, which contained $500 worth of personal property, featured a carpeted parlor with a mahogany sofa, dresser, and card table; a portrait on the wall and damask curtains; and a tea set and two Britannia spittoons.[44] Other houses were similarly or even more lavishly appointed. The average brothel in Ward 11 contained $536 of personal property, though it was not uncommon for the fanciest establishments—like Maggie Hamilton's house, described as "one of the most magnificently furnished establishments in the Monumental City"—to have $1,000 or more in furnishings and other personal property.[45] Brothels' furnishings and décor were so reminiscent of middle-class domestic spaces that observers sometimes mistook them for respectable houses. Historian Katherine Hijar has noted, for instance, that two brothel scenes painted by Baltimore-based artist Henry Bebie were for many years miscategorized in archives as generic depictions of domestic life.[46]

By imitating genteel settings, brothels became sites that provided male clientele with experiences beyond sexual services. They became homey spaces in which men could "enjoy the comforts of connubial feelings" and be "well entertained," not only by "charming lady boarders" but by their fellow clients.[47] Harry W. Davies and O. K. Hillard's excursions to Annette Travers's house at 70 Davis Street exemplify the ways in which men used brothels as homosocial as well as heterosexual spaces. Hillard "had a girl" named Anna Hughes at Travers's house, and his friend Davies accompanied him on visits to her. Davies noted that the two "seemed very much pleased at meeting, and hugged and kissed each other for about an hour." Davies sat with them and drank wine, and following Hillard's display in the parlor, he and Davies departed. While Hillard returned later to "pass the night" at the house on Hughes's request, his initial departure suggests that purchasing sex was not a requirement for visiting the brothel. In fact, on another trip to Travers's house, Hillard spent most of his visit in the parlor chatting with Hughes, Davies, and a grocer friend of his about politics and Abraham Lincoln's passage through Baltimore.[48] For him and for many other male visitors to brothels, the availability of sexual services was a significant but not exclusive part of their appeal. Brothels were comfortable spaces where men could socialize, forge commercial relationships with one another, and experience some of the positive aspects of courtship—affection and attachment—without the obligations or the imperative for sexual restraint that usually accompanied it.

Theoretically at least, the degree to which brothels adopted the trappings of middle-class parlors had the potential to make them uniquely problematic spaces in the economy and society of the Early Republic. Historians have attributed growing concerns about prostitution in the nineteenth century in part to anxieties about the shifting economic order. Amy Dru Stanley, for instance, linked an increase in antiprostitution reform sentiment following the Civil War to a growing discomfort over what commercial sex suggested about free-market capitalism, namely, that "the triumph of free labor did not safeguard even the most intimate sexual bonds from the marketplace."[49] Baltimore had not yet witnessed the triumph of free labor during the period covered by this essay, but it had experienced the rise of capitalism. By the latter decades of the antebellum period, its residents were already familiar with capitalism's potential to render laborers interchangeable with one another and to value the profitable over the personal.[50] Prostitution in all its forms was disturbing in part because it represented the depersonalizing tendencies of capitalism, for it made sex a commercial transaction rather than an expression of intimacy. With the emergence of the brothel, however, commercial sex went a step further. Rather than removing intimacy from the equation, the denizens and keepers of brothels used its pretenses to sell sex. Not only did they recognize the profitability of intimacy, but they were able to transform this otherwise ineffable emotion into a commodity with concrete exchange value.[51] Furthermore, they did so in establishments that closely resembled the very kind of domestic space—the middle-class home—that antebellum Americans idealized as havens from the harsh realities of self-interested profiteering and market competition. In so doing, they did more than merely offend the morality of nineteenth-century Americans; they called into question the very idea that there were any limits to capitalism's infiltration of urban life and the sacrosanct domestic sphere.

Yet, while businesses based on the sale of intimacies confirmed some of Baltimoreans' worst anxieties about the potential for market incursions into personal relationships, urban dwellers evinced little in the way of sustained concern about the presence of prostitution in their city. In practice, local courts from the 1840s onward treated houses of ill fame as businesses to be regulated rather than nuisances to be suppressed. Provided that they did not severely disrupt the peace of their neighborhoods, keepers of bawdy houses generally found themselves subjected to a progressive system of fines that functioned as de facto licensing fees. Incidents in which houses of ill fame encroached on newly fashionable neighborhoods or violated community standards by, for example, allowing married or particularly young women to frequent them, often resulted in public uproar and in suppressive action by local authorities. Generally speaking, however, popular outcry against houses of ill fame was sporadic, targeted, and not directed specifically at brothels as spaces of sexual commerce. Newspaper, police, and personal commentaries on prostitution usually fixated on it as a moral issue while seldom distinguishing it from other, noncommercial forms of extramarital sexuality. In fact, the economic dimensions of prostitution went virtually unmentioned in popular literature and personal writing, and few people directly criticized the sex trade for introducing market forces where none belonged.

Popular commentators' fixation on the moral rather than economic aspects of prostitution reflected a general concern with illicit sexuality, but it also reflected the savvy of Baltimore's brothel keepers. Many madams and prostitutes attracted clients by promoting the fiction that they and their establishments were not profit driven, intentionally obscuring the aspect of the business that involved trading sex for money. Madams and prostitutes used this strategy to temper criticism from reformers and middle-class male clients that their labor violated the genteel ideal of the separation of domestic and commercial spheres. Establishments that were explicit about their commercial nature were regarded as crass and unfit to serve clients seeking a refined experience. Likewise, prostitutes who made it clear that they were working women who expected payment for their attentions were widely derided as "low." Men could and did commodify women in the course of purchasing their sexual services, but women who were blunt about commodifying their own labor for the sake of economic gain at men's expense drew criticism and sometimes a violent response.[52] When discussing Eliza Randolph's house, for instance, "Free Loveyer's" 1859 brothel guide remarked, "This lady keeps a first class house, but we don't like her arrangements. It's either treat, trade, or travel. Gentlemen are not over fond of such disgusting language, especially from such pretty young ladies." The author concluded the entry with, "Oh, you little fellows,/Don't us whores see fun," suggesting that that Randolph's women took advantage of and condescended to their clients. "Whores" was not generally a term that applied to women who worked in high-end houses of prostitution. Rather, it situated women within the class of prostitutes most subject to violence and intimidation in Baltimore's sexual marketplace.[53]

In contrast, the establishments that garnered the most praise featured "ladies" like Anna Hughes, who did not complain when her paramour, O. K. Hillard, departed without purchasing her services, despite the fact that he had spent an hour kissing and cuddling her. Truly genteel brothels were those whose female residents were welcoming and affectionate toward men but did not make commercial demands on them. Madams and their boarders had to create an environment that could fulfill a complex and often contradictory set of male desires, particularly the desire to be able to "shop" for and purchase immediate access to a wide variety of women while still maintaining the fantasy that the women were genuinely attracted to them. The allure of a high-end prostitute was her ability to maintain the veneer of flirtatious affection while still subtly encouraging her "beau" to spend his money. Thus, madams who sought to make their businesses among the most profitable in the sex trade were in the somewhat unusual position of having their success as business proprietors depend to a great extent on their ability to appear unconcerned at all with monetary matters.

In this regard, the sale of champagne, wine, and other spirits within brothels proved especially strategic, as it allowed "hostesses" to make money, even if "gentlemen callers" wished only to sit in the parlor, flirt with the women of the house, and talk with fellow visitors. The *Directory to the Seraglios* touted several of the houses in Baltimore as fine places in which to drink and socialize. Margaret Hamilton's establishment on Frederick Street, for instance, had "good wines constantly on hand." Maggy King's house in Watch-House Alley (so named because it was home to the Central District Watch-House) featured "Good wines &c. of the very best brands."[54] While the pious among the middle class would hardly regard drinking as a respectable activity, within the world of brothels the type of alcohol offered was a crucial sign of status. The sale of champagne and fine wines marked such establishments as being of the highest class and added to their profits; if the wine's intoxicating effects loosened men's purse strings, so much the better.[55]

High-end brothels' reliance on supplies of good wine and liquor created opportunities for other businesses in the area even as it helped to preserve brothels' aura of noncommercialized respectability. It was not unheard of for brothel keepers to stock and sell their own spirits. In 1830, for instance, Catherine Peduze, who worked as a prostitute and madam for at least twenty-two years during the antebellum period, was charged both with keeping a disorderly house and selling liquor illegally. Peduze was fined twenty-four dollars for the latter offense, a penalty that likely did not cancel out the profits of illegal liquor sales, even though it was steep for the period.[56] Other brothel keepers, perhaps hoping to avoid large fines and the attention of the authorities, refrained from selling liquor directly and instead placed orders with nearby taverns and groggeries. When Ann Power was charged with keeping a house of ill fame in 1840, for instance, one of her clients testified that Power never stocked liquor in her establishment. Rather, she made it clear to her clients that it could be sent for upon request.[57] Thus, though taverns and grog shops in the western part of the city did not themselves serve as sites of prostitution as commonly as their eastern counterparts did, they nevertheless operated symbiotically with local brothels.

Baltimore's theaters also profited from their proximity to the city's houses of ill fame. Both long-standing venues like the Front Street and Holliday Street Theaters and new venues such as the Baltimore Museum and the Roman Amphitheater were popular locations for "fancy" prostitutes and streetwalkers alike to solicit clients, a fact of which theater managers were well aware. Some venues responded with sporadic attempts to discourage the use of their spaces as sites for the negotiation of sexual exchange; the Howard Athenaeum, for instance, noted in its advertisement for the farce *The Queen* that unescorted gentlemen wishing to attend would have to pay a 50 percent markup of the general admission price and that unescorted women would not be admitted at all.[58] But many theater owners in the antebellum period actively encouraged solicitation, offering discounted admissions to working women and setting aside seating or even entire tiers of the theater as meeting places for them and their potential clients.[59] John B. Ray, a private officer at the Holliday Street Theater who later became a watchman, testified that the theater's third tier was reserved for prostitutes and their clients. Ray said he had often observed women of the town gathered there.[60] Especially for women unaffiliated with particular brothels but reluctant to solicit on the streets, access to these third tiers was crucial to drumming up clientele, and some women went to great lengths to gain admittance. When the officers at the Roman Amphitheater denied admission to one particularly well-known prostitute, she used blackface to sneak into the "colored" section of the theater.[61]

Restaurant and tavern keepers likewise made catering to prostitutes and their potential customers a significant part of their business model. For example, Alonso Welch (or Welsh) and his wife, Susan (alias Creamer), were presented to the City Court a handful of times in the early to mid-1850s on charges relating to keeping a house of ill fame and, in Alonso's case, selling liquor without a license. The "house" referred to in the charges was an eating establishment, the Parisian Restaurant, located in the basement of the Commercial Building on the corner of Second and Gay Streets. In 1852, witnesses testified before the Baltimore City Court that the Welches' establishment had the reputation of being a bawdy house. By "bawdy house," however, the witnesses did not mean that the Welches ran a brothel or that they allowed sex on their premises. One witness, a hackman named John Valentine, admitted that he had eaten at the Welches' establishment several times over a period of years and had never seen anything "wrong" occurring there.[62] Rather, the source of the Parisian Restaurant's ill repute stemmed from its status as a favorite hangout for prostitutes. Hack drivers who operated around Barnum's Hotel testified that they had frequently picked up women from known brothels and brought them back and forth to the Welches' eatery, and had taken women from the eatery to the city's theaters. Randall Meacham, who ran a counting room on Gay Street, confirmed that the restaurant was a supper club for prostitutes and fashionable women. Other accounts suggested that it was also a hangout of various "gentlemen" looking to buy sex and of hack drivers hoping for a drink or a potential fare. Thus, while the Welches may not have been explicitly involved in the sale of sex, they—and those who ran similar businesses—profited significantly from catering to prostitutes and their suitors and offering a likely place where they could meet.[63]

Additionally, the presence of brothels in a particular neighborhood could create demands for other, far less glamorous forms of labor within the service economy. In order to maintain the appearance of gentility and cleanliness, brothels required domestic labor such as washing. Prostitutes whose job was to behave like ladies (even when they were themselves from lower-class or middling backgrounds) did not perform these duties, and not every brothel employed live-in domestic servants. It is perhaps no coincidence then that many brothels were located amid clusterings of dwellings that housed women, often African Americans, who gave their occupation as washwomen in census records.[64] Locating their establishments in neighborhoods populated by poorer laborers may have been a means by which madams minimized legal interference, but it also served a practical purpose for prostitutes and laborers.[65] Even as brothels became more refined, they depended on the labor of poor Baltimoreans to maintain their gentility and that of their inhabitants. In all likelihood, the small groups of washwomen and other service workers who resided around brothels made their livings in part by taking laundry from prostitutes and performing other services for commercial-sex establishments.

Perhaps most significantly, the expansion of brothel prostitution provided opportunities for those who owned the properties out of which high-end prostitutes operated. Despite having fairly substantial personal wealth, many—perhaps the majority of—women who kept brothels and assignation houses did not own the buildings in which they and their boarders dwelled. Very few women listed in the census had recorded real property holdings, and court records confirm that there was a small but influential group of persons in the city who made a business of renting their properties for use as bawdy and assignation houses. Beginning in the late 1840s, prosecutions for this offense became relatively commonplace, though it is not entirely clear whether this kind of arrangement became more common as the antebellum period progressed or whether the sudden appearance of "renting" cases was simply the result of the authorities' taking a greater interest in pursuing cases against brothel owners. Quite likely, it was both.[66] As the demand for prostitution and other forms of commercial sex rose with population increase and the commercial development of the city, opportunities arose for men and women alike to purchase dwellings—often inexpensive alley houses—and lease them for bawdy purposes. Their dealings with prostitutes put them at risk of presentment by the grand jury, but they, like so many of their tenants, found that the costs of prosecution seldom erased their profits.

In many cases, the profits from renting out brothels were not extraordinary; the majority of the accused property owners entered the brothel-renting business on a small scale. For instance, Priscilla Howard, who was one of the few African American women to be indicted for the offense of renting a house to be used as a brothel, appeared in court only once. Howard was charged with leasing a dwelling at 153 Caroline Street to Margaret Fay. Similarly, Rosanna Calder, a widowed Irish immigrant living in Fells Point, was indicted in 1855 for renting a bawdy house to an unnamed woman. Calder was a grocer with several children and fairly substantial real and personal property holdings, and she lived almost directly adjacent to a grouping of houses of ill fame. East Baltimore's sexual economy continued to be dominated by taverns, boardinghouses, and lager houses, and the brothels that Howard and Calder rented out could hardly be classed as top-tier establishments.[67] Nevertheless, Howard's and Calder's cases demonstrate both that the trend of specialization in commercial sex had spread eastward in Baltimore by the 1850s and that its financial benefits were not limited to the fanciest class of houses.

Brothels of all types generated income sufficient to make them reliable tenants, and women like Howard and Calder likely saw renting their properties for that purpose as a relatively safe way to generate income from their surplus properties.[68]

In other instances, however, property owners made a sizable business out of renting properties to sex workers. In four sample years of court cases between 1849 and 1859, ten people (two women and eight men) appeared in court multiple times on charges of renting bawdy houses. Though a few of these landlords were likely quite wealthy, most were middling persons for whom renting houses to be used as brothels was a path to upward mobility (provided they could avoid excessive fines for doing so).[69] Andrew Fitzpatrick, a grocer who kept a shop on the corner of Canal and Silver Streets in Old Town, was one of the most prolific offenders and opportunists. In the four sample years, Fitzpatrick faced thirteen counts of renting houses of ill fame to eleven different proprietors, male and female. Lewis Goldsmith, who along with his wife Martha rented out several houses for bawdy purposes, worked at the customs house, and other property owners had occupations that ranged from sailors, hatters, and teachers to dry goods importers and real estate brokers. The rise of brothel prostitution provided diverse groups of Baltimoreans with opportunities for commercial advancement through indirect participation in the commercial sex trade.[70]

The discussion of the wide variety of persons involved—directly or indirectly—in early Baltimore's sex trade highlights a central contention of this essay. Over the course of the Early Republic and antebellum periods, prostitution and the sex trade changed a great deal from the world that William Darlington and "Rustic" observed in the early decades of the century. Commercial sex expanded geographically and became increasingly specialized in terms of the spaces it occupied and the types of labor it required from the women employed in it. One thing remained consistent, however: it was never a marginal form of commerce. The growth of the commercial sex trade was intimately tied to the development of transportation infrastructures and changes in the service economy more broadly, and it in turn shaped the businesses around it and created its own demands for domestic service and labor. In short, prostitution was deeply integrated into the broader economy of urban America.

As this essay suggests, the boom in the sex trade derived at least in part from the advent of brothels that imitated middle-class domestic spaces, a fact that highlights the complicated relationship between early capitalism and the "private" sphere of intimacy. On one hand, capitalism as many nineteenth-century Americans understood it depended on the world of the domestic to soften the harsh realities of competition and safeguard bonds of affection and virtue. On the other hand, capitalism created dislocations—for men and women—that promoted the commodification of sex and certain forms of romantic courtship and intimacy at a level never before witnessed in American life. The juxtaposition of these two realities raises important questions about how Americans navigated the contradictions that resulted from the emergence of the market economy as well as why they grappled with those contradictions at particular moments. What this essay suggests is that women involved in the sex trade played a significant role in minimizing the potential fallout from high-end brothels' co-optation of courtship rituals and gentility by successfully commodifying emotion. At the same time, prostitutes and madams conducted themselves and their establishments in a way that obscured the commercial nature of their work and thus allowed men to "shop" for and project their sexual fantasies onto women while maintaining their fantasies of desirability and gentility. The fiction that brothels were domestic rather than economic spaces—and, remarkably, the means by which prostitutes and madams promoted it—helped to make prostitution an exceedingly profitable business. By examining prostitution as a business, rather than fixating on it as a primarily moral problem, historians can learn much about some of the many ways ordinary women shaped the culture of early capitalism.

CHAPTER 10

Economies of Print in the Nineteenth-Century City

PAUL ERICKSON

A Cincinnati bookseller's scrapbook on the book trade in Ohio raises questions about the historiography of American business. A late nineteenth-century article from a trade magazine evaluating the "leading book dealers in Columbus" pasted into the scrapbook lists ten businesses, four of which were newsstands (three in hotels, one at the train depot). The anonymous evaluator praised various stores for their enterprising spirit or their attractive window displays, and then added, "L. T. Thraw is a one-armed man who keeps a barber shop and attends strictly to business. . . . All the Hotel News-stands pay more attention to cigars than to any other line." The same scrapbook contains several obituaries of J. R. Hawley, the "Nestor" of Cincinnati's book dealers, who died in 1904. The obituaries recount how his bookstore, which opened in 1861, was a frequent stop for U.S. presidents—from Johnson to McKinley—when visiting the Queen City. Yet they also hint at Hawley's other lines of business. One notes that his bookstore was also "for many years the headquarters of the sporting celebrities who came to Cincinnati. Grandpa Hawley was agent for the A.G. Spalding company and supplied the Reds with their uniforms."[1]

Bookstores in nineteenth-century Ohio cities were also barbershops, cigar stores, and outfitters of professional baseball teams. Or was it the other way around? If three of the leading book dealers in Columbus were more concerned with their traffic in cigars than books, would people at the time have thought of them as the city's leading book dealers? To which business was the one-armed L. T. Thraw strictly attending—that of selling books, or cutting hair and shaving beards? Put another way, was one business peripheral to the other, or were they mutually reinforcing?

While many historians have argued that wholesalers and retailers were purveyors of limited kinds of (often related) goods, it is clear that the reality of economic practice in nineteenth-century America was much more varied than we realize. Booksellers were no exception, as they often dealt in a variety of goods in addition to printed matter. Since their first appearance in North American cities and towns, bookstores sold stationery and writing implements alongside books and periodicals. But books have often found themselves jockeying for position on store shelves with other materials not even tenuously related to the practices of reading and writing, ranging from musical instruments to knives and razors.[2] In the antebellum decades, in the heart of the boom in newspaper production and what has been called the "first paperback revolution," readers often purchased inexpensive reading material from newsstands or street vendors that sold a range of other items, participating in a larger economy of print that did not segregate books and newspapers from other types of goods.[3]

Most models of the book trade employed by scholars working in the field of the history of the book draw on Robert Darnton's famous 1982 diagram of what he called the "communications circuit," which links authors to publishers to printers (and their suppliers) to shippers to booksellers to readers (and binders).[4] While there have been revisions to this model since, the general framework has remained influential, particularly given that many book historians are primarily interested in individuals' "literary" roles in this cycle—as authors, publishers, booksellers, and readers. This essay examines the "communications circuit" not as an instance of communication, but rather as an example of the economy of print. As such, it emphasizes individuals' economic roles in the circuit—as producers, manufacturers, retailers, and consumers—rather than the positions they assumed with respect to a particular culturally charged artifact, the book. Scholars who study the print trades, whether as a mode of literary practice or as an area of economic activity, frequently tend to treat the links in this circuit as actors holding self-contained, easily defined roles who abide by agreed-upon, mutually beneficial economic practices, as is common to many scholars of other modes of business practice.

Models based on the "chain" or "circuit" metaphor imply a neatly staged process in which goods pass through a system in orderly fashion. But such models fail to take into account overlaps and tangles in the links in the chain, areas in which different activities in the realm of production, distribution, and retail exchange are performed by the same person. While the literature on the history of the print trades often emphasizes linkages between prominent publishing houses, respectable book stores, and elite readers, this essay examines the economies of print that actually existed on the ground—or, more accurately, on the street—of the nineteenth-century American city. Focusing on the range of economic activities in which bookselling barbers, sidewalk smut-peddlers, and anti-obscenity crusaders engaged, instead of homing in on particular forms of economic activity, helps to clarify the nature of the antebellum print trades. Examining the messy, overlapping realms of business practice among low-level entrepreneurs on the margins of respectability in the print trades shows that many of the other sectors of the economy on which these publishers and booksellers depended (such as transportation, hospitality, and prostitution) were not as separate as they are portrayed by many historians. Looking beyond the success of a particular publishing firm or the edification of a specific group of readers, this essay offers portraits of printers, street vendors, and pornographers who operated in the shadow of the law. Their stories trouble the stable categories of retail trade and individual careers on the margins of nineteenth-century capitalism. Whether the materials they sold were deemed illicit or respectable, these entrepreneurs all in some ways capitalized on economic activity that took place in the messy margins of the communication sector of the economy, blending print and nonprint goods as crucial parts of their businesses. Considered narrowly, this essay suggests new avenues for research that take into account the importance of nonbook materials to "book people" active in the print trades in nineteenth-century America, and urges scholars to include under the umbrella of the business of print individuals who might not be considered "book people" at all, indicating the slipperiness of the boundaries of what we refer to as the "book trade." Yet when considered more broadly, the activities of nineteenth-century entrepreneurs of print also tell us much about how low-level urban retailers in a range of sectors went about trying to earn a living.

The print trades in antebellum American cities were largely, although not entirely, male worlds. While large numbers of young women worked in book binderies and in workshops that colored engravings and lithographs, most people involved in the typesetting, printing, and retail sale of books were men. Yet, particularly in the worlds of job printing and the production of scandalous and obscene materials, there were few stable occupational boundaries. Young men working in the print trades performed a variety of tasks, from printing and assembling packages of books and broadsides to making deliveries and selling books and prints on the street or at newsstands.

In taking on these varied roles, they often straddled the line between legitimate and shadowy business practices. As the first two vignettes offered below illustrate, consumers encountered printed materials in the larger context of other consumer goods, and print vendors worked as independent dealers, acquiring materials from a range of wholesalers, often selling legal and obscene materials at the same time. These young men often conducted their business in plain sight: to the uninitiated, these street-level retail practices would have appeared unremarkable. Because these producers and consumers created modes of retail sale and reading experience that simultaneously seemed like other transactions and often required specific and secret knowledge on the part of consumers, reformers used these transactions to chart the boundaries of morality, legality, and legitimacy.

Brewster Maverick was one of these young men in 1840s New York. A markedly enthusiastic and omnivorous reader, he is also the kind of reader rarely encountered in scholarly studies of reading practices. Yet he was not just a reader—he was a flexible, multitalented worker in antebellum New York's thriving print trades. Without question his reading was informed by the materials he helped produce, but it is just as likely that his unique position in the world of job printing informed what he chose to read and how he read it. Brewster Maverick was born in 1831 in New York City; his father was an engraver and copper-plate printer, and his uncle was a job printer. A small pocket diary that he kept during 1847 outlines how he spent his time: studying law under the tutelage of two Manhattan lawyers; helping out in his uncle's shop; distributing type or delivering broadsides, menus, or other printed items to customers in lower Manhattan; and buying and reading plays. Sixteen-year-old Maverick was something of a theater fanatic. On the very first page of his diary he listed "plays bought at Taylor & Co.," most of them popular offerings on the antebellum New York stage.[5] The entry for June 12, 1847 includes a list labeled "Residence of Comedians," offering the home addresses of most of the major stars of New York's theater (perhaps Maverick would visit to try to get autographs on some of the plays he had purchased). Most historians of reading do not think of play scripts as typical reading material for nineteenth-century readers, especially for teenaged boys. Likewise, most historians of consumer culture do not consider printed plays as commodities that people purchased as part of their theatergoing experience, or that the young Maverick would be a consumer of such things. Yet Maverick's enthusiasm for going to plays and for reading the scripts of the plays he saw points not only to the blurry line between the print trades and the entertainment business in antebellum New York City but also to the need for historians of these worlds to acknowledge the unexpected paths that commerce in the nineteenth-century world of ideas actually took. Plays were publicized in the newspapers and on broadsides; perhaps Maverick's uncle printed some of those posters in his shop. Theatergoers were able to purchase the script of a play they were going to see or had already seen, perhaps with a view to performing the play at home themselves.[6] Thus print created a market for the theater, which in turn opened the market for a specific kind of print. Maverick situated himself at the intersection of the print trades and the larger culture industry in the antebellum city: printing broadsides, attending theaters, and then buying copies of the plays.

Between recipes for lemonade and various chemical parlor tricks, Maverick recounted his visits to the theater in the terse prose of easily distracted adolescent masculinity: May 3, 1847—"Got my hair cut. Had no work. Went to see Forrest. He played *Jack Cade* and *Invisible Prince*." His reading (and theatergoing) was of a decidedly sensational variety. He had a girlfriend named Mary, whom he visited on his own, without adult supervision. He gadded about town with his friends Alex and Dodger, and occasionally wrote in Bowery slang.[7]

Maverick's entries for May 18 and 24, 1847 offer a glimpse of his multiple points of engagement with the popular print culture of antebellum New York. On May 18, he wrote, "Stayed at home all day. Finished Palais Royal. Went to the Winter's. Commenced picture scrap book. Leather cover. Got a Evening Post."[8] His entry for May 24 reads, "Helped uncle distribute type. Sent Deeds to Washington. Seen Booth in Hamlet. Took home Mrs. Beaumont's cards. Seen a Chinaman." So, in the space of a week, he finished a popular historical novel, started a scrap book for printed images, bought a newspaper, distributed type in his uncle's job printing shop, sent printed material from the shop to Washington, saw a popular actor (Edwin Booth) in a play of which Maverick almost certainly owned a copy, and brought home calling cards printed for another customer. And, apparently, saw a Chinese man in the street.

This avid consumption of print came at a price—a price that his work as a producer of print apparently did not fully support. Maverick frequently noted having to ask his uncle for money, only to be rebuffed; these incidents are often followed in the diary by the summation, "Uncle mad." Maverick periodically offers glimpses into his financial situation: on December 2, 1847, he received one dollar from his grandmother, and on January 1, 1848, he had $20.36 on hand (not bad for a seventeen-year-old boy in antebellum New

York). Throughout the summer of 1847, Maverick was constantly borrowing both money and books from family and friends, reflecting his active engagement in the urban economy of reading (June 18: "Read book Dodger lent me. Did not like it."). His reading included some serious works—he borrowed John Marshall's life of George Washington from his law tutor on July 31—but tended toward lighter and occasionally racy fare, including Thomas Haliburton's *Sam Slick*, Samuel Lover's *Handy Andy: A Tale of Irish Life*, *The Adventures of the Chevalier de Faublas: The French Don Juan*, and *The Secret Passion* (most likely Robert F. Williams's novel of that name, which was part of a series of novels featuring William Shakespeare as a character).[9]

Both his consumption of such a wide range of printed materials and his family's professional role in New York's print trades would have made Brewster Maverick acutely aware of the fact that the production and distribution of printed material were economic activities central to the emerging capitalist system in the antebellum city (the printing and book trades were among the largest employers in the economy of 1840s New York).[10] Yet Maverick's personal use of print almost purely for entertainment purposes calls attention to a mode of engaging with print culture that goes beyond the role of "reader." It is worth noting that Maverick spent almost all his time consuming or producing printed material, yet in his diary he never recorded purchasing an actual book—he bought plays and newspapers and scrapbooks, but he borrowed all of the books he noted having read. Maverick clearly thought about print as part of a broader spectrum of leisure and commercial activities, and print for him was situated within a much larger world of commodities.

This participation in the economy of print rendered Maverick simultaneously a consumer and producer of a commodity, rather than just a boy who liked to read. Brewster Maverick did not compile a library of the play scripts and cheap paper-covered novels that he bought, and he did not expand at great length in his diary about his responses to individual texts. He read a few serious books, but the vast majority of adolescent Brewster's reading unsurprisingly skewed toward the light and racy. His multiple modes of engagement with print culture also indicate a flexibility and blurriness of boundaries in the realm of print that people at the time took for granted—cheap paperback series offered everything ranging from sensational true crime novels to Shakespeare and Pope. For Maverick, broadsides and calling cards and newspapers and play scripts and books did not occupy discrete niches of experience, but were rather all combined together in his daily involvement in the world of print capitalism in antebellum New York.

Another male teenager in 1840s New York, Edward Scofield, occupied a distinctly more tenuous role in the economy of print than did Brewster Maverick, and his story offers a different perspective on the street-level retail trade in the antebellum city. He left no surviving diary or any list of books he bought or read. In fact, it is unclear whether he knew how to read at all. Scofield is familiar to us today because in 1842, during the first of what would become a series of municipal crackdowns on the production and sale of obscene books and prints in New York City, he got himself arrested. Scofield, a newsboy who lived on Nineteenth Street, was apprehended by an alderman for selling obscene books and images that he had received from Cornelius Ryan, a book dealer with a stall on Wall Street.[11] Scofield testified that "said books are kept by Ryan in a Tin Box under his stand."[12] Scofield's arrest touched off a tremendous crackdown on New York's pornography dealers by George Matsell, the chief of police.[13] The affidavits in the court records from these prosecutions outline a two-tiered structure in the smut trade: some dealers acted primarily as wholesalers, selling small quantities of books and prints to young boys working as sidewalk venders, who marked up the products to whatever extent they could. Other booksellers conducted a retail trade out of their own bookshops, stalls, or carts. Some dealers—like Cornelius Ryan—probably did both, acting as a supplier to street peddlers while also selling retail from the "tin box" under the counter. It is also important to keep in mind that while some printers and wholesalers may have specialized in sexually explicit material, the retailers—both stall keepers such as Cornelius Ryan and street venders such as Edward Scofield—would have sold both respectable and obscene publications at the same time. Aside from the risk of criminal prosecution that dealing exclusively in sexually explicit material would have posed, street-level retail traders simply would not have had enough business in the smut trade alone. Thus the trade in standard printed material, at least at the retail level, was interwoven with the traffic in obscene materials.

These diversified businessmen—almost entirely concentrated in a small section of lower Manhattan—formed an extensive network of interconnected economic relationships in which people would have dealt with multiple partners. Edward Scofield, for instance, did not purchase his wares only from Cornelius Ryan; he testified that he had bought books (namely, *The Lustful Turk*, *Fanny Hill*, and *The Curtain Drawn Up*, works advertised on the flyer shown in Figure 10.1) from William Bradley, who kept a book stand at the corner of South and William Streets; James Jones at South and Fulton;

Charles Huestis at the corner of Ann and Nassau; Francis Kerrigan at South Street and Burling Slip; and a man named Childs, who had a print shop in Nassau near Fulton.[14] The deposition went on to state, "Deponent further says that said Books are generally sold to boys who again dispose of them to Strangers and others about the Hotels."[15]

In his 1858 *History of Prostitution*, William Sanger offered one of the clearest descriptions we have of how young men sold obscene materials on the streets of New York, a vignette that points to the ubiquity of obscene materials in the public spaces of the antebellum city:

> Boys and young men may be found loitering at all hours round hotels, steam-boat docks, rail-road depots, and other public places, ostensibly selling newspapers or pamphlets, but secretly offering vile, lecherous publications to those who are likely to be customers. . . . The vendors have a trick which they frequently perform. . . . In a small bound volume they insert about half a dozen highly-colored obscene plates, which are cut to fit the size of the printed page. Having fixed upon a victim, they cautiously draw his attention to the pictures by rapidly turning over the leaves, but do not allow him to take the book into his hands, although they give him a good opportunity to note its binding. He never dreams that the plates are loose, and feels sure that in buying the book he buys the pictures also. When the price is agreed upon, the salesman hints that, as he is watched, the customer had better turn his back for a moment while taking the money from his pocket-book, and in this interval he slips the plates from between the leaves and conceals them. The next moment the parties are again face to face, the price is handed over, and the book he had seen before is handed to the purchaser under a renewed caution, and is carefully pocketed.[16]

This mode of street-level retail sale, in which young boys carried respectable books and obscene prints at the same time, indicates the interpenetration of the two spheres of the book trade. Sanger's account also illustrates the porosity of the boundaries between different forms of illicit behavior. The vendor Sanger describes seamlessly slips from the near-commission of one crime—selling obscene prints—to that of fraud (although a form of fraud that the customer would likely be embarrassed to rectify). This scam would have

PRIVATE CIRCULAR, FOR GENTLEMEN ONLY.

GENUINE FANCY BOOKS!

BEAUTIFULLY PRINTED! ELEGANTLY COLORED PLATES! HANDSOMELY BOUND!

Every work named on this Circular is printed from new type, on *fine paper*, handsomely illustrated with BEAUTIFUL COLORED PLATES, and richly bound in cloth. They can be sent either by *Mail or Express*, with perfect safety, and done up in such a manner as to defy detection.

Persons ordering can rest assured that their orders will be promptly and faithfully attended to.

EVERY WORK NAMED IS EXACTLY AS REPRESENTED.

FANNY HILL, Her Life and Amours, 10 colored plates, . . $2 00
ROSE DE AMOUR, The French Courtesan, 10 colored plates, . . 2 00
LUSTFUL TURK, or Love in the Harem, 10 colored plates, . . 2 00
TWO COUSINS, Their Confessions, 10 colored plates, . . 2 00
SILAS SHOVEWELL, His Amours with the Nuns, 10 colored plates, ... 2 00
CURTAIN DRAWN UP, or The Education of Laura, 10 colored plates, ... 2 00

VOLUPTUOUS CONFESSIONS IN BED, 5 colored plates, . . $1 00
MADAME CELESTINE, Her Intrigues, 5 colored plates, . . 1 00
CICILY MARTIN, The Woman of Pleasure, 5 colored plates, . . 1 00
CABINET OF VENUS UNLOCKED, 5 colored plates, . . 1 00
FLASH AND FRISKY SONGSTER, 5 colored plates, . . 1 00

FANNY HILL

LARGEST SIZE, 24 COLORED PLATES—THE LARGEST WORK EVER PRINTED OF THE KIND—IT IS A SPLENDID VOLUME, ... $5 00

FRENCH TRANSPARENT PLAYING CARDS. The finest article in the FANCY STYLE that has ever been produced—they can be played with the same as a common card by persons unacquainted with them—and by holding them to the light you have 52 BEAUTIFULLY COLORED FANCY PICTURES, Price $2 00

FRENCH "SAFES," OR "CONDOMS," *Warranted.*—The *only certain Preventive against Disease or Pregnancy.* Manufactured from fine transparent India Rubber—they cover the *Penis* entire, and increase the pleasures. Price, single, 50 cts., one dozen $3 00

PRINTS OF VARIOUS SIZES, ... From 50 cts. to $2 00 each.

TOBACCO BOXES, Double covers, illustrated, Price $3 00

CIGAR CASES, 10 illustrations, secret drawer, ... 3 00

☞ Recollect, none of the above can be had at our office in New York. All orders must be sent by mail, and they will receive early and prompt attention, and the articles ordered forwarded to their destination, in the most compact, reliable and expeditious manner.

Figure 10.1. This sales circular, most likely from the 1860s, advertises *Fanny Hill*, *The Lustful Turk*, and *The Curtain Drawn Up*, as well as other popular obscene titles not mentioned in Edward Scofield's indictment, as well as condoms, explicit prints, and novelty cigar cases and tobacco boxes that would have had erotic images concealed inside. The emphasis in all cases on the inclusion of colored plates (and the accompanying high prices) shows the sophisticated production methods that were brought to bear on obscene materials. "Private Circular, for Gentlemen Only: No. 2" (New York, 186-); collection of the American Antiquarian Society.

depended on the vendor's judgment of individual sellers: Did they look like they knew what they were doing? Were they big and strong enough to present a threat? Could the boy outrun his mark if he was chased?

Although Sanger here focuses on the use of obscene prints in the book vendor's ruse, such prints were not only used as bait but also were actively sold. A customer who had been tricked in this way once would not fall for the same scam again, and if he was determined to buy explicit images, such an interaction would only give him more knowledge of how to go about purchasing them in the future. As Sanger details elsewhere in his text, the trade in obscene books and prints also indirectly helped fuel another dubious form of capitalist activity: prostitution. Sanger's claim, a common one in the period, was that the easy availability of obscene books and prints led young women into sexual indiscretion, which increased the ranks of prostitutes on the city's streets. "There can be but one opinion as to the share obscene and voluptuous books have in ruining the character of the young, and they may justly be considered as causes, indirect as it may be, of prostitution."[17]

Obscene materials that Scofield and other boys bought from vendors like Cornelius Ryan were exchanged privately, but in public places, a transactional mode that created a world of those "in the know" on both sides of the law. Although some news items of the period complained about dirty pictures being shown to women on the street, for the most part this corner of the print economy in New York was almost entirely male, one in which Scofield (or Maverick) would easily find a place. And antebellum discourses about this economy stress how *open* and inclusive, not how *hidden*, it was. Indeed, immediately after singling out a particular publisher in Nassau Street, the *New York Sporting Whip* noted, "Nearly every stand that lumbers up the sidewalks is plentifully furnished with those things, together with libidinous books with most revolting and disgusting contents."[18] Of course, this availability would wax and wane, depending on the political climate in antebellum New York City and the attendant waves of prosecution of obscenity-related offenses. But this trade was carried on relatively openly, often on public sidewalks: consumers with recherché tastes in printed matter found the goods they were looking for to be readily available, even if most readers would not have sought out such items.

In calling attention to Nassau Street, the *Whip* reinforced a long-standing impression that a very specific area of lower Manhattan—the blocks in the immediate vicinity of Nassau and William Streets where they intersect with Fulton and Ann—was the city's "smut district." Writing of the shops selling old and new books that clustered around the corner of Ann and Nassau Streets, Helen Horowitz notes, "For the most part, these dealers did not make erotica a specialty. But in this world of men struggling to get by, erotic texts and illustrations made their way into their batches of books and prints, and they sold them willingly."[19] This mixture of illicit and respectable items in the stock of dealers in this neighborhood mirrors the way in which this smaller smut district (really only two blocks) was situated within the larger printing district in lower Manhattan, much like the intermixed commercial geographies that supported brothels, mock auction houses, dealers in used clothing, and the like. Only a block away from the city's largest and most prominent newspaper and book printing offices on Park Row, these smaller wholesale and retail vendors that supplied street dealers like Edward Scofield were not distinct from the legitimate sectors of the city's printing industry. Rather, they were tightly woven into the fabric of the trade, as is indicated in the sales circular for Thomas Ormsby in Figure 10.2: Ormsby set up his business on Nassau Street, firmly within Manhattan's cheap publication district, but diversified his offerings to include a range of "articles not connected with the trade."

It was within this world that Edward Scofield made a place for himself as a vendor of obscene texts—and, perhaps more importantly, of nonbook objects like explicit prints. We do not know what he thought of the books and images that he sold. We do know that he found this business, a modest enterprise, sufficiently lucrative to return to it after being arrested once. Scofield escaped punishment in 1842 by providing evidence to the police about his suppliers (although, as Donna Dennis notes, he did spend several months in jail until his mother could gather enough money to post a bond guaranteeing that he would return to give testimony).[20] In 1847, the *National Police Gazette* reported that Edward Scofield had again been arrested, this time for selling erotic books, along with a directory to local brothels, in the lobby of the Astor House hotel on Broadway.[21] According to the indictment, he was offering for sale copies of *Fanny Hill* (one of the books he had been selling in 1842) priced at two dollars, which indicates that it was likely an edition that included obscene illustrations.[22] Scofield had once again obtained his stock from one of the burgeoning group of pornographers in lower Manhattan, and he was once again working as an independent contractor in this highly flexible economic sector. If he tried to avoid punishment by giving up his suppliers, as he did in 1842, it did not work. The teenaged boy was tried, convicted of selling obscene books, and sentenced to six months in jail—a

THOMAS ORMSBY'S

Commission Bureau and

GENERAL PURCHASING AGENCY,

84 Nassau Street, New-York.

Books, Cards, Law Books, Blank Books, Stationery, Envelopes, Playing Cards, Prints, Cheap Publications, Fancy Goods, Gloves, Foils, Guns and Sporting Articles, Letter and Printing Papers, Watches, Jewelry, Silver and Plated Ware, and

MERCHANDISE OF EVERY DESCRIPTION,

Purchased and Forwarded to any part of the United States or Canadas at the Lowest Rates.

CATALOGUES SENT FREE. **REFERENCE GIVEN WHEN REQUESTED.**

Any Information required promptly transmitted without charge.

The undersigned, long and favorably known in the BOOK AND CHEAP PUBLICATION business, being in daily receipt of orders from his old customers and numerous friends to furnish them with many articles not connected with the trade, has, in order to insure the wants of all, and afford greater facilities for so doing, opened at 84 NASSAU STREET, NEW YORK, A GENERAL PURCHASING AGENCY for the especial accommodation of any who may be pleased to favor him with their patronage.

His long experience in buying, and familiarity with merchandise of every description, warrants him in assuring all parties that they can rely on his selections, both as to quality and price, and rest assured that he will not spare either trouble, care or judgment in his endeavors to satisfy their wishes and protect their interest, in the purchasing of any book or article they may be in want of.

To parties living in inland towns, or those wishing many articles that can only be procured in New York City, it is a great advantage, as they can have any goods they may wish purchased and sent to their address, either by mail or express, and at the same price (if not lower) than they could buy were they on the spot themselves.

All orders attended to with the utmost promptitude, carefulness and accuracy, and forwarded to their destination in the most compact, reliable and expeditious manner.

THOMAS ORMSBY, *General Purchasing Agent,*
84 NASSAU STREET, NEW YORK.

He would be pleased to call your attention to the following list of **BOOKS WHICH ARE BOOKS**—having just issued new editions in the most superb style—the Printing, Binding and Illustrations surpassing that of any that have heretofore been offered to the public.

THE MARRIAGE BED;
Or, Wedding Secrets, Revealed by the Torch of Hymen.

Being a full Explanation of the Matrimonial Duties of both Bride and Bridegroom on the Eve of Marriage; Containing *Facts of Vital Importance* to the Married and Unmarried; With Practical Remarks on its Proper Seasons: How to Choose a Partner; Mysteries of Generation; Causes and Cure of Sterility; Abuse and Economy of the Generative Organs; Effects of Excessive Indulgence; Consequences of Total Abstinence from Coition, &c. Disclosing SECRETS AND HINTS to *Lovers, Husbands and Wives worth knowing*. Illustrated with Six Colored Engravings, printed from Steel Plates. Neatly and handsomely bound. **Price 50 Cents.**

A COMPANION TO THE ABOVE.

WOMAN'S FORM;
Or, Female Beauties.

Being a Complete Analysis and Description of every part of Woman's Form, and showing her Perfect Capacities for the Purposes of *Love, Procreative Duties and Happiness*. Illustrated with *Five Beautiful Colored Pictures* of the most perfect Female Forms. Containing nearly 200 pages of reading. Handsomely and neatly bound. **Price only 50 Cents.**

ADVICE TO HUSBANDS & WIVES.
The Only True Guide to Happiness.

4 Colored Plates. 200 pages. **Price 50 Cents.**

THE WEDDING NIGHT;
Or, Advice to Timid Bridegrooms.

8 Colored Plates; neatly bound. **Price 50 Cents.**

THE LOVE ORACLE;
Or, Counselor to the Sex.

Being a complete Fortune Teller and Interpreter to all questions upon the different events and situations of life, but more especially relating to all circumstances connected with Love, Courtship and Marriage. By LE MARCHAND. Illustrated cover, printed in colors. **Price 25 Cents.**

COURTSHIP MADE EASY;
Or, The Mysteries of Making Love Fully Explained.

With specimen Love-Letters; containing also a Treatise on the General Qualifications necessary for Marriage, and the Proper Age and Condition for Wedlook, &c., &c. By a Widower who has been thrice married, but is still young enough to be an especial favorite of the ladies. **Price 13 Cents.**

THE DICTIONARY OF LOVE.

Containing a definition of all the terms used in the History of the Tender Passion, with rare quotations from the Ancient and Modern Poets of all Nations; together with specimens of Curious Model Love-Letters, and many other interesting matters appertaining to Love, never before published; the whole forming a remarkable Text-Book for all Loves, as well as a Complete Guide to Matrimony, and a Companion of Married Life. Translated in part, from the French, Spanish, German and Italian, with several Original Translations from the Greek and Latin. By THEOCRATUS JUNIOR. Handsomely bound in Cloth. **Price One Dollar.**

ANECDOTES OF LOVE.

Being a True Account of the Most Remarkable Events connected with the *History of Love in all Ages*. By MADAME LOLA MONTEZ, *Countess of Landsfeldt*. These romantic and surprising anecdotes really contain all events connected with the history of the tender passion. It is precisely the kind of book which a man will find it impossible to relinquish until he has read it through from the first to the last chapter. Bound in Cloth. **Price One Dollar.**

ARTS OF BEAUTY;
Or, Secrets of a Lady's Toilet.

With hints to Gentlemen on the *Art of Fascinating*. By MADAME LOLA MONTEZ, *Countess of Landsfeldt*. Cloth, gilt Side. **Price 50 Cents.**

THE LAWS OF LOVE.

A Complete *Code of Gallantry*. 12mo., paper. Containing concise rules for the conduct of a Courtship through its entire Progress, Aphorisms of Love, Rules for telling the Characters and Dispositions of Women, Remedies for Love, and an Epistolary Code. **Price 25 Cents.**

On receipt of the price, either in CASH or STAMPS, copies of any of the above named books will be sent to any part of the United States or Canadas, either by Mail or Express, securely and neatly packed, POST PAID.

Address **THOMAS ORMSBY,**
General Purchasing Agency,
84 Nassau Street, N. Y.

Figure 10.2. This sales circular for Thomas Ormsby's "general purchasing agency" indicates the flexibility that dealers in racy materials adopted in their business practices. The books advertised here are primarily sex manuals (most of them illustrated), but their availability along with gloves, guns, sporting goods, and jewelry points to the porous borders between the "book trade" and activity in other retail sectors. "Thomas Ormsby's Commission Bureau and General Purchasing Agency" (New York, 1861); collection of the American Antiquarian Society.

sentence that was, as Dennis notes, "the heaviest penalty imposed for an obscenity offense in antebellum New York."[23]

Brewster Maverick and Edward Scofield were young men just embarking on their careers in the print industry in antebellum New York. In contrast, more established men held positions in the print trades that straddled the line between the production and sale—and, as we shall see, destruction—of printed material. Together, their stories illustrate the extent to which the print trades played a crucial role in clarifying just what constituted legitimate economic activity in nineteenth-century America. These economies of print extended beyond the boundaries of the trade itself and became interwoven into the larger economic fabric of the antebellum city. Printers not only opened themselves to prosecution by publishing racy and outright obscene materials; they also circulated information about other sectors of the economy of reading that reformers seized on in order to more clearly define the boundaries of acceptable business practice in the period. And both Maverick and Scofield also engaged in careers that were within the world of print but not exclusively defined by its boundaries. All of the publishers discussed here conducted their business in an uncertain legal environment. Given the lack of clear obscenity laws on the books, dealers in sexually explicit materials were never entirely clear on what they could get away with, and were left to gauge the direction of the political wind. Periodic antismut campaigns would result in abundant arrests, but between these outbursts of reformist sentiment, publishers and retailers could operate in relative peace.

Erastus Elmer Barclay was a low-level entrepreneur in the economy of print who, over the course of a career that spanned almost fifty years, managed to avoid anything that resembled success. The bibliographer Thomas McDade lamented in a 1956 article that "Barclay is practically unnoticed in the history of the publishing field. I have found only two references to the man or his publications. He is omitted from all lists of Philadelphia publishers; he appears in no indexes, bibliographies, or references which have come to my attention."[24] In the five decades since McDade's article, the situation has not changed.[25] E. E. Barclay was a prolific (if peripatetic) publisher of lurid sensational narratives, most of them claiming to offer stories of what we would now call "true crime" or other forms of scandal. These books were almost always published in short pamphlet form, often with colored covers and eye-catching cover images usually depicting the impending close of some unfortunate's life. Barclay filed for his first copyright in 1841 and would spend the next forty-five years eking out a living on the lower rungs of the cheap publishing world.[26]

Barclay's publications were sensational, but never sexually explicit (although he did have a long-standing interest in stories involving women dressing as men). Rather, his primary approach to the economy of print was to cut numerous corners, which differentiated him from the more upstanding firms of the day. Unlike Scofield, who operated in the street and competed for territory with other independent peddlers, Barclay hired his own salesmen and gave them exclusive territory. They distributed broadside sheets door to door that advertised his novels and then returned to sell copies.[27] In addition, he appears never to have had a storefront from which he retailed books. Furthermore, rather than starting the pagination of his books with page number one, as was standard practice, Barclay began his novels with page number nineteen (on rare occasions pagination started with an even higher number). Presumably he did this in order to make his short publications seem longer to customers who glanced at the last page to see how much reading matter they were getting for their pennies.[28] Barclay's mobility also differentiated him from more reputable publishing firms. After a slow start in New York City, Barclay moved to Cincinnati in 1846 and then to Philadelphia in 1849. At some point along the way, he became a close friend of the sensational novelist George Lippard, after whom he named his son. (George Lippard Barclay later joined his father in the family business, writing pamphlets on catastrophes such as the Chicago fire of 1871 and on explorers such as Stanley, Livingstone, and DuChaillu).[29] The senior Barclay returned to Cincinnati in 1856, then moved back to Philadelphia in 1858.

Yet, to judge by his novels' title pages, he was even more mobile. In order to give readers the impression of greater access to local knowledge and hence boost the popularity of his books, he used standard publication conventions to his advantage, frequently identifying the place of publication as a city located close to the events described in the narrative. For instance, the title page of *Dark and Terrible Deeds of George Lathrop: Who, After Passing Through the Varying Degrees of Crime, Was Finally Convicted and Hung in New Orleans, June 6, 1848, for the Robbery and Murder of His Father, June 8, 1847* gives New Orleans as its place of publication and lists the Rev. W. Stuart as the publisher, even though the other side of the title page indicates that the work was copyrighted in Ohio by E. E. Barclay. If his imprint is to be believed, Barclay was prolific, doing business in New Orleans, Richmond, Charleston,

New York, Cincinnati, Philadelphia, and Frankfort, Kentucky, which would have both generated local interest in the vicinity of those sites and perhaps given readers farther afield the sense that they were reading something more akin to reportage than fiction.[30]

Another Barclay title—*The Entwined Lives of Miss Gabrielle Austin, Daughter of the Late Rev. Ellis C. Austin, and of Redmond, the Outlaw, Leader of the North Carolina "Moonshiners,"* by Bishop Edward Crittenden of North Carolina (1881)—provides evidence of some of Barclay's other questionable yet ingenious business practices. Many of Barclay's narratives focused on a real criminal or actual event—Lewis Richard Redmond was a real moonshiner who shot and killed a revenuer in Transylvania County, North Carolina, in 1876—while wrapping the real incident in entirely fictitious garb. This title, too, evinces another favorite practice of Barclay's: presenting a respectable but fictitious man (usually a minister, sometimes a judge or a lawyer, and in this case a Methodist bishop) as the author. *Fearful Adventures in Pennsylvania's Wilds; or, The Startling Narrative of Adelaide Lane* (1856), for example, was "Written by herself at the suggestion of the Rev. Barry Hillyard, Pastor of the M.E. Church, Shattucksburg, McKean Co., Pa." While there is a McKean County in Pennsylvania, there is no evidence of a town named Shattucksburg having existed there. Barclay was not alone in using many of these business strategies, but they were the tactics that cheap publishers resorted to in order to stake out territory in the low-rent district of the print economy, in a much different way than larger and more established publishers of the day.[31]

With the end of the Civil War, Barclay recognized new economic opportunities, broadening his line of offerings to include cookbooks, health manuals, songsters, and "dream books"—essentially gambling manuals—as well as a number of books on actual crimes, such as the assassinations of James Fisk and President Garfield. Barclay also began catering to the growing German immigrant community, publishing many of his titles in both English and German and providing captions for the crude illustrations he commissioned in both languages, so that he needed only to print one run of plates for use in both the German and English editions. The firm continued for some time after Barclay's death in 1888 under his wife's supervision, ultimately issuing at least 160 unique titles. Two pamphlets appeared in Barclay's name in 1896 with a Cincinnati address belonging to Andries Nielen, a "publisher of ephemeral literature" whose entry in the city directory read, "A. Nielen's Publishing House: The Cash Buyers Agency, Clocks, Bronzes, Crockery, Household Goods, Musical Novelties, Publishers for Agents."[32] Thus Barclay's idiosyncratic business, on the fringe of respectable publishing, wound up being absorbed by an even more idiosyncratic business: a publisher who sold household items or a dealer in household items who for some reason also published books.[33]

While E. E. Barclay's business practices might have been questionable—occasionally shortchanging readers and publishing salacious or violent tales but never running afoul of the law—there was little question about what business Jeremiah Farrell was in. Farrell was the subject of what may be the single most damning two sentences in the more than 2,900 volumes that make up the collection of credit reports compiled on American businessmen by R. G. Dun and Company during the nineteenth century. An entry for January 31, 1871 describes Farrell thus: "Bad man, bad business, bad habits, bad character. Not recommended."[34] This for a man who, in the 1870 Federal Census, reported his worth at $8,000.[35] Yet Farrell—one of New York City's most prolific publishers of obscene books and prints—had not always been viewed as such a bad businessman. Even if members of New York's business community knew the source of Farrell's income—and, by all descriptions that we have of his bookstore, it would have been impossible not to—their opinion of him was slow to turn. In 1862, an ad run by Farrell in a sporting newspaper announced, "BOOKS! BOOKS!! BOOKS!!! SPORTING ARTICLES, CARDS AND PRINTS . . . All books, Sporting and Fancy Articles you may see advertised, will be furnished to order."[36] As declared in this ad, Farrell was selling not only racy books but also contraceptives and sex toys—"sporting and fancy articles."

In 1863, Farrell, then twenty-six years old, bought out the business of his associate in New York's pornography world, Frederic A. Brady (who did business under the name Henry S. G. Smith and Company), for a whopping $5,000, including his stock of obscene books and some of his stereotype plates.[37] In his early years Farrell was the ideal Dun and Company businessman. An August 1864 credit report, the first entry on Farrell, described the Irish immigrant as a "smart active business man, doing a successful business. Buys and sells for cash, asks very little credit, worth fully $15,000 and adding to his worth, correct and honest in his dealings, prompt in his payments. Credit good."[38] In 1866, three years after expanding his business to become the second-largest smut dealer in New York (and thus in the nation), Farrell continued to get good reviews from the credit reporters: "Has fair means for the business he is doing and is considered very good for all he buys."[39] Clearly the reporter knew what line of goods Farrell sold—"the business he is doing"—yet was primarily interested in Farrell's capitalist bona fides, not his moral probity.

Yet his reputation would soon take a rapid turn, along with his business fortunes. A report from December 21, 1867 noted that Farrell "pays his way but is a man of bad character. He is the publisher of obscene books in which," the report noted begrudgingly, "he manages to do a good business." Three years later, on November 5, 1870, a report expanded further: "Deals in obscene books and pictures, is intemperate and unreliable, of disreputable character and unworthy of credit."[40] As Farrell's business reputation began to suffer, other storm clouds gathered. Starting in 1868, a remarkably energetic man named Anthony Comstock declared war on New York City's smut industry. As Donna Dennis notes, Farrell was the only one of the major New York pornographers who kept his own storefront and ran ads inviting customers to come examine his stock, making him particularly vulnerable to prosecution.[41] Having identified four major producers of obscene books in the city, Comstock first set his sights on William Haynes and Frederic Brady but soon turned his attention to Farrell. Before police officers responding to a complaint filed by Comstock (who visited Farrell's shop and bought an obscene book) could arrest him, an officer who was on the publisher's payroll allegedly gave him a tip: "Jerry, [we] have a warrant for you. If you don't want to be taken get out of the way."[42] Farrell fled. Pursuing the case, Comstock arrested Farrell's store clerks, who led him to Farrell's printer, Thomas Holman, a Yonkers man who posed as a religious publisher. In the back room, police seized six tons of stereotype plates, pages for nearly 50,000 volumes, and account books showing that over the previous four years Holman had printed more than 140,000 books for Farrell.[43]

Dun agents in New York clearly sensed the wind's direction. On July 12, 1871, six months after his epically bad credit report, another report described Farrell as "intemperate" and "not safe to trust over night." Before Comstock or the police could actually catch up with Farrell to file charges, on May 11, 1872 the publisher was found dead in his home at 159 Adams Street in Brooklyn, apparently a suicide. He was thirty-five. Helpfully, the final entry in his Dun record, dated June 6, 1872, reads simply, and in larger-than-usual handwriting, "Dead."

Farrell's rise and fall illustrate several points about capitalism and the print trades in nineteenth-century America. As Janet Farrell Brodie notes, Jeremiah Farrell oversaw a complex production network, having his books printed by Thomas Holman in Yonkers and subcontracting their binding to

Charles and Joseph Darrow in lower Manhattan.[44] That the Darrows would task their female employees with binding obscene books along with the rest of their licit publications indicates that the production of obscene materials may have been socially marginal but not segregated as a business practice. This might suggest, too, that the women who worked in book binderies and likely colored obscene plates risked their livelihoods should they object to the subject matter of the texts and pictures that they encountered in their production lines. Brodie writes, "Using the techniques that propelled American publishing to master production of cheap books as well as more expensive volumes, Darrow and Farrell exhibited the traits of progressive businessmen," a fact that was not lost on the credit reporters for the Dun agency.[45]

In treating the stereotype plates he purchased from Brady as fungible assets, Farrell's business practices were entirely in line with those of other postbellum publishers, as was his practice of subcontracting the printing and binding of his books. So was his practice of selling nonbook items—"fancy goods"—alongside the printed material in his shop at 15 Ann Street. The only thing that distinguished Farrell from his colleagues in the print trades in lower Manhattan was the sexually explicit nature of his line of goods, which, like etiquette books and popular biographies, catered to its own particular market. But from the perspective of the mainstream of nineteenth-century business practice, this was only an issue insofar as it exposed Farrell to legal prosecution and thus financial insecurity. Indeed, Farrell's very first Dun report, recorded in August 1864, described him as a "smart active business man, doing a successful business . . . correct and honest in his dealings, prompt in his payments."[46] Yet in just under six years, he was deemed "not safe to trust overnight."[47]

What changed during this time was not the business Farrell conducted, nor was it the awareness of that business—by all accounts, anybody who walked into his store in 1864 would have known that he sold sexually explicit books and prints as well as condoms and other nonprint items. What did change in the intervening years, and proved likely the cause of Farrell's fading financial situation, was the appearance of another concerted antismut campaign in New York. In other words, his business became more marginal because the margin moved, not because Farrell started doing something different.

The Dun records for Farrell's peers in the smut trade show a similar tendency. A September 1852 report on George Akarman, another prominent New York wholesaler in obscene materials, states, "We learn that he is a smart shrewd business man, very attentive and industrious and an excellent financier. Has been prompt in meeting his engagements. . . . His actions of late have not been looked upon very favorably and those who formed a good opinion of him think otherwise. His associations are bad."[48] Similarly, a September 1859 report on Frederic Brady (who would later sell his business to Farrell), remarked, "We learn from others that his character does not stand well on account of his connection with the sale of obscene books for which he was arrested and imprisoned some time ago. He is supposed, however, to be worth significant property and can buy all he wants on good terms."[49] In both cases, fairly serious moral reservations—Brady had been arrested and imprisoned for obscenity, Akarman's "associations are bad"—were outweighed in the marketplace by shrewd business sense and the possession of sufficient capital to "buy all he wants on good terms." Farrell's case illustrates the changeable nature of life on the margins of respectable business practice. With a shift in the political and moral climate in the city—or with the rise of an unaccountably energetic antismut crusader—business practices that one year drew praise for being "correct and honest in his dealings, prompt in his payments" would in another year result in the grand slam of credit report calumny: "Bad man, bad business, bad habits, bad character." Perhaps Farrell was simply foolish, or arrogant, to trade in obscene books and prints as openly as he did. Or perhaps his changing fortunes illustrate that the influence of moral and legal regulation on nineteenth-century capitalist practice was not as consistent as we have come to think. The lack of clear antiobscenity laws, and the fluctuation in the enforcement of those laws that were on the books, placed entrepreneurs like Farrell in a doubly tenuous position. Farrell must have known that he was operating in violation of the law—after all, the man he purchased his business from had gone to jail for selling the very books whose plates Farrell purchased. But in all its particulars save for that of subject matter, Farrell's business looked like any other publishing business of the time, and the agents who monitored his credit seemed not to care what sort of books he sold as long as he could pay his bills—until, that is, shortly before 1870, when Anthony Comstock encouraged them to care a great deal.

It may be unusual to think of Comstock as an entrepreneur in the economy of print, yet his shadow looms over the entire world of publishing in the second half of the nineteenth century. While he began his crusade against sellers of obscene books in the late 1860s and by 1872 had put out of business the three biggest pornographers in New York, the sweeping powers granted to him by the 1873 amendment to the Post Office Act that came to bear his name, the "Comstock Act," changed the business practices of all printers who came even close to flirting with the boundaries of respectability for the rest of the nineteenth century.

Comstock was another man who built a career out of print capitalism, simply from the other side of the ledger. His career would have been impossible without the work of printers like Jeremiah Farrell and street vendors like Edward Scofield. Approaching the print trades from another angle, Comstock worked both *through* print and *on* print to more clearly define the boundaries of acceptable business practice and hence to bolster his own image as a crusader and reformer. Born in 1844 in New Canaan, Connecticut, into a rigid Congregationalist family, Anthony Comstock was cast adrift after the end of the Civil War (which he spent in abstemious annoyance in Florida). Poorly educated, he was mired in low-end clerical jobs in Connecticut when a five-dollar gift from a friend enabled him to take his chances in New York. Finding work as a porter and then a clerk in a Manhattan dry goods store, Comstock led a fairly sedate existence until 1868, when a friend of his bought a brothel directory from a dealer of obscene books (perhaps an updated version of the guide sold by Edward Scofield). Consulting the directory, Comstock's friend visited a brothel, where he promptly contracted a venereal disease. Comstock discovered that his friend had purchased the book from a man named Charles Conway. He visited Conway's store himself, purchased an obscene book, and then returned with police in tow to arrest Conway for violating recently passed state obscenity laws.[50] This led him to other smut peddlers in lower Manhattan and more arrests, all of which were carried out in his spare time. Yet in 1871, when he married Margaret Hamilton and bought a small house in Brooklyn, he was still making only twenty-seven dollars a week as a dry goods salesman and was going into debt to support his new reform activities.

This would change in 1872 when Comstock appealed to the recently formed Young Men's Christian Association (YMCA) with an unprecedented business opportunity. William Haynes, the city's foremost producer of erotica, had just died (with Comstock hot on his heels), and the reformer found himself presented with an opportunity to buy Haynes's stock and take the books out of circulation. Morris Jesup, one of the wealthiest men in New York and a board member of the New York YMCA, saw Comstock's hastily scrawled appeal and gave Comstock $650 to help in his work.[51] From that point on, Comstock was a force of nature. In 1873 the twenty-eight-year-old

Comstock testified before Congress to reform the postal laws. Bringing along armloads of smut as exhibits, he argued for the prohibition of obscene materials in the mails, including any nonbook items of a sexual nature (such as condoms or dildos) and any items or materials that might be used to induce an abortion, as well as any information about where or how to procure contraception or an abortion.[52] Made a special agent of the U.S. Post Office (although an unpaid one), Comstock became one of the few law-enforcement officers in the country with truly national authority. As Andrea Tone notes, "these were extraordinary powers for a struggling clerk-turned-reformer to wield."[53] Late in 1872, the YMCA formed its Committee for the Suppression of Vice and hired Comstock to run it on an annual salary of $3,000, which doubled his income from his job selling dry goods "and raised him securely into the ranks of the middle class."[54] This new calling drew Comstock from the dry goods trade into a career firmly situated in the world of print. As the cover illustration of Comstock's 1880 book *Frauds Exposed* (Figure 10.3) makes clear, his primary concern was with the production and circulation of printed matter. In the autumn of 1873, when the committee was detached from the YMCA and renamed the New York Society for the Suppression of Vice (NYSSV), Comstock gave up his foundering career as a dry goods clerk and took on the excoriation of vice as his sole livelihood. While his interests would turn later in the 1870s to fighting lotteries and fortune-tellers, Comstock had lifted himself into the middle class by basing his career on marginalizing a segment of the print trades that, until his friend came home from a brothel with a venereal disease, operated relatively openly in America's cities (despite occasional crackdowns).

Anthony Comstock's success in putting small-scale (and pornographic) publishers out of business lay in a crucial insight: that the trade in erotic books was inseparable from the trade in nonbook materials. In a letter from Comstock read to the House of Representatives by Clinton Merriam, the New York congressman who introduced the act, Comstock claimed, "For be it known that wherever these books go, or catalogues of these books, there you will ever find, as almost indispensable, a complete list of rubber articles for masturbation or for the professed prevention of conception."[55] In one of Comstock's earliest prosecutions carried out after the formation of the NYSSV, he arrested Leander Fox for mailing obscene books and circulars and seized "1000 rubber articles and various other vile articles, 100 photos [and] 50 books."[56] Comstock was able to make a persuasive case that businessmen like Leander Fox and Jeremiah Farrell were not only publishing large num-

Figure 10.3. The vignettes on the cover of Anthony Comstock's 1880 book *Frauds Exposed* may display scenes of reform, but they also depict the distribution (by mail) and destruction of printed matter. Comstock liked to present himself as a crusader against bad men—such as the criminal on the way into his cell—but the other half of the upper vignette clearly shows that Comstock's real crusade was against bad *books*, which were to be countered both by burning and by the writing of *good* books, such as this one. Anthony Comstock, *Frauds Exposed; or, How the People Are Deceived and Robbed, and Youth Corrupted* (New York: J. Howard Brown, 1880); collection of the American Antiquarian Society (copy inscribed to the library by the author).

bers of obscene books and prints but also selling condoms, "rubber goods for ladies," and abortifacients, because they sold more than books.

In her study of contraception in America, Andrea Tone writes that the relative lack of success of NYSSV agents in arresting people for distributing contraceptives resulted from a type of tunnel vision: "Ignoring the intricacies of the contraceptive industry, agents pursued a select group of birth control sellers—those whose activities most closely resembled their stereotypes of smut peddling."[57] That is to say, they approached the trade in sexual goods and contraceptives as though it were a branch of the book trade, which in many respects it was. Comstock wrote in *Frauds Exposed*, "When I undertook the great and all-important work of suppressing by legal process this hydra-headed monster, what did I find? I found a business systematized, and systematically carried on."[58] He found book publishers who ran bookstores and published catalogs of their title lists who also had thriving businesses manufacturing and selling condoms and dildos—enterprises that were "systematically" integrated with their activities in the print trades.

Comstock is thought of today as a crusader against anything to do with sex, but thinking of his career as a capitalist enterprise rather than a moral crusade makes clear that his primary dedication was to shaping the production, distribution, and sale of certain types of printed matter and nonprint goods and earning a living by doing so. In his anti-vice campaigns he trumpeted his attempts to prohibit the distribution of all goods of a sexual nature, especially contraceptives. But the trade in those goods was often carried out by publishers and frequently indistinguishable from the print trade. By invoking the specter of nonprinted items, Comstock was able to more effectively push the production and sale of sexually explicit *printed* matter firmly into the shadow of the law.

The short biographical vignettes offered here help illuminate several aspects of lives lived on the margins of capitalist enterprise in the world of print in the nineteenth century. All of the men depicted in this essay were involved in the production or sale of printed matter other than books. As such, they help remind us that the economy of print was expansive and included nonbook materials as well. The printed cards that Brewster Maverick delivered, the obscene images that Jeremiah Farrell had printed in Yonkers and that Edward Scofield sold on the streets of lower Manhattan, and the contraceptives that Farrell purveyed and Comstock pursued were part of a complex chain of producers, distributors, and consumers. All of these things were central to the functioning of the print trades in nineteenth-century America.

Like other retail trades, the boundaries of the print industries in terms of what was made and what was sold were rarely as neat as the term "print trades" would indicate.

The boundary between legitimate and illicit enterprise was similarly blurry. Knowing his readership, Erastus Barclay published racy books with misleading title pages and fiddled with page numbers to dupe his readers. At the low prices he charged, it is likely that few readers felt terribly cheated, and he never strayed over the line into obscenity. Yet the "dream books" that he published later in his career would have gained Anthony Comstock's condemnation had they been more widely marketed. Jeremiah Farrell bought a pornography business from Frederic Brady, who had gone to jail in the wake of an obscenity charge only a few years earlier. Yet Farrell was relatively open in his sale of not only obscene books and prints but also a range of contraceptives and sex toys. And he was quite successful, too—that is, until Anthony Comstock came to his store, bought an obscene book, and obtained an arrest warrant for Farrell, who apparently decided that he would rather die than go to prison. Barclay's line of books was relatively innocuous, yet still clearly several steps below the stock of the "legitimate" publishers of the day. Farrell's publications were more extreme, yet for several years he was able to sell smut quite openly in lower Manhattan and was much more successful at it than Barclay ever was. But when Comstock emerged as a participant in the economy of print, the line separating the tolerated from the illicit shifted, and Farrell was either unable or unwilling to recalibrate his business to bring it in line with the new market pressures.

The flexibility of day-to-day occupational practice within the print trades highlighted in these men's careers complicates the stability of the boundaries of what contemporary scholars often consider to be a single industry. The proliferation of cheap printed material in nineteenth-century America created entertainment for young men like Brewster Maverick (and jobs for his father and uncle), provided employment for Edward Scofield, and offered entrée into the middle class (however tenuously) for men like E. E. Barclay, Jeremiah Farrell, and Anthony Comstock.

Yet each of these men's modes of professional engagement in the world of print was wildly different. Maverick and Scofield were limited to particular occupational roles because of their age (and Maverick would go on to a more full-fledged career in the print trades). Barclay published unconventional works and conducted his business in an unconventional way, changing locations with startling frequency. Comstock built a career on print by attacking a specific segment of the print trades (only later would he write books of his own). Jeremiah Farrell had perhaps the most conventional entrepreneurial career in the print trades: he bought out a successful publisher and wholesaler, partnered with subcontractors to produce his goods, advertised through the mail, and had a retail outlet in the nation's largest city. Yet he published and sold works that ruined his reputation and destroyed his career.

The business enterprises in which these men participated remain largely unremarked by scholars. In the absence of business records for any of these individuals, how can we know what role illicit material, or nonprinted materials, played in their bottom line? Our lack of knowledge of the contours of this sector of the economy of print constitutes a call for further investigation. What did it mean for publishers or booksellers to actively engage in selling other kinds of goods? And how did selling books or other forms of print change how businesses of various types were perceived? Were the people Comstock went after primarily publishers, or were they really contraceptive dealers who decided to list a few books on their advertising circulars to give their businesses a veneer of legitimacy? By examining the lives of entrepreneurs and laborers who worked within economies such as cheap print, we gain new insight into how murky were the boundaries of capitalist enterprise in the nineteenth-century city. By selling more than books (or, in the case of Barclay, less), these men's careers shake the stability of the categories we use to describe nineteenth-century capitalism.

CHAPTER 11

Back Number Budd

An African American Pioneer in the Old Newspaper and Information Management Business

ELLEN GRUBER GARVEY

Americans in the mid- to late nineteenth century felt overwhelmed by the abundance of cheap printed matter in circulation. It was full of valuable information, but how should they store it and find unindexed material again? "Many beautiful, interesting, and useful thoughts come to us through the newspapers, that are never seen in books, where they can be referred to when wanted. When they are gone they are lost. If one should keep a regular file of one of our principal papers, as the *Tribune* or *Herald*, in a few years it would be found to be valuable. . . . But they cannot be bought," noted E. W. Gurley in 1880, advising his readers to keep scrapbooks of the newspaper items that mattered to them to get around the problem.[1] But one man *did* keep regular files of principal and more obscure papers, understood and helped to define their value, and made a living by offering them for sale.

The career of Robert M. Budd, an African American man known as Back Number Budd, weaves through the movement of print from the 1860s to the early 1930s. As users were starting to see newspapers as data, he developed technologies to organize, store, and access that information. As a business owner, Budd worked with materials that others considered valueless. He found marginal spaces to work from and advertised in innovative ways. He made a business of creating value from discarded materials, using a network of more marginal workers like hotel cleaning staffs to rescue old newspapers on their way to the trash.

Although every city had rag and old paper collectors who resold these materials for reprocessing into more paper, Budd instead understood that newspapers could be reprocessed into more information. He converted them into valuable goods by creating a system to sort and access them. As an innovative black businessman, he was on both the cutting edge and the margin. Because he worked with newspapers and was in contact with newspaper workers, reporters found his business a worthwhile subject to write about. Their curiosity extended to his personal and family life, and so he made surprising appearances in the newspapers.

A top-hatted visitor on the way to the theater in New York around 1885 might have been intrigued by the Civil War-era headlines of newspapers on display at the head of a staircase. Heading down the steps, he would have entered one of the cramped Tenderloin-area basements where Budd kept shop from 1881 to 1905. He would have climbed over the shoeshine stand, squeezing past the youths or men leafing through dime novels. After edging along the papers stacked precariously close to the gas lamps, he might have overheard an outraged customer complaining that a dog-eared five-year-old newspaper ought to be worth less, not more, than a crisp new one. How could he have guessed that the proprietor of this cluttered venue was pioneering new ways of commodifying information?[2] Prices for news and information were mutable and negotiable, not rigidly straightforward. Newspaper items themselves had often already recirculated through the press, with "scissors editors" picking up and reprinting articles from one another's papers, paying only in acknowledgment of the source paper, if that. Sometimes prices were tied to the materiality of the paper: the day's news was free for the reading from the big newspaper boards posted outside the offices of daily newspapers or could be listened to when it was read aloud there. It cost only a penny or two to buy a fresh paper. New services offered smaller quantities of more specialized news for a higher price, and sped its delivery. For example, in 1882 Dow Jones started publishing its targeted business news bulletins throughout the day and distributing them on the floor of the New York Stock Exchange, and then in 1897 sped up delivery by using a stock ticker. Clipping services became popular by the 1900s, sending subscribers envelopes of clippings from the current papers on topics of their choice, decentralizing the acquisition of information. Newspaper reports touted the efficiency of the clipping services' rows of "girls" scanning newspapers for their assigned keywords, marking them, and sending them on to be clipped, stamped with the name of the service, and sent along to the subscribers. But unless a scissors editor decided to reprint just the item the reader wanted, it was difficult to retrieve again from the torrent of printed old news or information. New media were starting to address this problem by compiling information into data in new ways: by 1905, for example, horseracing sheets codified, updated, and regularly published tables of information on horses' past performance that would otherwise have had to be painstakingly dug out from old newspapers. But even then, actual copies of old newspapers usually seemed more like trash than treasure.[3]

While the new modes of extracting and reselling data from newspapers began to make that information valuable, the used papers themselves were on a distinctly lower plane. Although used book dealers sometimes sold a run of an old newspaper or periodical sets, Budd's entire basement and, later, warehouse full of newspapers were of a different order. His enterprise was associated less with dealings in other used goods—like furniture and books—than with the business of rags and bones and ashes collected for reprocessing—"downcycling," in today's parlance. Its function as an information repository, available for mining for new information, was harder for Budd's contemporaries to see. As I will discuss in this essay, Budd asserted his place in the capitalist economy as a businessman selling valuable information and resources, but his work was not recognized in this light by the businesses with which he dealt.

Budd built up his back number newspaper business in a period when newspapers did not publish indexes, and only a few kept indexes for their own use. Storing masses of unindexed newspapers was impractical. If a reader anticipated wanting an item again, he or she could clip and paste it into a scrapbook. Otherwise, as Gurley had noted, it was gone. Even if they stacked or bound some magazines, libraries and reading rooms often disposed of their back issues of the daily press. Budd sought to offer a comprehensive collection of newspapers, and his warehouse held millions of newspapers and magazines. The collection suffered two major fires, one in 1895 and a more devastating one in 1922, though he was still in business in 1931. He died in 1933.[4]

Born in 1852 in Washington, DC, Budd got his start as a child selling newspapers to the Union soldiers in camps near Washington during the Civil War. Soldiers offered him an extravagant three dollars—and sometimes even five—for each of his remaining copies of newspapers describing the battles in which they had fought. "The boys were willing to pay almost anything for them for the sake of getting the news," he later explained.[5] He said he had started out as an underaged drummer boy, but he was barred from that position when authorities discovered he was too young to serve. He became a camp follower instead, selling newspapers and riding back from the front on ambulances and carts carrying the dead.[6]

After the war, he continued to sell papers, first in Washington, then in Philadelphia, and finally in New York. Budd's battlefield experience and his customers' requests suggested to him that there was money in old newspapers. In New York in the early 1880s, he first combined a shoeshine and newspaper stand selling the day's papers with his back number newspaper business, and kept the shoeshine stand within his establishment for many years. He worked very long hours, keeping his newsstand open from 6 o'clock in the morning until 10 o'clock at night, seven days a week. He stockpiled millions of old papers, cramming them into his tunnellike twenty-four-foot by sixty-five-foot gaslit basement in an old wooden building on Broadway and Thirty-Second Street. This store and seven or eight others he moved to within a few blocks of one another were located in New York's Tenderloin, the area of prostitution and gambling; pool halls and oyster houses; many theaters, like Wallacks, Daly's, and the Eagle; and some hotels, like Gilsey House—from whose staffs he bought old papers. Black residential enclaves existed a little to the west and slightly to the north—Budd and his first wife, Hattie, lived for a time on West Forty-Seventh Street, on the northern edge of the Tenderloin.[7] While there would have been great advantages to Budd in occupying space downtown, where most of his clients were—newspapermen on Newspaper Row, near City Hall, and lawyers, who congregated near the downtown courts—the attraction of the Thirty-Second Street area for Budd was surely that rents were initially lower than in a downtown location.[8] In the early 1890s, newspapers like the New York *Tribune* and the *Herald* moved uptown from Newspaper Row, and the Thirty-Second Street area was renamed Greeley Square in honor of the *Tribune*'s former publisher. But as the area developed into an upscale business and shopping district (Macy's arrived nearby in 1902), rents rose precipitously.

Although later reports depict Budd as wealthy or having made a fortune from his newspaper sales, an 1884 glimpse into his home in the West 40s reveals something of the lives of striving black people. Black married women often continued to work outside the home, unlike white women who occupied similar social positions in their communities. Although his wife was described as the "queen of New York colored society," she worked as a laundress.[9] She told one of her employers, the actress Florence Marryat, that her husband had promised that if she had a baby she would no longer have to work. Marryat found the couple living in a tastefully decorated four-room apartment, adorned with a photograph of Robert Budd in a red velvet frame.[10]

Budd moved from one location to another around Greeley Square until 1905. From then on, he conducted all of his business out of a warehouse in Ravenswood, Queens (now in Astoria), a former horsecar barn he had acquired by 1886 to store papers. With optimism painful in hindsight, he described it as fireproof. Astoria was a barren area, no longer a neighborhood of wealthy people's houses, and not yet the industrial area it would become. He moved his residence there as well and lived adjacent to his warehouse, possibly in one of the decaying mansions on the river. In some respects the location was ill-suited to his business. His closeness to the river would have left his papers vulnerable to rats. At the time he moved there, he later recounted, his Italian neighbors kept goats that occasionally got in and nibbled at the papers. But it was expedient to keep both his Astoria warehouse and Manhattan location. Ferries ran directly across the East River from Ravenswood to Thirty-Second Street and Thirty-Fourth Street in Manhattan, while a spur of the elevated train met the ferry on the Manhattan side and ran up to Greeley Square, near his shop and the newspaper offices clustered nearby.[11]

Budd's choices of location shaped both his rent bill and his opportunities for obtaining his stock. Budd's methods for acquiring papers were both within and outside conventional market channels. Budd took advantage of his location in the Tenderloin with its numerous hotels. Beyond keeping the day's unsold papers from his own newsstand, he paid hotel cleaning staffs by the pound for old newspapers and magazines they collected from hotel lobbies and their newsstands.[12] In paying by the pound, Budd aligned himself with the kinds of used paper dealers who bought paper to be pulped; very likely he also competed with them. He contracted with clubs to buy their daily newspaper files by the month.[13] He also devised less conventional methods for increasing his stock of papers, taking advantage of the fact that they might be worth little to those he obtained them from. So he staked bets on elections with files of newspapers. He reported that his wagers on the election of Benjamin Harrison brought him files of six magazines and newspapers and 244 other files.[14] He also bartered for papers, for example, offering 70,000 envelopes, addressed "to the lady of the house" for "files of any New York papers or for any kind of old paper." As his business became better known, other papers came to him free of charge, directly from publishers who put him on their subscription lists, evidently seeing value in having, in effect, an offsite repository.[15] By 1888, he was continually advertising for old books, magazines, and newspapers and traveling "considerably to purchase them." Each week he also put away "a number of copies of the daily papers and current periodicals." He bought and sold bound volumes of newspapers and magazines as well. In 1888 he was reported to have a million and a half papers; a year later he advertised that he had "2,178,777 copies in stock," spotlighting a level of specificity that suggested a minute attention to his inventory. His bookkeeping system for tracking sales allowed him to audit his holdings, so that he was keenly aware of when he had only a single copy left and could take steps to acquire more, and charge accordingly.[16]

Budd set uniform prices based on the age of the newspapers, adding surcharges based on rarity. In 1887, he was asking five cents for a week-old copy of most papers, and eight cents for week-old copies of five-cent papers. The price rose to ten cents for month-old papers, and five cents for each additional month; fifty cents for year-old papers, and twenty-five cents for each additional year. Rare papers fetched even higher prices.[17] When a reporter who sought articles from a few months earlier was unable to find them in a library, he was directed to Budd's establishment. Budd located them easily and then shocked him by charging "ten times their original price."[18] Other reporters marveled at Budd's ability to command such prices for papers that had once been worth only a penny, and marveled also that he stuck to his rates (an issue surely on the mind of any reporter who had just tried to bargain with him). One sympathetic account noted, "It frequently happens that persons come to purchase papers several years old and expect to get them at face value. When they learn of the advanced price, it is amusing to hear them threaten to complain to the publisher and write to the editor and do other dreadful things, but as a general rule, they end by paying Budd's prices, as they know they cannot procure them elsewhere." Budd, a shrewd businessman who had carved a niche for himself in the market for information, forced everyone, including white men, to accept his valuations, scaled according to his own price through current and careful recordkeeping.[19]

Negotiations like these may have been amusing to reporters, but Budd felt slandered by them. He defended his practices in an advertising booklet published in 1889: "It is often said that my business is a trust and a swindle, and an outrage because I charge $2.50 for a copy of any paper 7 years old, which only cost me 1½ cents." He explained in great detail how much money he invested in his stock of papers to produce an income of five hundred dollars a year. He summed up, "As can be seen from my Sales from the last 7 years that only one thirty-second . . . of the Papers I have are sold, and out of this I must get the money to pay my rents, help and my own work Day and Night. Then would you call this a Trust?"[20] He wanted not only to silence his critics but also to have them acknowledge his innovative and extensive enterprise. His booklet asserts, "Is this not a great enterprise? Does it not deserve Success? Is not my experience in Newspaper Business since 1863 worth at these late dates of my life, a few dollars? or would you have me work during my old age or bad health? I begin to think you all would. But as I have had the enterprise to accomplish what no other dealer in the world ever attempted, I can stand being called a trust. . . . My address can never be forgotten. It is BACK NUMBER BUDD, New York City, USA."[21] Budd's advertising booklet was titled "Back Number Budd's Directory," perhaps to lend it more gravitas. It was hardly intended to seduce customers. Rather, it addressed a hostile reader who thought Budd had an unfair monopoly on information—just when the Sherman Antitrust Act was working its way through Congress—and who wanted him to work into old age (as, in fact, he went on to do). Like white writers who imagined lazy black people lounging instead of working and white legislators who enacted the notorious Black Codes of the post-Reconstruction South to enforce freedpeople's labor, Budd's hostile reader could not recognize his hard work. Race shaped this discussion about value, competition, success, and independence. White men rarely would have been required, as Budd evidently felt he was, to show everyone their books. Budd's careful recordkeeping allowed him to make an argument about his business acumen, but this close scrutiny of his books seems a race-based invasion of privacy.

Budd presided over an unparalleled storehouse and exchange center of the nation's documents. While newspaper reading rooms like the Merchants' Exchange Reading Room, located in the New York Stock Exchange, catered to the men involved in the exchange with a broad selection of the press from the United States and abroad, its collection was geared to news of the moment, and it disposed of older papers. Moreover, using the reading room required a substantial investment: in 1864, its dues were twenty-five dollars per year. Some subscription libraries kept a select stock of newspapers. But unlike these exclusive repositories with gatekeepers screening their collections, Budd's collection was vastly inclusive: the *Amusement Bulletin* and the black paper the *Pittsburgh Courier* were not likely to be in the stacks at the select libraries.

Journalists do not seem to have accused Budd of being a devious schemer or running a trust. Instead, reporters often framed their anecdotes of high prices Budd received for particular copies of papers as a story of Budd creating riches from waste, almost by chance: "He has a business that grows while he sleeps, and grew from almost nothing," one asserted.[22] This article appeared after Budd's response to white hostility in his advertising booklet. Like those who ignored the labor of Jewish old clothes and rag dealers and instead imagined them coining money from waste or from illicit activities, whites continued to ignore the hard work and business acumen that built Budd's business. The casual racism of some articles contributed to this framing, positioning Budd's enterprise as below the level of legitimate business.[23]

The daily paper depended for its value on freshness and up-to-dateness and its readers' sense that they were reading at the same time as their neighbors and fellow citizens. Old newspapers conventionally were worth far less than the current day's paper. In the nineteenth century, old papers were likely to be recycled via one of many modes, all of which ignored their printed content and reduced them to paper for wrapping fish or other goods; insulating clothing, shoes, bedding, and walls; cutting into dress patterns and quilt backings; folding into hats for printers and newsboys; lining trunks, drawers, shelves, and baskets; stocking the kindling and outhouse pile; shredding to make papier-mâché goods; and pulping to produce new paper.[24] Budd's business depended on a different underlying economy—an information economy. Budd discovered that there was value in age. Like modern archivists or special collections librarians, Budd understood that he could not predict what would later interest people, but he recognized the papers' potential value.

E. W. Gurley wrote that "a regular file of one of our principal papers" would become valuable after a few years. It is worth examining why this is so. Value accrued to Budd's copies of the newspapers as other people disposed of them or reused them for their paper and not their news. Michael Thompson's *Rubbish Theory: The Creation and Destruction of Value* offers a theory of the life cycle of mass-produced objects such as souvenirs. Thompson takes the decorative machine-woven Stevengraph pictures as a case study. These inexpensive ornaments embodied transient value when they originated as souvenirs from the 1879 York Exhibition in England; many people bought them and displayed them as attractive signs of modern technology, as souvenirs of attending the exhibition, and then as souvenirs of the settings shown in their pictures. By the mid-twentieth century, Stevengraphs were no longer a novelty, but a sign of distastefully outmoded Victorian preferences. They were oppressively familiar and therefore devalued, becoming simply rubbish that people threw out. It was only years later, after many had been disposed of and they were no longer being made, that the remaining Stevengraphs became scarce and therefore potentially valuable. Their scarcity made them unfamiliar, curious objects.[25]

Newspapers travel a condensed version of this path. Today's newspaper has obvious value: it carries news of the moment and notices of events planned for that day or the day after. When the day is over, it is no longer today's paper, and a new "today's paper" supplants it on the top of the stack. As it moves farther down the stack, it speaks less and less to the needs of the day. The papers seem more like a stack of waste, and even the most indolent housekeeper will eventually dispose of them. As one nineteenth-century account of newspapers explained, "A daily paper lasts but for a day; then it is dead and another takes its place. To know how completely a daily paper dies when its day's work is done, so to speak, suppose you try to buy a copy three months old, or a year old. You remember three months ago there were hundreds of thousands of copies printed and distributed. You suppose that you can get a copy at the office of the paper, at any rate. But no; all more than three months old have been destroyed."[26] Budd was unique among commercial reusers of out-of-date newspapers for his attention to the content as well as the paper.

When a single copy survives general disposal over the decades or centuries, it, like the surviving Stevengraph, becomes unfamiliar and novel. When it is discovered, people want to examine it and keep it. A curiosity, it may arouse nostalgia or seem like a window into the past. Beyond their traveling the usual rubbish-to-valuable cycle, newspapers contain specific information that people want to find and that has otherwise vanished. Budd sold the unacknowledged cost of storing and searching them. His advertising booklet exhorted his customers not to "waste your time and room filing papers and only using them twelve times a year, when you can obtain back numbers of all Papers from any day in any year from 1833 to date." Since most people did not take the time to file the papers, it was in that middle period—when most people threw newspapers out for a lack of space—that papers became valuable for their rarity. Beyond simply saving papers, Budd organized them so that he could find individual issues when they were called for.

The relationship between value and price, worth and cost, was complicated both by the rubbish life-cycle economy and by advertising's subsidy of newspapers, so that the penny or two a customer paid for the current day's newspaper did not reflect the newspaper's production cost (and possibly not even the cost of paper and ink). But the 1895 fire at Budd's warehouse demonstrated how slippery cost and value were in relation to old newspapers: it revealed that insurance companies had been unwilling to consider his collection as anything but waste paper, and so he received no compensation for his loss. As he complained to *Printer's Ink*, an advertising trade weekly, "In the eyes of the insurance people, my stock is nothing but 'junk.'"[27] Their insistence on classifying his materials as junk—as old things with diminished value from which dealers mysteriously generated money—may have had a racial dimension as well, since many junk dealers were black. Moreover, his ventures in acquiring such paper goods as the envelopes addressed "to the lady of the house," which he sought to trade for newspapers, complicated any description of his stock and its quantification.

Census takers indicated similar unease about the value of old newspapers when they described his occupation. The 1900 census ambiguously designated him as a "paper dealer," and only in 1910 was he transformed into "proprietor, news store," while in 1920 his used newspapers perhaps seemed so hard to categorize that the census taker called it a stationery business. Budd repurposed old newspapers not as material for pulping, but as a data source. Insurance companies and others, however, insisted on seeing only the wastepaper and not its transformation.[28]

In addition to the value Budd contributed by storing bulky, vulnerable materials, Budd's prices crucially reflected the value added in creating a system to organize the papers so they could be located again. His storerooms seemed densely cluttered with stacks and bundles of papers, but, as in stores dealing in used clothing with their bundles of clothes, the chaotic appearance was deceptive. The papers were bundled and arranged chronologically on shelves, organized and retrievable through what he described as "a simple system of my own. All the papers of a given date are arranged in bundles, according to States and localities, with a separate tag on each bundle. In this way, either my men or I can put our hands upon any paper we want inside a minute or two."[29] His "bump of order must be well developed," another journal commented, evoking the phrenological system of classifying character traits.[30] He could reach back into bundles of the Boston *Advertiser* or the *New York World*, to pull out the correct date, others noted.

The transformation from trash to treasure, the instability of value, and the potential of the scorned and marginal to reveal astonishing worth are themes that appear repeatedly in nineteenth-century popular writing, in works that illuminate the cultural assumptions of their period. In his popular "Acres of Diamonds" speech, for example, Russell Conwell told his listeners to look to their own disregarded backyards for wealth. Other stories of valueless material recontextualized also remained popular, such as the story of

Dick Whittington's cat that was published in many nineteenth-century collections and school readers and appealed to the sense that riches lurked in the commonplace.[31] Valueless material, relocated, reshaped, or reinterpreted, could lead to wealth. News accounts reinforced the idea that riches might more literally lurk in the newspaper—a lawsuit might turn on a piece of evidence lost in the stacked papers of the past, or an old paper might hold evidence of a crime. Like other "rags-to-riches" narratives, these transformation stories suggested that the key was pluck and intelligence, more than luck. But Horatio Alger's heroes hawk today's papers, not yesterday's. They may shop at the old clothes dealer, but they do not start as one or become one. Used goods in the nineteenth century, whether clothes or junk or papers, were so tainted by their association with ethnic or racial outsiders that they were largely excluded from the rags-to-riches narrative.

Budd helped to shape the demand for his services through innovative advertising. Even his name, "Back Number Budd," alerted anyone who heard it to the nature of his business. He used it in most of his print advertising, signed correspondence and checks with it, and claimed to have copyrighted it. Into his Broadway storefront, he drew curious customers by selecting from his files of all the New York dailies issued during the Civil War and "occasionally on anniversaries of battles exhibits in front of his place papers of that time, giving accounts on both sides, and other interesting mementoes."[32] In a period when advertising was often hailed as the mark of a progressive businessman, he advertised in periodicals directed variously to journalists, book dealers, and bibliophiles. Because he was always building his stock, his ads displayed his willingness both to buy and to sell. The *Back Number Budd's Directory* advertising booklet included ads from a neighboring confectionery and a gentlemen's clothing store, which presumably paid him in some way for the advertising space, though perhaps he extended this favor for their help in accepting packages for him. Their ads, along with a useful table for deriving the cross-streets from New York's avenue addresses on the front cover, also made *Back Number Budd's Directory* seem more like an almanac or informational booklet than a simple advertisement.

Budd created another advertisement that inserted his business into the history of newspapers by reprinting a 1789 *Ulster County Gazette* and a *Gazette of the United States* that carried news of George Washington's inauguration. He bought up old stereotyped plates of an edition sold for the 1876 centennial celebration. In an era before photographic technology for creating a facsimile of the paper existed, the centennial edition was a transcription of the words of the original, in the format of the original, reset in nineteenth-century type (though that was not obvious to many collectors later, who believed it was the 1789 copy). He further distinguished his reprint copies from originals by his ads on the back and by a copyright notice he inserted.[33] His *Gazette of the United States* adds, on the edge of the first page, "Gen. Geo. Washington's Inauguration, Our First President, 1789," with the possessive pronoun firmly asserting Budd's equal ownership of the nation's past. His reprinting work registers an understanding that both the physical form of the item, or at least a gesture to it, and the information it contained were valuable. People wanted the tangible connection to the past, even in reproduction. They certainly would have wanted to keep such an advertisement around—and dealers in rare printed matter have continued to have to explain that these are not originals.

The newspaper dealer staked out space in other print media as well. For a time, he called his business Back Number Budd and Sons, and listed each of his sons on a separate line in *Trow's New York City Directory*. Even the infant Reason Budd received a separate line, until his death at age three. As someone accustomed to noticing the value of column inches, perhaps Budd understood these listings as a tactic to garner extra space on the directory page. His practice reflected fatherly pride and aspiration as well. Although none of the newspaper articles about his business mention his sons, he saw them as part of the business and included their names, even as young children, on his letterhead.[34]

Each of the many articles that appeared about Budd alerted potential customers that they had a place to go to locate old periodicals as needed. He showed off his stock to reporters, introducing them to novelties. Among the special issues in his possession, which he brought forth for the press, was the *Vicksburg Daily Citizen* set into type July 3, 1863, printed on wallpaper.[35] His own advertising and the many articles about him noted that he had runs of newspapers dating back to 1833, another way of flattering reporters by dignifying New York press history and legitimating his own profession. Since 1833 marked the founding of the *New York Sun*, often hailed as the first of the city's penny papers, choosing that date also marked his ties to the city's journalistic history.

Writing articles about Budd's business allowed reporters to celebrate the value of their own newspapers. So a *New York World* reporter exulted in 1886, "a glance at Mr. Budd's books . . . serves to indicate something of the wonderful growth of *The World* within the past four years. . . . From Feb[ruary]

20 to Nov[ember] 30 of the present year, he has sold 5,614 *Worlds*, or nearly twice as many as any other paper on his list."[36] Magazines even advertised that he collected their issues. The *Amusement Bulletin* boasted that Budd was laying in copies of their weekly for the value of its illustrations.[37]

What was the market that Budd created and primed? His renown drew many kinds of clients. Some sought out his stock for nostalgia or personal interest—much like Budd's earliest customers on the Civil War battlefields. "It is nothing unusual to see an old soldier in Budd's purchasing a paper containing an account of some action in which he was engaged," one reporter noted.[38] Some of the old soldiers were more purposeful: General Ulysses S. Grant bought a month's worth of papers in June 1885, perhaps for work on his memoir. By 1895, Budd occasionally scanned through and clipped his newspapers for clients as well, making a commissioned scrapbook in 1892 for Helen Gould on the death of her father, the financier and railroad magnate Jay Gould, and another on the first wedding of Astor family heir Jack.[39]

Serialized fiction in newspapers and magazines brought in new customers, and Budd praised "the long stories the papers have been publishing for the last few years. People get so interested in them toward the end"—presumably having first encountered the serial part way through—"that they can't wait till they are published as books, and so they come to me for the back numbers."[40] He sold dime novels and other used books as well, though newspaper reporters rarely noted this part of his business.[41]

Some sales inspired publicity themselves, and spread news of his business. Jake Sharp, a corrupt railroad magnate convicted of bribing an alderman, paid the high sum of a hundred dollars in 1886 for a selection of old papers, for reasons about which New Yorkers could only speculate: "Some said he intended to make a 'boodle' scrap book," while others thought he was looking for material on which to base libel suits against newspapers. In this case, the reporter seemed to gloat about the high price Sharp was forced to pay.[42] Even rumors of high prices brought publicity. Budd was reported to have been offered $10,000 to complete a file of two years of the *Leavenworth Journal* covering the time leading up to the establishment of Kansas as a free state on behalf of the Kansas Historical Society.[43] The Kansas Historical Society's records do not show evidence of any such sale, but the newspapers' reprinting of the story added to Budd's renown.[44]

Although Budd's dealings with the famous and infamous and occasional high-priced sales drew press attention, his bread-and-butter clients were reporters and lawyers, for whom information was an essential commodity. The pairing of newspaper reporters seeking background information for their stories and lawyers seeking physical evidence exemplifies the crucial doubleness of newspapers: they are both data and mere sheets of paper. Reporters often paid to read Budd's papers on the premises. They thus treated the newspaper as a vehicle for information and used his storehouse as a library or reading room—substituting it for those libraries and reading rooms that failed to save newspapers. From Budd's they took away the information they needed, in the form of notes, that they would then reprocess into new articles. When they actually purchased papers, it was for the convenience of keeping or transferring the words at a later date.

Lawyers who wanted documentation of dates of events or notices, however, needed the materiality of the news item on paper—physical evidence that it had been published on a specific date. So if one had failed to save the all-important item—the iconic precious clipping, or the clipping related to a bequest that would have been worth a thousand dollars—Budd's vast storehouse of newspapers might supply it. Lawyers therefore not only bought the old papers but sometimes paid Budd to swear to a newspaper's authenticity. The reputation Budd had earned in legal circles as a supplier of authenticated records evidently overrode the common nineteenth-century devaluation of African American testimony.

Budd's inventory was considered so comprehensive that plaintiffs assumed they could produce the relevant evidentiary newspapers by drawing on his stock. In one 1896 legal case, Stephen Fisk testified that he had learned of his wife's previous marriage and divorce only when he read about it in a series of articles in an 1867 or 1868 newspaper, the *Citizen*. Concluding that he "was wedded to infamy," he broke off relations with her. Seeking an annulment thirty years later, Fisk explained, "I have not preserved the copies of those papers, and I have been unable to get them, due to the fact that Back-Number Budd's place was burned up . . . while I was preparing for the suit. I made a search for these papers, and my counsel made a search for them, prior to the burning up of Back-Number Budd's place, and that was the place where we finally made up our minds we would get them."[45] While he claimed to have been devastated by having his name dragged through the mud by the newspaper thirty years earlier, he lost the case because he could not present the physical evidence—the newspaper item—to prove that an injury resulted from his wife's failing to tell him of her previous marriage.

While this case and other stories about his business show that Budd's newspaper collection was a unique and irreplaceable resource, it was also—

along with scrapbooks, clipping services, library cataloging systems, filing systems, and even pigeonhole desks—a mode of thinking about information, how to amass it, collate it, and find it again. These are the foundations of more recent filtering of information via digital methods, namely, Google, Lexis/Nexis, blogging, personal sharable note-taking applications such as Evernote and Zotero, and the like. Each technology contributes to our understanding that pieces of information—whether in the form of articles, books, or snippets—are detachable, movable, and classifiable under multiple headings.[46]

Back Number Budd conceptualized newspapers as piles of printed paper that would become valuable over time, and that people would buy if the papers were properly sorted and stored so they could access an item from an already known date. The alternative was to search through files, paper by paper. It was up to the purchaser to decide whether to view the newspaper item as movable data or as concrete evidence, fused to the date-stamped materiality of the paper. The newspaper clipping services or bureaus, which coexisted with Budd and outlasted him, instead framed their task as organizing and sorting the information in the current newspapers.[47] Clipping bureaus began in the 1880s and started to take hold in the 1890s. Employees at these bureaus scanned and clipped items from current newspapers for material on topics specified by clients, who periodically received packets of clippings by mail or courier. Budd's scrapbook-making work for clients participated to an extent in the same project, with the special advantage that he had ready access to old newspapers. Clipping services clipped only the day's or week's papers and offered "back number work" only at a steep premium. The possibility of making similar use of Budd's business appears only in fragments; a 1909 report mentions that one of New York's then-separate subway companies, the Interborough Rapid Transit Company, "gathered the data for its recent proposal from the archives of Back Number Budd."[48]

Clipping services were not the only cause of the decline of Budd's business. The first of two fires, in April 1895, burned the Ravenswood warehouse he had described as "fireproof." The fire started in the warehouse, and by the time firemen arrived the store was ablaze. Budd was in his Manhattan store at the time. "When he reached the scene, his home and labor of thirty-two years were represented by a heap of blackened timbers and burned and water-soaked newspapers. His collection was considered to be one of the most valuable in this country."[49] He had believed that his papers were too tightly packed to burn, but was proven wrong. He did, however, salvage some of the papers themselves, and since he was in constant negotiations to buy as well as sell papers, he succeeded in buying files of many of the works he had lost, bought back some that he had previously sold, built a new warehouse, and continued in business. He left Manhattan's Greeley Square area in 1905 and was operating solely out of Queens after that—and so his business was no longer very convenient for either reporters or lawyers. The Queens fire, too, and the publicity about it, may have given some people the impression that he had gone out of business. In 1899, when Budd still had a shop in the West 30s, Sherwin Cody, a Chicago journalist, wrote, "In New York there was once a little old shop, kept by a queer old mulatto, known as 'Back Number Bud,' [*sic*] who charged a dollar and a half for a one cent paper, less than a year old. This shop of 'Back Number Bud's' was, a few years ago, the only place in New York City where back numbers of newspapers could be purchased at any price; and in smaller cities no copies whatever could be obtained, except by chance."[50]

The second conflagration, a three-alarm fire on a bitterly cold night in December 1922, was much more devastating. Before the fire, Budd's business card proclaimed that he had "6,278,183 copies on hand." The fire spread from the two-story warehouse to his home and destroyed both, with some help from his son Robert Jr.'s motorcycle and its gas tank, stored in an adjoining shed.[51] Seventy years old by then, Budd rushed back into the building to attempt to save some of his papers.[52] Learning from the previous fire, he succeeded in rolling out a barrel of his correspondence about purchasing periodicals.[53] He stayed in business until the early 1930s—one 1931 report asserted that his enterprise was "regarded as the most extensive privately owned collection of 'back numbers.'"[54] But his operation was not what it had been, and he no longer enjoyed visibility in the press. Several articles from the 1920s call him "the late Back Number Budd," and by his actual death in 1933 his son Robert Jr. had sold most of what was left of Budd's collection, keeping some dime novels. He had long shown pride in the span of his work. The 1895 article about his first fire reported that he had been in business for thirty-two years, dating his business to 1863 when he was an eleven-year-old Civil War newsboy in Washington, rather than to his opening the New York store in 1881 or his 1870s newsstand in Philadelphia. His 1889 advertising booklet had asked if his customers would have him work into old age. The fires and the precarious nature of his business perhaps were what caused him to have to do so.

Budd's two fires highlight another facet of his relationship to newspapers: the frequency with which he appeared as the subject of newspaper stories. Because his business both served reporters and attributed high value to their own productions, they wrote about him in articles that in turn helped advertise his business. Budd and his business are unusual for repeatedly appearing in the white press in a period when most white editors assumed they had no black readers or that black people warranted mention only as criminals. The existence of a record, then, is part of his story. All of the articles about his business mention his race. A few reporters cast his conversation in improbable minstrel dialect, but most treated him respectfully, presumably because they relied on his services.

At the same time, Budd and his family were the objects of what media critics writing of the late twentieth-century context have called black hypervisibility. The *St. Paul Daily Globe* referred to him as a "New York Celebrity" when they covered his shooting of a janitor in 1887.[55] Elsewhere Budd and his family were treated like comic celebrities, with Budd's marital complexities discussed in newspapers scattered around the country. The *St. Louis Republic*, for example, reported on a fight between Hattie Budd and Robert's girlfriend (later his wife) Mary Trice and the subsequent warrant for Hattie Budd's arrest.[56] The *Brooklyn Eagle* followed the saga further, reporting on Budd's arrests for nonsupport and his counter-proceedings against his wife, charging her with being involved with other men and paying her support payments in pennies, many of which were bad.[57] The *New York Evening World* chimed in with the news that he was not only living with Trice but had two children with her, one of them still living at the time of the 1894 court case.[58]

By the time Budd's older son, Robert Jr., eloped with an Italian neighbor against both families' wishes in 1912, Budd was less often in the news, and information about the event was confined to papers more local to Astoria. Budd's departure from the spotlight is still more evident in the surprising paucity of coverage of Robert Jr.'s murder of his father-in-law in 1920 and his subsequent acquittal on the grounds of self-defense.[59] Tensions between Robert Jr. and the family of his estranged wife ran high. When Back Number Budd's business burned down in 1922, Budd suggested that arson might have caused it, but police do not seem to have pursued the accusation. As Budd faded from visibility and hypervisibility to low visibility in the press, the dwindling number of newspaper articles about him after the turn of the century suggests that newspaper reporters no longer relied so heavily on his storehouse of information.

Newspaper reports had framed Budd's hard-won success as the product of good luck rather than the skill and planning that some reporters found difficult to credit to a black man. It is his failures, rather, that might be better explained by bad luck and prevailing ideas of race and value. Back Number

Budd took pride in having started his business with only eight dollars. In other words, he was undercapitalized. His description of his business practices in his advertising booklet demonstrates how thin a margin he worked on, even if projecting an image of success made for good publicity. After the 1895 fire, insurance coverage offered no help, because insurance companies classified his stock as junk—perhaps because they assumed black men dealing in used goods were junk dealers.

Budd could only draw from his own resources and ingenuity to rebuild. In the 1890s, good fortune had brought newspaper offices like the *Tribune* into the transportation-rich, low-rent area where he had initially set up his business, and he thrived. As department stores and other higher-class businesses arrived as well and drove rents up, he moved several times within a few blocks, though transporting so many papers must have been a massive undertaking. His frequent moves—four locations in eight years—made him hard to find and made writers like Cody assume he was out of business. Budd finally severed his connection with the more expensive midtown location and operated exclusively from his quarters across the river, where reporters were far less likely to drop in, whether to buy papers or pay to read them on the premises, and less likely to give him free publicity by writing about him.

Although his business continued to be unique, forms of competition of a completely different order emerged: newspapers deepened their internal morgues or clipping files, the New York Public Library set up a new reading room for newspapers and periodicals in its new building on Forty-Second Street and decided it was worthwhile to save old issues, and clipping bureaus offered information seekers more specialized and directed services. Budd had proudly listed his sons in his ads, but with the possible exception of Robert Jr., they did not join him in the enterprise.

He persevered for decades, buying and selling by mail as well as to in-store customers. Even near the end of his life, after the second fire and into the Depression era, Back Number Budd continued to sell old papers and dime novels. He no longer shined shoes as he had early in his career, but he sold shoelaces and the miscellaneous goods of a junk dealer, reduced to the insurance companies' earlier valuation. And he still displayed the sign that had announced the extent of his stock in his heyday: "Anything ever published, 1833 to date."[60]

Conclusion

BRIAN P. LUSKEY AND WENDY A. WOLOSON

The contributors to this volume offer interpretive frameworks for studying previously neglected markets and the people who created, negotiated, and debated them. The authors illuminate how these economies worked, identify who participated in them, and clarify the ways Americans appraised value and legitimacy in the nineteenth century. These essays give us a better sense of how Americans actually lived their lives in the nineteenth century and how they coped with and contributed to capitalist transformation.[1] Although these historical subjects can be elusive, when light is shed on them we can see that the people engaged in these countless, everyday transactions existed at the nexus—and not the fringe—of commercial activity. In some instances, they comprised distinct markets unto themselves and in other cases they were enmeshed in larger commercial networks that could be highly localized or extremely far-flung.

What the people featured in this essay collection did was important in their own right and also has ramifications for historians today. For instance, having a better understanding of the immigrant exploitation business in New York City forces us to rethink how we see the transportation revolution, and by knowing more about the domestication of prostitution in Baltimore we come to see the culture of business travelers in a new way. People involved in stolen goods rings and engaged in fraudulent marketing practices impelled authorities to police their activities and change public policy. Those who were engaged in legal occupations such as dealing in used clothes initiated a cultural response, with critics attempting to articulate categories of self and other, pure and contaminated, genteel and crude. Finally, there was the economic contribution—horse thieves, newspaper dealers, and cotton pilferers alike were intimately tied to larger commodity chains that kept the economy going.

What becomes clear is that the entrepreneurs described in these essays were quite skilled and brought to bear their knowledge of human nature, law, geography, and the market. Without any formal apprenticeship system, alliances defined by occupation, or prescriptive literature to consult, they had to become experts in their own fields of endeavor, often drawing upon networks defined by geographical proximity and kinship. If they operated illegally, they also had to know how to evade the authorities or gain their cooperation, and they employed a variety of strategies to do so. They also had to understand market psychology in order to capitalize on people's desires, anxieties, and weaknesses to reap the greatest profit: they had to know their marks and their markets.

Another theme running through this collection is how much we still do not know. Contemporaries largely disregarded these entrepreneurs or found it more efficient to consider them in the aggregate—as workers, customers, or criminals. Leaving little documentation, these people and what they actually did remain elusive. Source material on petty retail trades and informal economies, to say nothing of prostitution, swindling, thieving, and other illegal endeavors, is hard to locate, and the information that can be found often exists in fragments, leaving scholars to make inferences and rely on impressions where concrete data do not exist. This accounts in part for why these economies and their participants have gotten short shrift by historians. But a seeming dearth of source material is no reason for turning a blind eye to the life and work of petty entrepreneurs, especially when it comes at the risk of constructing a narrative that is concerned primarily with history's most visible people.

Historians and cultural geographers working on similar aspects of British history have taken the lead and provide instructive examples for scholars examining the United States. Focusing on secondhand markets, their work is broad, deep, and interdisciplinary.[2] Digital archives such as *London Low Life* and *Old Bailey Online* help to continue the nineteenth-century work of the journalist Henry Mayhew, who depicted in exacting detail the lives of London's small-scale tradesmen, from blind bootlace sellers and street-sellers of birds' nests to destroyers of vermin (James Francis's kindred spirits, no doubt).[3] There are very few Americans who chronicled the lives of their down-and-out contemporaries with such care and detail—Philadelphia's "Night Hawk" of the late 1820s, New York's George Foster writing during the late antebellum era, and James McCabe after the Civil War are among the most notable and reliable.[4] Most other contemporary accounts come from the perspectives of the politicians, reformers, and authorities whose descriptions of people outside of their own cohort helped to shade these people and their economies in the first place.

Scholars interested in illuminating elusive economic activities have to be as ambitious, creative, and adaptive as their subjects. Although these people often did not maintain business records (or did not save them), some of their transactions and activities can be found, in glimpses, in the records kept by others. Commodities dealers moving scrap materials from junk dealers to industry, for example, often kept ledger books, and large companies certainly recorded these dealings. Diaries, too, often capture the quotidian aspects of everyday life that might otherwise be overlooked. Records of arrest and prosecution often contain highly detailed accounts of theft, fraud, gambling, and other illegal activities and are invaluable in singular cases and also in the aggregate, useful for those seeking to quantify the true scale and measure of these markets' effect on the economy as a whole. Government records located in city archives and historical societies—including mayors' court reports, minutes of city council sessions, and license applications—reveal instances of both compliance with and disobedience to authorities. Documents found in the collections of the National Archives and Records Administration, such as those generated by bankruptcy courts, the Customs House, and the State Department, similarly contain traces of these people and their commercial dealings. For instance, official inventories enumerate the amounts and kinds of cargo carried in ships, records of the Union army document trading with horse thieves, and bankruptcy records serve as commercial narratives of failed businesses and the debtors who ran them into the ground. Although we have to rely in large part on records kept by people other than our subjects, we can nevertheless glean important information from them. The vast and rich source base from which these essays draw is suggestive and invites more archival discovery.

Scholars must employ a variety of methodologies to piece together the narratives of those they wish to study. Theories from material culture studies enable us to consider the importance of artifacts that carry physical traces recording their interactions with people (such as shinplasters with notes scrawled on them). Sources such as contemporary budget studies and prices current provide an economic perspective, helping us quantify the costs of the small things of everyday life (such as the amount that prostitutes paid for their cosmetics, contraceptives, and clothing). Cultural geographies help us reimagine what people did by tracking the places they traveled and where their stuff went, including the circulation of stolen goods (based on police blotters), the location of shops (listed in directories), and the movement of individuals (from census records, prison intake ledgers, and other name-rich sources).

There is much still to be done. As co-organizers of the initial "Capitalism by Gaslight" conference, we were thrilled about the enthusiastic response to our call for papers. And as coeditors of this resulting collection, we are buoyed by the quality and thoughtfulness of the essays. But this volume tells only part of the story. Women's contributions to the economy obviously went far beyond them being prostitutes and brothel owners. They also ran boardinghouses, did piecework in their homes, became skilled barterers, wrote self-published memoirs, worked as fortune-tellers and passers of counterfeit notes, ran junk shops, and performed many other necessary yet forgotten tasks that kept their families in food and clothing. Children, too, are absent here, yet were important contributors to the nineteenth-century economy. In addition to being indispensable laborers on rural farms, they were essential to the growth of urban economies, honing their skills as newsboys, rag pickers, metal scrappers, fruit peddlers, and dock thieves. We also need to illuminate other economic activities, including what was occurring in the South among slaves and poor whites and among the land speculators, gold diggers, and settlers out West.

Americans were risk-takers and profit-makers. In mock auction houses, the elegant parlors of brothel madams, public markets, and bookstores and on city streets, docks, and the high seas, they sought survival, courted success, and negotiated the rules of exchange. What unites these diverse essays is that they refreshingly blur the distinctions we have used to define and make sense of capitalist transformation. We urge readers to consider this volume as the beginning of a much longer conversation that confounds and complicates yet ultimately begins to clarify our understanding of the cultural history of capitalism by bringing light to the shadows.

NOTES

INTRODUCTION

1. "Mayoral proclamation . . ." *Philadelphia Inquirer*, June 2, 1862; "Death of a Well-Known Character," *Evening Telegraph* (Philadelphia), December 9, 1864.

2. See, for instance, *The Cambridge Economic History of the United States*, Stanley L. Engerman and Robert E. Gallman, ed., vol. 2, *The Long Nineteenth Century* (Cambridge: Cambridge University Press, 2000).

3. A few prominent examples of this voluminous literature include Sean Wilentz, *Chants Democratic: New York City and the Rise of the American Working Class, 1788–1850* (New York: Oxford University Press, 1984); Christine Stansell, *City of Women: Sex and Class in New York, 1789–1860* (New York: Alfred A. Knopf, 1986); Mary H. Blewett, *Men, Women, and Work: Class, Gender, and Protest in the New England Shoe Industry, 1780–1910* (Urbana: University of Illinois Press, 1988); Christopher Clark, *The Roots of Rural Capitalism: Western Massachusetts, 1780–1860* (Ithaca, NY: Cornell University Press, 1990); Charles Sellers, *The Market Revolution: Jacksonian America, 1815–1846* (New York: Oxford University Press, 1991); John Lauritz Larson, *The Market Revolution in America: Liberty, Ambition, and the Eclipse of the Common Good* (Cambridge: Cambridge University Press, 2010).

4. Important works in this genre include Lawrence B. Glickman, *Buying Power: A History of Consumer Activism in America* (Chicago: University of Chicago Press, 2009); William Leach, *Land of Desire: Merchants, Power, and the Rise of a New American Culture* (New York: Pantheon Books, 1993); Elaine S. Abelson, *When Ladies Go A-Thieving: Middle-Class Shoplifters in the Victorian Department Store* (New York: Oxford University Press, 1989); Stuart M. Blumin, *The Emergence of the Middle Class: Social Experience in the American City, 1760–1900* (New York: Cambridge University Press, 1989); Susan Porter Benson, *Counter Cultures: Saleswomen, Managers, and Customers in American Department Stores, 1890–1940* (Urbana: University of Illinois Press, 1986); Kathy Peiss, *Cheap Amusements: Working Women and Leisure in Turn-of-the-Century New York* (Philadelphia: Temple University Press, 1986); and Richard Wightman Fox and T. J. Jackson Lears, *The Culture of Consumption: Critical Essays in American History, 1880–1980* (New York: Pantheon Books, 1983).

5. Michael Zakim and Gary J. Kornblith, introduction and Jean-Christophe Agnew, afterword, to *Capitalism Takes Command: The Social Transformation of Nineteenth-Century*

America, ed. Michael Zakim and Gary J. Kornblith (Chicago: University of Chicago Press, 2012), 1–12, 277–284; Jeffrey Sklansky, "The Elusive Sovereign: New Intellectual and Social Histories of Capitalism," *Modern Intellectual History* 9 (2012): 233–248.

6. For the installation of gaslight lamps on city streets, see Peter Baldwin, *In the Watches of the Night: Life in the Nocturnal City, 1820–1930* (Chicago: University of Chicago Press, 2012), 15–20.

7. Rosanne Currarino, "Toward a History of Cultural Economy," *Journal of the Civil War Era* 2, no. 4 (December 2012): 564–585 (quotations on 573–575). For some examples of "cultural economy" upon which our work builds, see Jane Kamensky, "The Exchange Artist's Wife" (keynote address for the "Capitalism by Gaslight" conference, presented at the McNeil Center for Early American Studies, June 7, 2012); Zakim and Kornblith, *Capitalism Takes Command*; Joshua D. Rothman, *Flush Times and Fever Dreams: A Story of Capitalism and Slavery in the Age of Jackson* (Athens: University of Georgia Press, 2012); Brian P. Luskey, *On the Make: Clerks and the Quest for Capital in Nineteenth-Century America* (New York: New York University Press, 2010); Wendy A. Woloson, *In Hock: Pawning in America from Independence Through the Great Depression* (Chicago: University of Chicago Press, 2009); Seth Rockman, *Scraping By: Wage Labor, Slavery, and Survival in Early Baltimore* (Baltimore: Johns Hopkins University Press, 2009); Ellen Hartigan-O'Connor, *The Ties That Buy: Women and Commerce in Revolutionary America* (Philadelphia: University of Pennsylvania Press, 2009); Jane Kamensky, *The Exchange Artist: A Tale of High-Flying Speculation and America's First Banking Collapse* (New York: Viking, 2008); Stephen Mihm, *A Nation of Counterfeiters: Capitalists, Con Men, and the Making of the United States* (Cambridge, MA: Harvard University Press, 2007); Timothy Gilfoyle, *A Pickpocket's Tale: The Underworld of Nineteenth-Century New York* (New York: W. W. Norton, 2006); Scott A. Sandage, *Born Losers: A History of Failure in America* (Cambridge, MA: Harvard University Press, 2005); Michael Zakim, *Ready-Made Democracy: A History of Men's Dress in the American Republic, 1760–1860* (Chicago: University of Chicago Press, 2003); Jackson Lears, *Something for Nothing: Luck in America* (New York: Viking, 2003); Edward Balleisen, *Navigating Failure: Bankruptcy and Commercial Society in Antebellum America* (Chapel Hill: University of North Carolina Press, 2001); Ann Fabian, *Card Sharps and Bucket Shops: Gambling in Nineteenth-Century America*, 2nd ed. (New York: Routledge, 1999); Nan Enstad, *Ladies of Labor, Girls of Adventure: Working Women, Popular Culture, and Labor Politics at the Turn of the Twentieth Century* (New York: Columbia University Press, 1999); and Jackson Lears, *Fables of Abundance: A Cultural History of Advertising in America* (New York: Basic Books, 1994).

8. In addition to the works cited in note 7, our collection joins a scholarly project that is underway in sociological and anthropological work on these economies in the present day, such as Sudhir Alladi Venkatesh, *Off the Books: The Underground Economy of the Urban Poor* (Cambridge, MA: Harvard University Press, 2006); Sudhir Alladi Venkatesh, *Gang Leader for a Day: A Rogue Sociologist Takes to the Streets* (New York: Penguin, 2008); and Howard Karger, *Shortchanged: Life and Debt in the Fringe Economy* (San Francisco: Berrett-Koehler, 2005). And while our evidence comes mainly from the

history of the United States, we also see this book as part of a growing literature that charts the history of these economies in other places and periods. See, for instance, the opportunities we now have to compare the experiences of street sellers and the cultural debates about their position in the societies of nineteenth-century London, Rio de Janeiro, and Philadelphia in the work of Stephen Jankiewicz, "A Dangerous Class: The Street Sellers of Nineteenth-Century London," *Journal of Social History* 46, no. 2 (Winter 2012): 391–415; Patricia Acerbi, "Slave Legacies, Ambivalent Modernity: Street Commerce and the Transition to Free Labor in Rio de Janeiro, 1850–1925" (PhD diss., University of Maryland, College Park, 2010); and Candice L. Harrison, "The Contest of Exchange: Space, Power, and Politics in Philadelphia's Public Markets, 1770–1859" (PhD diss., Emory University, 2008).

9. The conference, "Capitalism by Gaslight," was held in conjunction with the Library Company exhibition of the same name (http://www.librarycompany.org/shadow economy/).

CHAPTER 1. THE LOOMIS GANG'S MARKET REVOLUTION

The author would like to thank Darcie Caswell, Kevin Schlottmann, Allison Abra, the participants in the Capitalism by Gaslight conference at the Library Company of Philadelphia in June 2012, and the editors of this volume for being the most recent in a long line of smart scholars whose research and writing assistance have contributed materially to this essay.

1. The Loomis Gang has been fertile territory for local historians since the late nineteenth century. Accounts of their lives and criminal activities have appeared in newspapers, in manuscripts in local historical societies, and as published books and articles. See, for example, "The 'HUDDLE' 60 Years Ago, Number 6," *Waterville Times* (Waterville, NY), March 30, 1876; "The 'HUDDLE' 60 Years Ago, Number 8," *Waterville Times*, April 20, 1876; "The Loomis Gang," *New York Sun*, May 21, 1879; Carl Carmer, *Listen for a Lonesome Drum: A York State Chronicle* (New York: Farrar and Rhinehart, 1936); Leon A. Dapson, "The Loomis Gang," *New York History* 19, no. 3 (July 1938): 269–279; Harold William Thompson, *Body, Boots and Britches: Folktales, Ballads, and Speech from Country New York* (Philadelphia: Lippincott, 1939); John B. Hoben, "Roscoe Conkling and the Loomis Gang," *New York History* 22, no. 4 (October 1941): 437–449; Bruce J. Dew, "The Loomis Gang Again," *New York Folklore Quarterly* 10, no. 3 (Autumn 1954): 195–197; Roy Gallinger, *Oxcarts Along the Chenango* (Sherburne, NY: Heritage Press, 1965); Norman R. Cowen, *Loomis Family History* (Waterville, NY: Waterville Historical Society, 1983); George Walter, *The Loomis Gang* (Utica, NY: North Country Books, 1985); Isabel Bracy, "Family of Crime: The Loomis Gang" (unpublished manuscript, 1991, Colgate University Special Collections, Hamilton, NY); and Fuller Torrey, *Frontier Justice: The Rise and Fall of the Loomis Gang* (Utica, NY: North Country Books, 1992). Several fictionalized or semifictionalized accounts of the Loomises have also been published; see Charles Brutcher, *Joshua: A Man of the Finger Lakes* (Syracuse, NY: privately published, 1925);

Harriet McDoual Daniels, *Nine Mile Swamp: A Novel of Old New York State and the Outlaw Loomis Gang* (New York: Grosset and Dunlap, 1941); and John Brick, *Rogues' Kingdom* (Garden City, NY: Doubleday, 1965).

2. Sellers, *The Market Revolution*. For a more specific discussion on the market revolution in upstate New York, see Paul E. Johnson, *A Shopkeeper's Millennium: Society and Revivals in Rochester, New York, 1815–1837* (New York: Hill and Wang, 1978); Mary P. Ryan, *Cradle of the Middle Class: The Family in Oneida County, New York, 1790–1865* (New York: Cambridge University Press, 1981); and Carol Sheriff, *The Artificial River: The Erie Canal and the Paradox of Progress, 1817–1862* (New York: Hill and Wang, 1996).

3. See Lears, *Something for Nothing*, 3.

4. See Rothman, *Flush Times and Fever Dreams*.

5. "The 'HUDDLE' 60 Years Ago, Number 8."

6. Daniel E. Wager, *Our County and Its People: A Descriptive Work on Oneida County, New York*, Part 2 (Boston: Boston History Company, 1896), 16.

7. "The 'HUDDLE' 60 Years Ago, Number 8." See also Daniel E. Wager, *Our County and Its People: A Descriptive Work on Oneida County, New York*, Part 1 (Boston: Boston History Company, 1896), 537–538. For a more complete genealogy of the Osborn family, see http://www.osborne-origins.org (accessed May 10, 2012).

8. Wager, *Our County*, Part 1, 223, 194, 227, 539–541; Thomas A. Rumney, "A Search for Economic Alternatives: Hops in Franklin County, New York During the Nineteenth Century," *Middle States Geographer* 31 (1998): 23–34; and Paula Baker, "The Culture of Politics in the Late Nineteenth Century: Community and Political Behavior in Rural New York," *Journal of Social History* 18, no. 2 (Winter 1984): 167–193.

9. Wager, *Our County*, Part 2, 17. See also Wager, *Our County*, Part 1, 537–543; and "Hon. Amos O. Osborn, Death of One of the Oldest and Most Prominent Citizens of Waterville," *Waterville Times*, October 2, 1896. Amos O. Osborn's career as an amateur naturalist was recognized when a fossil that he discovered locally was named *Proscorpius Osborni* in his honor. His scientific interests led him to join the American Museum of Natural History, the New York Agricultural Society, the American Association for the Advancement of Science, and the Geological Society of America. His career as a local historian peaked in 1851 when he wrote the chapter on Sangerfield for a volume of local history. See Pomroy Jones, *Annals and Recollections of Oneida County* (Rome, NY: Published by the author, 1851), 401–427. For more on the rural cemetery movement of which Amos O. was a part, see Thomas Bender, "The 'Rural' Cemetery Movement: Urban Travail and the Appeal of Nature," *New England Quarterly* 47, no. 2 (June 1974): 196–211; and John F. Sears, *Sacred Places: American Tourist Attractions in the Nineteenth Century* (New York: Oxford University Press, 1989), 87–121.

10. Sheriff, *Artificial River*, 5. See also Whitney R. Cross, *The Burned-Over District: The Social and Intellectual History of Enthusiastic Religion in Western New York, 1800–1850* (Ithaca, NY: Cornell University Press, 1950).

11. Harry L. Watson, *Liberty and Power: The Politics of Jacksonian America*, 2nd ed. (New York: Hill and Wang, 2006), 186.

12. Wager, *Our County*, Part 2, 17.

13. Amos O. Osborn's social, political, and economic position was also profoundly similar to that of the Rochester businessmen who led Charles Finney's revival in 1830–1831; see Johnson, *Shopkeeper's Millennium*.

14. "The 'HUDDLE' 60 Years Ago, Number 6"; "The 'HUDDLE' 60 Years Ago, Number 8"; and "A Resident 'Native' Replies To 'Exile,'" *Waterville Times*, April 6, 1876. See also Walter, *Loomis Gang*, 17–18; and Torrey, *Frontier Justice*, 33–35. For genealogical information on Rhoda Loomis, see Anna S. Mallett, *John Mallett, the Huguenot, and His Descendants, 1694–1894* (Harrisburg, PA: Harrisburg Publishing Company 1895).

15. "The Celebrated Loomis Farm," *Waterville Times*, June 8, 1900; Walter, *Loomis Gang*, 16–18; Torrey, *Frontier Justice*, 2–3, 10–12.

16. Walter, *Loomis Gang*, 18–20; Torrey, *Frontier Justice*, 35–36; Wager, *Our County*, Part 1, 223, 194, 227.

17. Torrey, *Frontier Justice*, 41–43. For more on counterfeiting in the Early Republic, see Mihm, *A Nation of Counterfeiters*.

18. Torrey, *Frontier Justice*, 17.

19. Walter, *Loomis Gang*, 38–40.

20. Ryan, *Cradle of the Middle Class*, 15.

21. Ibid., 233.

22. Torrey, *Frontier Justice*, 15.

23. "The Loomis Gang," *New York Sun*, May 21, 1879. See also Thompson, *Body, Boots and Britches*, 87; Torrey, *Frontier Justice*, 41; and Walter, *Loomis Gang*, 27–28.

24. For more on the relationship between middle-class family imagery and commercial sex, see Katie Hemphill's essay in this volume.

25. Karl Polyani, *The Great Transformation* (New York: Farrar and Rinehart, 1944), 133. See also Kathryn Kish Sklar, *Catharine Beecher: A Study in American Domesticity* (New York: W. W. Norton, 1976).

26. Torrey, *Frontier Justice*, 13–32, 54–56.

27. Ibid., 13–32.

28. George W. Walter, "Chips and Shavings," *Madison County Leader* (Morrisville, NY), September 27, 1945; Torrey, *Frontier Justice*, 20–22.

29. Ann Norton Greene, *Horses at Work: Harnessing Power in Industrial America* (Cambridge, MA: Harvard University Press, 2008), 110–163.

30. "The Loomises' Foe," *St. Paul Daily Globe* (St. Paul, Minn.), April 24, 1893.

31. William G. Roy, *Socializing Capital: The Rise of the Large Industrial Corporation in America* (Princeton, NJ: Princeton University Press, 1997), 79.

32. See Pauline Maier, "The Revolutionary Origins of the American Corporation," *William and Mary Quarterly*, 3rd ser., 50, no. 1 (January 1993): 51–84; Ronald E. Seavoy, *The Origins of the American Business Corporation, 1784–1855: Broadening the Concept of Public Service During Industrialization* (Westport, CT: Greenwood, 1982); and James Willard Hurst, *The Legitimacy of the Business Corporation in the Law of the United States, 1780–1970* (Charlottesville: University Press of Virginia, 1970).

33. "Twenty-First Annual Report of the Prison Association of New York, Part 1, Transmitted to the Legislature, January 22, 1866," *London Quarterly Review*, American ed., 122, no. 243 (January 1867): 48. For more on the increasing organization of urban crime in this period, see Gilfoyle, *A Pickpocket's Tale*.

34. "Twenty-First Annual Report of the Prison Association of New York," 48, 50.

35. Edward F. Underhill, *Proceedings and Debates of the Constitutional Convention of the State of New York, Held in 1867 and 1868 in the City of Albany* (Albany, NY: Weed, Parsons, 1868), 1001–1002. See also Baker, "Culture of Politics in the Late Nineteenth Century."

36. This amendment never went into effect, however, because for myriad reasons the voters of New York State rejected the proposed constitution in 1869.

37. Greene, *Horses at Work*, 110–163; and Mark R. Wilson, *The Business of Civil War: Military Mobilization and the State, 1861–1865* (Baltimore: Johns Hopkins University Press, 2006).

38. Thomas Grey to George Weeks, July 2, 1864; and Thomas Grey to George Weeks, July 9, 1864, Record Group 92, Entry 225, Box 15, National Archives and Records Administration, Washington, DC.

39. See Milton C. Sernett, *North Star Country: Upstate New York and the Crusade for African American Freedom* (Syracuse, NY: Syracuse University Press, 2002), 225, and James S. Pula and Cheryl A. Pula, eds., *"With Courage and Honor": Oneida County's Role in the Civil War* (Utica, NY: Eugene Paul Nassar Ethnic Heritage Studies Center, 2010), ix.

40. Torrey, *Frontier Justice*, 128.

41. Mary P. Ryan, *Civic Wars: Democracy and Public Life in the American City During the Nineteenth Century* (Berkeley: University of California Press, 1997), 135–183.

42. Hoben, "Roscoe Conkling," 442–443. See also Torrey, *Frontier Justice*, 48–55, 144–145; Walter, *Loomis Gang*, 124–128; and Dapson, "Loomis Gang," 276–277.

43. Ann-Marie Szymanski, "Stop, Thief! Private Protective Societies in Nineteenth-Century New England," *New England Quarterly* 78, no. 3 (September 2005): 407–439, 422. See also Anthony S. Nicolosi, "The Rise and Fall of New Jersey Vigilante Societies," *New Jersey History* 86, no. 1 (February 1968): 29–53; and Matthew Luckett, "The 'Wide Awake Citizens': Anti Horse-Thief Associations in South Central Wisconsin, 1865–1890," *Wisconsin Magazine of History* 91, no. 2 (Winter 2007/2008): 16–27. Indeed, the activities of the Sangerfield Vigilance Committee more nearly resembled those of contemporary anti-horse thief organizations in the West; its actions would have been more typical of Kansas in the 1860s than of New York. See Cindy Higgins, "Frontier Protective and Social Network: The Anti-Horse Thief Association in Kansas," *Journal of the West* 42, no. 4 (Fall 2003): 63–73; and James David Drees, "The Army and the Horse Thieves," *Kansas History* 11, no. 1 (March 1988): 35–53.

44. Hoben, "Roscoe Conkling," 441–445; Torrey, *Frontier Justice*, 153–167; Walter, *Loomis Gang*, 153–184.

45. "Lynch Law in Oneida County," *New York Times*, June 18, 1866; and "The Loomis Family Mobbed," *New York Times*, June 21, 1866. See also Torrey, *Frontier Justice*, 168–185; and Walter, *Loomis Gang*, 185–210.

46. "A Band of Horse Thieves Extending from Maine to Indiana," *Clearfield Republican* (Clearfield, PA), July 28, 1880; and "A Horse Thief Gang," *Troy Daily Times* (Troy, NY), July 10, 1880.

47. Rothman, *Flush Times and Fever Dreams*, 178, 180.

48. "Twenty-First Annual Report of the Prison Association of New York," 50.

49. Hoben, "Roscoe Conkling," 446–449.

50. "The Loomises' Foe," *St. Paul Daily Globe*, April 24, 1893.

CHAPTER 2. THE PROMISCUOUS ECONOMY

1. William Chambers, *Things As They Are in America* (London: William and Robert Chambers, 1854), 307; George Rogers Taylor and George G. Foster, " 'Philadelphia in Slices' by George G. Foster," *Pennsylvania Magazine of History and Biography* 93, no. 1 (January 1969): 29, 55–60; Archibald Maxwell, *A Run Through the United States, During the Autumn of 1840* (London: H. Colburn, 1841), 2:166.

2. "Shopping, and Where It is Done," *North American* (Philadelphia), September 21, 1859; "The N. York Commercial of Friday . . . ," *North American*, December 20, 1841; W. Williams, *A Hand-Book for the Stranger in Philadelphia* (Philadelphia: George S. Appleton, 1849), 77–79; *Rae's Pictorial Directory and Panoramic Advertiser: Chestnut Street, from Second to Tenth Streets* (Philadelphia: Julio H. Rae, 1851); Dell Upton, *Another City: Urban Life and Urban Spaces in the New American Republic* (New Haven, CT: Yale University Press, 2008), 145–179; Sarah Leigh Jones, " 'A Grand and Ceaseless Thoroughfare': The Social and Cultural Experience of Shopping on Chestnut Street, Philadelphia, 1820–1860" (MA thesis, University of Delaware, 2008).

3. "South Street," *Public Ledger* (Philadelphia), July 6, 1844. On Southwark, see Emma Jones Lapsansky, *Neighborhoods in Transition: William Penn's Dream and Urban Reality* (New York: Garland Publishing, 1994), 71–100; Bruce Laurie, "Fire Companies and Gangs in Southwark: The 1840s," in *The Peoples of Philadelphia: A History of Ethnic Groups and Lower-Class Life, 1790–1940*, ed. Allen F. Davis and Mark H. Haller (Philadelphia: Temple University Press, 1973), 71–88.

4. "South Street." "Frippery," in addition to connoting an excessive or misplaced sense of fashion, was also a store where used clothes were sold.

5. Tamara Plakins Thornton, "Capitalist Aesthetics: Americans Look at the London and Liverpool Docks," in *Capitalism Takes Command*, ed. Zakim and Kornblith (Chicago: University of Chicago Press, 2012), 184.

6. Luskey, *On the Make* (New York: New York University Press, 2010), esp. 83–118; Michael Zakim, "The Business Clerk as Social Revolutionary; or, A Labor History of the Nonproducing Classes," *Journal of the Early Republic* 26, no. 4 (Winter 2006): 563–603; Dell Upton, "Commercial Architecture in Philadelphia Lithographs," in *Philadelphia on Stone: Commercial Lithography in Philadelphia, 1828–1878*, ed. Erika Piola (University Park: Pennsylvania State University Press, 2012), 153–175.

7. "Philadelphia Market," *The Ariel* (Philadelphia), August 22, 1829.

8. Seth Rockman, *Scraping By: Wage Labor, Slavery, and Survival in Early Baltimore* (Baltimore: Johns Hopkins University Press, 2009); Woloson, *In Hock*; Mihm, *A Nation of Counterfeiters*; Hartigan-O'Connor, *The Ties That Buy*; Serena Zabin, *Dangerous Economies: Status and Commerce in Imperial New York* (Philadelphia: University of Pennsylvania Press, 2009); Dylan Penningroth, *The Claims of Kinfolk: African American Property and Community in the Nineteenth-Century South* (Chapel Hill: University of North Carolina Press, 2003), 45–78; Betty Wood, *Women's Work, Men's Work: The Informal Slave Economies of Lowcountry Georgia* (Athens: University of Georgia Press, 1995).

9. I use the term "promiscuous" in this chapter not to conflate plebeian economic activities with licentiousness but rather to evoke its meaning for nineteenth-century Americans: lacking order or method, indiscriminate, mixed or amalgamated, casual, ungoverned—all of which imply a kinetic quality that was central to antebellum understandings of capitalism.

10. Arjun Appadurai, "Commodities and the Politics of Value," in *The Social Life of Things: Commodities in Cultural Perspective*, ed. Arjun Appadurai (Cambridge: Cambridge University Press, 1986), 57.

11. Zakim and Kornblith, *Capitalism Takes Command*; Joyce Appleby, *The Relentless Revolution: A History of Capitalism* (New York: W. W. Norton, 2010). For the attempts made by social and moral authorities to establish order and regulate promiscuity in the marketplace, see Jeffrey Sklansky, *The Soul's Economy: Market Society and Selfhood in American Thought, 1820–1920* (Chapel Hill: University of North Carolina Press, 2002); Amy Dru Stanley, *From Bondage to Contract: Wage Labor, Marriage, and the Market in the Age of Slave Emancipation* (Cambridge: Cambridge University Press, 1998); David Montgomery, *Citizen Worker: The Experience of Workers in the United States with Democracy and the Free Market During the Nineteenth Century* (Cambridge: Cambridge University Press, 1993), 52–114; Balleisen, *Navigating Failure*.

12. John Fanning Watson, *Annals of Philadelphia: Being a Collection of Memoirs, Anecdotes, and Incidents of the City and Its Inhabitants . . .* (Philadelphia: E. L. Carey and A. Hart, 1830), 219. The literature on secondhand retailing is more developed for Europe than for America during the eighteenth and nineteenth centuries, including Beverly Lemire, "Consumerism in Preindustrial and Early Industrial England: The Trade in Second-Hand Clothes," *Journal of British Studies* 27 (1988): 1–24; Lemire, "The Theft of Clothes and Popular Consumerism in Early Modern England," *Journal of Social History* 24 (1990): 255–276; Penelope Lane, "Work on the Margins: Poor Women and the Informal Economy of Eighteenth and Early Nineteenth-Century Leicestershire," *Midland History* 22 (1997): 85–99; Madeleine Ginsburg, "Rags to Riches: The Second-Hand Clothes Trade, 1700–1978," *Costume* 14 (1980): 121–135; Lemire, *The Business of Everyday Life: Gender, Practice and Social Politics in England, c. 1600–1900* (Manchester, UK: Manchester University Press, 2005), 82–109; Jon Stobart and Ilja Van Damme, eds., *Modernity and the Second-Hand Trade: European Consumption Cultures and Practices, 1700–1900* (Hampshire, UK: Palgrave Macmillan, 2010); Laurence Fontaine, ed., *Alternative Exchanges:*

Second-Hand Circulations from the Sixteenth Century to the Present (New York: Berghahn, 2008). For more on Jewish secondhand clothing dealers, see Adam Mendelsohn's essay later in this volume.

13. Rockman, *Scraping By*, 173. As Rockman and others have shown, these flexible consumer practices produced and reflected a complicated set of gendered divisions. On the gendering of these economies, see my discussion of hucksters below and Katie Hemphill's and Will Mackintosh's essays in this volume.

14. Daily Occurrence Docket (1787–1790), Guardians of the Poor, Philadelphia City Archives (hereafter PCA); Simon P. Newman, *Embodied History: The Lives of the Poor in Early Philadelphia* (Philadelphia: University of Pennsylvania Press, 2003), 36–37.

15. On the overlapping of commerce and charity, see Alice Taylor, "'Fashion Has Extended Her Influence to the Cause of Humanity': The Transatlantic Female Economy of the Boston Antislavery Bazaar," in *The Force of Fashion in Politics and Society: Global Perspectives from Early Modern to Contemporary Times*, ed. Beverly Lemire (Farnham, UK: Ashgate, 2010), 115–142; Julie Roy Jeffrey, "'Stranger, *Buy* . . . Lest Our Mission Fail': The Complex Culture of Women's Abolitionist Fairs," *American Nineteenth Century History* 4, no. 1 (Spring 2003): 1–24; Bruce Dorsey, *Reforming Men and Women: Gender in the Antebellum City* (Ithaca, NY: Cornell University Press, 2002), 33–39.

16. In this way, this essay suggests, secondhand was not only an economic strategy but had a range of cultural meanings. On the one hand, secondhand provided poorer consumers a way to engage, within constraints, with a "world of goods" too often equated with middling and elite consumption practices. On the other, as Vivienne Richmond shows in her recent study of Victorian England, by lowering the bar of entry to the world of goods, secondhand served further to marginalize the poorest members of society who were unable to dress fashionably with used clothing; Richmond, *Clothing the Poor in Nineteenth-Century England* (Cambridge: Cambridge University Press, 2013). See also Lemire, *Business of Everyday Life*; Stobart and Van Damme, *Modernity and the Second-Hand Trade*; John Styles, *The Dress of the People: Everyday Fashion in Eighteenth-Century England* (New Haven, CT: Yale University Press, 2007).

17. Sean Patrick Adams, "Warming the Poor and Growing Consumers: Fuel Philanthropy in the Early Republic's North," *Journal of American History* 95, no. 1 (June 2008): 72.

18. Mathew Carey, *Advices and Suggestions to Increase the Comforts of Persons in Humble Circumstances* (Philadelphia: n. p., 1832).

19. James Mease, *On the Utility of Public Loan Offices and Savings Funds, Established by City Authorities* ([Philadelphia?]: n. p., 1836), 2–3.

20. *Report of the Library Committee of the Pennsylvania Society for the Promotion of Public Economy* (Philadelphia: S. Merritt, 1817), 19.

21. Woloson, *In Hock*, 112; Adams, "Warming the Poor," 72–73.

22. "Accommodating," *Public Ledger*, June 6, 1840; City Council Records, 1811: 294, Baltimore City Archives. See also Newman, *Embodied History*, 31–32; Margaret B. Tinkcom, "The New Market in Second Street," *Pennsylvania Magazine of History and Biography*

82, no. 4 (October 1958): 393–394; Charles William Janson, *The Stranger in America: Containing Observations Made During a Long Residence in That Country . . .* (London: Printed for James Cundee, 1807), 180.

23. Candice L. Harrison, "'Free Trade and Hucksters' Rights!' Envisioning Economic Democracy in the Early Republic," *Pennsylvania Magazine of History and Biography* 137, no. 2 (April 2013): 147–177; Gergely Baics, "Is Access to Food a Public Good? Meat Provisioning in Early New York City, 1790–1820," *Journal of Urban History* 39, no. 4 (July 2013): 643–668.

24. "Those on their way to the Bedford Springs . . . ," *Aurora* (Philadelphia), July 31, 1828; Baldwin, *In the Watches of the Night*, 112.

25. For ongoing debates about the "swinish multitude" in Baltimore's streets, see City Council Records, 1824: 409, 1825: 173, 178, 179, 1842: 458, 1843: 342, 1844: 463, 1847: 438, 713, 1849: 894, 1850: 478, 1851: 676, Baltimore City Archives (hereafter BCA). See also Catherine McNeur, "The 'Swinish Multitude': Controversies over Hogs in Antebellum New York City," *Journal of Urban History* 37, no. 5 (September 2011): 639–660.

26. "Woman-Pelicans," *Sun* (Baltimore), October 18, 1839.

27. "A Peep at the Markets," *Sun*, August 23, 1839; "Watermelons," *North American*, June 30, 1847.

28. City Council Records, 1824: 337, BCA. On the tradeoff between convenience and long-term planning, see Rockman, *Scraping By*, 173–185. For more on mock auctions, consult Corey Goettsch's essay in this collection.

29. Consider the reemergence of debates over forestalling, an ancient market infraction most often associated with hucksters and itinerants that acquired new significance and scale in antebellum America, particularly after the Panic of 1837. "Provisions," *Sun*, August 23, 1837; "Flour Speculators," *Sun*, November 14, 1837; "Forestalling in the markets, alias *huckstering* . . . ," *Sun*, November 6, 1838; "Beef," *Sun*, April 6, 1839; "Tabitha Squaretoes, the Mermaid," *Sun*, January 11, 1840; "Forestalling," *Sun*, September 28, 1841; "A Poor Man," *Sun*, October 13, 1841; "Forestalling," *Public Ledger*, November 27, 1838; "Forestalling," *North American*, April 10, 1839; "Household Markets," *North American*, May 13, 1847.

30. Stansell, *City of Women*, 50–51, 204–206.

31. City Council Records, 1824: 482, BCA. As Wendy Woloson notes, junk dealers, not pawnshops or secondhand stores, were "the true movers of stolen goods." Woloson, *In Hock*, 128–129.

32. "Judge Todd's Charge," *Pennsylvania Inquirer and Daily Courier* (Philadelphia), November 10, 1838. For more on sex, commerce, and space in antebellum cities, see Katie Hemphill's chapter in this volume.

33. Donna Dennis, *Licentious Gotham: Erotic Publishing and Its Prosecution in Nineteenth-Century New York* (Cambridge, MA: Harvard University Press, 2009); David M. Henkin, *City Reading: Written Words and Public Spaces in Antebellum New York* (New York: Columbia University Press, 1998), 110–113; Patricia Cline Cohen, Timothy J. Gilfoyle, and Helen Lefkowitz Horowitz, *The Flash Press: Sporting Male Weeklies in 1840s New York*

(Chicago: University of Chicago Press, 2008), 93–94; and Paul Erickson's essay in this volume.

34. City Council Records, 1827: 424, BCA; Graham Russell Hodges, *New York City Cartmen, 1667–1850* (New York: New York University Press, 1986). As Hodges notes, cartmen likewise viewed their contributions to the urban economy through the lens of the public good, serving as a reminder that the concept of the public good was both potent and pliable in the antebellum period.

35. At the time, only forty-eight watchmen patrolled Baltimore. "Mayor's Communication," *Patriot* (Baltimore), February 19, 1817; City Council Records, 1828: 423–425, BCA.

36. Minutes of the Common Council of Philadelphia, December 17, 1810, PCA; Singleton to Watson, August 4, 1826, Joseph Watson Papers, Historical Society of Pennsylvania (hereafter JWP, HSP).

37. Licensing also served a range of fiscal uses for money-strapped municipal governments, but few contemporaries saw its commercial and social dimensions as discrete. As one jurist noted in 1876, "Custom has much to do in determining whether certain classes of exactions are to be regarded as taxes or as duties imposed for regulation." Thomas M. Cooley, *A Treatise on the Law of Taxation* (Chicago: Callaghan, 1876), 396–397. For a short discussion of licensing as an instrument of regulation, see William J. Novak, *The People's Welfare: Law and Regulation in Nineteenth-Century America* (Chapel Hill: University of North Carolina Press, 1996), 90–95, 172–177.

38. *A Statistical Inquiry into the Condition of the People of Colour, of the City and Districts of Philadelphia* (Philadelphia: Kite and Walton, 1849), 17–18; Gary B. Nash, *Forging Freedom: The Formation of Philadelphia's Black Community, 1720–1840* (Cambridge, MA: Harvard University Press, 1988), 149–150; Christopher Phillips, *Freedom's Port: The African American Community of Baltimore, 1790–1860* (Urbana: University of Illinois Press, 1997), 108–113, 203.

39. *City Characters; or, Familiar Scenes in Town* (Philadelphia: G. S. Appleton, 1851), 5; *The Cries of Philadelphia: Ornamented with Elegant Wood Cuts* (Philadelphia: Johnson and Warner, 1810).

40. Samuel Otter, *Philadelphia Stories: America's Literature of Race and Freedom* (New York: Oxford University Press, 2010), 81–88.

41. "The Presentment of the Grand Jury of Union District [South Carolina]," *American Farmer* (Baltimore), November 13, 1839; "Desultory Observations, on Diverse Matters," *American Farmer*, August 21, 1839.

42. Jennifer Hull Dorsey, *Hirelings: African American Workers and Free Labor in Early Maryland* (Ithaca, NY: Cornell University Press, 2011), 84; Ira Berlin, *Slaves Without Masters: The Free Negro in the Antebellum South* (New York: New Press, 1974), 241–243; Paul A. Gilje and Howard B. Rock, "'Sweep O! Sweep O!': African-American Chimney Sweeps and Citizenship in the New Nation," *William and Mary Quarterly* 51, no. 3 (July 1994): 507–538.

43. "An Ordinance for the Admission and Regulation of Pawnbrokers" (1838), *Ordinances of the Mayor and City Council of Baltimore* (Baltimore: John D. Toy, 1838), 93–96;

"An Ordinance Regulating Pawn Brokers" (1824), *Digest of the Acts of Assembly, and the Ordinances, of the Commissioners and Inhabitants of the Kensington District of Northern Liberties* (Philadelphia: Joseph Rakestraw, 1832), 27–28; Woloson, *In Hock*, esp. 122–153.

44. "Presentment of the Grand Jury," *Poulson's American Daily Advertiser* (Philadelphia), November 1, 1820.

45. Mayor's Correspondence, 1824: 831, BCA.

46. "Autobiography of a Fip Shin-Plaster," *Sun*, March 2, 1838. Object narratives were rare in antebellum America, although James Fenimore Cooper did compose a well-known one, "Autobiography of a Pocket-Handkerchief," for *Graham's Magazine* in early 1843. There was, however, a long tradition in British literature of narrating the life of goods from which the anonymous author of the shinplaster piece could draw. Mark Blackwell, ed., *The Secret Life of Things: Animals, Objects, and It-Narratives in Eighteenth-Century England* (Cranbury, NJ: Associated University Presses, 2007).

47. "Autobiography of a Fip Shin-Plaster." For more on shinplasters, consult Joshua Greenberg's essay in this volume. For more on the "promiscuous circulation" of paper money in urban economies, see Henkin, *City Reading*, 137–165. On the relationship between money, cleanliness, and race, see Michael O'Malley, *Face Value: The Entwined Histories of Money and Race in America* (Chicago: University of Chicago Press, 2012).

48. Private business interests solved this dilemma before the state did. Scott Sandage notes that "as commerce moved faster and farther, credit agents trumped individual self-control with institutional surveillance" in the 1840s. Sandage, *Born Losers*, 111.

49. On "good society," see "The Night Hawk, No. 22," *Mechanics' Free Press* (Philadelphia), April 25, 1829 (hereafter *MFP*); Blumin, *The Emergence of the Middle Class*, 122. I am grateful to Matthew Osborn for sharing his research on the Night Hawk, including the identity of the author. Osborn, "The First Batman: Identity and Popular Romanticism in the Early Republic" (paper presented at the annual meeting for the Society for Historians of the Early American Republic, Philadelphia, Pennsylvania, July 14–17, 2011).

50. Nathaniel Lightner to Watson, July 2, 1825, JWP, HSP.

51. A. Porter to Watson, October 20, 1825, JWP, HSP.

52. George Bartram to Watson, January 10, 1828, Lightner to Watson, July 2, 1825, JWP, HSP.

53. Charles Williams to Watson, December 16, 1824, JWP, HSP. For other instances, see Henry Kelly to Watson, June 23, 1825, Charles Mitchell to C. J. Coxe, September 30, 1825, Charles Mitchell to Watson, July 16, 1827, JWP, HSP.

54. Joseph Williams to Watson, November 17, 1825, JWP, HSP.

55. Lightner to Watson, January 4, 1826, Cummins to Watson, October 22, 1827, JWP, HSP.

56. As Stephen Mihm notes, arguably the most effective "passers" of counterfeit money were those unaware they were doing so. Mihm, *Nation of Counterfeiters*, 209–259.

57. "Proceedings of a numerous and respectable meeting . . ." (ca. 1823–1828), William Smith to Watson, August 22, 1825, JWP, HSP. On the prevention of horse theft, see Lightener to Watson, July 2, 1825; Westcott to Watson, May 23, 1825; E. H. Cummins to

Watson, October 22, 1827; Roland Diller to Watson, September 9, 1825; Lightner to Watson, March 18, 1826; Thomas Mott to Watson, October 26, 1824; Smith to Watson, August 22, 1825; Jesse Sharp to Watson, August 8, 1825; M. T. Simpson to Watson, March 22, 1826; Westcott to Watson, January 14, 1825, JWP, HSP; *Constitution of the Centre-Square Association of Montgomery County, for the Recovery of Stolen Horses, and Detection of Thieves* (Norristown, PA: J. Winnard, 1821); *Constitution and Rules of the Union Association of Newtown and Parts Adjacent in Delaware County, for Detecting Horse Thieves, and the Recovery of Horses and Other Stolen Property: Adopted and Subscribed January 3, 1835* (Newtown, PA: Wm. Sloanaker, 1835).

58. "An Operative Citizen" [William Heighton], *The Principles of Aristocratic Legislation, Developed in an Address, Delivered to the Working People of the District of Southwark, and Townships of Moyamensing and Passyunk . . .* (Philadelphia: J. Coates, 1828); "Unlettered Mechanic" [William Heighton], *An Address, Delivered Before the Mechanics and Working Classes Generally, of the City and County of Philadelphia . . .* (Philadelphia: Printed at the Office of the *Mechanics' Gazette*, 1827); "A Fellow-Laborer" [William Heighton], *An Address to the Members of Trade Societies, and to the Working Classes Generally . . .* (Philadelphia: Published by the Author, 1827); David Ricardo, *On the Principles of Political Economy and Taxation* (London: J. Murray, 1817), 1–48. Ricardo's influence on Americans was the greatest of all European economists, according to Paul K. Conkin, *Prophets of Prosperity: America's First Political Economists* (Bloomington: Indiana University Press, 1980), 30.

59. Louis H. Arky, "The Mechanics' Union of Trade Associations and the Formation of the Philadelphia Workingmen's Movement," *Pennsylvania Magazine of History and Biography* 76, no. 2 (April 1952): 142–176; Alexander Saxton, "Problems of Class and Race in the Origins of the Mass Circulation Press," *American Quarterly* 36, no. 2 (Summer 1984): 211–234; Timothy Helwig, "Black and White Print: Cross-Racial Strategies of Class Solidarity in *Mechanics' Free Press* and *Freedom's Journal*," *American Periodicals* 19, no. 2 (2009): 117–135.

60. The Night Hawk was influenced by exposés of Paris and London in the mid-1820s, such as the memoir of the former head of Paris's undercover detective agency, Eugène François Vidocq, first published in English in 1828. The relatively recent advent of criminal court reportage in newspapers also served as an inspiration for the Night Hawk's style and subject matter. Eugène François Vidocq, *Memoirs of Vidocq, Principal Agent of the French Police Until 1827* (London: Printed for Hunt and Clarke, 1828); Saxton, "Origins of the Mass Circulation Press," 211–234.

61. As Jeffrey Sklansky has shown, the popularity of melodrama in the 1820s and 1830s provided the literary influence for William Leggett, whose critiques of corruption and capitalists shared many features with the Night Hawk. Jeffrey Sklansky, "William Leggett and the Melodrama of the Market," in *Capitalism Takes Command*, ed. Zakim and Kornblith, 203–210. See also Osborn, "First Batman."

62. "The Night Hawk, No. 1," *MFP*, July 5, 1828.

63. "The Night Hawk, No. 41," *MFP*, January 2, 1830.

64. “The Night Hawk, No. 36,” *MFP*, November 14, 1829; “The Night Hawk, No. 52,” *MFP*, March 27, 1830.

65. “The Night Hawk, No. 23,” *MFP*, May 9, 1829. On police reforms after Dallas, who resigned after less than a year to pursue greater political ambitions, see David R. Johnson, *Policing the Urban Underworld: The Impact of Crime on the Development of the American Police, 1800–1887* (Philadelphia: Temple University Press, 1979), 12–40.

66. “The Night Hawk, No. 34,” *MFP*, October 17, 1829. On contemporaneous efforts to interpret the nocturnal landscapes of the city, see Baldwin, *In the Watches of the Night*, esp. 75–103. See also Katie Hemphill’s discussion in this volume of Fells Point in Baltimore, a neighborhood roughly analogous to the Northern Liberties both in its social composition and in popular attitudes toward it.

67. “The Night Hawk, No. 42,” *MFP*, January 9, 1830.

68. “The Night Hawk, No. 15,” *MFP*, December 27, 1828. See also Luskey, *On the Make*, 177–205.

69. “The Night Hawk, No. 53,” *MFP*, April 3, 1830. On the politicization of fashion, see Linzy A. Brekke, “‘The Scourge of Fashion’: Political Economy and the Politics of Consumption in the Early Republic,” *Early American Studies: An Interdisciplinary Journal* 3, no. 1 (Spring 2005): 111–139. Matthew Osborn shows that the author of the Night Hawk was also the author behind “Peter Single,” another *MFP* column that focused extensively on the political meanings and pitfalls of fashion. Osborn, “First Batman.”

70. “Foreign Fashions—No. 2,” *MFP*, May 2, 1829.

71. “The Night Hawk, No. 40,” *MFP*, December 26, 1829.

72. “The Night Hawk, No. 40,” *MFP*, December 26, 1829; “The Night Hawk, No. 41,” *MFP*, January 2, 1830.

73. Dell Upton, “‘Another City’: The Urban Cultural Landscape in the Early Republic,” in *Everyday Life in the Early Republic*, ed. Catherine E. Hutchins (Winterthur, DE: Henry Francis DuPont Winterthur Museum, 1994), 61–117; Wendy Bellion, *Citizen Spectator: Art, Illusion, and Visual Perception in Early National America* (Chapel Hill: University of North Carolina Press for the Omohundro Institute of Early American History and Culture, 2011); Nick Yablon, *Untimely Ruins: An Archaeology of American Urban Modernity, 1819–1919* (Chicago: University of Chicago Press, 2009); Carl Smith, *City Water, City Life: Water and the Infrastructure of Ideas in Urbanizing Philadelphia, Boston, and Chicago* (Chicago: University of Chicago Press, 2013).

CHAPTER 3. THE ERA OF SHINPLASTERS

1. Before the passage of Illinois’s free banking act in 1851, all banks needed special legislative approval. For more on the free banking era in Illinois, see Andrew J. Economopoulos, “Illinois Free Banking Experience,” *Journal of Money, Credit and Banking* 20, no. 2 (May 1988): 249–264; and George William Dowrie, “The Development of Banking in Illinois, 1817–1863,” *University of Illinois Studies in the Social Sciences* 2, no. 4 (December 1913): 2–181.

2. "The Na-Chu-Sa-House," *Dixon Telegraph* (Dixon, IL), December 10, 1853. The name Nachusa was taken from the Winnebego term Nada-chu-ra-sah, or head-hair-white, the name for town founder John Dixon.

3. William D. Barge, *Early Lee County: Being Some Chapters in the History of the Early Days in Lee County, Illinois* (Chicago: Barnard and Miller, 1918), 103–104.

4. "New Money," *Milwaukee Sentinel* (Milwaukee, WI), June 8, 1841, reprinted from the *Chicago Democrat*. Italics in original.

5. In this essay, I concentrate on notes from regulated banks and quasi-legal unregulated entities. Stephen Mihm has examined the variety of counterfeit bank notes in circulation and their important and lasting ramifications for the culture of paper money in *A Nation of Counterfeiters*.

6. Frederick W. Seward, *Reminiscences of a War-Time Statesman and Diplomat 1830–1915* (New York: G. P. Putnam's Sons, 1916), 22.

7. "Mr. Beverley Lee; or, The Days of the Shin-Plasters," in George P. Morris, *The Little Frenchman and His Water Lots, with Other Sketches of the Times* (Philadelphia: Lea and Blanchard, 1839), 137.

8. See Bessie Louise Pierce, *A History of Chicago: The Beginning of a City 1673–1848* (Chicago: University of Chicago Press, 1937), 149–170; and Charlotte Reeve Conover, *The Story of Dayton* (Dayton: Greater Dayton Association, 1917), 133–134, for good examples.

9. For just a few examples, see Wendell A. Wolka, *Indiana Obsolete Notes and Scrip* (Iola, WI: Society of Paper Money Collectors, 1978); Wendell A. Wolka, *A History of Nineteenth Century Ohio Obsolete Bank Notes and Scrip* (Iola, WI: Society of Paper Money Collectors, 2004); and Chester L. Krause, *Wisconsin Obsolete Bank Notes and Scrip* (Iola, WI: Society of Paper Money Collectors, 1994).

10. Richard H. Timberlake, "The Significance of Unaccounted Currencies," *Journal of Economic History* 41, no. 4 (December 1981): 853–866.

11. On some of the controversies around late eighteenth-century paper money, see Farley Grubb, "State Redemption of the Continental Dollar, 1779–90," *William and Mary Quarterly* 69, no. 1 (January 2012): 147–180; and Woody Holton, "Primitive Accumulation," *Labor: Studies in Working-Class History of the Americas* 6, no. 3 (Fall 2009): 21–36.

12. Endless accounts of cash shortages exist for the period, but for two typical examples, see Lucy Maynard to Libbit and Able Pipper, December 3, 1839, quoted in John Mack Faragher, *Sugar Creek: Life on the Illinois Prairie* (New Haven, CT: Yale University Press, 1986), 135; and Roxanna Stowell to Dexter Whittemore, June 1835, quoted in Thomas Dublin, "Women and Outwork in a Nineteenth-Century New England Town: Fitzwilliam, New Hampshire, 1830–1850," in *The Countryside in the Age of Capitalist Transformation*, ed. Steven Hahn and Jonathan Prude (Chapel Hill: University of North Carolina Press, 1985), 64.

13. "The Era of Shinplasters," *New York Times*, October 12, 1857.

14. Bray Hammond, *Banks and Politics in America: From the Revolution to the Civil War* (Princeton, NJ: Princeton University Press, 1957), 227–250. For an alternative view of money, politics, and the government during these years and especially treasury notes,

see Richard Timberlake, *Monetary Policy in the United States: An Intellectual and Institutional History* (Chicago: University of Chicago Press, 1993), 13–27.

15. *The History of a Little Frenchman and His Bank Notes. "Rags! Rags! Rags!"* (Philadelphia: Pub. for the author by Edward Earle, 1815). The story obviously resonated with later generations and saw multiple reprints. The *Journal of Banking* introduced one version in 1842, noting that the story was from 1815 and "at that time, as now, the banks were in a state of suspension, but then every body that chose made money out of paper, and notes for the fractional parts of a dollar took the place of silver change." "The History of a Little Frenchman and His Bank Notes," *Journal of Banking* (February 16, 1842), 259.

16. *The History of a Little Frenchman and His Bank Notes*, 4–5.

17. Ibid., 8.

18. Joseph B. Felt, *An Historical Account of Massachusetts Currency* (Boston: Perkins and Marvin, 1839), 222.

19. For some examples, see H. A. Gray, "Early Boston Shinplasters," *Numismatist* 28, no. 7 (July 1915): 260–261.

20. William Goold, "John Taber and Son of Portland, and Their Paper Money," *Collections and Proceedings of the Maine Historical Society*, 2nd ser., 9 (January 1898): 128–132.

21. Iowa was not alone here. Arkansas also amended its constitution in 1846 to outlaw banks of issue. See Matt Rothert, *Arkansas Obsolete Notes and Scrip: The State That Outlawed Banks* (North Attleboro, MA: Society of Paper Money Collectors, 1985). Texas outlawed banks of issue in 1845, but allowed the Commercial and Agricultural Bank of Galveston to keep its 1835 charter until it expired in 1855.

22. Erling A. Erickson, "Money and Banking in a 'Bankless' State: Iowa, 1846–1857," *Business History Review* 43, no. 2 (Summer 1969): 182.

23. "Wisconsin," *Wisconsin Territorial Gazette and Burlington Advertiser* (Burlington, Wisconsin Territory [Iowa]), December 9, 1837.

24. "The Shinplaster Era," *Chicago Daily Tribune*, November 11, 1857.

25. Quoted in H. Earl Cook, "Iowa's First Banking System," *Annals of Iowa* 32 (1955): 607.

26. John Anthony Muscalus, *Album of Georgia County and City Scrip* (Bridgeport, PA: Historical Paper Money Research Institute, 1975).

27. John Anthony Muscalus, *Pennsylvania Borough and City Scrip* (Bridgeport, PA: Historical Paper Money Research Institute, 1975).

28. "Cockroaches vs. Shinplasters," *The Huntress* (Washington, DC), July 22, 1837. The story was reprinted from the *New Orleans Picayune*. I want to thank Jessica Lepler for helping me analyze this anecdote.

29. "Shin-plasters," *New-Yorker*, June 24, 1837.

30. *Laws of the Commonwealth of Massachusetts in Relation to Banks and Banking* (Boston: Press of the Centinel and Gazette, 1836).

31. "Kentucky," *The American Jurist and Law Magazine, for July and October, 1834* (Boston: Lilly, Wait, 1834), 509.

32. "Law of Pennsylvania," *Luzerne County Gleaner* (Wilkes-Barre, PA), April 11, 1817.

33. "Wilkes-Barre Academy," *Luzerne County Gleaner*, May 1, 1818.

34. Seward, *Reminiscences of a War-Time Statesman and Diplomat*, 21.

35. Frederick W. Seward, *Autobiography of William H. Seward, from 1801 to 1834 with a Memoir of His Life, and Selections from His Letters from 1831 to 1846* (New York: D. Appleton, 1877), 357–359.

36. *The Perpetual Laws of the Commonwealth of Massachusetts from the Establishment of Its Constitution in the Year 1780, to February, 1807*, IV (Boston: Thomas and Andrews, 1807), 294.

37. Nathaniel Ames, *The Diary of Dr. Nathaniel Ames of Dedham, Massachusetts* (Camden, ME: Picton Press, 1998), 919 and 1093–1094.

38. Nathaniel Ames Daybook, April 10, 1805, Dedham Historical Society.

39. See David Henkin, *City Reading: Written Words and Public Spaces in Antebellum New York* (New York: Columbia University Press, 1998), 137–165; and Robert Gamble's essay in this volume.

40. Timberlake, "Significance of Unaccounted Currencies," 865.

41. Ibid., 862.

42. "Bank Commissioners' Report," *United States Commercial and Statistical Register* (Philadelphia), February 5, 1840.

43. "Kentucky," 510. The charter explicitly prohibited issuing notes. See *Acts Passed at the First Session of the Forty-Second General Assembly for the Commonwealth of Kentucky* (Frankfort, KY: Albert G. Hodges, 1834), 499–500.

44. For a more developed discussion of the relationship between politics and general incorporation laws, see L. Ray Gunn, *The Decline of Authority: Public Economic Policy and Political Development in New York State, 1800–1860* (Ithaca, NY: Cornell University Press, 1988), 222–245.

45. Charlotte Reeve Conover, *The Story of Dayton* (Dayton, OH: Greater Dayton Association, 1917), 133–134.

46. Robert W. Steele and Mary Davis Steele, *Early Dayton: With Important Facts and Incidents from the Founding of the City of Dayton, Ohio to the Hundredth Anniversary, 1796–1896* (Dayton, OH: U. B. Publishing House, 1896), 167.

47. "Thomas Morrison," Dayton, OH, 12½¢, January 31, 1838, http://currency.ha.com/c/item.zx?saleNo=329&lotIdNo=63011 (accessed June 5, 2013).

48. "Small Notes," *Financial Register of the United States* (Washington, DC), January 17, 1838.

49. "The Shin-Plaster Currency in Court," *Extra Globe* (Washington, DC), June 7, 1838.

50. "Our Whig Shin Plaster Corporation," *Democratic Free Press* (Detroit, Michigan Territory), September 5, 1838.

51. "Mayor Jones," *Detroit Free Press*, February 29, 1840.

52. "A Just Rebuke," *Ohio Statesman* (Columbus), April 26, 1843.

53. *Acts of a Local Nature, Passed at the First Session of the Thirty-Sixth General Assembly of the State of Ohio Begun and Held in the City of Columbus, December 7, 1837* (Columbus, OH: Samuel Medary Printer to the State, 1838), 277.

54. "A Just Rebuke," *Ohio Statesman*, April 26, 1843. See also "Presented as a Nuisance," *Two Worlds* (New York), May 7, 1843.

55. A similar but somewhat satirical indictment of passing bank paper was issued by the Grand Jury of Grant County, Wisconsin, in 1853. This was followed by the citizens of Hazel Green, also in Grant County, voting to prohibit using paper money for property purchases. See "Bank Paper in the West," *Milwaukee Daily Sentinel*, April 18, 1853.

56. Henry Dacre, *Sober Second Thoughts* (New York: Henry Robinson, 1838).

57. "The Undersigned Citizens of Chillicothe," *Scioto Gazette* (Chillicothe, OH), August 17, 1843. For more back and forth over banking regulation in Chillicothe, see "Bank Reform," *Scioto Gazette*, September 20, 1838.

58. "The Better Currency," *Ohio Statesman*, June 2, 1841 and "The Better Currency," *Cleveland Daily Herald* (Cleveland, OH), April 26, 1841. For other articles in the "Better Currency" discussion, see *Scioto Gazette*, June 9, 1842; *Daily Scioto* (Chillicothe, OH), October 14, 1846; *Ohio Statesman*, March 5, May 12, June 2, June 6, June 23, 1841, and August 9, 1843; *Cleveland Daily Herald*, January 28, January 31, and September 16, 1840.

59. "Taking the Pledge," *Brooklyn Eagle* (Brooklyn, NY), June 26, 1843.

60. "The Undersigned Citizens of Chillicothe," *Scioto Gazette*, July 13, 1843. A similar meeting occurred in Hillsborough just a week earlier.

61. On the Free Banking Era, see Arthur J. Rolnick and Warren E. Weber, "New Evidence on the Free Banking Era," *American Economic Review* 73, no. 5 (December 1983): 1080–1091; and Jay C. Shambaugh, "An Experiment with Multiple Currencies: The American Monetary System from 1838–1860," *Explorations in Economic History* 43, no. 4 (October 2006): 629.

62. See "The Era of Shinplasters," which ran in the *New York Times* during the height of the Panic of 1857 as both a remembrance of the currency woes of the Panic of 1837 and a warning that another wave of money uncertainty might be coming.

63. "Shinplasters," *Brooklyn Eagle*, March 14, 1851.

64. "What the Country Gained by Discrediting Shinplasters," *Chicago Daily Tribune*, February 12, 1858.

65. Bridgeton was not incorporated until 1865, and its population was only 6,830 as late as the 1870 federal census.

66. Helen McKearin and George Skinner McKearin, *Two Hundred Years of American Blown Glass* (New York: Crown Publishers, 1958), 125.

CHAPTER 4. THE RAG RACE

1. Quotation from James Fenimore Cooper, *The Redskins* (New York: Burgess and Stringer, 1846), 54. On New York's growth rate, see Wilentz, *Chants Democratic*, 109. For a selection of impressions of New York in the middle decades of the century, see Kenneth T. Jackson and David S. Dunbar, eds., *Empire City* (New York: Columbia University Press, 2002), 143–254. On filth in city streets, see Tyler Anbinder, *Five Points: The*

19th-Century New York City Neighborhood That Invented Tap Dance, Stole Elections, and Became the World's Most Notorious Slum (New York: Free Press, 2001), 82–83. On grand retail emporia, see Robert Hendrickson, *The Grand Emporiums: The Illustrated History of America's Great Department Stores* (New York: Stein and Day, 1979), 25–149; Deborah S. Gardner, "'A Paradise of Fashion': A.T. Stewart's Department Store, 1862–1875," in *A Needle, A Bobbin, A Strike: Women Needleworkers in America*, ed. Joan M. Jensen and Sue Davidson (Philadelphia: Temple University Press, 1984), 60–80.

2. O.S. Fowler, "Hereditary Descent: Its Laws and Facts Applied to Human Improvement," *American Phrenological Journal* 10, no. 4 (April 1848): 117. Such urban commercial clusters were not unusual. Nassau Street, for example, gained notoriety as the center of the city's "smut district."

3. Horatio Alger, Jr., *Ragged Dick; or, Street Life in New York with the Boot Blacks* (Philadelphia: Loring, 1868), 45–49.

4. For a selection of these depictions, see "Further of the Investigations—The Custom House Officers Too Sharp for the Old Clothes Men," *New York Herald*, July 8, 1841; George Foster, *New York in Slices* (New York: W.F. Burgess, 1849), 13–16, 30, 32–33; Professor Ingraham, "Glimpses at Gotham—No. IV," *The Ladies Companion* 10, no. 4 (April 1839): 291; Anonymous, *The Family of the Seisers* (New York: J.M. Elliott, 1844), 32, 147; Cornelius Mathews, "The Ghost of New York," *United States Magazine, and Democratic Review* 16, no. 79 (January 1845): 10, 74; Henry Morford, *The Days of Shoddy* (New York: T.B. Peterson and Brothers, 1863), 182; Fowler, "Hereditary Descent," 117; Charles Loring Brace, *The Dangerous Classes of New York* (New York: Wynkoop and Hallenbeck, 1872), 195–196; "The Pawnbrokers and the Savings Banks," *Merchants' Magazine and Commercial Review* 20 (June 1849): 669; Walt Whitman, "Our City," *New York Aurora* (New York), March 28, 1842, in *Walt Whitman of the New York* Aurora, *Editor at Twenty-Two*, ed. Joseph Jay Rubin and Charles H. Brown (State College, PA: Bald Eagle Press, 1950), 18; Richard Stott, *Workers in the Metropolis: Class, Ethnicity, and Youth in Antebellum New York City* (Ithaca, NY: Cornell University Press, 1990), 186n50; Irving Allen, *The City in Slang: New York Life and Popular Speech* (New York: Oxford University Press, 1993), 201; Frederic Jaher, *A Scapegoat in the Wilderness* (Cambridge, MA: Harvard University Press, 1994), 222; Rudolf Glanz, *Jews in the Old American Folklore* (New York: Waldon Press, 1961), 100–103, 147–165; Louise A. Mayo, *The Ambivalent Image: Nineteenth-Century America's Perception of the Jew* (Cranbury, NJ: Fairleigh Dickinson University Press, 1988), 111–112.

5. George Sala, *Dutch Pictures* (London: Tinsley Brothers, 1861), 322; Henry Mayhew, *London Labour and the London Poor*, vol. 1 (London: George Woodfall and Sons, 1851), 368; Beverly Lemire, *Dress, Culture and Commerce: The English Clothing Trade before the Factory, 1660–1800* (New York: Palgrave Macmillan, 1997), 75–77, 79–85; Beverly Lemire, "Consumerism in Preindustrial and Early Industrial England: The Trade in Secondhand Clothes," *Journal of British Studies* 27, no. 1 (January 1988): 14–17.

6. "The Jewish Clothesman," *London Jewish Chronicle* (hereafter *JC*), December 21, 1849; Todd Endelman, *The Jews of Georgian England, 1714–1830* (Ann Arbor: University of Michigan Press, 1999), 182–185; Anne and Roger Cowen, *Victorian Jews Through British*

Eyes (Oxford: Littman Library of Jewish Civilization, 1998), 4–8; Anon., *A View of London* (London, 1804), 107.

7. Historians of Anglo-Jewry have paid some attention to Jews and old clothing in the eighteenth century. See, for example, Harold Pollins, *Economic History of the Jews in England* (Rutherford, NJ: Farleigh Dickinson University Press, 1982), 66–69; Endelman, *Jews of Georgian England*, 179–183.

8. On shadow economies, see Thomas Buchner and Philip R. Hoffmann-Rehnitz, eds., *Shadow Economies and Irregular Work in Urban Europe* (Berlin: LIT, 2011), 3–36.

9. See Lemire, *Dress, Culture and Commerce*, 75–77.

10. Claude Lévi Strauss, *Totemism* (Boston: Beacon Press, 1963), 89.

11. While I know of no dedicated study focused on the secondhand clothing trade, several essays in this volume, particularly those by Robert Gamble and Ellen Garvey, have begun to redress this gap in the literature. Wendy Woloson has discussed the interrelationship of the trade with pawnbroking. See Woloson, *In Hock*, 62–64, 71–73. By contrast the subject has received considerable attention in England. Several scholars have examined the trade as a case study of the penetration of consumerism into preindustrial Britain. See, for example, John Styles, *The Dress of the People* (New Haven, CT: Yale University Press, 2008); Madeleine Ginsburg, "Rags to Riches: The Second-Hand Clothes Trade 1700–1978," *Costume* 14 (1980): 121–135; Lemire, "Consumerism in Preindustrial and Early Industrial England;" Beverly Lemire, "Shifting Currency: The Culture and Economy of the Second Hand Trade in England, c.1600–1850," in *Old Clothes, New Looks*, ed. Alexandra Palmer and Hazel Clark (New York: Bloomsbury Academic, 2005): 29–48; Miles Lambert, "'Cast-Off Wearing Apparell': The Consumption and Distribution of Second-Hand Clothing in Northern England During the Long Eighteenth Century," *Textile History* 35, no. 1 (May 2004): 1–26.

12. Ginsburg, "Rags to Riches," 122–123, 127; Lemire, "Trade in Secondhand Clothes," 1–6.

13. Peter P. Hinks, *To Awaken My Afflicted Brethren: David Walker and the Problem of Antebellum Slave Resistance* (University Park: Pennsylvania State University Press, 1997), 66–68. On the Jewish population in Boston, see Jonathan D. Sarna, Ellen Smith, and Scott-Martin Kosofsky, eds., *The Jews of Boston* (New Haven, CT: Yale University Press, 2005), 343.

14. See John Marshall, *Jews in Nevada: A History* (Reno: University of Nevada Press, 2008), 107. On Chinese laundries in the gold fields of California, see Susan Lee Johnson, *Roaring Camp: The Social World of the California Gold Rush* (New York: W. W. Norton, 2000), 125–127. On Chinese immigrants and the clothing trade, see *Chinese Immigration: The Social, Moral, and Political Effect of Chinese Immigration* (Sacramento, CA: State Printing Office, 1876), 151; Otis Gibson, *The Chinese in America* (Cincinnati, OH: Hitchcock and Walden, 1877), 55.

15. Irish laborers may have been first drawn to the area in large numbers to work on the extension of the nearby St. Katherine's Docks in 1827–1828. H. J. Dyos, "Some Social Costs of Railway Building in London," *Journal of Transport History* 3, no. 1 (1957): 29n2;

Mayhew, *London Labour*, 1:109–111, 2:45–46. For Irish migration and settlement in London, see Jerry White, *London in the Nineteenth Century* (London: Cape, 2007), 130–131, 133–134; Lynn Hollen Lees, *Exiles of Erin: Irish Migrants in Victorian London* (Ithaca, NY: Cornell University Press, 1979), 44–50, 56–60, 67–68, 80; "Father Mathew in Rag-Fair," *Times* (London), August 30, 1843; "Ireland," *Times*, June 19, 1834: 6; "Letter from Moses Moses," *JC*, March 16, 1855; Parliamentary Papers (hereafter PP), 1847, q. 990. For the image of Irish migrants, see Roger Swift, "Heroes or Villains?: The Irish, Crime, and Disorder in Victorian England," *Albion* 29, no. 3 (1997): 399–421.

16. This impression is reinforced by a sample of court records. On Irish employment patterns in London, see Lees, *Exiles of Erin*, 92–100.

17. In Baltimore five of twenty-two Jewish household heads whose occupations were listed were involved in the dry goods and clothing business. Of these, four were of Dutch and English origin. Nine of eleven Jewish dry goods merchants in New Orleans were of Dutch origin. A somewhat weaker but still significant pattern was also evident in Philadelphia and Charleston. These data are extracted from Ira Rosenwaike, *On the Edge of Greatness: A Portrait of American Jewry in the Early National Period* (Cincinnati, OH: American Jewish Archives, 1985), 140–164. On the shortcomings of these data, see 165–170. For an early but uncorroborated claim that the first Jewish clothing dealers in Chatham Street had close ties with England, see John Stevens, "New York in the Nineteenth Century," *American Historical Magazine* 1, no. 5 (1906): 412. On a similar pattern in Syracuse, New York, in the 1840s and 1850s, see Jonathan S. Mesinger, "Peddlers and Merchants: The Geography of Work in a Nineteenth Century Jewish Community," (Department of Geography, Syracuse University Discussion Paper Series no. 38, 1977): 9.

18. Bertram Korn, *The Jews of Mobile, Alabama, 1763–1841* (Cincinnati, OH: Hebrew Union College Press, 1970), 40.

19. For the growth of New York, see Edwin G. Burrows and Mike Wallace, *Gotham: A History of New York City to 1898* (New York: Oxford University Press, 2000), 434; Wilentz, *Chants Democratic*, 24–27, 108–110; William Pencak, "Introduction: New York and the Rise of American Capitalism," in *New York and the Rise of American Capitalism*, ed. William Pencak and Conrad Edick Wright (New York: New York Historical Society, 1989), xii–xiii; Edward K. Spann, *The New Metropolis: New York City, 1840–1857* (New York: Columbia University Press, 1983), 1–44; Stott, *Workers in the Metropolis*, 7–24.

20. The stock description of Jewish hucksters cajoling out-of-towners into their stores formed part of a larger trope of bumpkins being tricked by weasely urbanites. Quotation from Glanz, *Jews in Old American Folklore*, 153. A California hat was a broad-brimmed felt hat.

21. Zakim, *Ready-Made Democracy*, 70. For colorful descriptions of the overlap between the trades of Chatham Street, see Brace, *Dangerous Classes of New York*, 195–196.

22. Lemire, "Shifting Currency," 34–40; Woloson, *In Hock*.

23. "Up the Spout," *Harper's New Monthly Magazine*, 19, no. 113, October 1859): 676.

24. In 1847 the chief of police counted 115 secondhand clothing stores, 215 junk shops, and 11 mock auction shops receiving stolen merchandise. "A Dark Picture," *Scientific*

American 2, no. 44 (July 24, 1847): 349. Quote from Burrows and Wallace, *Gotham*, 638. On mock auctions, see Corey Goettsch's essay in this volume. For earlier regulations governing secondhand dealers in New York, see New York (NY) Common Council, *A Law to Regulate Pawn-Brokers, and Dealers in the Purchase or Sale of Second-Hand Furniture, Metals or Clothes: Passed July 13th, 1812* (New York: John Hardcastle, 1812).

25. On middle-class culture, see Karen Halttunen, *Confidence Men and Painted Women: A Study of Middle-Class Culture in America, 1830–1870* (New Haven, CT: Yale University Press, 1983).

26. Quote from *Philadelphia Inquirer*, November 10, 1838; my thanks to Robert J. Gamble for sharing this with me. On clothing as a mark of respectability, see John F. Kasson, *Rudeness and Civility: Manners in Nineteenth-Century America* (New York: Hill and Wang, 1990), 117–121, 130. For women's clothing, see Halttunen, *Confidence Men and Painted Women*, 56–91. On fears about urban anomie, see Robert J. Gamble's essay in this volume; Paul A. Gilje, "Culture of Conflict: The Impact of Commercialization on New York Workingmen, 1787–1829," in *New York and the Rise of American Capitalism*, 249–267.

27. Quotation from Virginia Penny, *Employments of Women: A Cyclopaedia of Women's Work* (Boston: Walker, Wise, 1863), 135–136; For Penny's discussion of average wages, see xiii.

28. Anonymous, *One Hundred Years' Progress of the United States* (Hartford, CT: L. Stebbins, 1870), 309, 313–315.

29. Penny, *Employments of Women*, 135–136.

30. Famously the spendthrift Mary Todd Lincoln attempted to sell her wardrobe to a New York clothing dealer in 1867. "Among the Israelites," *Northern Monthly*, vol. 1 (June 1867): 117; Jesse Pope, *The Clothing Industry in New York* (Columbia: University of Missouri, 1905), 7; Susan Strasser, *Waste and Want* (New York: Metropolitan Books, 1999), 51, 60; Judith Greenfield, "The Role of Jews in the Development of the Clothing Industry in the United States," *Yivo Annual* 2 (1948): 181; Egal Feldman, "Jews in the Early Growth of New York City's Men's Clothing Trade," *American Jewish Archives* 12, no. 1 (1960): 5–7.

31. For evocative descriptions, see Penny, *Employments of Women*, 135–136; David W. Mitchell, *Ten Years in America: Being an Englishman's View of Men and Things in the North and South* (London: Smith, Elder, 1862), 58–59; my thanks to Shari Rabin for sharing this with me; R. P. Forster, *A Collection of the Most Celebrated Voyages and Travels* (Newcastle upon Tyne: Mckenzie and Dent, 1818), 209; William Whitecar, *Four Years Aboard the Whaleship* (Philadelphia: J. B. Lippincott, 1864), 31, 190; Arthur Hertzberg in *The Jews in America* (New York: Columbia University Press, 1997), 93; Rowena Olegario, "'That Mysterious People': Jewish Merchants, Transparency, and Community in Mid-Nineteenth Century America," *Business History Review* 73, no. 2 (June 1999): 165–166; Hasia Diner, *The Jews of the United States, 1654–2000* (Berkeley: University of California Press, 2006), 102. For Chatham Street abroad, see Martha Williams, *A Year in China* (New York: Hurd and Houghton, 1864), 194; Isaac Wiley, *China and Japan* (Cincinnati, OH: Walden and Stowe, 1879), 194.

32. PP, 1847, vol. 9 (Reports vol. 5), cmd. 666, 1847, "Reports from the Select Committee on Sunday Trading," q. 1438.

33. PP, 1847, q. 1124.

34. PP, 1847, q. 1129.

35. Mayhew, *London Labour*, 1:368.

36. PP, 1847, q.1129, 1152, 1157; pp, 1850, vol. 19 (Reports, vol. 11), cmd. 441, 1850, "Select Committee on the Sunday Trading Prevention Bill," q. 243, 245, 314; *JC*, March 16, 1855. For a striking description, see James Greenwood, "The City Rag Shop," *Saint Pauls Magazine* 12 (1873), 655–658.

37. "Abraham Simmons," *JC*, October 27, 1911: 33; Sala, *Dutch Pictures*, 332–337; "Effect of Cheap Fares," *Chambers's Edinburgh Journal* 2, no. 47 (1844): 334–335; John Mills, *The British Jews* (London: Houlston and Stoneman, 1853), 264–270; Mayhew, *London Labour* 1: 104–105, 368–369; 2: 26–29, 38–39; Watts Phillips, *The Wild Tribes of London* (London: Ward and Lock, 1855), 60, 63; Andrew Wynter, *Peeps into the Human Hive*, vol. 2 (London: Chapman and Hall, 1874), 277–286; George Sala, "Layard in London," *Illustrated London Magazine* 1 (1853): 228; from James Ewing Ritchie, *Here and There in London* (London: W. Tweedie, 1859), 120–122; *Hansard's Parliamentary Debates*, June 25, 1858: 418–420; Diana De Marly, *Working Dress: A History of Occupational Clothing* (New York: Holmes and Meier, 1986), 97; Lemire, "Consumerism in Preindustrial and Early Industrial England": 17–18; Ginsburg, "Rags to Riches," 124–125.

38. John Timbs, *Curiosities of London* (London: David Bogue, 1868), 484.

39. N.S. Dodge, "Rag Fair," *Harper's New Monthly Magazine* 35 (September 1867): 517; "Old Clothes and What Becomes of Them," *London Times*, November 3, 1864.

40. Sala, *Dutch Pictures*, 337–338.

41. Proceedings of the Central Criminal Court, October 27, 1851: 784–785.

42. On homespun, see Zakim, *Ready-Made Democracy*, ch. 1.

43. The classic studies of this are Endelman, *Jews of Georgian England* and V. D. Lipman, *Social History of the Jews in England, 1850–1950* (London: Watts, 1954).

44. Leo Hershkowitz, "Some Aspects of the New York Jewish Merchant and Community, 1654–1820," *American Jewish Historical Quarterly* 66 (1977): 10–34.

45. The advertisements placed by dealers in newspapers attest to the challenges of sourcing supplies. On the ideology of homespun in the Early Republic, see Zakim, *Ready-Made Democracy*, 11–36.

46. See, for example, Avraham Barkai, *Branching Out: German-Jewish Immigration to the United States, 1820–1914* (New York: Holmes and Meier, 1994); Hasia Diner, *A Time for Gathering: The Second Migration, 1820–1880* (Baltimore: Johns Hopkins University Press, 1992). On peddling, see Hasia Diner, "Entering the Mainstream of Modern Jewish History," in *Jewish Roots in Southern Soil: A New History*, ed. Marcie Cohen Ferris and Mark Greenberg (Lebanon, NH: Brandeis University Press, 2006), 86–108; Maxwell Whiteman, "Notions, Dry Goods, and Clothing: An Introduction to the Study of the Cincinnati Peddler," *Jewish Quarterly Review* 53, no. 4 (1963): 306–321; Lee Friedman, "The Problems of Nineteenth Century American Jewish Peddlers," *American Jewish Historical Quarterly* 44 (September 1954): 1–7.

47. Joseph T. Rainer, "The 'Sharper Image': Yankee Peddlers, Southern Consumers, and the Market Revolution," in *Cultural Change and the Market Revolution in America, 1789–1860*, ed. Scott C. Martin (Lanham, MD: Rowman and Littlefield, 2005), 97–98.

48. At times these tropes became intertwined with those of the folkloric wandering Jew. Rainer, "'Sharper Image,'" 97, 101–102, 105; Louis Schmier, "Hellooo! Peddlerman! Hellooo!," in *Ethnic Minorities in Gulf Coast Society*, ed. Jerrell Shofner and Linda Ellsworth (Pensacola, FL: Gulf Coast History and Humanities Conference, 1979), 79. On modern iterations of the mythology of the wandering Jew, see Richard I. Cohen, "The 'Wandering Jew' from Medieval Legend to Modern Metaphor," in *The Art of Being Jewish in Modern Times*, Barbara Kirshenblatt-Gimblett and Jonathan Karp, eds. (Philadelphia: University of Pennsylvania Press, 2008), 147–175. On peddlers in American folklore, see David Jaffee, "Peddlers of Progress and the Transformation of the Rural North, 1760–1860," *Journal of American History* 78, no. 2 (September 1991): 527–531.

49. Frederick Law Olmsted, *The Cotton Kingdom*, vol. 1 (New York: Mason Brothers, 1862), 45–46, 252.

50. Frederick Law Olmsted, *The Cotton Kingdom*, vol. 2 (New York: Mason Brothers, 1862), 165.

51. Strasser, *Waste and Want*, 78–80.

52. Ibid., 13, 70–71, 73, 81; Horace Greeley, *The Great Industries of the United States* (Hartford: J.B. Burr and Hyde, 1873), 588–589; Pope, *Clothing Industry*, 6–7. For an example of this, see Philip Kahn, Jr., *A Stitch in Time: The Four Seasons of Baltimore's Needle Trades* (Baltimore: Maryland Historical Society, 1989), xvii–xviii.

53. For an example of a peddler paid a monthly wage, see "Reflections of a New England Peddler" in *Memoirs of American Jews 1775–1865*, ed. Jacob Rader Marcus, (Philadelphia: Jewish Publication Society, 1955), 2:27.

CHAPTER 5. LICKSPITTLES AND LAND SHARKS

1. William Brown, *America: A Four Years' Residence in the United States and Canada* (Leeds: Printed for the author by Kemplay and Bolland, 1849), 3.

2. Ibid., 3.

3. Ibid., 4.

4. For an overview of the emergence of the penny press, see Patricia Cline Cohen, *The Murder of Helen Jewett: The Life and Death of a Prostitute in Nineteenth-Century New York* (New York: Knopf, 1998), 20–37. For the "flash press" of the 1840s, see *The Flash Press: Sporting Male Weeklies in 1840s New York*, ed. Patricia Cline Cohen, Timothy J. Gilfoyle, and Helen Lefkowitz Horowitz (Chicago: University of Chicago Press, 2008), 1–13. For an exploration of mock auctioneers, see the essay in this volume by Corey Goettsch.

5. Edwin G. Burrows and Mike Wallace, *Gotham: A History of New York City to 1898* (New York: Oxford University Press, 1999), xiv–xv.

6. The first quotation is from "Emigrants from Europe," *New York Herald*, June 14, 1845; the second is from "An Interesting Narrative: The Story of an Emigrant," *New York Herald*, May 29, 1856.

7. Raymond L. Cohn, *Mass Migration Under Sail: European Immigration to the Antebellum United States* (New York: Cambridge University Press, 2009), Table A4.1. Immigration from Europe, Calendar Year Estimates, 1819–1860, 96.

8. Robert Greenhalgh Albion, *The Rise of New York Port, 1815–1860* (New York: Charles Scribner's Sons, 1939), apps. 10 and 27, 401, 418.

9. Philip Taylor, *The Distant Magnet: European Migration to the U.S.A.* (London: Eyre and Spottiswoode, 1971), 108.

10. David M. Schneider, *The History of Public Welfare in New York State, 1609–1866* (Chicago: University of Chicago Press, 1938), 306–307.

11. See Novak, *The People's Welfare*, 19–50.

12. "European Paupers," *Catholic Telegraph* (Cincinnati, OH), June 23, 1836, 238.

13. Jonathan A. Glickstein, *American Exceptionalism, American Anxiety: Wages, Competition, and Degraded Labor in the Antebellum United States* (Charlottesville: University of Virginia Press, 2002), 187–191.

14. See Benjamin J. Klebaner, "The Myth of Foreign Pauper Dumping in the United States," *Social Service Review* 35, no. 3 (September 1961): 302–309.

15. Many articles complained of the rapid increase in the number of foreign-born paupers in urban almshouses in the 1830s, greatly outnumbering the native poor. See, for example, "Foreign Pauperism in the United States," *New-England Magazine* 7, no. 6 (December 1834): 497.

16. For an analysis of the reasons why the transatlantic indentured servant trade collapsed by 1820, see Farley Grubb, "The End of European Immigrant Servitude in the United States: An Economic Analysis of Market Collapse, 1772–1835," *Journal of Economic History* 54, no. 4 (December, 1994): 794–824. The illegal Atlantic slave trade also persisted, as examined by Craig Hollander in this volume.

17. The cabin fares are from Robert G. Albion, *Square Riggers on Schedule: The New York Sailing Packets to England, France, and the Cotton Ports* (Princeton, NJ: Princeton University Press, 1938), 235. The steerage fares are from Albion, *Rise of New York Port*, 340. The antebellum belief in the linkages between poverty, low moral character, and disease is clearly demonstrated in Charles E. Rosenberg, *The Cholera Years: The United States in 1832, 1849, and 1866*, rev. ed. (1962; repr., Chicago: University of Chicago Press, 1987), 148–149.

18. For example, see the lengthy memo from the New York Chamber of Commerce, the chief organ of the city's elite merchants, to the New York State Legislature, critiquing aspects of the bill that would eventually create the Board of the Commissioners of Emigration. Letter from R. B. Minturn to P. M. Wetmore, March 19, 1847, New York Chamber of Commerce and Industry Records, 1768–1984, Box 231, Folder 4: Immigration 1862–1867, Rare Book and Manuscript Library, Butler Library, Columbia University.

19. Stephen Fox, *Transatlantic: Samuel Cunard, Isambard Brunel, and the Great Atlantic Steamships* (New York: HarperCollins, 2003), 10.

20. Edith Abbott, *Immigration: Select Documents and Case Records* (Chicago: University of Chicago Press, 1924), 38.

21. Herman Melville, *Redburn, or His First Voyage* (New York: Harper and Brothers, 1850), 301.

22. Taylor, *The Distant Magnet*, 108.

23. Terry Coleman, *Going to America* (New York: Pantheon Books, 1972), 59.

24. New York State Legislature, *Report of the Select Committee Appointed by the Legislature of New-York, to Examine into Frauds upon Immigrants* (Albany: C. Van Benthuysen, 1847), 8.

25. Ibid., 2.

26. Ibid., 3.

27. "At no former period have there been so many emigrants arriving . . . ," *Brooklyn Eagle*, June 6, 1846.

28. New York State Legislature, *Report of the Select Committee*, 3.

29. Ibid., 4.

30. "More about Emigrants," *New York Herald*, June 15, 1845.

31. Railroad growth in the 1830s and 1840s in New York had been hampered by the success of the canal system, but lines began to consolidate in the early 1850s. The multiple lines that made up the Albany-to-Buffalo link would be consolidated as the New York Central in 1853. George Rogers Taylor, *The Transportation Revolution, 1815–1860* (New York: Holt, Winston and Rinehart, 1951; 1964), 84.

32. Irene D. Neu, *Erastus Corning: Merchant and Financier, 1794–1872* (Ithaca, NY: Cornell University Press, 1960), 62–80. While I cannot be entirely certain, "R. Schoyer" is quite possibly Raphael Schoyer, who was at times an engraver, artist, printer, wine merchant, and "jack-of-all-trades," and in the early 1860s would establish himself as an American merchant in Yokohama, Japan. See C. T. Assendelft de Coningh, *A Pioneer in Yokohama: A Dutchman's Adventures in the New Treaty Port*, ed. and trans. Martha Chaiklin (Indianapolis: Hackett Publishing, 2012), 108n1.

33. R. Schoyer to Erastus Corning, May 30, 1848, Erastus Corning Papers, Box 17, Folder 16: 1844–1852: Emigrant Business, 1844–1852. Albany Institute of History and Art, Albany, New York.

34. Ibid.

35. One of the best concise expositions about this culture remains a passage in Elliott J. Gorn's *The Manly Art: Bare-Knuckle Prize Fighting in America* (Ithaca, NY: Cornell University Press, 1986), 129–136.

36. "Emigrant Plundering," *New York Tribune*, August 2, 1853.

37. Paul A. Gilje, "On the Waterfront: Maritime Workers in New York City in the Early Republic, 1800–1850," *New York History* 70, no. 4 (October 1996): 398, 402.

38. "Violent Altercation—Probable Murder," *New York Times*, December 14, 1854.

39. David M. Scobey, *Empire City: The Making and Meaning of the New York City Landscape* (Philadelphia: Temple University Press, 2002), 136.

40. Denis Tilden Lynch, *"Boss" Tweed: The Story of a Grim Generation* (New York: Boni and Liveright, 1927), 119.

41. "The Pardoning Power," *New York Times*, January 22, 1859.

42. "Is Swindling Legal?" *New York Times*, January 25, 1859.

43. Friedrich Kapp, *Immigration and the Commissioners of Emigration of the State of New York* (New York: The Nation Press, 1870), 44–46.

44. Ibid., 46–49.

45. Ibid.

46. Ibid.

47. New York, vol. 340, p. 92, R.G. Dun and Company Credit Report Volumes, Baker Library Historical Collections, Harvard Business School.

48. *Proceedings of the Board of Alderman and Assistant Aldermen*, vol. 12: May 14, 1844–May 13, 1845 (New York: J.F. Trow, 1845), 396–400.

49. "Robbing Emigrant Passengers," *Subterranean* (New York), December 5, 1846.

50. "Robbing Emigrant Passengers," *Subterranean*, December 12, 1846.

51. "The Emigrants," *New York Tribune*, October 7, 1846.

52. "Passage of the Immigrant Bill," *New York Tribune*, May 6, 1847; reprinted from the *Albany Evening Journal*.

53. Kapp, *Immigration and the Commissioners of Emigration*, 126–127.

54. "Indignation Meeting," *New York Times*, August 7, 1855.

55. "Government Regulations for Emigrants to the United States," *The Merchants Magazine and Commercial Review* 38, no. 4 (April 1858): 517.

56. An explanation of how a runner for "immigrant hotels" lured newcomers in the 1880s can be found in "How Immigrants Are Swindled," *New York Times*, May 14, 1888.

57. See, for example, "How Emigrants Are Fleeced," *New York Times*, May 29, 1866.

58. "The Tammany Emigration Commission," *New York Times*, June 29, 1871.

59. Horatio Alger, Jr., *Ben the Luggage Boy; or, Among the Wharves* (Boston: A.K. Loring, 1870).

CHAPTER 6. "THE WORLD IS BUT ONE VAST MOCK AUCTION"

1. "July 2: Mock Auction Stores in Chatham Street—A Verdant Youth from the Country," *New York Herald*, July 3, 1845.

2. "The Peter Funk," *New York Sunday Morning Atlas*, May 3, 1840. The name Peter Funk originated in a satiric novel about business in New York City. See Asa Greene, *The Perils of Pearl Street* (New York: Betts, Anstice and Peter Hill, 1834), esp. chap. 7. In the story, Peter Funk is a character who helps auctioneers swindle purchasers.

3. M. Schele de Lere, *Americanisms; The English of the New World* (New York: Charles Scribner and Company, 1872), 299.

4. Until recently, business and financial historians focused almost exclusively on elite capitalists, and their histories portrayed capitalists and capitalism in a positive light. In these histories, markets were reliable and fair, and businessmen were benevolent do-gooders whose saintly deeds benefited everyone equally. See, for example, Allan Nevins, *John D. Rockefeller: The Heroic Age of American Enterprise*, 2 vols. (New York: C. Scribner

and Sons, 1940); Alfred Chandler, *The Visible Hand: The Managerial Revolution in American Business* (Cambridge, MA: Harvard University Press, 1977); Donald Adams, *Finance and Enterprise in Early America: A Study of Stephen Girard's Bank, 1812–1831* (Philadelphia: University of Pennsylvania Press, 1978); Howard Bodenhorn, *A History of Banking in Antebellum America: Financial Markets and Economic Development in an Era of Nation-Building* (New York: Cambridge University Press, 2000); Joseph Fenstermaker, *The Development of American Commercial Banking, 1782–1837* (Ph.D. diss., University of Illinois, 1963); Philip Scranton, *Proprietary Capitalism: The Textile Manufacture at Philadelphia, 1800–1885* (New York: Cambridge University Press, 1983); Glenn Porter and Harold Livesay, *Merchants and Manufacturers: Studies in the Changing Structure of Nineteenth-Century American Marketing* (Baltimore: Johns Hopkins University Press, 1971); Thomas Doerflinger, *A Vigorous Pursuit of Enterprise: Merchants and Economic Development in Revolutionary Philadelphia* (Chapel Hill: University of North Carolina Press, 1986); David Hounshell, *From the American System to Mass Production, 1800–1932: The Development of Manufacturing Technology in the United States* (Baltimore: Johns Hopkins University Press, 1984); Barbara Tucker and Kenneth Tucker, *Industrializing Antebellum America: The Rise of Manufacturing Entrepreneurs in the Early Republic* (New York: Palgrave Macmillan Press, 2008); Albert Fishlow, *American Railroads and the Transformation of the Ante-Bellum Economy* (Cambridge, MA: Harvard University Press, 1965); John Denis Haeger, *The Investment Frontier: New York Businessmen and the Economic Development of the Old Northwest* (Albany: State University of New York Press, 1981); Robert Swierenga, *Pioneers and Profits: Land Speculation on the Iowa Frontier* (Ames: Iowa State University Press, 1968). More recently, historians of capitalism have begun chronicling the misdeeds of many of America's leading business magnates and have painted a more nuanced picture of American capitalism, acknowledging that the nineteenth-century "captains of industry" also committed major acts of fraud and sometimes stifled economic development. See Richard White, *Railroaded: The Transcontinentals and the Making of Modern America* (New York: W. W. Norton, 2011); Kamensky, *The Exchange Artist*; Robert Shalhope, *The Baltimore Bank Riot: Political Upheaval in Antebellum Maryland* (Urbana: University of Illinois Press, 2009); Robert Sobel, *Panic on Wall Street: A History of America's Financial Disasters* (Washington, DC: Beard Books, 1999); Geoffrey C. Ward, *A Disposition to Be Rich: Ferdinand Ward, the Greatest Swindler of the Gilded Age* (New York: Random House, 2012); Scott B. McDonald and Jane E. Hughes, *Separating Fools from Their Money: A History of America's Financial Disasters* (New Brunswick, NJ: Transaction Publishers, 2007); David E. Y. Sarna, *History of Greed: Financial Fraud from Tulip Mania to Bernie Madoff* (New York: John Wiley and Sons, 2010). However, a lot of work remains to be done on the dark side of American capitalism.

5. Other historians have noted the role that auctions played in public debates about markets and regulations. For example, see Ellen Hartigan-O'Connor, "'Auctioneers of Offices': Patronage, Value, and Trust in the Early Republic Marketplace," *Journal of the Early Republic* 33, no. 3 (Fall 2013): 463–488; Joanna Cohen, "'The Right to Purchase Is as Free as the Right to Sell': Defining Consumers as Citizens in the Auction-House Conflicts of the Early Republic," *Journal of the Early Republic* 30, no. 1 (Spring 2010): 25–62.

However, these scholarly accounts do not discuss mock auctions, which figured prominently in nineteenth-century dialogues about auctions and capitalist practices.

6. In the vocabulary of confidence games like mock auctions, a "mark" is the person targeted by the con and who typically finds himself or herself at the bad end of a shady deal.

7. In this essay, I hope to contribute to a growing historiography on fraud, underground economies, and the culture of the market. See, for example, Mihm, *A Nation of Counterfeiters*; Gilfoyle, *A Pickpocket's Tale*; Wendy A. Woloson, *In Hock: Pawning in Early America from Independence through the Great Depression* (Chicago: University of Chicago Press, 2009), esp. 122–153; Dan Plazak, *A Hole in the Ground with a Liar on Top: Fraud and Deceit in the Golden Age of American Mining* (Salt Lake City: University of Utah Press, 2006); James W. Cook, *The Arts of Deception: Playing with Fraud in the Age of Barnum* (Cambridge, MA: Harvard University Press, 2001); Jean-Christophe Agnew, *Worlds Apart: The Market and the Theatre in Anglo-American Thought, 1550–1750* (New York: Cambridge University Press, 1986); Sandage, *Born Losers*; Serena Zabin, *Dangerous Economies: Status and Commerce in Imperial New York* (Philadelphia: University of Pennsylvania Press, 2009); Edward J. Balleisen, "Private Cops on the Fraud Beat: The Limits of Business Self-Regulation, 1895–1932," *Business History Review* 83, no. 1 (2009): 113–160.

8. On "creative destruction," or the tumultuous way that entrepreneurs change the economy, see Joseph Schumpeter, *Capitalism, Socialism, and Democracy* (orig. pub. 1942; New York: Routledge, 2013), esp. chap. 7. Though Schumpeter was mostly concerned with the way that entrepreneurs innovated while monopolistic corporations resisted change, I would amend Schumpeter's theory to include criminals who are also agents of creative destruction, as they were critical in creating new business practices and also in defining the rules of commerce. Indeed, the line between "swindler" and "entrepreneur" is sometimes murky.

9. See Joshua Greenberg's contribution to this volume.

10. Robert Albion, *The Rise of New York Port, 1815–1860* (New York: Charles Scribner's Sons, 1939), esp. 9–15; Edward K. Spann, *The New Metropolis: New York City, 1840–1857* (New York: Columbia University Press, 1981), 1–22; William Pencak, "Introduction: New York and the Rise of American Capitalism," in *New York and the Rise of American Capitalism: Economic Development and the Social and Political History of an American State, 1780–1870*, ed. Pencak and Conrad Edick Wright (New York: New-York Historical Society, 1989), xi–xx.

11. Albion, *Rise of New York Port*, 276–280; Albert Buck, *The Development and Organisation of Anglo-American Trade, 1800–1850* (New Haven, CT: Yale University Press, 1925), 141–145; Ray Bert Westerfield, "Early History of American Auctions: A Chapter in Commercial History," *Transactions of the Connecticut Academy of Arts and Sciences* 23 (May 1920): 173–174, 179.

12. Ira Cohen, "The Auction System in the Port of New York, 1817–1837," *Business History Review* 45, no. 4 (Winter 1971): 495.

13. Joanna Cohen, "'The Right to Purchase Is as Free as the Right to Sell,'" 60–62; Ira Cohen, "Auction System," 505–510.

14. *Reasons Why the Present System of Auctions Ought to Be Abolished* (New York: Alexander Ming, Jr., 1828), 4–5.

15. New-York Anti-Auction Committee, *Facts, Important to Be Known by the Manufacturers, Mechanics, and All Other Classes of the Community* (New York: n. p., 1831), 7, 19. Also see "A New-York Merchant," in *An Exposition of Some of the Evils Arising from the Auction System* (New York: Van Pelt and Spear, [1820?]), 6; Joshua Greenberg, *Advocating the Man: Masculinity, Organized Labor, and the Household in New York, 1800–1840* (New York: Columbia University Press, 2008), 52–55.

16. *Auctions Inconsistent with Regular Trade, and Injurious to the City: Addressed to the People of New-York* (New York: Van Winkle, Wiley and Co., 1817), 4–5. Also consult Hartigan-O'Connor, "Auctioneers of Offices," 463–488.

17. Circular by the Anti-Auction Committee, dated December 1828, Luther Bradish Papers, Box 7, New-York Historical Society; also see Westerfield, "Early History of American Auctions," 196–197.

18. *Auctions Inconsistent*, 14.

19. *Reasons Why the Present System of Auctions*, 15.

20. My understanding of auctions as a form of selling has been greatly enriched by Richard A. Cassady, Jr., *Auctions and Auctioneering* (Berkeley: University of California Press, 1967).

21. Ibid., 92–94.

22. Ibid., 113–126, 140, 164–167.

23. "Mock Auctions," *New York Herald*, December 12, 1843.

24. See "Mock Auctions," *United States' Telegraph* (Washington, DC), September 13, 1836; "Manœuvres at Mock Auctions," *New York Morning Herald*, April 9, 1838; "Mock Auctions," *New York Spectator*, August 23, 1838; "Mock Auction Trial," *New York Morning Herald*, September 13, 1838; "Burning at Mock Auctions," *Christian Secretary* (Hartford, CT), September 14, 1838; "Another Auction Shave," *New York Spectator*, October 22, 1838; "Auction Burning," *New York Morning Herald*, April 15, 1839; "Auction Fraud," *New York Sun*, May 18, 1839; "Auction Fraud," *New York Sun*, September 12, 1839; "Mock Auctions," *Public Ledger* (Philadelphia), November 7, 1839; "Auction Swindling," *New York Sun*, February 1, 1840; "Mock Auction Swindling in a New Style," *Charleston Mercury* (Charleston, SC), October 27, 1840; "Another Street Robbery," *New York Herald*, February 15, 1851; "'Peter Funk' Cornered," *New York Herald*, December 18, 1841; "Mock Auctions," *New York Herald*, December 12, 1843; "A Mock Auction Case," *New York Herald*, December 8, 1844; "Mock Auction Fraud," *New York Herald*, August 14, 1845; "Another Mock Auction Case," *New York Herald*, August 28, 1845; "Still Another," *New York Herald*, August 28, 1845; "Mock Auction Case," *National Police Gazette* (New York), January 17, 1846; "An Aggravated Mock Auction Case," *Public Ledger*, November 17, 1852; "Beware of Mock Auctions," *New York Herald*, March 12, 1849; "Mock Auctions Again," *New Orleans Daily Picayune*, January 25, 1851; "Another Mock Auction Swindle," *Boston Herald*, March 15, 1851; "'Done Brown' from Green, at a Mock Auction," *New York Herald*, April 15, 1851; "More of the Mock Auction Business," *New Orleans Daily Picayune*, February 8, 1852; "Mock Auction Fraud," *Maine Farmer* (Augusta, ME), March

4, 1852; "New York City," *New York Times*, May 28, May 29, 1852; "Mock Auction Swindle," *New York Daily Times*, July 13, 1852; "Another Swindle by a Mock Auctioneer," *New York Times*, July 28, 1852.

25. "Pick-Pockets and Picture-Pockets; or, Art Dodges and Artful Dodges," *Frank Leslie's Budget of Fun* (New York), April 1, 1860.

26. Ibid.

27. Indictment against Harlon E. Will and Elias Aaron for Obtaining Money under False Pretences, May 8, 1837, Reel 172, Box 332, New York District Attorney Indictment Records, Municipal Archives of the City of New York.

28. Indictment against Phineas Alden for Obtaining Money by False Pretences, August 16, 1838, Reel 181, Box 351, New York District Attorney Indictment Records, New York Municipal Archives.

29. "Another Auction Shave," *New York Spectator*, October 22, 1838.

30. "A Mock Auction Case," *New York Herald*, December 8, 1844. Also see "Another Mock Auction Case," *New York Herald*, August 20, 1845.

31. "A Mock-Auction Swindle," *New York Tribune*, August 2, 1856.

32. Indictment against John Crowe and Hugh O'Neil for Obtaining Money under False Pretences, November 21, 1837, Reel 176, Box 340, New York District Attorney Indictment Papers, New York Municipal Archives.

33. Ibid.

34. "A Victim," *New Orleans Daily Picayune*, November 16, 1849.

35. On bookkeeping's role in the creation of capitalist ideology, see Michael Zakim, "Bookkeeping as Ideology: Capitalist Knowledge in Nineteenth-Century America," *Common-Place* 6, no. 3 (April 2006): http://www.common-place.org/vol-06/no-03/zakim/.

36. "Mock Auction Swindling, in a New Style," *Charleston Mercury*, October 27, 1840.

37. "Joseph King Among the Peters," *New York Morning News*, December 2, 1845.

38. "Mock Auction Stores—Peter Funks—Increase of Fraud and Rascality—Expose of Rogues and Roguery," *New York Herald*, December 15, 1843.

39. In addition to the opening vignette in this chapter, see "Mock Auction Fraud," *Milwaukee Sentinel* (Milwaukee, WI), June 11, 1839; "Peter Funk and Jonathan," *New Orleans Daily Picayune*, October 11, 1845; "A Rich Mock Auction Case," *New York Herald*, December 12, 1845; "Peter Funks Operating on a Down Easter," *Boston Herald*, November 26, 1852; "Mock Auction Swindles," *New York Times*, April 26, 1855; "A 'Cute One' Overreached," *New York Times*, May 24, 1854; "A Yankee Swindled at a Mock Auction," *New York Tribune*, October 2, 1858; "Have We a Currency Among Us?," *Maine Farmer*, August 18, 1853; "Hints to Strangers—No. IV. Perils of New York," *Water-Cure Journal* 15, no. 5 (May 1853): 111; "Mr. Jones's Experience with Peter Funk," in *Cyclopaedia of Commercial and Business Anecdotes*, ed. Richard Miller Devins and Frazer Kirkland (New York: D. Appleton, 1865), 1:213–224.

40. For more on the Yankee, the "cute" Yankee, and the "shrewd" Yankee peddler, see Constance Rourke, *American Humor: A Study of the National Character* (New York: Harcourt Brace, 1931; repr., Tallahassee: Florida State University Press, 1959), 3–32; William R. Taylor, *Cavalier and Yankee: The Old South and American National Character*

(New York: George Braziller, 1961), 95–141; Joseph Rainer, "The Sharper Image: Yankee Peddlers, Southern Consumers, and the Market Revolution," *Business and Economic History* 26 (1997): 27–44; Francis Hodge, *Yankee Theatre: The Image of America on the Stage* (Austin: University of Texas Press, 1964), 41–59; Sarah Burns, *The Pastoral Inventions: Rural Life in Nineteenth-Century American Art and Culture* (Philadelphia: Temple University Press, 1989), 99–188; Richard L. Bushman, *The Refinement of America: Persons, Houses, Cities* (New York: Alfred A. Knopf, 1992), 353–402; Cook, *Arts of Deception*, 97, 99; David Jaffee, "Peddlers of Progress and the Transformation of the Rural North, 1790–1860," *Journal of American History* 78, no. 2 (September 1991): 511–535.

41. "Mock Auction Stores—Peter Funks—Increase of Fraud and Rascality—Expose of Rogues and Roguery," *New York Herald*, December 15, 1843.

42. "The Peter Funk," *New York Sunday Morning Atlas*, May 3, 1840. For examples of other stories using Peter Funks as Jews, see "The Jews," *American Phrenological Journal* 5, no. 9 (September 1843): 426; "Another Mock Auction Case," *New York Herald*, August 20, 1845; "Hints to Strangers—No. III. Perils of New York," *Water-Cure Journal* 15, no. 4 (April 1853): 87; "Big Mock Auctions," *Subterranean* (New York), February 20, 1847; "New York Correspondence," *Wisconsin Free Democrat* (Milwaukee, WI), February 5, 1851; "Beware of the Swindlers," *Milwaukee Sentinel*, June 28, 1858; Alvin F. Harlow, *Old Bowery Days: The Chronicles of a Famous Street* (New York: D. Appleton, 1931), 358; Lambert A. Wilmer, *Our Press Gang; or, A Complete Exposition of the Corruptions and Crimes of American Newspapers* (Philadelphia: J. T. Lloyd, 1859), 169; William M. Bobo, *Glimpses of New-York City, By a South Carolinian, (Who Had Nothing Else To Do)* (Charleston, SC: J. J. McCarter, 1852), 115–116; George G. Foster, *New York in Slices* (New York: W. F. Burgess, 1850) 8–16.

43. Woloson, *In Hock*, 25–27; also see Bobo, *Glimpses of New-York City*, 115–122; Foster, *New York in Slices*, 8–16; Harlow, *Old Bowery Days*, 358; James Henry McCabe, *The Secrets of the Great City, A Work Descriptive of the Virtues and Vices, The Mysteries, Miseries, and Crimes of New York City* (Philadelphia: National Publishing Company, 1868), 356–357.

44. See Woloson, *In Hock*, 31, 38, 70–76, 129.

45. "Sacking a Mock Auctioneer," *Newport Mercury* (Newport, RI), April 11, 1846.

46. "Mock Auctions," *New York Herald*, December 12, 1843.

47. "Peter Funk in New York," *New Orleans Daily Picayune*, December 23, 1857.

48. For more on violence and market morality, see Will Mackintosh's chapter in this volume; Paul A. Gilje, *Road to Mobocracy: Popular Disorder in New York City, 1763–1834* (Chapel Hill: University of North Carolina Press, 1987); Shalhope, *Baltimore Bank Riot.*

49. "Mock Auction Shops," *New York Herald*, August 14, 1845. Also see "Rogues at a Premium," *New York Herald*, December 11, 1843.

50. "Mock Auction Shops."

51. "Rogues at a Premium."

52. William H. Bell Diary, November 13, 1850, New-York Historical Society.

53. Ibid., December 23, 1850.

54. "An Ordinance for the Establishment and Regulation of the Police of the City of New York," *New York Herald*, March 21, 1843.

55. "Mock Auctions—A Good Idea," *New York Herald*, August 19, 1845; "Mock Auction Stores," *New York Herald*, July 18, 1845; "'Othello's Occupation Gone,'" *New York Herald*, September 2, 1845; "Mock Auctions," *New Orleans Daily Picayune*, September 5, 1845.

56. "Good," *New York Herald*, September 3, 1845; "Encouraging," *New York Herald*, September 4, 1845; "City Items," *New York Tribune*, September 18, 1845.

57. "Excitement Among the Peter Funks," *New York Herald*, September 26, 1845.

58. David Henkin, *City Reading: Written Words and Public Spaces in Antebellum New York* (New York: Columbia University Press, 1998), 39–68.

59. Charles H. Haswell, *Reminiscences of an Octogenarian of the City of New York (1816–1860)* (New York: Harper and Brothers, 1896), 395. For other examples of commentators gravitating toward the placards, see Barlow, *Old Bowery Days*, 357; "Intelligence Offices and Mock Auctions," *Advocate of Moral Reform* 12, no. 22 (November 16, 1846): 174; "Funk, (Peter)," Rev. E. Cobham, Jr., *Character Sketches of Romance, Fiction, and Drama*, ed. Marion Harland (New York: Selmar Hess, 1892), 54; "Taking a Sight: As Sung by P. Morris; With Great Applause," in *The New Popular Forget-Me-Not Songster* (Cincinnati: U. P. James, 185?), 25; "The Money Market," *Public Ledger*, August 9, 1848; Helen Campbell, *Darkness and Daylight: Or, Lights and Shadows of New York Life as Seen by a Woman* (Hartford: Hartford Publishing Company, 1895), 577; Bobo, *Glimpses of New-York City*, 115–116; "Peter Funk Going South," *New Orleans Daily Picayune*, October 16, 1846; "From Our Correspondent: New York," *Southern Patriot* (Charleston, SC), September 25, 1845; "The Auctions," *Barre Gazette* (Barre, MA), September 26, 1845; "Notes of a Southward Traveller: New-York," *Portsmouth Journal of Literature and Politics* 60, no. 49 (December 8, 1849): 2.

60. "Beware of Mock-Auctions," *Subterranean*, September 6, 1845.

61. "Big Mock Auctions," *Subterranean*, February 20, 1847.

62. "Beware of Yankee Doodle!," *Yankee Doodle* 1, no. 1 (October 10, 1846), 7. The emphasis is my own.

63. For more about Briggs, see "Harry Franco," *New York Times*, December 23, 1877; Hans Bergmann, *God in the Street: New York Writing from the Penny Press to Melville* (Philadelphia: Temple University Press, 1995), 140–142.

64. Harry Franco [Charles F. Briggs], "Peter Funk's Revenge," *Knickerbocker* (New York) 27, no. 1 (January 1846): 58. Fancy stocks were defined as follows: "These are, generally speaking, of no particular or known value, and represent worthless or embarrassed corporations, which have failed in the undertakings for which capital was contributed, and most generally have never paid a dividend, and are never expected to. Their real worth, or rather worthlessness, is so little known, that it seldom interferes with an unlimited expansion or contraction in prices, as according as the wealth or talent employed on either side may preponderate." A Reformed Stock Gambler, *Stocks and Stock-Jobbing in Wall-Street, with Sketches of the Brokers and Fancy Stocks* (New York: New York Publishing

Company, 1848), 13. This was not the only time that Briggs discussed mock auctions in his writing. He also wrote a brief chapter about mock auction swindling in his two-part novel about the Panic of 1837. See Harry Franco [Charles F. Briggs], *The Adventures of Harry Franco: A Tale of the Great Panic* (New York: F. Saunders, 1839), 1: 46. For more on the novel, see Andrew Lawson, "Men of Small Property: Harry Franco and Henry Ward Beecher in the Antebellum Market," *Common-Place* 10, no. 4 (July 2010), at http://www.common-place.org/vol-10/no-04/lawson/.

65. Franco [Briggs], "Peter Funk's Revenge," 58–61.

66. "Held to Bail," *New York Herald*, September 12, 1846; "More of the Mock Auction War," *New York Herald*, September 16, 1846; "Injunction on the 'Banners,'" *New York Herald*, September 25, 1846; "The Mock Auction War," *New York Herald*, October 2, 1846; "Arrest of a Mayor," *Trumpet and Universalist Magazine* 19, no. 17 (October 10, 1846): 67.

67. "The Mock Auction Case," *National Police Gazette*, November 7, 1846; "Vice Chancellor's Court: Warren Gilbert v. Andrew Mickle; 14th, 15th, and 29th Oct. 1846," *New-York Legal Observer* 5, no. 1 (January 1847): 10–14; "Warren Gilbert v. Andrew H. Mickle; In Chancery, New York, First Circuit, Before Vice Chancellor Sanford," *Pennsylvania Law Journal* 6, no. 1 (January 1847): 126–131. For more on Gilbert, consult *Doggett's New-York City Co-Partnership Directory for 1846 and 1847* (New York: John Doggett, Jr., 1846); and *Wilson's Business Directory of New-York City* (New York: [H. Wilson]; John F. Trow, 1850).

68. "A Dark Picture," *Scientific American* 2, no. 44 (July 24, 1847): 349.

69. Foster, *New York in Slices*, 36.

70. Stuart M. Blumin, introduction to *New York by Gaslight and Other Sketches*, ed. Stuart Blumin (Berkeley: University of California Press, 1990), 40–42. For more on Foster, also see George Rogers Taylor, "'Philadelphia in Slices' by George G. Foster," *Pennsylvania Magazine of History and Biography* 93, no. 1 (January 1969): 23–72; Stuart Blumin, "Explaining the New Metropolis: Perception, Depiction, and Analysis in Mid-Nineteenth-Century New York City," *Journal of Urban History* 11, no. 1 (November 1984): 9–38.

71. "Frauds in Trade," *New York Morning News*, October 1, 1845.

72. "The Financial and Commercial Prospect," *New York Herald*, December 9, 1856.

73. "'Commercial Delusions'—Speculations," *The American Review: A Whig Journal of Politics, Literature, Art and Science* 2, no. 4 (October 1845): 348. Also see "Affairs in Nebraska," *New York Herald*, May 9, 1857.

74. "Intelligence Offices and Mock Auctions."

75. See, for example, the stories appearing in just one New York newspaper: "Mock Auction Swindles," *New York Times*, March 23, 1853; "Mock Auction in Broadway Again," *New York Times*, October 24, 1853; "Mock Auction Swindle," *New York Times*, May 4, 1853; "The Mayor and the Mock Auctions," January 15, 1855; "An Alleged Mock Auction Swindle," *New York Times*, May 3, 1853; "Mock Auction Swindle—Another Settlement," *New York Times*, February 1, 1855; "Mayor's Black Book," *New York Times*, January 24, 1855; "Another Mock Auction Swindle," *New York Times*, January 23, 1855; "A Peter Funk Compelled to Disgorge," *New York Times*, January 6, 1855; "Another Broadway Mock

Auctioneer," *New York Times*, February 2, 1855; "Mock Auctions," *New York Times*, April 12, 1855; "Mayor's Black Book," *New York Times*, January 26, 1855; "Mayor's Black Book," *New York Times*, March 6, 1855; "More Mock Auctions—Be Careful," *New York Times*, February 14, 1855; "Mock Auction Swindle," January 19, 1858; "City Items," *New York Times*, April 9, 1858; "Mayor's Office," *New York Times*, January 19, 1858; "Mock Auction Swindles," *New York Times*, January 21, 1858; "Another Mock Auction Case," *New York Times*, February 18, 1859; "Arrest and Discharge of Mock Auctioneers," *New York Times*, August 7, 1862; "At the Mayor's Office," *New York Times*, April 24, 1860.

76. "Mock Auction Stores," *New York Herald*, July 24, 1848.

77. "Mock Auctions—Beware Peter Funks," *New York Times*, April 14, 1855. Also see "An Act to Punish Gross Frauds, and to Suppress Mock Auctions: Passed April 9, 1853," *Documents of the Board of Aldermen of the City of New York* 20 (1853): 524–526.

78. "A Mock Auctioneer Arrested Under the New Law and Held to Answer," *New York Herald*, April 23, 1853; "An Alleged Mock-Auction Swindle," *New York Daily Times*, May 3, 1853; "Swindling," "Another Charge," "Mock Auctions," *New York Herald*, May 22, 1853.

79. "Mock-Auctions in New York," *New York Times*, October 13, 1853.

80. Mock Auctions," *New York Times*, July 4, 1855.

81. Ibid.

82. "Waifs from New York," *Boston Saturday Evening Gazette*, January 8, 1859. Also see "Inefficiency of the Administration of Law in New York," *Boston Daily Courier*, January 3, 1859.

CHAPTER 7. UNDERGROUND ON THE HIGH SEAS

1. Several scholars have described this legislative progression. See Paul Finkelman, "Regulating the African Slave Trade," *Civil War History* 54, no. 4 (2008): 379–405; Matthew Mason, "Keeping Up Appearances: The International Politics of Slave Trade Abolition in the Nineteenth-Century Atlantic World," *William and Mary Quarterly* 66, no. 4 (2009): 809–832; Matthew Mason, *Slavery and Politics in the Early American Republic* (Chapel Hill: University of North Carolina Press, 2006); and Donald L. Robinson, *Slavery in the Structure of American Politics, 1765–1820* (Ann Arbor: University of Michigan Press, 1970).

2. James Monroe, "Special Message to the Senate and House of Representatives of the United States," December 17, 1819 (Online by Gerhard Peters and John T. Woolley, *The American Presidency Project*, http://www.presidency.ucsb.edu/ws/?pid=66495).

3. Some case records include first-person narratives in the form of letters, interrogations, or depositions, providing a vivid glimpse into the shadowy world of the slave traders themselves. Such accounts are otherwise rare, because slave traders were understandably reluctant to create a paper trail or leave other evidence of their crimes. But for other first-person narratives about the American slave trade, see Brantz Mayer, *Captain Canot; or, Twenty Years of an African Slaver* (New York: Appleton, 1854); and *Revelations*

of a Slave Smuggler: Being the Autobiography of Capt. Rich'd Drake (New York: Robert M. DeWitt, [c1860]). These works are extremely problematic, however. In both cases, secondary authors transcribed the texts, so the accounts are first-person in name only. Moreover, the secondary authors were very candid about their political motives for publishing the narratives, creating doubt about the veracity and accuracy of the material.

4. In my dissertation, titled "Against a Sea of Troubles: Slave Trade Suppressionism During the Early Republic" (Johns Hopkins University, 2013), I argue that Americans of the Early Republic took seriously the suppression of the transatlantic slave trade (legal and otherwise). Those I term "suppressionists" mounted an effort to extricate their fellow citizens from participating in the traffic and to eradicate the slave trade of foreign nations. I attribute the rise of the suppressionist movement to multiple causes, such as the increased support for philanthropic projects, the unique political dynamics of the Early Republic, and the fear of divine punishment. The suppressionist movement waned during the late antebellum period because suppressionist victories invited negative comparisons between the illicit transatlantic slave trade and the nation's legal domestic slave trade. Slaveholders regarded such comparisons as a threat to slavery itself. As a result, they withdrew their support for the movement to safeguard the institution of slavery. In time, the suppression of the illegal slave trade was relegated to being a cause célèbre of the small (and unpopular) abolitionist movement, enabling Americans to reemerge during the late antebellum period as, perhaps, the predominant slave traffickers of the Atlantic world.

5. These figures were ascertained from the data available at www.slavevoyages.org.

6. For more on Great Britain's efforts to secure commitments from the European maritime powers to abolish their national slave trades, see Christopher Brown, *Moral Capital: Foundations of British Abolitionism* (Chapel Hill: University of North Carolina Press, 2006); David Brion Davis, *The Problem of Slavery in the Age of Revolution* (Oxford: Oxford University Press, 1999); Seymour Drescher, *Abolition: A History of Slavery and Antislavery* (Cambridge: Cambridge University Press, 2009); Seymour Drescher, *Econocide: British Slavery in the Era of Abolition* (Chapel Hill: University of North Carolina Press, 2010); Adam Hochschild, *Breaking the Chains: Prophets and Rebels in the Fight to Free an Empire's Slaves* (New York: Houghton Mifflin Company, 2005); Jenny Martinez, *The Slave Trade and the Origins of the International Human Rights Law* (Oxford: Oxford University Press, 2012); Derek R. Peterson, ed., *Abolitionism and Imperialism in Britain, Africa, and the Atlantic* (Athens: Ohio University Press, 2010); and Hugh Thomas, *The Slave Trade: The Story of the Atlantic Slave Trade* (New York: Simon and Schuster, 1997).

7. The Spanish issued two royal *cédulas*, one in 1789 and the other in 1791, abolishing most price controls on imports. Consult David Eltis, *Economic Growth and the Ending of the Transatlantic Slave Trade* (New York: Oxford University Press, 1987), 36.

8. Robert Francis Jameson, *Letters from the Havana, During the Year 1820; Containing an Account of the Present State of the Island of Cuba, and Observations on the Slave Trade* (London: Printed for John Miller, 1821), 18. Presumably, the British efforts to suppress the slave trade contributed to this annual decrease.

9. Ibid., 32. David Eltis corroborates Jameson's observation about the decline in slave prices in Africa following the abolition of the Anglo-American slave trades in 1808. In fact, Jameson probably underestimated this price drop. Eltis calculates that the price of slaves in Africa dropped about 50 percent after 1808. David Eltis, *Economic Growth and the Ending of the Transatlantic Slave Trade* (New York: Oxford University Press, 1987), 41.

10. Jameson, *Letters from the Havana*, 31.

11. Malibran's incriminating letters are now stored with the other articles of his cases in the archives of the U.S. District Court for the Southern District of New York at the New York branch of the National Archives and Records Administration (hereafter NARA). The letters were translated and published in newspapers and are cited at the relevant places below.

12. Eugene Malibran to Francisco Mattheu, December 31, 1819, "Slave Trade," *City of Washington Gazette*, November 14, 1820.

13. Eugene Malibran to Adolphe Lacoste, January 1, 1820, "New York . . . ," *Boston Weekly Messenger*, November 9, 1820.

14. "From the Mirror . . . ," *Baltimore Patriot*, November 30, 1819.

15. "On the Slave Trade," *Daily National Intelligencer* (Washington, DC), October 31, 1818.

16. "To the Citizens of Baltimore Engaged in the Slave Trade to the Coast of Africa," *Christian Herald* (New York), October 16, 1816.

17. Mercantile ventures were extremely dependent on the availability of credit. It would, therefore, have been very difficult for merchants to conduct their businesses under a cloud of suspicion from the authorities, especially since convictions for slave trading could result in large fines and property seizures. Not surprisingly, then, merchants who were mentioned in the trial of the *Plattsburgh* took steps to clear their names. Specifically, John D'Arcy and Henry Didier, who in September 1819 had sold to Thomas Sheppard their shares of the *Plattsburgh*, published in newspapers a series of notarized documents attesting to their innocence. So even in Baltimore—the epicenter of the illegal slave trade—the two merchants had to prove their innocence to restore their full faith and credit. For example, see "The Schooner Plattsburgh," *Baltimore Patriot and Mercantile Advertiser*, February 21, 1821.

18. In terms of public service, Sheppard had served as captain in the Maryland militia in the War of 1812, president of the Columbia Fire Company, and member of the city council. He also enjoyed leadership in the merchant community, cofounding both the Baltimore Exchange Company and the National Mechanics' Bank.

19. The schooner *Plattsburgh* was built four years before its fateful voyage to Africa in 1819. She had a square stern, a round tuck, one deck, and two masts and measured slightly over 101 feet in length, nearly 24 feet in breadth, and 11 feet in depth. U.S. Customs Certification for the *Plattsburgh*, case no. 1214, "The Officers and Crew of the US Ship of War the *Cyane* vs. The Schooner *Plattsburgh* . . . ," p. 206; Supreme Court Appellate Case Files, Record Group 267; NARA, Washington, DC. The *Plattsburgh* was probably named in honor of the American victory at the Battle of Plattsburgh, New York, during the War of 1812.

20. The exploits of Thomas Boyle (1794–1825) during the War of 1812 led to a street in south Baltimore being named in his honor. I believe this essay offers the first evidence of his involvement in the illegal slave trade.

21. Emma Christopher, *Slave Ship Sailors and Their Captive Cargoes, 1730–1807* (New York: Cambridge University Press, 2006), 96. For more on British slave ship captains during the eighteenth century, see Stephen Behrendt, "The Captains in the British Slave Trade from 1785 to 1807," *Transactions of the Historic Society of Lancashire and Cheshire* 140 (1990), 79–140. For a monograph pertaining to an American slaver ship captain, see Ron Soodalter, *Hanging Captain Gordon: The Life and Trial of an American Slave Trader* (New York: Washington Square Press, 2006).

22. Christopher, *Slave Ship Sailors*, 101.

23. "Slave Trade and Piracy," *Weekly Recorder* (Chillicothe, OH), May 28, 1819; "A Friend of Humanity," *Evening Post* (New York), September 18, 1816.

24. Laurence M. Thomas, *Vessels of Evil: American Slavery and the Holocaust* (Philadelphia: Temple University Press, 1993), 4. Scholars from various fields have long debated how "ordinary" individuals can be impelled to commit deeds that they would have formerly considered to be "evil." However, I am particularly indebted to Christopher Browning, the author of *Ordinary Men: Reserve Police Battalion 101 and the Final Solution in Poland* (New York: HarperCollins, 1992), for his excellent scholarship on this topic, as well as his personal and professional guidance.

25. Lacoste was exceptionally young to be a captain, even of a small pilot boat like the *Science*. Presumably, Malibran hired the young Frenchman to serve as the captain of the *Science* because more senior sailors would not engage in the illegal slave trade, at least without being offered more money.

26. Adolphe Lacoste to James Blair, January 3, 1822, p. 2; case no. 576, box 9; Monroe Administration, 1817–1825; Petitions for Pardons (1789–1860); General Records of the Department of State, Record Group 59; NARA, College Park, MD.

27. *Charleston Directory, and Stranger's Guide, 1816* (Charleston, SC: Abraham Motte, 1816), 49.

28. Eleanor Florence Lacoste to James Monroe, undated, p. 1; case no. 576, box 9; Monroe Administration, 1817–1825; Petitions for Pardons (1789–1860); General Records of the Department of State, Record Group 59; NARA, College Park, MD.

29. Joseph de Valnais to Joseph Story, January 1821, p. 1; file entitled "Misc. Records of the Court"; U.S. District Court for the District of Massachusetts; Records of District Courts of the United States, Record Group 21; NARA, Waltham, MA.

30. Adolphe Lacoste to James Blair, February 6, 1822, p. 2.

31. Eugene Malibran to Adolphe Lacoste, January 1, 1820, "New York . . . ," *Boston Weekly Messenger*, November 9, 1820.

32. Ibid. It seems peculiar that Malibran would intentionally overload the *Science* with trading goods. Instead, I believe that Malibran's comment about the surplus was meant to reinforce his claim that he provided Lacoste with sufficient goods to trade for "a handsome and heavy cargo" of slaves. Malibran's comment also put pressure on Lacoste to drive hard bargains for slaves in Africa, because he supposedly had enough trading goods for two loads.

33. Joseph F. Smith to John Quincy Adams, June 12, 1822, p. 2; case no. 624, box 11; Monroe Administration, 1817–1825; Petitions for Pardons (1789–1860); General Records of the Department of State, Record Group 59; NARA, College Park, MD.

34. *The Baltimore Directory, for 1817–1818* (Baltimore: Printed by James Kennedy, 1817), 175.

35. "Loss of the Privateer Pike," *National Intelligencer*, September 6, 1814.

36. Hugh E. Davey to James Monroe, March 17, 1821, p. 3; unnumbered cases, box no. 16; Monroe Administration, 1817–1825; Petitions for Pardons (1789–1860); General Records of the Department of State, Record Group 59; NARA, College Park, MD.

37. Dorcas Smith to James Monroe, March 17, 1821, p. 2; unnumbered cases, box no. 16; Monroe Administration, 1817–1825; Petitions for Pardons (1789–1860); General Records of the Department of State, Record Group 59; NARA, College Park, MD.

38. W. G. D. Worthington to John Quincy Adams, August 18, 1822, p. 2; case no. 624, box 16; Monroe Administration, 1817–1825; Petitions for Pardons (1789–1860); General Records of the Department of State, Record Group 59; NARA, College Park, MD.

39. Ibid.

40. Joseph F. Smith to M. W. Maitts, August 24, 1821, p. 4; case no. 624, box 11; Monroe Administration, 1817–1825; Petitions for Pardons (1789–1860); General Records of the Department of State, Record Group 59; NARA, College Park, MD.

41. Dorcas Smith to James Monroe, April 1, 1822, p. 2; case no. 624, box 16; Monroe Administration, 1817–1825; Petitions for Pardons (1789–1860); General Records of the Department of State, Record Group 59; NARA, College Park, MD.

42. For the most part, the French did not share in the Anglo-American aversion to the transatlantic slave trade. In fact, even when the French Convention abolished the institution of slavery in 1794, the slave trade itself remained technically legal until Napoleon abolished it during his "Hundred Days" coup d'état. Under tremendous British pressure, the restored French monarchy agreed at the Congress of Vienna to prohibit the slave trade at some future date, which was determined eventually to be March 1818.

43. Ralph Clayton, *Cash for Blood: The Baltimore to New Orleans Domestic Slave Trade* (Bowie, MD: Heritage Books, 2002), 5.

44. Frederick Douglass, "The Internal Slave Trade," speech delivered in Rochester, New York, July 5, 1852. Published in Frederick Douglass, *My Bondage and My Freedom* (New York: Miller, Orton, and Mulligan, 1855), 447.

45. W. G. D. Worthington to J. Q. Adams, August 18, 1822, p. 3.

46. Joseph F. Smith to Peter Little, February 3, 1822, p. 1; case no. 624, box 11; Monroe Administration, 1817–1825; Petitions for Pardons (1789–1860); General Records of the Department of State, Record Group 59; NARA, College Park, MD.

47. Joseph F. Smith to James Monroe, February 21, 1822, p. 2; case no. 624, box 11; Monroe Administration, 1817–1825; Petitions for Pardons (1789–1860); General Records of the Department of State, Record Group 59; NARA, College Park, MD.

48. Seth Rockman, *Scraping By: Wage Labor, Slavery, and Survival in Early Baltimore* (Baltimore, MD: Johns Hopkins University Press, 2009), 75.

49. Joseph F. Smith to James Monroe, February 21, 1822, p. 3.

50. Thomas Jefferson to Richard Rush, June 22, 1819. Published in Thomas Jefferson, *The Writings of Thomas Jefferson,* ed. Paul Leicester Ford (New York: G. P. Putnam's Sons, 1899), 10:133. As the U.S. minister to Britain, Rush might have worried whether the depression that ensued after the Panic of 1819 would spur the illegal slave trade, which he was working diligently to end with his British counterparts.

51. Joseph de Valnais to Joseph Story, January 1821, p. 1.

52. Eugene Malibran to Adolphe Lacoste, January 1, 1820, "New York . . . ," *Boston Weekly Messenger,* November 9, 1820.

53. John T. Noonan, *The Antelope: The Ordeal of the Recaptured Africans in the Administration of James Monroe and John Quincy Adams* (Berkeley: University of California Press, 1977), 10.

54. "St. Jago de Cuba, Oct. 4, 1819," *Baltimore Patriot and Mercantile Advertiser,* December 6, 1819.

55. Testimony of John Fervor; case no. 1214, "The Officers and Crew of the US Ship of War the *Cyane* vs. The Schooner *Plattsburgh* . . . ," p. 156; Supreme Court Appellate Case Files; Record Group 267, NARA, Washington, DC.

56. Testimony of William Flowers; case no. 1214, "The Officers and Crew of the US Ship of War the *Cyane* vs. The Schooner *Plattsburgh* . . . ," p. 164; Supreme Court Appellate Case Files; Record Group 267, NARA, Washington, DC.

57. Testimony of John Fervor, 157.

58. Joseph F. Smith to James Monroe, February 21, 1822, p. 2. Judging by Smith's improved spelling in this particular letter, it seems likely that he either dictated these recollections to a second party or had someone proofread his letter. It is also conceivable that Smith's previous letters were written in a version of shorthand or that he improved his spelling during his time in prison.

59. It seems curious that the *Plattsburgh* would bring both rice and tobacco from Baltimore, only to reship with rice and tobacco on its voyage to Africa. Nevertheless, the rice that the *Plattsburgh* brought from Baltimore was sold, at least nominally, to a Spanish resident of Santiago de Cuba named Francisco Gerardo. It is possible that this rice was then reloaded on the *Plattsburgh.* But the tobacco that came from Baltimore in the *Plattsburgh* was sold legitimately in Cuba and shipped to the African coast in another vessel called the *Maria.*

60. The above quotes and information were taken from the Testimony of Frederick J. Rapp; case no. 1214, "The Officers and Crew of the US Ship of War the *Cyane* vs. The Schooner *Plattsburgh* . . . ," p. 181; Supreme Court Appellate Case Files; Record Group 267, NARA, Washington, DC.

61. Ibid., 182 and 184.

62. Ibid., 181–182.

63. Joseph F. Smith to James Monroe, February 21, 1822, p. 2.

64. Joseph F. Smith to M. W. Maitts, August 24, 1821, p. 2.

65. Joseph F. Smith to James Monroe, February 21, 1822, p. 2.

66. Ibid., 3.

67. Joseph F. Smith to unknown recipient, February 14, 1821, p. 2; case no. 624, box 11; Monroe Administration, 1817–1825; Petitions for Pardons (1789–1860); General Records of the Department of State, Record Group 59; NARA, College Park, MD.

68. Joseph F. Smith to James Monroe, February 21, 1822, p. 3.

69. Unknown writer to Manuel Gonzales, February 24, 1820, p. 1; case no. 1214, "The Officers and Crew of the US Ship of War the *Cyane* vs. The Schooner *Plattsburgh* . . . ," unknown page number; Supreme Court Appellate Case Files; Record Group 267, NARA, Washington, DC.

70. Joseph F. Smith to William Smith, February 23, 1820, p. 1; case no. 1214, "The Officers and Crew of the US Ship of War the *Cyane* vs. The Schooner *Plattsburgh* . . . ," p. 49; Supreme Court Appellate Case Files; Record Group 267, NARA, Washington, DC.

71. Hugh Thomas, *The Slave Trade: The Story of the Atlantic Slave Trade, 1440–1870* (New York: Simon and Schuster, 1997), 393.

72. James Monroe, U.S. Congress, House, *Message of the President of the United States at the Commencement of the First Session of the Sixteenth Congress*, 16th Cong., 1st sess., December 7, 1819, Foreign Relations: vol. 4, no. 312, p. 629. The *Cyane* was a famous warship in 1820, though the vessel was better known for its defeat than for its victories. The *Cyane* was built for the British navy in 1804. During the War of 1812, on February 20, 1815, the U.S.S. *Constitution* captured H.M.S. *Cyane* between Gibraltar and the Atlantic Islands. Badly damaged, the *Cyane* was brought to New York, where it was repaired at great expense and recommissioned for service in the U.S. Navy.

73. "Extract of a Letter from the Reverend Samuel Bacon to the Secretary of the Navy," March 21, 1820, U.S. Congress, House, *Report on the Slave Trade*, 16th Cong., 2nd sess., February 9, 1821, vol. 1, no. 59, p. 11.

74. Ibid., 11.

75. Edward Trenchard to Unknown Recipient, April 10, 1820, *A View of the Present State of the African Slave Trade* . . . (Philadelphia: William Brown, Printer, 1824), 33.

76. Andrews was remanded to New York. On September 13, 1820, he was indicted for violating the Slave Trade Act of 1800, which carried a maximum penalty of two years in prison and a $2,000 fine. In response, Andrews claimed that "he had been inadvertently drawn into the affair at a dinner party in Baltimore" and "was willing to give any lawyer two thousand dollars who would free him from this embarrassment." It was a fee that he could easily afford. Evidently, Andrews "admitted that he had made about fifteen thousand dollars" while participating in the illegal slave trade (a veritable fortune for a mere midshipman). Justice Henry Brockholst Livingston presided over Andrews's trial in September. During the proceedings, it was revealed that Andrews had made $200 per month in the slave trade, whereas "the usual wages on board merchant vessels is but fifteen dollars a month." *Judicial Cases Concerning American Slavery and the Negro*, ed. Helen Tunncliff Catterall, vol. 4, *Cases from the Courts of New England, the Middle States, and the District of Columbia* (Washington, DC: Carnegie Institution of Washington, 1936), 376. According to newspapers, the jury reached a verdict in the trial. However, when the court reconvened to hear it, the twelfth juror was "seized with fits and rendered

unable to appear." "Slave Trade," *Newport Mercury* (Newport, RI), September 23, 1820. Andrews's lawyer objected successfully to the impending verdict, causing Livingston to order a retrial. It is unclear when, if ever, this trial took place.

77. Testimony of Silas H. Stingham; case no. 1214, "The Officers and Crew of the US Ship of War the *Cyane* vs. The Schooner *Plattsburgh* . . . ," p. 170; Supreme Court Appellate Case Files; Record Group 267, NARA, Washington, DC.

78. Joseph F. Smith to M.W. Maitts, August 24, 1821, p. 3.

79. Joseph F. Smith to James Monroe, February 21, 1822, p. 3.

80. Joseph F. Smith to M. W. Maitts, August 24, 1821, p. 3.

81. Testimony of Silas H. Stingham, 174.

82. John Davis to George Blake, May 4, 1821, p. 2; case no. 624, box 11; Monroe Administration, 1817–1825; Petitions for Pardons (1789–1860); General Records of the Department of State, Record Group 59; NARA, College Park, MD.

83. Testimony of Silas H. Stingham, 175.

84. John Davis to George Blake, May 4, 1821, p. 3.

85. Testimony of Silas H. Stingham, 171.

86. "Boston, Saturday Morning," *Boston Daily Advertiser*, July 8, 1820.

87. James Monroe, *The Writings of James Monroe*, ed. Stanislaus Murray Hamilton (New York: G. P. Putnam's Sons, 1902), 6:144, 145–146.

88. "Slave Trade," *Vermont Republican* (Windsor, VT), June 19, 1820.

89. "Boston, Jan. 28," *New-York Gazette and General Advertiser*, January 31, 1821. These written motions are now contained in the respective casework for Lacoste and Smith in the NARA, Waltham, MA.

90. Despite Donald Canney's claim in *Africa Squadron: The U.S. Navy and the Slave Trade, 1842 to 1861* (Washington, DC: Potomac Books, 2006) that "there is no record of a trial for the Americans who were returned" from Africa by the *Cyane*, the casework for the trials of Joseph F. Smith and Adolphe Lacoste is available in the Records of the United States District Court for the District of Massachusetts, NARA, Waltham, MA. The files are entitled "U.S. vs. Joseph F. Smith," "U.S. vs. Adolphe Lacoste," and "Misc. Records of the Court" for 1820. The National Archives in Waltham also contains a timeline for the two trials in Docket Book No. 4 for the Circuit Court (October 1812–December 1821), case nos. 33–37.

91. According to the legal historian Laura Edwards, petitions for pardon served as an alternative appeals process in the Early Republic. They were formulaic in content, typically stressing the defendant's naivety and otherwise good conduct and the innocent family that would suffer should the punishment be carried out. Edwards also points out that petitioners tended to acknowledge the defendant's guilt, distinguishing "degrees of criminality and guilt that other conceptions of law did not." See Laura Edwards, *The People and Their Peace: Legal Culture and the Transformation of Inequality in the Post-Revolutionary South* (Chapel Hill: University of North Carolina Press, 2009), 60. Although the petitioners for Smith and Lacoste employed these standard conventions, they denied the guilt of the two captains until 1822, reflecting their belief that Monroe would not show mercy for slave traders.

92. Samuel D. Harris to J. Q. Adams, March 15, 1822, p. 1; case no. 576, box 9; Monroe Administration, 1817–1825; Petitions for Pardons (1789–1860); General Records of the Department of State, Record Group 59; NARA, College Park, MD.

93. James Monroe to J. Q. Adams and Dorcas Smith, undated; case no. 624, box 11; Monroe Administration, 1817–1825; Petitions for Pardons (1789–1860); General Records of the Department of State, Record Group 59; NARA, College Park, MD.

94. Originally printed in the *National Intelligencer*, April 2, 1822. Reprinted in "By the Mails," *Providence Gazette* (Providence, RI), April 10, 1822.

95. "Slave Trade; Death," *New Bedford Mercury* (New Bedford, MA), June 9, 1820.

96. "Slave Trade and Piracy," *Weekly Recorder*, May 28, 1819; "A Friend of Humanity," *Evening Post*, September 18, 1816.

97. Joseph F. Smith to James Monroe, February 21, 1822, pp. 4–5.

98. Ibid., 1–4.

99. Ibid., 4.

100. W. G. D. Worthington to J. Q. Adams, August 18, 1822, p. 3.

101. According to Warren Howard, between 1837 and 1862 only seven of the slave traders who were convicted under the Slave Trade Act of 1818 served time in prison. Howard wrote, "when, occasionally, a ship's officer did go to jail, he could almost invariably obtain executive clemency. Usually his fine was remitted if he pleaded poverty; frequently his sentence was reduced by many months." See William Howard, *American Slavers and the Federal Law, 1837–1862* (Berkeley: University of California Press, 1963), 189–190. Only two slaver captains were convicted under the Act of 1820: James Smith in 1854, who spent thirty-two months in prison before President Buchanan pardoned him, and Nathaniel Gordon, who was executed in 1862.

102. "Vermont . . . ," *Arkansas Gazette* (Little Rock, AR), August 3, 1824.

103. "Slave Trade," *Daily National Intelligencer*, June 2, 1820.

104. Equity Case Files of the United States Circuit Court for the Southern District of New York, 1791–1846, M884, "Eugene Malibran vs. The United States of America," U.S. District Court for the Southern District of New York, Records of District Courts of the United States, Record Group 21, NARA, New York.

105. Henry Wheaton, *Report of Cases Argued and Adjudged in the Supreme Court of the United States*, February Term, 1825, vol. 10 (New York: R. Donaldson, 1825), 142.

106. John Quincy Adams, *Memoirs of John Quincy Adams Comprising Portions of His Diary from 1795 to 1848*, ed. Charles Francis Adams (Philadelphia: J. B. Lippincott, 1875), 3:305.

CHAPTER 8. "SOME RASCALLY BUSINESS"

1. Jacob F. Schirmer Diary, August 21, 1835, South Carolina Historical Society, Charleston, SC (hereafter SCHS).

2. "Summary Punishment," *Charleston Courier* (Charleston, SC), August 22, 1835. The 1830–1831 and 1835–1836 city directories both listed R. W. Carroll as a hairdresser at 4

Queen Street; Morris Goldsmith, *Directory and Strangers' Guide, for the City of Charleston and Its Vicinity, from the Fifth Census of the United States* (Charleston: Printed at the Office of the Irishman, 1831); James Smith, *The Charleston Directory and Register for 1835–6* (Charleston: Daniel J. Dowling, 1835); Schirmer reported that Wood shipped as many as seventy-five bales in one season. Schirmer Diary, August 21, 1835, SCHS.

3. "Summary Punishment." Wood did not deal solely in stolen cotton. The *Charleston Courier* announced on August 24, "We are requested by the Sheriff of Charleston District to state that several Trunks, (removed from the late residence of R. W. CARROLL, in Queen street, containing articles supposed to have been stolen by and received from Negroes) have been left for the inspection of the public at the auction store of Mr. DUNN, Vendue Range. It is requested that all persons who may have lost, at that time, silver spoons, fine linen, and other articles of value, will go and examine the trunks, and claim their property, if found therein. The balance of articles, unclaimed, will be sold, and the amount paid over to the Intendant of the City, to be remitted to the Wife and Children of CARROLL." A later account of this episode similarly added that "several trunks were taken therefrom, which contained silver spoons, fine linen, ladies' apparel complete, bed drapery, etc." "We are requested . . . ," *Charleston Courier*, August 24, 1835; William L. King, *The Newspaper Press of Charleston, S.C.: A Chronological and Biographical History, Embracing a Period of One Hundred and Forty Years* (Charleston: Edward Perry Book Press, 1872), 150–151.

4. Eugene D. Genovese, *Roll, Jordan, Roll: The World the Slaves Made* (New York: Vintage Books, 1974), 599–600; Alex Lichtenstein, "'That Disposition to Theft, with Which They Have Been Branded': Moral Economy, Slave Management, and the Law," *Journal of Social History* 21, no. 3 (Spring 1988): 421.

5. Helen Tunnicliff Catterall, ed., *Judicial Cases Concerning American Slavery and the Negro* (Buffalo: W. S. Hein, 1998), 2:373.

6. "Summary Punishment." In May 1842 Jacob Schirmer remarked upon the trial of John K. Brown "for receiving stolen cotton from a Mr. Howard." Schirmer Diary, May 11, 1842, SCHS.

7. Grand Jury Presentment, Charleston District, May 1851, South Carolina Department of Archives and History (hereafter SCDAH).

8. "Summary Punishment."

9. Lacy K. Ford, *Deliver Us from Evil: The Slavery Question in the Old South* (New York: Oxford University Press, 2009), 481–504; William W. Freehling, *Prelude to Civil War: The Nullification Controversy in South Carolina, 1816–1836* (New York: Harper and Row, 1965), 340–348.

10. Grand Jury Presentment, Charleston District, May 1851, SCDAH.

11. Grand Jury Presentment, Charleston District, May 1852, SCDAH. Also see Grand Jury Presentments, Charleston District, January 1859, January 1860, SCDAH; George B. Eckhard, ed., *A Digest of Ordinances of the City Council of Charleston from the Year 1783 to Oct. 1844: To Which Are Annexed the Acts of the Legislature Which Relate Exclusively to the City of Charleston* (Charleston: Walker and Burke, 1844), 219–230; "Carolinian," *Charleston Courier*, March 4, 1835; and "A Friend to Good Order," *Charleston*

Courier, March 14, 1835. Frederick Law Olmsted noted an item in the *Charleston Standard* (Charleston, SC) from November 23, 1854, which stated, "This abominable practice of trading with slaves, is not only taking our produce from us, but injuring our slave property," adding that "the negroes will steal and trade, as long as white persons hold out to them temptations to steal and bring to them." See Olmsted, *A Journey in the Seaboard Slave States: With Remarks on Their Economy* (New York: Dix and Edwards, 1856), 441.

12. See David J. McCord, ed., *The Statutes at Large of South Carolina; Edited, Under Authority of the Legislature* (Columbia: A. S. Johnston, 1840), 7:407–408, 434–435, 454–455; Eckhard, *Digest of the Ordinances of Charleston, 1783–1844*, 171–172; and Lichtenstein, "That Disposition to Theft," 428–430.

13. "Main Guard House," *Charleston Mercury* (Charleston, SC), December 24, 1839.

14. See, for instance, Eric Williams, *Capitalism and Slavery* (Chapel Hill: University of North Carolina Press, 1944); Robert William Fogel and Stanley L. Engerman, *Time on the Cross: The Economics of American Negro Slavery* (Boston: Little, Brown, 1974); Herbert G. Gutman, *Slavery and the Numbers Game: A Critique of Time on the Cross* (Urbana: University of Illinois Press, 2003); Eugene D. Genovese, *The Political Economy of Slavery: Studies in the Economy and Society of the Slave South* (New York: Vintage, 1967); Genovese, *Roll, Jordan, Roll*; and James Oakes, *The Ruling Race: A History of American Slaveholders* (New York: W. W. Norton, 1998).

15. For studies of the international and domestic slave trades, see David Eltis, *Economic Growth and the Ending of the Transatlantic Slave Trade* (New York: Oxford University Press, 1987); Marcus Rediker, *The Slave Ship: A Human History* (New York: Viking, 2007); Stephanie Smallwood, *Saltwater Slavery: A Middle Passage from Africa to American Diaspora* (Cambridge, MA: Harvard University Press, 2007); Frederic Bancroft, *Slave Trading in the Old South* (orig. pub. 1931; repr. Columbia: University of South Carolina Press, 1996); Michael Tadman, *Speculators and Slaves: Masters, Traders, and Slaves in the Old South* (Madison: University of Wisconsin Press, 1989); Walter Johnson, *Soul by Soul: Life Inside the Antebellum Slave Market* (Cambridge, MA: Harvard University Press, 1999); and Steven Deyle, *Carry Me Back: The Domestic Slave Trade in American Life* (New York: Oxford University Press, 2006). The national and global nature of industrialization are illustrated in Joseph Inikori, *Africans and the Industrial Revolution in England: A Study in International Trade and Economic Development* (New York: Cambridge University Press, 2002).

16. See, for example, Seth Rockman, *Scraping By: Wage Labor, Slavery, and Survival in Early Baltimore* (Baltimore, MD: Johns Hopkins University Press, 2009); Mihm, *A Nation of Counterfeiters*; and Rothman, *Flush Times and Fever Dreams*.

17. See Genovese, *Roll, Jordan, Roll*, 587–612; Lichtenstein, "'That Disposition to Theft,'" 413–440; E. P. Thompson, *The Making of the English Working Class* (New York: Vintage, 1966); Peter Linebaugh, *The London Hanged: Crime and Civil Society in the Eighteenth Century* (London: Verso, 2003); Herbert Aptheker, *American Negro Slave Revolts* (New York: International Publishers, 1993); Kenneth M. Stampp, *The Peculiar Institution: Slavery in the Ante-Bellum South* (New York: Alfred A. Knopf, 1956); Linda Cooke Johnson, "Criminality on the Docks," in *Dock Workers: International Explorations in Comparative Labour History, 1790–1970*, ed. Sam Davies et al. (Burlington, VT: Ashgate Publishing Limited,

2000), 2:721–745; Gerald Mars, "Dock Pilferage," in *Deviance and Social Control*, ed. Paul Rock and Mary McIntosh (London: Tavistock Publications Limited, 1974), 209–228; Michael Grüttner, "Working-Class Crime and the Labour Movement: Pilfering in the Hamburg Docks, 1888–1923," in *The German Working Class, 1888–1933: The Politics of Everyday Life*, ed. Richard J. Evans (Totowa, NJ: Barnes and Noble, 1982), 54–79; Michael Stephen Hindus, *Prison and Plantation: Crime, Justice, and Authority in Massachusetts and South Carolina, 1767–1878* (Chapel Hill: University of North Carolina Press, 1980), 140–141; and Frederick Douglass, *My Bondage and My Freedom* (New York: Miller, Orton, 1857), 189–190.

18. Historian Jeffrey Bolster suggested the concept of antebellum southern waterfronts as "amphibious borderlands" while serving as a commentator for a panel session at the annual meeting of the Southern Historical Association in Baltimore, Maryland, in 2011.

19. Douglas R. Egerton, "Slaves to the Marketplace: Economic Liberty and Black Rebelliousness in the Atlantic World," *Journal of the Early Republic* 26, no. 4 (Winter 2006): 617–639.

20. For studies of slaves' "internal" or "informal" economies and plantation provision grounds, see Genovese, *Roll, Jordan, Roll*, 535–540; Philip D. Morgan, "Work and Culture: The Task System and the World of Lowcountry Blacks, 1700–1880," *William and Mary Quarterly*, 3rd ser., 39, no. 4 (October 1982): 563–599; Philip D. Morgan, "The Ownership of Property by Slaves in the Mid-Nineteenth-Century Low Country," *Journal of Southern History* 49, no. 3 (August 1983): 399–420; Sidney Mintz, *Caribbean Transformations* (New York: Columbia University Press, 1989); Ira Berlin and Philip D. Morgan, eds., *The Slaves' Economy: Independent Production by Slaves in the Americas* (London: Frank Cass, 1991); and Jeff Forret, "Slaves, Poor Whites, and the Underground Economy of the Rural Carolinas," *Journal of Southern History* 70, no. 4 (November 2004): 783–824.

21. Robert Pringle to John Erving, September 9, 1740, in *The Letterbook of Robert Pringle*, ed. Walter Edgar (Columbia: University of South Carolina Press, 1972), 2:243–244. Also see a similar letter to Erving on December 7, 1743, Edgar, *Letterbook of Robert Pringle*, 2:616; Court of General Sessions, Indictments, Charleston County, 1809-53A, SCDAH; Charleston Chamber of Commerce Award Book, case 2, June 5, 1823, SCHS. Also see Henry Averell v. William Rindge, Charleston District Court, Record of Cases, May Term, 1816, David M. Rubenstein Rare Book and Manuscript Library, Duke University (hereafter RL).

22. State v. Francis Deignan, Charleston District Court, Record of Cases, January Term, 1823, RL; "Robberies," *Charleston Courier*, May 10, 1830. Jacob Schirmer noted in December 1841 that on the "night of [the] 23rd a store on Boyce's Wharf was broken open and several Bags of Coffee stole." Schirmer Diary, December 20, 1841, SCHS; Schirmer Diary, August 22, 1833, SCHS. The *Charleston Courier* reported that the back of the store was broken open "by wrenching off the pad lock," demonstrating that even locked-up waterfront goods were subject to theft. "Caution," *Charleston Courier*, August 24, 1833; Goldsmith, *City Directory for 1830–31*. The 1835–1836 city directory listed Lafar as a cooper at 18 Vendue Range. Smith, *City Directory for 1835–36*.

23. The decision of the chamber of commerce arbitrators is unknown; James B. Campbell Legal Case Papers, folder 11/102/8, SCHS; Charleston Tax Records, 1860–1865,

Charleston Library Society, Charleston, SC (hereafter CLS). Also see Otis Mills and Company in the 1855, 1859, and 1860 city directories and in Ward Books, 1852–1856, Charleston County Public Library, Charleston, SC (hereafter CCPL); David M. Gazlay, *The Charleston City Directory and General Business Directory for 1855: Containing the Names of the Inhabitants, Their Occupations, Places of Business and Dwelling Houses: A Business Directory, a List of the Streets, Lanes, Alleys, the City Offices, Public Institutions, Banks, &c.* (Charleston: David M. Gazlay, 1855); Leonard Mears and James Turnbull, *The Charleston Directory: Containing the Names of the Inhabitants, a Subscribers' Business Directory, Street Map of the City, and an Appendix of Much Useful Information* (Charleston: Evans, Walker, 1859); W. Eugene Ferslew, *Directory of the City of Charleston, to Which Is Added a Business Directory* (Savannah: J. M. Cooper, 1860).

24. Journal, February 28, 1857, 424, and Cash Book, July 19, 1859, 92, Charles T. Mitchell Account Books, CLS. Workers deliberately broke bottles and barrels of beer as well. In February 1861, for instance, the owners of the *Samoset* paid the grocer Bancroft five dollars for breakage on casks of ale. Cash Book, February 16, 1861, 138, Charles T. Mitchell Account Books, CLS. The rules of the Charleston Chamber of Commerce prescribed a standard "Allowance for Leakage and Breakage." See *New Tariff Amended, or Duties Payable on Goods, Wares & Merchandize Imported into the United States of America: Likewise the Rates of Tonnage, Drawback, Tares, &c.* (Charleston: A. E. Miller, 1823), 24. Also see Johnson, "Criminality on the Docks," 2:724n8.

25. See Johnson, "Criminality on the Docks," 2:725; and Grüttner, "Working-Class Crime," 59.

26. Logbook of the Ship *Robin Hood*, February 9, 1833, Collections Research Center, Mystic Seaport, Mystic, CT.

27. *John H. Graver v. Steamer Palmetto*, February 15, 1853, Admiralty Minute Book, District of South Carolina, 5:282–283, National Archives and Records Administration (hereafter NARA), Atlanta.

28. Catterall, *Judicial Cases*, 2:415. The 1849 city directory listed J. F. Tiedeman as a grocer on Elizabeth Street, and Otto Tiedeman as a grocer on Boundary Street (later Calhoun Street). John H. Honour, *A Directory of the City of Charleston and Neck for 1849; Containing the Names, Residences and Occupations of the Inhabitants Generally: To Which Is Appended, a List of the Banks, Insurance Companies, Societies, Fire Department, Military, and Various Other Matters of General Interest* (Charleston: Printed by A. J. Burke, 1849).

29. Court of General Sessions, Indictments, Charleston County, 1823-55A, SCDAH.

30. Ibid.

31. Court of General Sessions, Indictments, Charleston County, 1826-4A, SCDAH.

32. See George Rogers Taylor, *Transportation Revolution, 1815–1860* (Armonk, NY: M. E. Sharpe, 1989); Ronald E. Shaw, *Canals for a Nation: The Canal Era in the United States, 1790–1860* (Lexington: University Press of Kentucky, 1991); Peter Way, *Common Labor: Workers and the Digging of North American Canals, 1780–1860* (Baltimore: Johns Hopkins University Press, 1997); F. A. Porcher, *The History of the Santee Canal* (Charleston: South Carolina Historical Society, 1903); *History of the Old Santee Canal* (Columbia: South Carolina Public Service Authority, n.d.); Walter Edgar, *South Carolina: A History*

(Columbia: University of South Carolina Press, 1998), 282–283; Sellers, *Market Revolution*; and Larson, *The Market Revolution in America.*

33. John G. Van Deusen, *Economic Bases of Disunion in South Carolina* (New York: Columbia University Press, 1928), 333, app. C. Also see Frederick Burtrumn Collins, "Charleston and the Railroads: A Geographic Study of a South Atlantic Port and Its Strategies for Developing a Railroad System, 1820–1860" (MA thesis, University of South Carolina, 1977), 100, Table V; and J. L. Dawson and H. W. DeSaussure, *Census of the City of Charleston, South Carolina, for the Year 1848* (Charleston: J. B. Nixon, 1849), 90–101.

34. Court of General Sessions, Indictments, Charleston County, 1830-20A, SCDAH; Goldsmith, *City Directory for 1830–31*; Smith, *City Directory for 1835–36.*

35. Occasionally, when planters desired their cotton to be guarded on the wharves at night, Charleston factors hired the same worker both to repair and guard the cotton, as when John Schulz paid a slave five dollars to mend and watch one hundred bales owned by Wade Hampton on February 28, 1817. Account Book, February 28, 1817, 22, John Schulz Account Books, South Caroliniana Library, Columbia, SC (hereafter SCL).

36. Petition, ND no. 1895, SCDAH. Also see Reeder and DeSaussure to A. H. Boykin, December 2, 1853, March 24, 1856, March 21, 1857, October 1, 1859, Boykin Family Papers, Southern Historical Collection, Chapel Hill, NC.

37. K. Boyce and Company Account Book, January 17, 1837, 114, SCHS.

38. Court of General Sessions, Indictments, Charleston County, 1835-9A, SCDAH.

39. Requesting exemption from militia duty to enable the protection of waterfront property during fires "and on all occasions where there is any sudden confusion in any portion of the City," Charleston's wharfingers stated in a petition to the state legislature in 1838 "that it frequently happens that goods of considerable value are allowed to remain on the wharf unstored during a part and often for the whole of a day." Petition, 1838 no. 117, SCDAH.

40. Though this petition was undated, it probably was written during the 1830s. It was not until the mid-1830s, for instance, that Ker Boyce and several other signers owned wharves. Petition, ND no. 1895, SCDAH.

41. Permitting slaves to cultivate cotton independently, complained South Carolina planters in 1816, enabled enterprising bondsmen to purchase and sell pilfered cotton "with impunity." Once entered onto the market, the petitioners argued, identifying and recovering the stolen cotton bales was "like looking of a drop of water lost in a river." Petition, 1816 no. 95, SCDAH, quoted in John Hope Franklin and Loren Schweninger, *Runaway Slaves: Rebels on the Plantation* (New York: Oxford University Press, 1999), 90. Also see Loren Schweninger, "Slave Independence and Enterprise in South Carolina, 1780–1865," *South Carolina Historical Magazine* 93, no. 2 (April 1992): 101–125.

42. Petition, ND no. 1895, SCDAH.

43. McCord, *Statutes*, 7:469. Also see Eckhard, *Digest of the Ordinances of Charleston, 1783–1844*, 221, 224; and "A Friend to Morals," in *Charleston Courier*, June 25, 1835.

44. In a separate deposition given on August 15, Levy claimed that he had seen yet another slave enter the Danielses' premises with a parcel of loose cotton; Court of General Sessions, Indictments, Charleston County, 1835-29A, 1835-42A, 1835-45A, SCDAH.

Though the 1835–1836 city directory confirmed that J. R. Daniels lived at 68 State Street, no occupation was given. Smith, *City Directory for 1835–36.*

45. Court of General Sessions, Indictments, Charleston County, 1835-29A-1835-46A, SCDAH. John Fraser and Company owned one slave in 1858, 1859, 1860, and 1862, and sixteen slaves in 1864. In 1864 the company was involved heavily in running the Union blockade of Charleston Harbor; Charleston Tax Records, 1860–1865, CLS; *List of the Tax Payers of the City of Charleston for 1858* (Charleston, SC: Steam Press of Walker, Evans, 1859); *List of the Tax Payers of the City of Charleston for 1859* (Charleston, SC: Steam-Power Press of Walker, Evans, 1860).

46. Court of General Sessions, Indictments, Charleston County, 1835-29A, SCDAH. Mary Daniels also pled guilty to further charges of trading cotton during the same session and was sentenced to an additional month's imprisonment. Court of General Sessions, Indictments, Charleston County, 1835-45A, SCDAH.

47. Court of General Sessions, Indictments, Charleston County, 1835-9A, SCDAH.

48. Petition, ND no. 5564, SCDAH; McCord, *Statutes*, 7:146; "Proceedings of Council," February 28, 1837, CCPL manuscript; "Proceedings of Council," April 4, 1837, *Charleston Courier*, April 18, 1837.

49. For examples of waterfront barriers, see Schirmer Diary, after July 1835, SCHS; "Proceedings of Council," August 25, 1840, *Charleston Mercury*, August 27, 1840; "Proceedings of Council," September 28, 1840, *Charleston Mercury*, October 1, 1840; and Vanderhorst Wharf Business Papers, folder 16, SCHS. For examples of night watchmen, see Patrick Scanlan in Gazlay, *City Directory for 1855*; and P. McWee, P. Sheen, and W. S. Smith in Ferslew, *City Directory for 1860*; Schirmer Diary, June 10, 1849, SCHS; and South Carolina Railroad Company Semi-Annual Report, January 1, 1840, Jane H. and William H. Pease Papers, Avery Research Center, College of Charleston, Charleston, SC.

50. For information on waterfront street lamps, see "Proceedings of Council," August 3, 1840, *Charleston Mercury*, August 5, 1840; "Proceedings of Council," December 12, 1842, *Charleston Mercury*, December 14, 1842; "Proceedings of Council," August 9, 1848, *Southern Patriot* (Charleston, SC), August 11, 1848; "Proceedings of Council," September 26, 1848, *Southern Patriot*, September 28, 1848; "Proceedings of Council," August 3, 1858, *Charleston Mercury*, August 5, 1858; "Proceedings of Council," August 17, 1858, *Charleston Mercury*, August 19, 1858; and "Proceedings of Council," October 26, 1858, *Charleston Mercury*, October 28, 1858; "All persons, unless duly . . . ," *Southern Patriot*, March 5, 1845.

51. "All persons, unless duly . . . ," *Southern Patriot*, March 5, 1845; "Proceedings of Council," August 26, 1845, *Southern Patriot*, August 28, 1845. Also see "Proceedings of Council," September 14, 1846, *Southern Patriot*, September 15, 1846.

52. These guardsmen were said to report to their posts at twilight, which could be as early as 5 o'clock during the peak commercial season, and remain there until relieved at around half past nine at night, at which time they reported to the Guard House unless impelled to return to the wharves by an emergency. "Proceedings of Council," February 15, 1847, *Southern Patriot*, February 16, 1847. Charleston police records reveal that these wharf patrols persisted into the 1850s. On February 26, 1856, for instance, Private Lyans "Could not be found on Post on Sunday Evenings [*sic*] Wharf Duty on Southern &

Commercial Wharves between Bells and not returning to the Guard House." On the same day, Private Sullivan was caught "Lying a Sleep [*sic*] on post Atlantic Wharf on a Bale of Cotton at 3/4 past 10 oClock P.M." And on March 13, 1856, Private Daly "Could not be found on his Post No. 7 Frazers [*sic*] Wharf near 4 oClock A.M." All three guardsmen were fined three dollars, and Private Sullivan was dismissed from duty at his own request. Charleston Police Records, February 26, 1856, March 13, 1856, CLS.

53. H. Pinckney Walker, ed., *Ordinances of the City of Charleston from the 19th of August 1844, to the 14th of September 1854; and the Acts of the General Assembly Relating to the City of Charleston, and City Council of Charleston, During the Same Interval* (Charleston: A. E. Miller, 1854), 72–73. Cotton sometimes disappeared from cotton presses. On December 24, 1859, commission merchant Charles T. Mitchell made an entry of $46.64 in his cash book "for 1 Bale of Cotton Short from Union press & to be deducted from their Bill." Less than a year later, Charles O. Witte recorded $52.63 in cash "collected from Union Press for 1 Bale missing." Cash Book, December 24, 1859, 106, Charles T. Mitchell Account Books, CLS; Cash Book, November 1, 1860, Charles O. Witte Estate Records, SCHS.

54. John R. Horsey, ed., *Ordinances of the City of Charleston from the 14th of September, 1854, to the 1st December, 1859; and the Acts of the General Assembly Relating to the City Council of Charleston, and the City of Charleston, During the Same Period* (Charleston: Walker, Evans, 1859), 16. The city council also passed an ordinance in March 1858 to license and regulate secondhand or junk shops, several sections of which seemed to be aimed at preventing the traffic of stolen goods. One provision, for instance, declared that shops were to be kept open only between sunrise and sunset, and were subject to police inspection at any time. Another stipulated that keepers of such shops were not permitted to trade with minors, apprentices, slaves, or free blacks without the permission of their guardians or owners. Ibid., 40–41.

55. Originally in the Mayor's Court, "The case was turned over to Magistrate Dingle for investigation." Officer Levy may have been either aforementioned police officer Moses E. Levy or Orlando Levy, a second lieutenant in the guard. Regardless, Levy regularly patrolled the wharves. See "Mayor's Court," *Charleston Mercury*, February 14, 1856; "Mayor's Court," *Charleston Mercury*, February 1, 1856; and Gazlay, *City Directory for 1855*.

56. Walker, *Ordinances of the City of Charleston, 1844–1854*, 45–48, 62–65, 159. Also see Charles Mackay, *Life and Liberty in America; or, Sketches of a Tour in the United States and Canada in 1857–8* (New York: Harper and Brothers, 1859), 195; and McCrady Motte and Company v. R. L. & W. E. Holmes, Admiralty Journal, U.S. District Court, Eastern District of South Carolina, Charleston, 1857–1861, 1–4, NARA, Atlanta.

57. Catterall, *Judicial Cases*, 2:318. According to Charleston's grand jurors in May 1851, "Slave property in this District, and especially in this City is every day decreasing in value . . . in consequence of the corrupt influence" of the white liquor dealers. Grand Jury Presentment, Charleston District, May 1851, SCDAH.

58. Christopher Fitzsimons to Mr. David Olivier, July 28, 1807, Christopher Fitzsimons Letterbook, SCL.

CHAPTER 9. SELLING SEX AND INTIMACY IN THE CITY

1. [William Darlington], "Journalissimo of a Peregrination to the City of Baltimore: Performed in the Year *domini* 1803," William Darlington Papers, New-York Historical Society. Thanks to Seth Rockman for sharing information about this citation.

2. "A Manuscript Account of a Journey from Wilmington to Baltimore and Back," 1818, p. 15. MS 523, Special Collections, Milton S. Eisenhower Library, Johns Hopkins University.

3. Numerous historians have acknowledged the presence of occasional prostitutes in urban marketplaces. For detailed discussions of prostitution as a common element of lower- and working-class youth culture, see Elizabeth Clement, *Love for Sale: Courting, Treating, and Prostitution in New York City, 1900–1945* (Chapel Hill: University of North Carolina Press, 1998); Timothy Gilfoyle, *City of Eros: New York, Prostitution, and the Commercialization of Sex, 1790–1920* (Chapel Hill: University of North Carolina Press, 1994); Judith Walkowitz, *Prostitution and Victorian Society: Women, Class, and the State* (Cambridge: Cambridge University Press, 1980).

4. Historian Katherine Hijar has noted that depictions of commercial sex establishments in popular culture often highlighted their bourgeois characteristics. Drawing on a variety of brothel guides, paintings, and published texts, Hijar argues that sporting male publications used surprisingly genteel language in their descriptions of brothels, which they cast as pseudo-domestic spaces that maintained many of the gender conventions of the American middle class. See Hijar, "Sexuality, Print, and Popular Visual Culture in the United States, 1830–1870" (PhD diss., Johns Hopkins University, 2008), 457–516.

5. Rebecca Yamin, "Wealthy, Free, and Female: Prostitution in Nineteenth-Century New York," *Historical Archaeology* 39, no. 1 (2005): 4–18, quotation on 4.

6. John Neal, *Randolph: A Novel* ([Philadelphia]: Published for whom it may concern, 1823), 60.

7. For discussions of Baltimore's economic expansion, see John Thomas Scharf, *History of Baltimore City and County, from the Earliest Period to the Present Day* (Philadelphia: Louis H. Everts, 1881); Gary Lawson Browne, *Baltimore in the Nation, 1789–1861* (Chapel Hill: University of North Carolina Press, 1980); Seth Rockman, *Scraping By: Wage Labor, Slavery, and Survival in Early Baltimore* (Baltimore: Johns Hopkins University Press, 2009).

8. Rockman, *Scraping By*, 23.

9. Scharf, *History of Baltimore City and County*, 513.

10. For a discussion of nineteenth-century maritime culture and sailors' experiences in boardinghouses, see W. Jeffrey Bolster, *Black Jacks: African American Seamen in the Age of Sail* (Cambridge, MA: Harvard University Press, 1997), esp. 186–187 and 228. On dockside prostitution, see Linda M. Maloney, "Doxies at Dockside: Prostitution and American Maritime Society, 1800–1900," in *Ships, Seafaring, and Society: Essays in Maritime History*, ed. Timothy J. Runyan (Detroit, Mich.: Wayne State University Press, 1987), 217–225.

11. The correspondent to the *Whip* claimed that Wilson had been a bawd for thirty-five years. Wilson appeared in Baltimore City Court at least as early as 1825 on charges of keeping a disorderly house: Baltimore City Court (Docket and Minutes), case no. 487, June Term, 1825 (C184-2), Hall of Records, Annapolis, Maryland. Wilson appeared in numerous court dockets thereafter on charges related to keeping a disorderly or bawdy house, and city directories indicate that she continued to operate her establishment as late as 1850. See *Matchett's Baltimore Director [sic], 1849 '50* (Baltimore: R. J. Matchett, 1849), 426. Available online from Archive.Org, http://archive.org/details/matchettsbaltimo1849balt (accessed December 21, 2013).

12. "Baltimore: Correspondent of The Whip," *The Whip* (New York), July 2, 1842, quoted in *The Flash Press: Sporting Male Weeklies in 1840s New York*, ed. Patricia Cline Cohen, Timothy J. Gilfoyle, and Helen Lefkowitz Horowitz (Chicago: University of Chicago Press, 2008), 190–191. Wilson's brothel was also listed as a tavern in the 1842 issue of *Matchett's Baltimore Director* ([Baltimore]: Baltimore Director Office, [1842]), 403.

13. "Vile Cribs," *The Viper's Sting and Paul Pry* (Baltimore), August 11, 1849. Only a few issues of the *Viper* are known to exist today, but their content suggests that the paper had a lengthier run.

14. "Depravity," *Sun* (Baltimore), June 13, 1839.

15. "A Bad Neighborhood," *Sun*, August 1, 1840.

16. Maryland Governor and Council (Pardon Papers, folder 106 [MSA S1061-15], Maryland Hall of Records, Annapolis (hereafter MHR), quoted in James D. Rice, "Laying Claim to Elizabeth Shoemaker," in *Over the Threshold: Intimate Violence in Early America*, ed. Christine Daniels and Michael V. Kennedy (New York: Routledge, 1999), 185–201.

17. William Sanger, *The History of Prostitution: Its Extent, Causes, and Effects Throughout the World* (New York: Harper and Brothers, 1869), 559–564.

18. William Sanger notes dissatisfaction with the restraints imposed by home life as a reason why young women entered the sex trade in his chapter on the causes of prostitution. See ibid., 451–548.

19. This claim is based on examinations of twelve sample years of court dockets from the Baltimore County Court of Oyer and Terminer (C-183), the Baltimore City Court (C-184), and the Baltimore City Criminal Court (C-1849) between 1813 and 1860 (court records exist somewhat sporadically for the years before 1852), MHR. See also Stansell, *City of Women*, 171–192.

20. For a selection of Harriet Carroll's appearances in Baltimore City Criminal Courts on charges of keeping a bawdy house, see Baltimore City Court (Docket and Minutes), cases no. 246 and 247, October Term, 1839 (C184-6); case no. 292, May Term, 1847 (C184-10), MHR.

21. Cynthia M. Blair, *I've Got to Make My Livin': Black Women's Sex Work in Turn-of-the-Century Chicago* (Chicago: University of Chicago Press, 2010). For an earlier study of black women's participation in the sex trade and commercial sex across the color line, see Judith Kelleher Schafer, *Brothels, Depravity, and Abandoned Women: Illegal Sex in Antebellum New Orleans* (Baton Rouge: Louisiana State University Press, 2009).

22. "Central Watch," *Sun,* August 25, 1837.

23. "Baltimore: Correspondent of The Whip," *The Whip*, July 2, 1842. Quoted in Cohen, Gilfoyle, and Horowitz, *Flash Press,* 190. "Central Watch," *Sun*, August 26, 1837; "Nuisances," *Sun,* November 16, 1839.

24. "Baltimore: Correspondent of The Whip."

25. On the coalescence of the middle class in Early Republic cities, see Blumin, *The Emergence of the Middle Class.*

26. A Baltimorean, *The Stranger's Guide to Baltimore, Showing the Easiest and Best Mode of Seeing All the Public Buildings and Places of Note* (Baltimore: Murphy, 1852), 15.

27. "Baltimore: Correspondent of The Whip."

28. Timothy Gilfoyle noted a similar shift from mixed-economic spaces to specialized commercial sex establishments in antebellum New York, though the process took place significantly earlier. Gilfoyle noted that bawdy houses began to supplant taverns and boardinghouses as the primary sites of commercial sex after 1820 and that they were a well-established part of the urban landscape by the late 1830s. *City of Eros*, 161–178. As I argue here, specialization in Baltimore was a significantly slower process, and one that occurred unevenly throughout the city.

29. For a history Baltimore's early institutional and commercial development, see Scharf, *History of Baltimore City and County.*

30. On clerks' participation in male sporting culture, see Patricia Cline Cohen's *The Murder of Helen Jewett* (New York: Knopf, 1999). See also Gilfoyle, *City of Eros.*

31. David Schley, "Making the Capitalist City: The B&O Railroad and Urban Space in Baltimore, 1827–1877" (PhD diss., Johns Hopkins University, 2013).

32. Scharf, *History of Baltimore City and County*, 513.

33. For a discussion of Barnum's Hotel and the rise of the hospitality industry more generally, see A. K. Sandoval-Strausz, *Hotel: An American History* (New Haven, CT: Yale University Press, 2007), 50–52.

34. Gideon Miner Davison, *The Fashionable Tour: A Guide to Travellers Visiting the Middle and Northern States and the Provinces of Canada* (Saratoga Springs, NY: G. M. Davison, 1830), 50.

35. Scharf, *History of Baltimore City and County*, 516. Famous visitors to Barnum's hotel included John Quincy Adams, James Buchanan, Andrew Jackson, Martin Van Buren, Jenny Lind, Eli Whitney, and Charles Dickens, among many others.

36. Free Loveyer, *Directory to the Seraglios in New York, Philadelphia, Boston and all the Principal Cities in the Union* (New York: Printed and published for the trade, 1859), 37. Thanks to Eric Robinson of the New-York Historical Society for his assistance with this source.

37. All of the data cited here has been collected from the 1850 and 1860 U.S. Federal Census Schedules for Baltimore City, Wards 10 and 11. See Seventh Census of the United States, 1850 (microfilm publication M432, 1,009 rolls); 1860 U.S. Census, population schedule (microfilm publication M653, 1,438 rolls), both in Records of the Bureau of the Census, Record Group 29, National Archives and Records Administration, Washington, DC. Available online at Ancestry.com.

38. Baltimore was not the only city in which hotels and prostitution were spatially and economically connected. See, for instance, Gilfoyle, *City of Eros*, 120–122.

39. I am drawing conclusions from a wide sampling of court records and examinations of the census, brothel guidebooks, and a small collection of firsthand accounts of visits to brothels.

40. Hijar, "Sexuality, Print, and Popular Visual Culture," 457–516.

41. Demographic information on prostitutes was derived primarily from examinations of U.S. Federal Census Records from 1850 and 1860.

42. William Sanger noted that in first-class New York houses of prostitution, "none of the disgusting practices common in houses of a lower grade are met with here. There is no palpable obscenity, and but little that can outrage propriety." Sanger, *History of Prostitution*, 550.

43. "Baltimore: Correspondent of The Whip."

44. Baltimore County Orphans' Court, Inventory, December Term, 1848 (C396-24), MHR.

45. U.S. Federal Census Schedule, 1860, Baltimore City, Ward 11. Available online from Ancestry.com.

46. Katherine Hijar, "Sexuality, Print, and Popular Visual Culture," 457–516. Patricia Cline Cohen's *The Murder of Helen Jewett* has also made a compelling case that prostitutes performed services beyond sex, including writing letters to clients, introducing them to one another, and carrying on both short- and long-term "romantic" relationships with them. For descriptions of similarly operated houses of prostitution in New York, see Sanger, *History of Prostitution*, 549–559.

47. Free Loveyer, *Directory to the Seraglios*, 37.

48. From the Pinkerton Detective Agency's records, published by Norma Cuthbert in *Lincoln and the Baltimore Plot, 1861: From the Pinkerton Records and Related Papers* (San Marino, CA: Huntington Library, 1949).

49. Amy Dru Stanley, *From Bondage to Contract: Wage Labor, Marriage, and the Market in the Age of Slave Emancipation* (Cambridge: Cambridge University Press, 1998), 219.

50. On labor and the relationship between slavery and capitalism in early Baltimore, see Rockman, *Scraping By*.

51. Theoretical scholarship on commodities has acknowledged the role of emotion in imbuing objects with value, while numerous historical studies have argued that the nineteenth century witnessed the rise of commodities designed to evoke or capture emotions (e.g., Victorian holiday cards depicting sentimental scenes). Relatively few studies, however, have acknowledged that emotion could itself be a commodity, independent of its physical representation in objects. See Arjun Appadurai, ed., *The Social Life of Things: Commodities in Cultural Perspective* (Cambridge: Cambridge University Press, 1988); Sonia Solicari, "Selling Sentiment: The Commodification of Emotion in Victorian Visual Culture," *Interdisciplinary Studies in the Long Nineteenth Century* 19, no. 4, available at http://www.19.bbk.ac.uk/index.php/19/article/view/458 (accessed December 22, 2013).

52. While Baltimore had no well-documented, large-scale brothel riots in the antebellum period, madams, prostitutes, and brothels themselves were often targets of vio-

lence by men who resented prostitutes' wealth or their own lack of access to their services. On brothel rioting and the motivations that drove it, see Gilfoyle, *City of Eros*, 76–91; Cohen, *Murder of Helen Jewett*, 82–85.

53. Free Loveyer, *Directory to the Seraglios*, 37.

54. Ibid. Margaret "Maggie" Hamilton led a particularly interesting life. Her move to Frederick Street, for instance, had been precipitated by a violent confrontation with another madam. Hamilton attempted to whip Eliza Simpson in a public market space; Simpson responded by drawing a gun and shooting Hamilton in the face. Hamilton recovered from her wounds and became one of the most prosperous madams in the city.

55. Sanger, *History of Prostitution*, 541, 551.

56. Baltimore City Court (Docket and Minutes), case no. 331, June Term, 1830 (C184-5); MHR.

57. "City Court," *Sun*, February 18, 1840.

58. Scharf, *History of Baltimore City and County*, 695; Patricia Click, *The Spirit of the Times: Amusements in Nineteenth-Century Baltimore, Norfolk, and Richmond* (Charlottesville, VA: University of Virginia Press, 1989).

59. For more information of prostitution in theaters, see Claudia D. Johnson, "That Guilty Third Tier: Prostitution in Nineteenth-Century American Theaters," *American Quarterly* 27, no. 5, Special Issue: Victorian Culture in America (December 1975): 575–584.

60. "Local Matters," *Sun*, November 20, 1852.

61. May's Dramatic Encyclopedia of Baltimore, MS 995, Roll 7, R.A. 3 1846; R.A. 5 1846, Maryland Historical Society, Baltimore.

62. "Local Matters," *Sun*, November 20, 1852.

63. Ibid. Welch appeared in court multiple times throughout the 1850s for charges related to keeping a bawdy and disorderly house and selling liquor without a license. In 1855, for instance, he was jailed for five counts of the latter offense. Baltimore City and County Jail (Docket), July 14, 1855 (C2057-13), MHR.

64. This information is derived from an examination of Wards 10 and 11 in the U.S. Federal Census Schedules for 1850 and 1860.

65. Given the lack of available evidence, poor and laboring people's attitudes toward having brothels in their neighborhoods are difficult to discern. What is clear, however, is that the poor could not easily mobilize the types of opposition that resulted in police action or legal prosecutions designed to suppress the sex trade. Historians of prostitution in the Progressive era have argued that brothels relocated or were driven to poor (and often primarily black) neighborhoods to minimize controversy and avoid prosecution. See, for example, Kevin Mumford, *Interzones: Black/White Sex Districts in Chicago and New York in the Early Twentieth Century* (New York: Columbia University Press, 1997); Mara Keire, *For Business and Pleasure: Red-Light Districts and the Regulation of Vice in the United States, 1890–1933* (Baltimore: Johns Hopkins University Press, 2010).

66. In 1841, Hannah Smithson's assignation house was the target of a particularly strenuous prosecution after it was alleged that married women were frequenting her establishment to cheat on their husbands. The public outcry over Smithson's establishment prompted the indictment of her landlord, Samuel Goldsmith. Goldsmith's was the first

case I have found in which a landlord was indicted for renting a house to be used as a house of ill fame, but such charges became common in the years following his case. In 1848, the Maryland Court of Appeals upheld the city's right to prosecute the landlords of brothels in State v. Smith, 6 Gill 425.

67. While cities like New York seldom prosecuted the keepers or landlords of top-tier houses, Baltimore's annual presentments of bawdy house keepers typically included everyone from the lowest to the most affluent madams.

68. For Priscilla Howard's case, see Baltimore City Criminal Court (Docket), case no. 487, January Term, 1855 (C1849-4); for Calder's, see Baltimore City Criminal Court (Docket), case no. 886, May Term, 1852 (C1849-1) MHR. By the 1860 Census, Calder owned $8,000 of real property and $900 of personal property. As more specialization began to occur in East Baltimore, Orleans Street in particular became a hub of second-class commercial sex establishments.

69. Gilfoyle, *City of Eros*, 45.

70. Andrew Fitzpatrick, Baltimore City Criminal Court (Criminal Docket), cases no. 838–845, May Term, 1849, MSA C-1849. Lewis and Sarah Goldsmith, Baltimore City Criminal Court (Criminal Docket) cases no. 222–227, January Term, 1855, MHR.

CHAPTER 10. ECONOMIES OF PRINT IN THE NINETEENTH-CENTURY CITY

1. Davis Lawler James, Scrapbook, 1838–1933, American Antiquarian Society, Worcester, MA.

2. The practices of publishers and booksellers run counter to the narrative of increasing specialization offered by Stuart Blumin, Glenn Porter, and Harold Livesay. Porter and Livesay focus on increasing specialization in *roles* in the trade in manufactured goods—between manufacturer, merchant, wholesaler, jobber, and retailer. Blumin, on the other hand, focuses more on specialization in the retail sector—that is, in the *kinds* of goods that retailers sold. As this essay will show, the print trades represented a smaller-scale mode of manufacturing that lent itself to flexibility in roles, and printed goods often found a home on shelves and in catalogs with entirely different types of goods. See Glenn Porter and Harold C. Livesay, *Merchants and Manufacturers: Studies in the Changing Structure of Nineteenth-Century Marketing* (Baltimore: Johns Hopkins University Press, 1971), 17–22; and Blumin, *The Emergence of the Middle Class*, 78–83.

3. John Tebbel, "A Brief History of American Bookselling," in *Bookselling in America and the World*, ed. Charles B. Anderson (New York: Quadrangle, 1975), 12.

4. Robert Darnton, "What Is the History of Books," *Daedalus* 111, no. 3 (1982): 68.

5. Brewster Maverick pocket diary, 1847, New-York Historical Society. The plays he purchased include *Irish Attorney, How to Pay the Rent, Boots at the Sivan*[?], *Invisible Prince, Dead Shot, Charles 2nd of England, Charles 12th of Sweden, Loan of a Lover, Nervous Man, Used Up, William Tell, London Assurance, Macbeth Travestie*, and *Day After the Wedding*.

6. The world of amateur theatricals in the nineteenth century was remarkably robust. See Mary Isbell, "Amateurs: Home, Shipboard, and Public Theatricals in the Nineteenth Century" (PhD diss., University of Connecticut, November 2012); John W. Frick, *Theatre, Culture and Temperance Reform in Nineteenth-Century America* (Cambridge: Cambridge University Press, 2008); Eileen Curley, "Recording Forbidden Careers: Nineteenth-Century Amateur Theatricals," in *Scrapbooks, Snapshots and Memorabilia: Hidden Archives of Performance*, ed. Glen McGillivray (New York: Peter Lang, 2011), 229–248; and Lawrence W. Levine, *Highbrow/Lowbrow: The Emergence of Cultural Hierarchy in America* (Cambridge, MA: Harvard University Press, 1990).

7. Maverick pocket diary, 1847. See the entries for May 10, 1847: "Seen my Mary." May 14, 1847: "Went to see Mary. Treated rather cool." May 17, 1847: "Went to the Office. Asked Uncle for 75 cents. Would not give it to me. Left the Office. Vell, vot of it."

8. Ibid., May 18, 1847. The book he finished is most likely John H. Mancur's *The Palais Royal*, a historical romance set during the French Revolution which was published in New York in 1845.

9. Sam Slick was a comic character invented by Thomas Chandler Haliburton who appeared in numerous novels, almanacs, and joke books through the 1830s and '40s. It is impossible to know what title or edition Maverick might have been reading, but it was likely an edition of Haliburton's first use of Slick, *The Clockmaker; or, The Sayings and Doings of Samuel Slick, of Slickville* (New York: William H. Colyer, 1840). Samuel Lover, *Handy Andy: A Tale of Irish Life* (New York: D. Appleton, 1843); Jean-Baptiste Louvet de Couvray, *The Adventures of the Chevalier de Faublas: The French Don Juan*, written by himself (Boston: Irving, 1843–1844); Robert F. Williams, *The Secret Passion* (New York: Burgess, Stringer, 1847).

10. Brewster Maverick would forgo a career in the law. Instead, he took over his father's engraving business and added lithography to their range of offerings. He died in 1898, but the lithography firm of Maverick and Wissinger survived into the early twentieth century. For more on the significance of the print trades in antebellum New York City, see Allan Pred, *The Spatial Dynamics of U.S. Urban-Industrial Growth, 1800–1914: Interpretive and Theoretical Essays* (Cambridge, MA: MIT Press, 1966), 174–175.

11. Scofield gave his address as being on Nineteenth Street, although there are no families by that name that appear in any New York City directories from the early 1840s that I have been able to find, which is unsurprising given the family's apparent poor economic circumstances. Of course, Scofield may also have lied about his home address.

12. Helen Lefkowitz Horowitz, *Rereading Sex: Battles over Sexual Knowledge and Suppression in Nineteenth-Century America* (New York: Knopf, 2002), 211.

13. Ironically, in 1856 Matsell would take over the *National Police Gazette* and was responsible for shifting the newspaper's focus from accounts of criminal prosecutions to sex scandals and prostitution.

14. It is impossible to know what editions of these books Scofield would have been selling, since they were mainstays of the antebellum erotica trade, and many editions of obscene books that were available in the antebellum United States were imported. Most works of erotica, whether imported or domestically produced, either had no publication

information on the title page or included deliberately misleading information. John Cleland's *Memoirs of a Woman of Pleasure,* more commonly known as *Fanny Hill,* became one of the most commonly reprinted erotic books in the Anglophone Atlantic world in the wake of its 1748 publication. John Benjamin Brookes's *The Lustful Turk; or Lascivious Scenes in a Harem* was first published anonymously in 1828. *The Curtain Drawn Up; or The Education of Laura* was written by the French Revolutionary Comte de Mirabeau and appeared in various translations in the early nineteenth century. It is likely that all three of these particular editions sold by Scofield were printed in New York by Richard Hobbes, a publisher of erotica who was arrested for obscenity in 1842.

15. Deposition dated August 18, 1842; District Attorney Indictment Papers, Court of General Sessions, 1790–1879, reel 212, box 413 (September 28, 1842), New York City Municipal Archives and Records Center.

16. William W. Sanger, *The History of Prostitution: Its Extent, Causes, and Effects Throughout the World* (New York: Harper and Brothers, 1858), 521–522.

17. Sanger, *History of Prostitution,* 522.

18. "Obscene Pictures," *New York Sporting Whip,* November 11, 1843.

19. Horowitz, *Rereading Sex,* 244.

20. Donna Dennis, *Licentious Gotham: Erotic Publishing and Its Prosecution in Nineteenth-Century New York* (Cambridge, MA: Harvard University Press, 2009), 145.

21. "Police Items," *National Police Gazette* (New York), April 17, 1847: "Officers Doyle and Parrison, of the 4th ward, arrested, Saturday, a young man by the name of Edward Thomas Scofield, whom the officer found in the vestibule of the Astor House, offering for sale obscene books; he was conducted before Justice Drinker, and in default of bail in $500, he was committed to the Tombs."

22. Ibid. Dennis's and Horowitz's books, along with Timothy Gilfoyle's *City of Eros* and E. Haven Hawley's doctoral dissertation, when taken together, offer the best understanding we have ever had of the workings of the pornography trade in nineteenth-century New York, and represent models of a new strain of book history that is addressing itself to different texts, marginal publishers, and unknown readers. See Gilfoyle, *City of Eros*; and Elizabeth Haven Hawley, "American Publishers of Indecent Books, 1840–1890" (PhD diss., Georgia Institute of Technology, 2005).

23. "General Sessions," *National Police Gazette,* May 29, 1847: "Edward Thomas was next placed upon his trial on an indictment of having, on the 9th of April, offered to sell obscene books. The testimony in this case was so conclusive the jury found a verdict of guilty, and the court sentenced him to the penitentiary for the term of six months." Dennis, *Licentious Gotham,* 146.

24. Thomas M. McDade, "Lurid Literature of the Last Century: The Publications of E. E. Barclay," *Pennsylvania Magazine of History and Biography* 80, no. 4 (October 1956): 463. The only other work to mention Barclay in any detail is Edmund Lester Pearson, *Queer Books* (Garden City, NY: Doubleday, 1928).

25. This lack of interest on the part of scholars is understandable: his papers do not exist, no library holds a comprehensive collection of his publications, and he never pub-

lished works by any prominent authors (save for George Lippard, whose rediscovery by scholars is a phenomenon of the last twenty-five years).

26. This twenty-four-page pamphlet, *The Narrative and Confessions of Lucretia P. Cannon Who Was Tried, Convicted, and Sentenced to Be Hung at Georgetown, Delaware, with Two of Her Accomplices, Containing an Account of Some of the Most Horrible and Shocking Murders and Daring Robberies Ever Committed by One of the Female Sex*, essentially set the pattern for most future Barclay titles, which can be played like a version of the game *Mad-Libs*: "Narrative of [Woman's name] who did [a bad thing] and [was convicted/murdered/executed/drowned] in [someplace that you haven't been]."

27. While subscription publishing was in its heyday during Barclay's active period in business, subscription publishers sold a very different kind of book—typically long works of history or travel, often illustrated and in deluxe bindings. Nobody would have mistaken Barclay's agents for typical subscription book agents.

28. Barclay's first publications were priced at seven and one-half cents, with prices gradually increasing over the nineteenth century to twelve cents, then fifteen, and finally reaching twenty-five.

29. E. E. Barclay was very active in the fraternal organization Lippard founded, the Brotherhood of the Union. See John Bell Bouton, *The Life and Choice Writings of George Lippard* (New York: H. H. Randall, 1855). In 1852, when Lippard was traveling in Ohio and western Pennsylvania to promote the Brotherhood, Barclay was handling his business for him in Philadelphia. See letter from Lippard to E. W. C. Greene, dated Cleveland, July 14, 1852 (Gratz Manuscript Collection, case 6, box 23, Historical Society of Pennsylvania). George Lippard Barclay died of tuberculosis in 1886, preceding his father in death by two years.

30. The practice of listing cities other than that of the copyright holder as places of publication on title pages was relatively common in cheap nineteenth-century publishing circles, where publishers often partnered with other firms as their "agents" in other cities. But Barclay did not structure his business in this way, and it is clear that his use of other cities as places of publication was intended to mislead potential readers.

31. The practice of presenting fictional narratives as having been written by a trustworthy narrator, such as a clergyman, was a standard practice in British and American letters. But Barclay's dedication to the practice set him apart. Of all of the Barclay titles that I have examined, the only books that have the name of a real person listed as author or editor are those by E. E. Barclay's friend George Lippard and those by his son, George Lippard Barclay.

32. McDade, "Lurid Literature of the Last Century," 464.

33. While no papers from Barclay remain, it is clear that his cheap paper-covered books did not make him a rich man. The 1870 Federal Census lists the value of his real estate as only $500—not much success for a man who had been running his own publishing house for thirty years. *1870 United States Federal Census*, 6th Ward, 17th District, Philadelphia County, PA, p. 205 (Provo, UT: Ancestry.com Operations, 2009).

34. Credit report for "Jeremiah H. Farrell," New York, vol. 196, p. 919, R. G. Dun Co. Collection, Baker Library Historical Collections, Harvard Business School (entry dated January 31, 1871).

35. Given that this household included eleven people, this amount may sound more impressive than it was in practice. In addition to Jeremiah and his wife, Adelaide, their Brooklyn house accommodated six children (Kate, Emma, Jeremiah, Josephine, George, and Mary Ellen); an eighty-five-year-old woman named Mary Carney, perhaps Adelaide's mother; a servant named Julia Shurden; and a boy of seventeen named Jeremiah Griffin whose connection to the family is unclear. *1870 United States Federal Census*, 4th Ward, Brooklyn, Kings County, NY, p. 96 (Provo, UT: Ancestry.com Operations, 2009).

36. "BOOKS! BOOKS!! BOOKS!!!," *New York Clipper*, February 1, 1862.

37. Dennis, *Licentious Gotham*, 160. According to the accounting of the sale (the tally and receipts have survived), Farrell actually paid close to $6,000 for Brady's stock, plates, and store fixtures ($5,918.92).

38. Credit report for "Jeremiah Farrell," New York, vol. 196, p. 919, R. G. Dun Co. Collection, Baker Library Historical Collections, Harvard Business School (entry dated August 27, 1864). I have fully spelled out the many abbreviations and shorthand usages common in the Dun records.

39. Farrell credit report, May 10, 1866.

40. These reports from Dun bear witness to the lack of specialization that characterized entrepreneurs like Farrell. He was a publisher but also sold at retail and via mail order. Haven Hawley has noted that throughout his career as a publisher, Farrell only attempted to copyright a single work: *The Horse Car Railroad Guide and Directory for the Cities of New York, Brooklyn and Jersey City.* The copyright application was filed in 1867, in partnership with a Boston-based publisher of cheap books named H. L. Williams. It does not appear that the book was ever published. See Hawley, "American Publishers of Indecent Books," 447–448.

41. Dennis, *Licentious Gotham*, 243.

42. Quoted in ibid., 250.

43. The same investigation led to Charles and Joseph Darrow, binders operating in lower Manhattan who had bound all of Farrell's books, employing about forty young women in their bindery. Ibid., 251. See also Hawley, "American Publishers of Indecent Books."

44. Janet Farrell Brodie, *Contraception and Abortion in Nineteenth-Century America* (Ithaca, NY: Cornell University Press, 1994), 455.

45. Ibid., 456.

46. Farrell credit report, August 27, 1864.

47. Farrell credit report, July 12, 1871.

48. Credit report for "George Akarman," New York, vol. 268, p. 554, R. G. Dun Co. Collection, Baker Library Historical Collections, Harvard Business School (entry dated September 29, 1852).

49. Credit report for "Frederic A. Brady," New York, vol. 192, p. 581, R. G. Dun Co. Collection, Baker Library Historical Collections, Harvard Business School (entry dated September 30, 1859). Following an obscenity charge in early 1858, in May of that year Brady bought the business of H. Long and Brothers, a more mainstream publisher, perhaps hoping to draw less attention to himself.

50. In 1874, after Comstock had him arrested for the third time, Conway attacked the reformer with a knife, severely slashing his face. The most thorough treatment of Comstock's life—although with a decidedly Freudian early twentieth-century bent—is Heywood Broun and Margaret Leech, *Anthony Comstock: Roundsman of the Lord* (New York: Albert and Charles Boni, 1927). See also Hawley, "American Publishers of Indecent Books"; Dennis, *Licentious Gotham*; Horowitz, *Rereading Sex*; and Nicola Beisel, *Imperiled Innocents: Anthony Comstock and Family Reproduction in Victorian America* (Princeton, NJ: Princeton University Press, 1997).

51. Broun and Leech, *Anthony Comstock*, 84. Jesup, a banker, was one of the founders of the YMCA, as well as of the Five Points House of Industry and the American Natural History Museum, where he served as president for twenty-five years.

52. The act passed by Congress read, "That no obscene, lewd, or lascivious book, pamphlet, picture, paper, print, or other publication of an indecent character, or any article or thing designed or intended for the prevention of conception or the producing of abortion, nor any article or thing intended or adapted for any indecent or immoral use or nature, nor any . . . book, pamphlet, advertisement or notice of any kind giving information, directly or indirectly, where, or how, or of whom, or by what means either of the things before mentioned may be obtained or made . . . shall be carried in the mail, and any person who shall knowingly deposit or cause to be deposited, for mailing or delivery, any of the herein-before-mentioned articles or things, or any notice, or paper containing any advertisement relating to the aforesaid articles or things . . . shall be deemed guilty of a misdemeanor." (Quoted in Beisel, *Imperiled Innocents*, 39–40.) Every offense carried a fine of at least $100 and at most $5,000, or a sentence at hard labor from one to ten years.

53. Andrea Tone, *Devices and Desires: A History of Contraceptives in America* (New York: Hill and Wang, 2001), 7.

54. Horowitz, *Rereading Sex*, 374.

55. Quoted in Beisel, *Imperiled Innocents*, 40.

56. Ibid., 227n56.

57. Tone, *Devices and Desires*, 28.

58. Anthony Comstock, *Frauds Exposed, or, How the People Are Deceived and Robbed, and Youth Corrupted, Being a Full Exposure of Various Schemes Operated Through the Mails, and Unearthed by the Author in a Seven Years' Service as a Special Agent of the Post Office Department and Secretary and Chief Agent of the New York Society for the Suppression of Vice* (New York: J. H. Brown, 1880), 389.

CHAPTER 11. BACK NUMBER BUDD

1. E. W. Gurley, *Scrap-Books and How to Make Them: Containing Full Instructions for Making a Complete and Systematic Set of Useful Books* (New York: Authors' Publishing, 1880), 9.

2. My composite fictional visitor is male because I have seen no signed accounts of women visiting the Manhattan establishment.

3. "Dow Jones History," December 20, 2013, http://www.dowjones.com/history.asp. For more on clipping services and their relationship to "scissors editors," see Ellen Gruber Garvey, *Writing with Scissors: American Scrapbooks from the Civil War to the Harlem Renaissance* (New York: Oxford University Press, 2013), chaps. 1 and 7; Ryan Goldberg, "Frank H. Brunell: The Father of Form," *Daily Racing Form*, August 12, 2010, http://www.drf.com/news/frank-h-brunell-father-form.

4. "An Odd but Profitable Business," *New York World*, December 18, 1888, repr. in *Back Number Budd's Directory*, 1889 (New York: s.n.), 7; John S. Grey, "Back Number Budd," *Printers' Ink: A Journal for Advertisers*, 23, no. 11 (June 15, 1898): 35–36; Wendell Phillips Dodge, "Budd, 'The Back-Number King,'" *Chicago Defender*, February 7, 1914, repr. from *Technical World Magazine*; "A Flood of Congratulations for Mr. Morton," *New York Tribune*, November 10, 1888.

5. "New York Letter," *Literary World*, 29, no. 5 (March 5, 1898): 73.

6. Budd's parents seem to have been free. His mother, Henrietta Peale, and his father, Eugene Budd, were born possibly in France or French-speaking Canada.

7. Marcy Sacks notes that the move of more black people to midtown was marked by black churches that followed their constituents to midtown in the 1880s and 1890s. See Marcy S. Sacks, *Before Harlem: The Black Experience in New York City Before World War I* (Philadelphia: University of Pennsylvania Press, 2006).

8. In 1874, land in his area went for $70 per square foot, but it soon rose: in 1906 it was $250 per square foot, closer to the rates downtown, and by 1909, $350 per square foot. Stephen Jenkins, *The Greatest Street in the World: The Story of Broadway, Old and New, from the Bowling Green to Albany* (New York: Putnam, 1911), 252–254.

9. "Back Number Budd's Wife," *Brooklyn Eagle* (Brooklyn, NY), November 15, 1891.

10. The British actress Florence Marryat, reminiscing on her three-month trip to the United States in 1884, used her visit to Hattie Budd (whom she misnames Kitty) as a foil to other more insulting portrayals of black people. Hattie Budd walked with her and Marryat reports that she "quite forgot what other people might think of my walking with a coloured woman, in the interest I felt in her chatter." *Tom Tiddler's Ground* (London: S. Sonnenschein, Lowrey, 1886), 209–210.

11. "New York Letter"; Charles Grutzner, Jr., "If What You Want Was Published Within Past 98 Years, He Has It, Back-Number Budd Says," *New York Amsterdam News* (New York, NY), September 2, 1931. According to notices in the *Brooklyn Eagle*, he also sold copies of that paper near the ferry.

12. "Odd but Profitable Business"; Grey, "Back Number Budd," *Printer*'s *Ink*, 35–36.

13. Dodge, "Budd, 'The Back-Number King.'"

14. "A Flood of Congratulations for Mr. Morton."

15. Grey, "Back Number Budd."

16. "The Color Line in Newspapers: What the Negro Race Has Accomplished in American Journalism; A Peculiar Character and His Popular Specialty," *The Journalist* 4, no. 26 (March 19, 1887): 4; "Robert M. Budd," Advertisement, *Casper's Directory of the American Book, News and Stationery Trade* (Milwaukee, WI: C.N. Caspar, 1889), 1395.

17. "Color Line in Newspapers."

18. "New York Letter."

19. "Color Line in Newspapers."

20. *Back Number Budd's Directory,* 1–4.

21. *Back Number Budd's Directory,* 4.

22. "An Odd Way to Gain Money," *Baltimore American* (Baltimore, MD), June 1, 1891.

23. For Jewish secondhand clothing dealers, see Adam Mendelsohn's chapter in this volume. For example, one patronizing account had Budd speaking in improbable dialect, at odds with other accounts, saying, "Paper am a great ting to stand de fire and water," as he spread out newspapers to dry after his first fire. "Budd Is Digging in the Ruins," *New York Tribune,* June 16, 1895.

24. Thanks to the members of the SHARP-L listserv for information on these uses of newspapers, August 15 to August 18, 2008, SHARP-L archives, https://list.indiana.edu /sympa (accessed December 22, 2013).

25. Michael Thompson, *Rubbish Theory: The Creation and Destruction of Value* (New York: Oxford University Press, 1979), 13–33.

26. Sherwin Cody, *Four American Poets: William Cullen Bryant, Henry Wadsworth Longfellow, John Greenleaf Whittier, Oliver Wendell Holmes; A Book for Young Americans* (New York: Werner School Book, 1899), 44.

27. "Back Number Budd," *Printer's Ink,* 35–36.

28. "'Back Number' Budd's Great Loss: He Will Not Give Up His Business However," *New York Tribune,* April 26, 1895.

29. "Back Number Budd," *Printer's Ink,* 36.

30. "Color Line in Newspapers."

31. The rat-catching cat, common in London, is packed off on a trading voyage to a rat-infested land with no cats. Dick wins a fortune for his now valuable recontextualized cat.

32. "Color Line in Newspapers."

33. "Another Issue of Ulster Gazette," *Kingston Daily Freeman* (Kingston, NY), April 28, 1923.

34. "Budd, Back Number and Sons, News," *Trow's New York City Directory* (New York: John F. Trow), listings from 1894 to 1904. Thanks to Reginald Pitts for help in learning more about the Budd family.

35. "Budd Is Digging in the Ruins."

36. "Jake Sharp Buys Old Papers," *New York World* [date obliterated], 1886.

37. [Miscellany column], *Amusement Bulletin* (New York) 1, no. 2 (October 12, 1889): 10.

38. "Color Line in Newspapers."

39. [Miscellany column], *Amusement Bulletin;* "'Back Number Budd': The Prosperous Business of an Enterprising Colored Man; Over a Million Copies of Old Newspapers Collected on an Original Capital of $8—Relics of Old New York," *Idaho Statesman*

(Boise, ID), July 29, 1986, repr. from the *New York World.* Scrapbooks of Gould's obituary clippings that may be the ones referred to are in Helen Gould's papers at the New-York Historical Society.

40. "Back Number Budd, New York Letter," *Los Angeles Herald* (Los Angeles, CA), April 10, 1898.

41. His display card in *Trow's New York City Directory* for 1905–1906 advertises, "Bought and sold novels or Any periodicals."

42. "Jake Sharp Buys Old Papers."

43. "A Valuable File," *Hyde Park Herald* (Chicago, IL), July 8, 1887.

44. Correspondence with Pat Michaelis, Kansas Historical Society, April 9, 2013 and April 17, 2013.

45. Stephen R. Fisk against Mary M. Fisk, *Supreme Court of the State of New York*, First Department, Appellate Decision, 1896, p. 21, sec. 62.

46. For more on late nineteenth-century practices for managing information, see Garvey, *Writing with Scissors.*

47. For a substantial fee, Budd was willing to search through a year's papers for a desired article. He reported charging a hundred dollars for such a search ("Back Number Budd's Loss," *American Stationer*, 37, no. 19 (May 9, 1895): 857.

48. "Personal and Impersonal," *Brooklyn Eagle*, July 4, 1909.

49. "Back Number Budd's Great Loss: Fifteen Million Copies of Publications Covering Many Years, Destroyed by Fire," *New York Times*, April 25, 1895.

50. Cody, *Four American Poets*, 45.

51. "'Back Number Budd' Loses Historic Collection," *New York Times*, December 19, 1922.

52. "'Back Number Budd' Sees Entire Fortune Destroyed by Fire," *Daily Star* (New York), December 19, 1922.

53. Charles Grutzner, Jr., "'Paper, Mister? One Thousand Dollars!' 'Back Number' Budd, 79 Year Old Negro, Has Prints Since 1833 in Storeroom Here," *Daily Star* (Long Island, NY), September 18, 1931.

54. Grutzner, "'Paper, Mister?'"

55. "Back Number Budd: A New York Celebrity Gets into Trouble," *St. Paul Daily Globe* (St. Paul, MN), July 6, 1887.

56. "Gossip from Gotham: New York as Seen by Our Representative," *St. Louis Republic* (St. Louis, MO), November 19, 1891.

57. "Back Number Budd's Marital Troubles," *Brooklyn Eagle*, October 24, 1892; "She Stood the Pennies," *Brooklyn Eagle*, December 18, 1893.

58. "'Back Number' Budd's Divorce," *New York Evening World,* January 19, 1894; "Paid Her $3 in Pennies: 'Back Number' Budd's Wife Says He Spends $50 a Week," *New York Evening World,* November 3, 1892.

59. "Mulatto in Fight over Italian Wife Kills Her Father," *Brooklyn Eagle*, July 22, 1920; "Witnesses Say Budd Shot to Save Self," *Brooklyn Eagle*, July 28, 1920.

60. Grutzner, "If What You Want."

CONCLUSION

1. We wish to highlight, in addition to the works cited in the Introduction, the important work on capitalism in this period arising from discussions taking place at Cornell University's History of Capitalism Initiative, the Program in Early American Economy and Society at the Library Company of Philadelphia, the Program on the Study of Capitalism at Harvard University, and others (see Jennifer Schuessler, "In History Departments, It's Up with Capitalism," *New York Times*, April 6, 2013).

2. See, for example, Nicky Gregson and Louise Crewe, *Second-Hand Cultures* (New York: Berg, 2003).

3. *London Low Life* is a commercial archive from Adam Matthew Digital (http://www.amdigital.co.uk/m-collections/collection/london-low-life/); the *Proceedings of the Old Bailey, 1674–1913*, available for free, presents fully searchable text from London's central criminal court (www.oldbaileyonline.org). The first edition of Mayhew's three-volume work was published in 1851, and its full title is *London Labour and the London Poor; A Cyclopaedia of the Conditions and Earnings of Those That* Will *Work, Those That* Cannot *Work, and Those That* Will Not *Work . . .* (London: George Woodfall and Son, 1851). Mayhew published a companion volume a decade later dedicated to criminals: *Those That Will Not Work . . . Comprising, Prostitutes, Thieves, Beggars . . .* (London: Charles Griffin, 1861).

4. See *The Mechanics' Free Press* (Philadelphia); Matthew Warner Osborn, "The First Batman: Identity and Popular Romanticism in the Early Republic" (paper presented at the Society for Historians of the Early American Republic Annual Meeting, 2011); Stuart M. Blumin, ed., *New-York by Gaslight and Other Sketches by George G. Foster* (Berkeley: University of California Press, 1990); and James D. McCabe, *The Secrets of the Great City* (Philadelphia: Jones Brothers, 1868).

CONTRIBUTORS

Paul Erickson received his PhD in American studies from the University of Texas at Austin and is currently Director of Academic Programs at the American Antiquarian Society in Worcester, Massachusetts.

Robert J. Gamble is currently visiting assistant professor of history at the University of Kansas and received his PhD in history from Johns Hopkins University in 2014. His current book project, "Civic Economies: Commerce, Regulation, and Public Space in the Antebellum City," traces the relationship between capitalism and urban governance in Baltimore and Philadelphia between 1790 and 1860.

Ellen Gruber Garvey is the author of two prize-winning books: *Writing with Scissors: American Scrapbooks from the Civil War to the Harlem Renaissance* (2013) and *The Adman in the Parlor: Magazines and the Gendering of Consumer Culture* (1996). She is professor of English at New Jersey City University, where she also edits *Transformations: The Journal of Inclusive Scholarship and Pedagogy.*

Corey Goettsch is a PhD candidate at Emory University. His doctoral dissertation is about fraud in nineteenth-century New York City and how it relates to the expansion of American capitalism.

Joshua R. Greenberg is professor of history at Bridgewater State University and author of *Advocating the Man: Masculinity, Organized Labor, and the Household in New York, 1800–1840* (2009). He is currently working on a study of antebellum paper money and economic culture.

Katie M. Hemphill is assistant professor of history at the University of Arizona and is currently writing a history of commercial sex and its regulation in nineteenth-century Baltimore.

Craig B. Hollander received his PhD in nineteenth-century US history from Johns Hopkins University. He is currently the Behrman Postdoctoral Fellow in the department of history at Princeton University.

Brian P. Luskey is associate professor of history at West Virginia University. He is the author of *On the Make: Clerks and the Quest for Capital in Nineteenth-Century America* (2010) as well as several articles on class, ambition, labor, and consumer culture. He is currently writing a book about the cultural economy of Civil War America.

Will B. Mackintosh is assistant professor of history at the University of Mary Washington. His work focuses on the cultural naturalization of capitalism during the long nineteenth century. In addition to his research on the Loomis Gang, he is currently working on a cultural and intellectual history of the origins of tourism in the United States.

Adam Mendelsohn is associate professor of Jewish studies and the director of the Pearlstine/Lipov Center for Southern Jewish Culture at the College of Charleston. He specializes in the history of Anglophone Jewish communities in the period prior to eastern European mass migration and is the author of the forthcoming book *The Rag Race: How Jews Sewed Their Way to Success in America and the British Empire.*

Brendan P. O'Malley is lecturer at Brooklyn College and doctoral candidate in history at the Graduate Center of the City University of New York. He is coeditor, with Michael Stewart Foley, of *Home Fronts: A Wartime America Reader* (2008).

Michael D. Thompson earned his PhD in history from Emory University in 2009, and is UC Foundation Assistant Professor of American History at the University of Tennessee at Chattanooga. He is the author of the forthcoming book titled *Working on the Dock of the Bay: Labor and Enterprise in an Antebellum Southern Port*, a project that was awarded the 2011 Hines Prize from the College of Charleston's Program in the Carolina Lowcountry and Atlantic World.

Wendy A. Woloson is assistant professor of history at Rutgers University–Camden. In addition to having published several articles on the history of consumer culture and secondary markets, she is the author of two books, *Refined Tastes: Sugar, Consumers, and Confectionery in Nineteenth-Century America* (2000) and *In Hock: Pawning in America from Independence Through the Great Depression* (2009). Her current book project is about the history of cheap goods in America.

INDEX

ACKNOWLEDGMENTS

Although we have both been interested in economic history's dark and hidden corners for some time, it has taken us years to pull our ideas together into something resembling a cohesive whole. Finally, we had a great idea: why don't we get other people to do most of the work for us? We are delighted to be able to thank those people here.

Our first collaborators, Jo Cohen, Paul Erickson, Jeff Forret, Josh Greenberg, Candice Harrison, and Ellen Hartigan-O'Connor, were the game participants at two sessions of the Society for Historians of the Early American Republic conference in 2007 in Worcester, Massachusetts. Ed Balleisen and Tim Gilfoyle offered astute comments, and Tim set a high bar for performative commentary when he skillfully patched together his own shinplaster using a couple of greenbacks and some transparent tape. Since then, we have continued to lure these folks and other innocent bystanders into the conversation. They have generously—and patiently—allowed us to pick their brains. Our abettors have included Sean Adams, Ken Cohen, Ann Fabian, Kathy Hilliard, Alison Isenberg, Jess Lepler, Jen Manion, Stephen Mihm, Marina Moskowitz, Sharon Ann Murphy, Simon Newman, Emily Pawley, Phil Scranton, and Billy Smith. These ongoing conversations—and especially those with Paul, Josh, Ellen, and Stephen—have been enormously helpful.

Gaining momentum and encouraged by cosponsors John Van Horne, director of the Library Company of Philadelphia, and Dan Richter, director of the McNeil Center for Early American Studies, we colluded with still more presenters, commenters, and audience members at the "Capitalism by Gaslight" conference in 2012. Jane Kamensky kicked off the proceedings with a provocative keynote address, and sessions were adeptly guided by Cathy Matson, Kathy Peiss, Michelle McDonald, and Roderick McDonald, who offered incisive commentary and, in some cases, light entertainment. In addition to the essayists whose work is included here, Andrew Cohen, Colin Johnson, Jamie Pietruska, and Michael Ross contributed mightily to the program with rich and rewarding essays on smugglers, hoarders, fortune-tellers, and keepers of lying-in hospitals that they are repurposing for other projects.

We are especially grateful to those who have put their faith in the two of us. Most of all, we would like to thank the contributors to this volume, who have worked tirelessly to bring these histories to light. Bob Lockhart, Dan Richter, and two anonymous readers for Penn Press have given us the critical feedback and support necessary to make this book possible. Not to be left in the shadows, Ashley Whitehead Luskey and David Miller are the partners in crime we know we can always count on.